STUDIES IN BAPTIST HISTORY AND THOUGHT
VOLUME 18

Marianne Farningham

A Plain Woman Worker

STUDIES IN BAPTIST HISTORY AND THOUGHT
VOLUME 18

Marianne Farningham Hearn, 1834-1909

A full listing of titles in this series
appears at the end of this book

STUDIES IN BAPTIST HISTORY AND THOUGHT
VOLUME 18

Marianne Farningham

A Plain Woman Worker

Linda Wilson

Foreword by Ian M. Randall

WIPF & STOCK · Eugene, Oregon

Wipf and Stock Publishers
199 W 8th Ave, Suite 3
Eugene, OR 97401

Marianne Farningham
A Plain Woman Worker
By Wilson, Linda
Copyright©2007 Paternoster
ISBN 13: 978-1-60608-019-1
Publication date 6/6/2008
Previously published by Paternoster, 2007

This Edition Published by Wipf and Stock Publishers
by arrangement with Paternoster.

STUDIES IN BAPTIST HISTORY AND THOUGHT

Series Preface

Baptists form one of the largest Christian communities in the world, and while they hold the historic faith in common with other mainstream Christian traditions, they nevertheless have important insights which they can offer to the worldwide church. *Studies in Baptist History and Thought* will be one means towards this end. It is an international series of academic studies which includes original monographs, revised dissertations, collections of essays and conference papers, and aims to cover any aspect of Baptist history and thought. While not all the authors are themselves Baptists, they nevertheless share an interest in relating Baptist history and thought to the other branches of the Christian church and to the wider life of the world.

The series includes studies in various aspects of Baptist history from the seventeenth century down to the present day, including biographical works, and Baptist thought is understood as covering the subject-matter of theology (including interdisciplinary studies embracing biblical studies, philosophy, sociology, practical theology, liturgy and women's studies). The diverse streams of Baptist life throughout the world are all within the scope of these volumes.

The series editors and consultants believe that the academic disciplines of history and theology are of vital importance to the spiritual vitality of the churches of the Baptist faith and order. The series sets out to discuss, examine and explore the many dimensions of their tradition and so to contribute to their on-going intellectual vigour.

A brief word of explanation is due for the series identifier on the front cover. The fountains, taken from heraldry, represent the Baptist distinctive of believer's baptism and, at the same time, the source of the water of life. There are three of them because they symbolize the Trinitarian basis of Baptist life and faith. Those who are redeemed by the Lamb, the book of Revelation reminds us, will be led to 'fountains of living waters' (Rev. 7.17).

Series Editors

Anthony R. Cross, Fellow of the Centre for Baptist History and Heritage, Regent's Park College, Oxford, UK

Curtis W. Freeman, Research Professor of Theology and Director of the Baptist House of Studies, Duke University, North Carolina, USA

Stephen R. Holmes, Lecturer in Theology, University of St Andrews, Scotland, UK

Elizabeth Newman, Professor of Theology and Ethics, Baptist Theological Seminary at Richmond, Virginia, USA

Philip E. Thompson, Assistant Professor of Systematic Theology and Christian Heritage, North American Baptist Seminary, Sioux Falls, South Dakota, USA

Series Consultant Editors

David Bebbington, Professor of History, University of Stirling, Scotland, UK

Paul S. Fiddes, Professor of Systematic Theology, University of Oxford, and Principal of Regent's Park College, Oxford, UK

† Stanley J. Grenz, Pioneer McDonald Professor of Theology, Carey Theological College, Vancouver, British Columbia, Canada

Ken R. Manley, Distinguished Professor of Church History, Whitley College, The University of Melbourne, Australia

Stanley E. Porter, President and Professor of New Testament, McMaster Divinity College, Hamilton, Ontario, Canada

For Ian with thanks for all the help.

Contents

Foreword	xiii
Preface	xvii
Abbreviations	xix

Chapter 1
A Plain Woman Worker — 1
Tracing Changes within Evangelicalism — 4
Women of Faith — 6
Themes in Marianne's Writings — 7
Spirituality — 8
Sources — 9
   A Working Woman's Life — 10
The Book — 13

Chapter 2
Marianne's Life Journey — 14
Beginnings — 14
Early Childhood Memories — 16
Eynsford Chapel — 19
   Chapel Life — 20
Rebecca Hearn's Death — 22
Early Christian Experience — 25
Education — 26
Bristol — 28
The Start of Marianne's Writing Career — 29
Gravesend — 31
The Move to Northampton — 32
Northampton in the Later Nineteenth Century — 33

College Street Chapel	34
Teaching in Northampton	36
Engagement	37
Full-time Writing Career	40
Eva Hope	41
Marianne's Girls' Class	42
Further Developments	42
12 Watkin Terrace	43
The Hearn Family	46
Friendship	48
Breakdown	51
A Cottage in Barmouth	53
End of Marianne's Life	56

Chapter 3
Afraid to be Singular? Marianne and the Role of Women — **60**

Grace Darling – A Role Model	61
Afraid to be Singular	63
The Fear of Wasted Lives	65
Women and Domesticity	67
Evangelicalism and Feminism	74
Motherhood	76
Women and Work	80
Work is a Blessing	81
Working Women Make Happy Homes	83
Single Women and Work	86
Women's Rights	88
Women and the Church	92
Conclusion	94

Chapter 4
'A Great Work': Marianne and Sunday Schools — **97**

The Sunday School Movement	98
The College Street Class	99
First Lessons	101
Building Community: The Nature of the Class	102
Active Participation	106
Mutual Benefit	107

Contents   xi

  Development of the Class   109
Conversion and Church Membership   110
Retirement   114
Sunday School as a Third Sphere   114
'Unfilled hearts and unemployed hands'   116
The Challenge of Sunday School Teaching   119
Marianne as Pastor   121
Sunday Schools in the Late Nineteenth Century   122
Other Sunday School Involvement   123
Conclusion – the Sunday School Queen   125

Chapter 5
Marianne and Public Life   128
Writing, Editing, and the Public Sphere   129
Marianne as Writer   131
The Shortcomings of Journalism   133
Hymns   135
Eva Hope   139
Writing Male Lives   143
The *Sunday School Times*   145
  Marianne as Editor   147
  Issues Addressed by Marianne   149
Women and Public Speaking   151
  Preparation for Public Speaking   153
  The Transition to Public Speaking   153
  Giving Lectures   155
Northampton School Board   161
  Marianne's Work on the Board   166
  Marianne's Proposals   166
  Assessing Marianne's Contribution   169
Education Committee   170
Conclusion   171

Chapter 6
Marianne's Spirituality   173
The Heart of Spirituality   174
Focus on Jesus   176
The Importance of Joy   177

Conversion: The Gateway to a Relationship with God 178
Developing the Relationship: Personal Devotions and Prayer 182
   The Practice of Devotions 182
   Varieties of Prayers 184
   Realistic Patterns of Prayer 185
Developing the Relationship: The Role of the Bible 186
The Cross 189
Developments in Spirituality: Marianne's Brighton Experience 191
Marianne and Developments in Evangelical Theology 195
   The Development of Marianne's Theology: Heaven, Hell and 'the larger hope' 199
   Heaven 203
Unorthodox Beliefs 206
Doubts and Difficulties 208
Changing Attitudes to Leisure and the Use of Time 211
Marianne's Attitude to the Sabbath 215
Evangelicalism and Ecumenism 218
Was Marianne's Spirituality Gendered? 221
Conclusion 224

Chapter 7
Conclusion 226
Marianne and Women 226
Marianne and Sunday Schools 228
Public Life 228
Spirituality and Theology 229
Changes within Evangelicalism 230
A Plain Working Woman 231
The Last Word 233

Bibliography 235

Index 242

Foreword

Rosemary Mitchell has suggested in her *DNB* article on Marianne Farningham (1834-1909) that she was one of the most influential female members of the Baptist community in the nineteenth century. Many Baptists, and other evangelicals, reading that statement, might well respond 'Marianne who?' In fact, as Linda Wilson ably demonstrates in this splendid study, Farningham's influence stretched well beyond the Baptist denomination. But she was brought up, and a remained a Baptist. For much of her adult life she was a prominent member of College Street Baptist Chapel, Northampton. She was a friend of leading Baptists such as J.C. Carlile, and wrote a biography of the most famous nineteenth-century Baptist of them all, C.H. Spurgeon.

Linda Wilson takes up major aspects of Marianne Farningham's many-faceted life and thought: her views of the role of women; her educational work; her public life, for example as a popular lecturer; and her spirituality. Her fame in her life-time was due mainly to her writings. She contributed thousands of articles and poems to the Christian press in Britain and published several biographies and a number of other books, for example novels. After some years as a school teacher she became a full-time journalist on the staff of the *Christian World*, one of the leading British Christian weeklies of her period. Later she added the editorship of the *Sunday School Times*. Farningham was a prolific, nationally-known and highly popular author, and Linda Wilson evaluates both the content of her work and also the way in which she helped to shape the culture of nineteenth-century Nonconformity.

In the course of this examination of Farningham's life and work, a number of stereotypes of Victorian evangelicalism, including generalisations about Victorian evangelical women, are challenged with particular effectiveness. As Linda Wilson notes, the important process of rediscovering the lives of Nonconformist women from the nineteenth century is still at a comparatively early stage, with historians of women's lives having been slow to engage in careful study of the actual effects of Christian belief and ecclesiastical historians having neglected female contributions. Linda Wilson, in taking on this task, argues convincingly that Farningham can, as her views developed, be termed a moderate feminist. There has been an assumption that feminism and the evangelicalism of this period were not compatible. Farningham is an example of an evangelical who encouraged women to have their own careers. There were of course many Victorian evangelical women who engaged in voluntary philanthropic work, but Farningham wanted women to see paid work as valid.

Within the town of Northampton, Marianne Farningham was known principally for her work as an educator. After her death, the *Northampton Independent* spoke of her as the town's 'most notable woman'. Having been a teacher during her early years in Northampton, she was later appointed as member of – and the only woman on – the Northampton School Board. In College Street Chapel she was active as leader of a class of young women. Linda Wilson, in her detailed examination of Farningham's position as the leader of what became (from small beginnings) a class of almost two hundred young women, makes the intriguing suggestion that her role can be compared to that of a youth pastor, or a leader of a form of alternative church. Farningham was part of a Baptist community in England that held conservative views about women in leadership, but Linda Wilson argues that Farningham's eagerness to connect herself with Catherine Booth indicates sympathy for women preachers. A striking feature of the College Street class was that it had a substantial working-class element. K.D.M. Snell included Farningham in a list of 'outstanding figures in the annals of working-class or religious history'.

Northampton was also famous politically for returning the first avowedly atheist MP, Charles Bradlaugh, to Parliament. Bradlaugh was the founder of the National Secular Society, and an advocate of contraception. For some people Northampton became tainted by this apparent affirmation of secularism. But for Farningham, as a Northampton resident and as someone with Liberal sympathies, the town had 'insisted on sending Mr Bradlaugh to Parliament, not because it was less religious, but because it cared more strongly for liberty than most'. Her own sympathies were broad, contrary to the widespread impression that Victorian evangelicals were narrow and rigid, and in some respects, as Linda Wilson clearly shows, her thinking broadened in the later decades of her life. She seems, for example, to have moved away from a rigid sabbatarianism.

In the final, fascinating major chapter, looking at Farningham's spirituality, Linda Wilson draws the threads of her life together in exploring what was the foundation for all her action and writings. The essence of her spirituality is seen to have been relationship with Christ. A significant event in her spiritual journey was the huge Brighton Convention of 1875, which paved the way for the Keswick Convention. Farningham found the Brighton meetings, with their stress on deeper consecration, fresh and helpful, especially the addresses by an American Quaker, Hannah Pearsall Smith. Also, before the Brighton Convention, she had been wrestling with the issue of the eternal punishment of the impenitent. Hannah Pearsall Smith believed in the 'larger hope', as it was called, and Farningham found her thinking moving in this direction.

Linda Wilson, in this book, combines a vivid, probing and comprehensive account of the life of Marianne Farningham with a consistent critical engagement with writers whose work impinges on her topic. Farningham deserves the admirable quality of treatment found in this volume. She had a significant personal influence and is also someone whose life, as analysed here, illuminates nineteenth-century Baptist and wider evangelical Nonconformist culture and the role of women within that culture.

Ian M. Randall
International Baptist Theological Seminary, Prague and
Spurgeon's College, London
January 2007

Preface

I first encountered Marianne Farningham through reading her autobiography and other material whilst researching my doctorate, and I found her so intriguing that I promised myself I would take the time as soon as possible to study her more closely. This I have been doing, whenever other commitments allowed, over a period of several years, resulting in this book. It has been a long time gestating, and that it is here at all is thanks to the advice and encouragement of many people, and I am grateful for all the help I have received.

Series editor Anthony R. Cross suggested that this volume would fit well within the series, and he has been both helpful and tolerant of delays. Ian Randall, Ruth Gouldbourne and Tim Larsen all read a draft of the completed manuscript and made helpful comments. Ruth also listened, via email and over occasional lunches, to the continuing saga of research and writing, and gave welcome support. David Bebbington encouraged me to continue when the task seemed too daunting, and also made invaluable comments on some draft chapters.

Research like this would not be possible without helpful and knowledgeable librarians in a variety of libraries including the Bodleian, the British Library, Northampton Library and Special Collections at the University of Birmingham. Fiona Maclellan at the University of Northampton kindly arranged for me to use its Library resources when it was closed for building work. Other institutions have been equally helpful, including the Bristol and Northampton Record Offices.

Friends and colleagues in Bristol Christian Fellowship have been supportive and tolerant of the extent to which writing has occupied much of my time in the last couple of years. Laura and Nick have also encouraged me, as has my husband Ian who, with me, has lived with Marianne for some time now, and who has also done much of preparation for publication. Thanks to anyone else who I've forgotten.

Some of the material in this book has been previously published, and is included here by permission. An earlier version of part of Chapter 3, 'Afraid to be Singular: Marianne Farningham and the Role of Women', is included in S. Morgan, *Women, Religion and Feminism in Britain, 1750-1900*, Palgrave

Macmillan, 2002. Another part of Chapter 3 and some of Chapter 6 were first published as 'Marianne Farningham: Work, Leisure and the Use of Time' in R. Swanson, ed, *The Use and Abuse of Time in Christian History*, Studies in Church History, Volume 37, Boydell and Brewer, 2002, and previously given as a paper at the Ecclesiastical History Society Summer Conference in 1999.

Other sections were delivered as papers, and I am grateful for the opportunities for discussion thus provided. These include 'Good lessons could be learnt: Marianne Farningham and the use of biography in the late nineteenth century', a paper given at the Ecclesiastical History Conference in 2000. Excerpts from Chapter 4 were delivered as a paper entitled 'Not so much a class as a sisterhood: Marianne Farningham and her girls' class, 1867- 1901', at the Christian Youth Movements Conference in February 2006, and material from Chapter 5 as 'Marianne Farningham: A Public Life' at the Christianity and History Forum Conference in April 2007. 'Women and their Saviour: Marianne Farningham and nineteenth-century evangelical spirituality', a paper given at a day conference of the West of England and South Wales Women's History Network in June 2005, later became part of Chapter 6.

Abbreviations

CW	*Christian World*
DNB	*Dictionary of National Biography*
SST	*Sunday School Times*

Chapter 1

A Plain Woman Worker

Marianne was born as Mary Ann Hearn, on 17 December 1834, in a small village in Kent. Later she took its name, Farningham, as her nom-de-plume. By the time she died, in March 1909, Marianne had contributed thousands of articles and poems to the Christian press, published a handful of biographies, undertaken several lecture tours, taught, for many years, a class of young women in College Street Baptist Chapel, Northampton, and been for a while the only woman on the Northampton School Board. Yet in many ways, in the words of one obituarist, 'Her life was uneventful to the public eye. She was just a plain woman worker.'[1] So why choose to investigate the writings and life of this particular woman, practically unknown to us today?

One reason is that although she has been largely forgotten, her writing and editing career made Marianne's name familiar to many of her contemporaries. One Northampton newspaper suggested in 1907 that their town was famous 'all over the world... as the home of Miss Marianne Farningham Hearne',[2] and in the same year the *Freeman and Baptist Times* claimed that she was 'known and loved throughout the English-speaking world'.[3] Whilst these assertions might have been slight exaggerations, they were firmly based on truth. Marianne was enough of a public figure, for instance, to merit a short obituary in the *Times*, which described her as being 'for half a century well known and very popular among a large section of the religious public',[4] whilst as early as 1877 the *Western Daily Press* could describe her as a 'well-known author'.[5] She produced copy on a regular basis for the weekly newspaper the *Christian World,* which at its peak around 1880 had a circulation of 130,000, and a readership probably four times that size.[6] The young author's first piece for the paper was published in its inaugural number in 1857, and Marianne continued sending contributions until shortly before her death. Her writing covered a wide

---

[1] J.C. Carlile, 'Marianne Farningham, the Woman and her Work' in *The Freeman and Baptist Times*, 26 March 1907.
[2] *Northampton Independent* 20 April 1907.
[3] *Freeman and Baptist Times* 13 December 1907.
[4] *Times* 17 March 1909.
[5] *Western Daily Press* 13 November 1877.
[6] J. Munson, *The Nonconformists* (London: SPCK, 1991), p. 73. Compare this with the current circulation of *Christianity*, of around 30,000, (*Christianity,* November 2006.)

range of subjects and included poetry, prose pieces and serialised fiction. She also contributed to, and from 1885 edited, the *Sunday School Times and Home Educator*, another Christian weekly from the same stable, aimed at Sunday school teachers and parents. In addition, many of her short pieces were later published as collections in book form, with titles such as *Girlhood*, *Boyhood* and *Homely Talks about Homely Things*. Further works, mainly biographies, were published under the pseudonym of 'Eva Hope', a name wryly described by its owner as 'about the weakest we could have found'.[7] She also wrote hymns, some for general use and others specifically for children, many being composed for particular occasions such as weddings. Marianne thus had a wide readership, and, if often sentimental, was an accessible writer, as well as a prolific one. Her name appeared in print in many dissenting households at least once a week for over fifty years, and would thus have been extremely familiar in evangelical Nonconformist circles.

Although Marianne has been noticed by historians of Nonconformity, they have rarely acknowledged her importance. John Briggs, however, is aware of her as both a prolific writer and an influential educator,[8] and more recently, Rosemary Mitchell has suggested in her *DNB* article that Marianne was 'one of the most influential women members of the nineteenth century Baptist church'.[9] Yet this has not been generally recognised even amongst historians of Baptists and evangelicals. One exception is the work of Shirley Burgoyne Black, who in 1988 produced 'A Farningham Childhood', an introduction to the early chapters of Marianne's autobiography.[10] There is also an unpublished study of her life in the form of an MA thesis by Barbara Evans and Helen Rogers has used Marianne as an example of the relationship between working-class fathers and daughters, but there has never been a major study of the writer.[11]

Marianne's prominence was demonstrated when she was introduced to the Baptist preacher and notable Victorian Charles Spurgeon, in the summer of 1867. They were exact contemporaries in age and Marianne had recently been

---

[7] M. Farningham, *A Working Woman's Life* (London: James Clarke, 1907), p. 131. For a comprehensive list of her published work, see the Bibliography.

[8] J.H.Y. Briggs, *The English Baptists of the Nineteenth Century* (A History of English Baptists, 3; Didcot: The Baptist Historical Society, 1994), p. 279 and pp. 319-20.

[9] R. Mitchell, 'Hearn, Mary Ann (Marianne Farningham) (1834-1909)', *Oxford Dictionary of National Biography* (Oxford: Oxford University Press, 2004), www.oxforddnb.com/view/article/33789, accessed 4 July 2005.

[10] S.B. Black, *A Farningham Childhood* (Sevenoaks: Darenth Valley Publications, 1988), *The Baptist Quarterly,* March 1989, p. 52.

[11] M.A. Evans, 'Marianne Farningham (1834-1909) Aspects of the Life of a Victorian Woman' (unpublished MA dissertation, University of Leicester, 1994); H. Rogers, ' "First in the House": Daughters on Working-Class Fathers and Fatherhood' in T. L. Broughton and H. Rogers (eds) *Gender and Fatherhood in the Nineteenth Century* (Palgrave, 2007).

appointed as a full-time salaried contributor to the *Christian World*, after ten years of part-time work. Many years later, she recalled the occasion for her autobiography:

> Between the afternoon and evening services Mr Whittemore introduced me to Mr Spurgeon.
> 'So you are the great Marianne Farningham,' he said.
> And I replied 'So you are the great Charles Spurgeon.'
> After this, and the tea we had together, we were friends for the rest of the years.[12]

Such a comment by Spurgeon, even in jest, was an indication of just how well known the name of Marianne Farningham was. Further evidence of her fame comes from a much later stage in her life, when the future prime minister, Lloyd George, referred to her influence. He was a man with whom Marianne had some sympathies in areas such as education and foreign policy. While they were sharing a public platform in the little Welsh town of Barmouth, a few years before her death, Lloyd George confessed in his speech that Marianne's weekly writings had been one of the influences that had shaped his character. As a youngster, he recalled, he used to look forward to the appearance of the next edition of the *Christian World*. When it arrived, the first thing he did 'was to turn up Miss Hearn's articles and sweet bits of poetry'.[13] Her life may have been comparatively uneventful, but her influence was far-reaching, as a writer and as a role model although, in Lloyd George's case at least, it seems her advice was not always followed.

Marianne's popularity was also demonstrated by the way people crowded in to hear her speak when, for several years running, she undertook lecture tours, considering topics such as 'The Women of Today' and 'The Rush and Hush of Life'. The latter she remembered having given over two hundred times to many thousands of listeners.[14] In addition, for many years, she noted that hardly a week went by without receiving 'letters of appreciation and thanks from strangers',[15] an indication of a responsive readership, engaging with and considering themselves helped by her reflections on life and faith. Marianne especially hoped to influence her younger readers. As someone whose main church activity was leading a thriving class for teenage and young adult girls, she had a particular concern with encouraging that age group in their faith, and it appears that she had at least some degree of success. One correspondent wrote on the occasion of the jubilee of the *Christian World* to thank her for her

---

[12] Farningham, *Life*, p. 148.
[13] *CW* 25 March 1909, account of sermon at Barmouth following Marianne Farningham's death. Lloyd George's mother was a Baptist, and he was for a time a member of a Welsh Baptist Church in London. See the *Baptist Monthly* March 1899, p. 1.
[14] Farningham, *Life*, p. 165.
[15] Farningham, *Life*, p. 266.

book *Girlhood*: 'My aunts gave it to me when I was sixteen, and it was my monitor in many ways... your book strengthened my principles and helped me to view life and its responsibilities in a different light; in fact I cannot express all it did for me'.[16] Similarly, the Rev Charles Brown, who was President of the Baptist Union at the time of Marianne's death, and who took her funeral, recalled how as a young boy he had been influenced by *Boyhood* and how later the *Sunday School Times* 'was his constant companion, and through it she ministered to him'.[17] Such appreciative comments from her readers, combined with her wide readership, indicates that as well as reflecting the popular evangelical culture she lived in and wrote for, Marianne also helped to shape its attitudes, making a significant contribution to nineteenth-century Nonconformity. Mitchell is justified in claiming that her influence was widespread. Yet, in many ways, she was ordinary, and that, too, is a positive reason for studying her and her understanding of how faith can be worked out in everyday lives. Ian Randall has suggested that evangelical spirituality is a 'spirituality of ordinary people',[18] and therefore there is value in studying the life and writings of a woman who, despite her fame, reflected the beliefs and experience of many ordinary church members.

Tracing Changes within Evangelicalism

Marianne's life spanned slightly longer than the 64 years of Victoria's reign. Because she was active within the evangelical world for over half a century, her work sheds light on Nonconformist evangelicalism, especially that of Baptist congregations, during an extremely long period. In investigating her life and writings, our understanding of the Victorian world as a whole is enhanced, as evangelicalism was one of the dominant influences shaping English society and culture in the long nineteenth century. Evangelical values overlapped to a considerable extent with middle-class values, whilst its strictures were often the orthodoxy which rebels rejected and the norm from which people deviated. Whether through their adherence to or their reaction against it, many people constructed their identity and purpose within the framework of evangelical faith.

It would be helpful to briefly discuss the term 'evangelical'. Whilst an exact definition of evangelicalism has proved problematic, David Bebbington's frequently quoted 'quadrilateral' has gained much acceptance in recent years, and has the advantage of asserting that evangelicalism was as much a way of life as a system of beliefs. His four pillars of conversionism, activism, biblicism, and crucicentrism remain a useful template for describing

---

[16] Farningham, *Life,* pp. 266-67.
[17] *CW* 25 March 1909.
[18] I.M. Randall, *What a Friend we have in Jesus* (London: Darton, Longman & Todd, 2005), p. 15.

evangelicalism.[19] Indeed, it is now impossible to discuss evangelical spirituality without referring to this framework.[20] Not all Nonconformists were evangelical, and not all evangelicals were Nonconformists, but the Baptist chapels where Marianne made her home were included within what Clyde Binfield has called mainstream evangelical Nonconformity, along with Congregationalists and Wesleyan and Primitive Methodists.[21]

Her base was both evangelical and Nonconformist, and the Baptists, along with other evangelical networks, underwent change during the nineteenth century, a process which is reflected in Marianne's personal history. One prominent Baptist minister, John Carlile, who became editor of the *Baptist Times*, commented on some aspects of this process of change in his long memorial to Marianne in the *Freeman and Baptist Times*.

> Miss Hearn illustrated in her own experience the development of the Baptist denomination during recent years. Beginning among the Strict, she became less strict, broader in her sympathies, and less Calvinistic. Love was more to her than law. She had learnt the great lesson, that the affirmations of the Churches are greater than their differences. She was a friend to people of all sects, and a well-wisher to all creeds, though she never departed from the Baptist church.[22]

In this comparatively open attitude to fellow-Christians of other denominations, and to variety in doctrine, Marianne was in tune with the papers she wrote for, and their editors, especially James Clarke. The second editor of the *Christian World*, under whose leadership the paper prospered, Clarke from time to time had disagreements with evangelicals of a stricter persuasion. Nonconformist evangelicalism, always a broad umbrella, was gradually heading for the polarisation which took place in the early twentieth century between liberals and conservatives.[23]

Not only the Baptist world, but evangelical church culture, underwent

---

[19] D.W. Bebbington, *Evangelicalism in Modern Britain* (London: Unwin Hymen, 1989), pp. 3-17. Other attempts to define evangelicalism include I.C. Bradley, *The Call to Seriousness* (London: Cape, 1976), pp. 20-22, and B. Hilton, *The Age of Atonement* (Oxford: Clarendon, 1988), p. 7.

[20] A small selection of such references indicate the widespread recognition of the importance of this definition, for example, D. Gillett, *Trust and Obey, Explorations in Evangelical Spirituality* (London: Darton Longman Todd, 1993), p. 8; M. Noll, *The Rise of Evangelicalism* (Leicester: Inter-Varsity Press, 2004), p. 16.

[21] C. Binfield, *So Down to Prayers, Studies in English Nonconformity 1780-1920* (London: J.M. Dent & Sons, 1977), p. 7. Munson in *The Nonconformists*, p. 3, still chose these four denominations as representing the majority of Nonconformity at the end of the century.

[22] J.C. Carlile, 'Marianne Farningham The Woman and her Work', *The Freeman and Baptist Times* 26 March 1909.

[23] Bebbington, *Evangelicalism*, pp. 181-84.

significant changes, reflecting those in society at large, during the fifty or so years spanned by Marianne's career. John Wolffe has suggested that the period of greatest influence was in the middle of the century, with a 'loss of momentum' in the later Victorian years,[24] although this was rarely apparent to those who were living at the end of the century, as Marianne's cheerful optimism demonstrates.[25] The complex relationship between evangelicalism and culture led to considerable changes within the churches, and it is possible to trace some of these developing attitudes in Marianne's writings during the latter part of the century. Attitudes to keeping the Sabbath, and the debate over the existence of hell, are two of several topics in which changes can be traced in this way.[26]

The years when Marianne was writing were also important ones for the growth of opportunities for women. During this period women were for the first time admitted to higher education, including the study of medicine; whilst the Married Women's Property Acts gradually gave such women full legal control of all their property, whether owned at marriage or acquired subsequently. With the 1869 Municipal Franchise Act, single women householders were enabled to vote in local elections. The following year they were eligible both to vote in and stand for the new School Boards,[27] and in 1894 these voting rights were finally extended to married women. As Helsinger, Sheets and Veeder have highlighted, these were not years in which there was a clearly agreed and accepted attitude to men and women's roles: rather there was an ongoing debate over the 'Woman Question', with a diversity of opinions and arguments.[28] Marianne was certainly aware of some of these discussions and the variety of opinions expressed, and had her own views on the subject, which developed over time. Through the reciprocal relationship of reader and columnist, no doubt her writings reflected many of the opinions of her readers, especially concerning domesticity, but it is also likely that in some areas, such as attitudes to work, some of her readers' perspectives would have been challenged and possibly changed by Marianne's comments.

Women of Faith

There is a further important reason for uncovering the history of Marianne

---

[24] J. Wolffe, ed, *Evangelical Faith and Public Zeal* (London: SPCK, 1995), pp. 7-10.
[25] This is perhaps seen most clearly in M. Farningham, *Nineteen Hundred* (London: James Clarke, 1892). In her preface she describes the book as a 'little dream, of what, I hope, may be in the near future'.
[26] See Chapter 7.
[27] See Chapter 4.
[28] E.K. Helsinger, R.L. Sheets and W. Veeder, *The Woman Question: Society and Literature in Britain and America 1837-1883* (Chicago: University of Chicago Press, 1983), p. xiv.

Farningham: such study is part of the important process of rediscovering the lives of Nonconformist women of faith from the nineteenth century, a process that is still at a comparatively early stage.. Historians of women's lives have been slow to come to terms with the pervasive effects of religious belief in the lives of women of previous generations, and ecclesiastical historians have likewise often been reluctant to explore the female regions of their territory.[29] Some useful studies of individual women have emerged recently, although often they are of public figures already well known, such as Anne Stott's excellent biography of Hannah More.[30] There are also several investigations of Josephine Butler, and an interesting discussion by Sue Morgan of the rather less well known late nineteenth-century purity campaigner, Elise Hopkins.[31] Historians have come to realise that it is both difficult and inappropriate to discuss these women's lives without considering their religion, which was an integral part of both their formation and their mature lives. Leading the way in this field is the excellent work by Davidoff and Hall on the mid-century Victorian middle classes.[32] Much work remains to be done, however, on those who were well-known in their day but are now largely forgotten. Marianne is one of these women, and recovering her history and influence is a small contribution to this larger picture.

There are thus several significant reasons for choosing to study Marianne. In her beliefs, her simple faith, and the changes she gradually came to embrace, her life reflects the spiritual pilgrimage of many of her Nonconformist contemporaries, and may have helped to shape the attitudes of some of them through frequent exposure to her writing. She was both a role model and a companion on the journey for many evangelicals, men as well as women.

Themes in Marianne's Writings

In her autobiography, written towards the end of her long life, Marianne recalled her childhood longing for significance.[33] She described a monthly magazine she had read as a child which included a series of articles

---

[29] G. Malmgreen, *Religion in the Lives of English Women 1760-1930* (London: Croom Helm, 1986), p. 1.

[30] A. Stott, *Hannah More The First Victorian* (Oxford: Oxford University Press, 2003).

[31] S. Morgan, *A Passion for Purity: Ellice Hopkins and the politics of gender in the late Victorian church.* (Bristol: Centre for Comparative Studies in Religion and Gender, 1999). An interesting addition to the literature on Josephine Butler is L.S. Nolland, *A Victorian Christian Feminist: Josephine Butler, the Prostitutes and God* (Carlisle: Paternoster, 2004).

[32] L. Davidoff and C. Hall, *Family Fortunes: Men and Women of the English Middle Class 1780-1850* (London: Routledge, 1987).

[33] For issues surrounding the use of autobiographies, see this chapter, pp. 10-13.

on men who had been poor boys, and risen to be rich and great. Every month I hoped to find the story of some poor ignorant *girl*, who, beginning life as handicapped as I, had yet been able by her own efforts and the blessing of God upon them to live a life of usefulness, if not of greatness. But I believe there was not a woman in the whole series.[34]

In this short reminiscence the main themes in Marianne's life are evident, themes which can be traced in the private and public aspects of her life, as well as through her writings: faith, work and the lives of women. Because she was writing at a popular level, her attitudes to these themes of women, work and faith, can help to shed light on the beliefs and practices of ordinary Christians. Whilst she is interested in everyone, men and women, her attitudes towards women are particularly illuminating in the light of the public debate and changes in the place of women during the years she was writing. Her opinions about women's lives form one of the themes which will be traced through her writings and her life, whether in her public role as a lecturer and School Board member, or in her private life.

The importance of work is also indicated by this passage, clothed in the typically Victorian language of 'usefulness', and linked with the idea of reaching one's potential through a mixture of faith and hard work. Perhaps in choosing this passage, Marianne is suggesting that she has actually done what it seemed in her childhood that only boys could do. Through her own aspiration, and effort, she became, if not rich or great, someone who had contributed her share of work to the common good. Her working-class origins are also evident from this passage: she considered herself 'handicapped' by her background, probably a reference to her early rather sporadic education. She maintained a sympathy all her life with those from poor backgrounds.

Spirituality

The final theme, perhaps less clear in this passage, but for Marianne the heart of her experience, was that of faith. The quotation refers to the 'blessing of God', which could be merely a pious platitude, but in the context of her personal belief means much more, and was a consistent theme, expressed in the way she lived as much as in her words. Her spirituality gave coherence to all that she wrote and taught. People, she often insisted in her writing, needed a combination of their own efforts, and God's involvement, for their lives to be worthwhile. At the end of her life she could declare that 'The power of Christ, and all that is claimed for it is the realest thing in life, the realest thing in the world... His help is real, whatever your need may be'.[35] Marianne's understanding of faith was first and foremost a practical one.

---

[34] Farningham, *Life*, p. 44. Her italics.
[35] Farningham, *Life,* p. 279.

Marianne herself would not have employed the term 'spirituality', which only became common within evangelical circles towards the end of the last century. It will be used to encompass not just her devotional life, but the way faith is worked out in practice. James Gordon, following Gordon Wakefield, has argued that a definition of evangelical spirituality must include 'the impact of doctrine on experience and moral practice' and not just a discussion of devotional habits.[36] Alister McGrath, in a short paper on evangelical spirituality, has argued for a similar use of the word that, drawing on Protestant activist heritage, understands it as 'life in the world orientated towards God'.[37] This is the sense in which the term will be used in this book. Ian Randall uses the term in a similar sense, and his recent exploration of evangelical spirituality has provided a helpful starting point for the exploration of Marianne's expression of faith.[38]

Several other themes could be traced throughout Marianne's writing, such as the love of nature, or the importance of family, but most of these can be included within the three aspects mentioned. This book will study these major themes through her writing and practice, to evaluate how her attitudes and opinions changed and developed over the years, and to explore the relationship between her writing and the evangelical public.

Sources

Investigating Marianne Farningham's life has presented a dilemma with regard to source material. On the one hand, there is an abundance of material. Her prose pieces, fiction and poems in the *Christian World* over many years form a major part of her output, and through these one can track change and maturing in her own attitudes, beliefs and interests, as well as developments within the evangelical world. Then there was her work as editor of the *Sunday School Times*, including many fascinating editorials and her separate publications as Eva Hope, consisting mainly of biographies of a decidedly variable quality. There is, in addition, her fascinating autobiography, written towards the end of her long life and full of anecdotes, comments and reflections which say much about their author's preferences, opinions and experiences. Whilst all these sources provide a rich and varied mine in which to delve, there is an obvious disadvantage: they were all written by Marianne herself. Tracking down evidence of her life in other places has supplemented this material with newspaper articles, wills, minutes of School Board meetings and suchlike, but

---

[36] G. Wakefield, ed., *A Dictionary of Christian Spirituality* (London: SCM Press, 1983), pp. 361-63. J.M. Gordon, *Evangelical Spirituality, from the Wesleys to John Stott* (London: SPCK, 1991), p. vii.

[37] A.E. McGrath, *Evangelical Spirituality: past glories, present hopes, future possibilities* (London: St Antholin's Lectureship Charity, 1993), p. 7.

[38] Randall, *What a Friend*, Chapter 1.

with little of the detail of her life from other people. The friendships which were so important to her do not seem to be reflected in the written evidence that remains to us. For instance, she wrote of Spurgeon that they 'were friends for the rest of the years',[39] yet there is no documentary evidence of correspondence between them, and no reference to her in his own autobiography. Similarly, in later life she developed an acquaintance with the feminist thinker and campaigner Frances Power Cobbe which she valued, but there is no evidence in Cobbe's writing that such a friendship existed. It thus became clear that a biography might be problematic, yet the wealth of material available could provide a window on Victorian life, and especially female evangelical life, which would be extremely valuable. This, then, is the approach I have taken: to use her writings as a source of comment, conscious or unconscious, upon a variety of themes, already suggested: the changing nature of evangelicalism, including theology, practice and spirituality; women's role in private, public and in the church; and the development of Sunday schools. Marianne's writings, which provide a rich vein for such a mining operation, are supplemented wherever possible by the other available sources such as Board minutes.

A Working Woman's Life

One of the most useful sources is Marianne's autobiography, *A Working Woman's Life*, which provides an invaluable insight into her life and her spirituality. This *Life* includes a wealth of childhood memory, an insight into an era that was long gone by the time she recorded it. The *Freeman* called her accounts of her childhood and of the early days of the *Christian World* 'an exquisite idyll of Nonconformity'.[40] Yet there are some rather obvious difficulties with using an autobiography as a source. As Landow has indicated, there is a sense in which any autobiography is a performance, a construction for the benefit of an audience.[41] The inclusion of some parts of an individual's life, and the omission of others, combined with a perceived need to explain oneself to the imagined audience, can all create a bias. Even where the intention is to be honest, if written with the hindsight of old age, recollections are inevitably an interpretation and reconstruction of the past as much as a record of it. Memory itself can be uncertain, and writers often create a narrative which, with hindsight, gives purpose and meaning to their lives. As with other historical sources, not all the information given is entirely dependable and the conclusions drawn from it are, therefore, provisional, but this is true of all history. As Noll has commented, autobiographies 'offer the best place to

---

[39] Farningham, *Life*, p. 148.
[40] *Freeman*, 13 December 1907.
[41] Landow, G.P., ed, *Approaches to Victorian Autobiography* (Athens, Ohio: Ohio University Press, 1979) p. xxv.

ascertain what individuals concluded about their own experience'.[42] This work, however, gives a keen insight into the motives and world-view of the author, especially when used alongside other writings and sources. It is a significant source in its own right for an understanding of aspects of nineteenth century society and of Marianne's own life. Indeed, without it this study would have been impoverished. Whilst there are some difficulties in using autobiographic material, the advantages are considerable.

The style of her autobiography is informal and friendly, leading the reader to feel like a friend receiving a letter, rather than a stranger reading about someone she has never met, over one hundred and fifty years after many of the events recorded. There is also no suggestion of apology. Whilst she is modest about her own abilities and achievements, she does not justify her choice of life as a writer, but on the contrary, celebrates it, declaring that it 'was too dear to me ever to be given up'.[43] This is interesting, as Elizabeth Winston has argued that prior to 1920 female autobiographers tend to make a point of justifying their lifestyle and behaviour to their readers, especially if they have had successful careers.[44] This might indicate that Marianne is unusual in her self-confidence. Carole Jenkins however, commenting specifically on nineteenth-century autobiographies of working women, argues that women writing after 1850 demonstrate a pride in their own life or work.[45] She also traces a development from spiritual autobiographies in the earlier part of the century, which focused extensively on spiritual experience, through to a more secular style of writing, which may or may not have a religious content. In this context, Jenkins mentions Marianne, as being one of several women writing with a greater self-confidence, and expressing herself in vernacular rather than religious vocabulary.[46] She was typical of the growing assurance of working women, which in 1907 was still unusual enough to be noteworthy.

Winston also suggests that the very act of writing a memoir involved a conflict of values, and in this respect Marianne does seem to reflect convention. Certainly, in a brief foreword to her memoirs Marianne confessed 'I have had frequent misgivings while writing this autobiography... it has appeared very egotistical to do it'.[47] Not sure if her life would be as interesting to read as it was for her who lived it, she explains that it was the encouragement of friends

---

[42] M.A. Noll, *The Rise of Evangelicalism: the Age of Edwards, Whitfield and the Wesleys* (Leicester, IVP, 2004), p. 277.

[43] Farningham, *Life*, p 139.

[44] E. Winston, 'The Autobiographer and her Readers: From Apology to Affirmation' in E.C. Jelink, ed, *Women's Autobiography: Essays in Criticism* (Bloomington & London: Indiana University Press, 1980), p. 93.

[45] C. Jenkins, 'The major silence: autobiographies of working women in the nineteenth century', in J.B. Bullen, ed, *Writing and Victorianism* (Addison Wesley Longman, Harlow, 1997), p. 45.

[46] Jenkins, 'The major silence', p. 43.

[47] Farningham, *Life*, p 5.

which provoked her to record her experiences. This might be seen as the traditional apology for going into print at all, except that the tone of the book itself carries no such hint. She wrote that 'in some respects' writing the book 'has been a pleasant task' and her writing does give that impression. There is also evidence that she had for some years considered writing her autobiography. Contributing to the *Hearne Family History* in 1897 Marianne let slip that she meant to 'write my Reminiscences before I go, as I have lived in most interesting times and played my little part in them, for about ten years as a lecturer, and always as a writer',[48] so it is perhaps a little disingenuous to blame her friends for its production. Perhaps it would be truer to say that she had intended to write it, and others persuaded her that it would really be worthwhile, but that is only speculation. In her apology for writing, therefore, Marianne is conventional. Even in the writing of her autobiography, she displayed a mixture of both conventional and unconventional attitudes, a feature which marked out so much of her life.

According to Winston, women writing their autobiographical accounts 'were modest and self-effacing, they understated their achievements, disclaimed interest in personal recognition' and never 'affirmed their achievements without apology', the emphasis only changing to an affirmation of their achievements later in the twentieth century.[49] Whilst this description would fit many spiritual autobiographies written earlier in the nineteenth century, it was far from accurate in Marianne's case. Here was a woman who was quite happy to name-drop her acquaintance with famous people and to mention the large circulation of her writings. Whilst she often expressed surprise that she had been so successful, there was no hint of an apology for her earning power and her abilities, her public role or her successful journalistic career. Marianne was untypical in that respect. There was also, Winston has argued, a sense in which women writing autobiographies before 1920 felt the need to defend their support for 'cultural stereotypes which inhibit women from fully realizing their potentialities'.[50] The implication is that there was some dishonesty in the way women portray themselves, constructing a persona which would be acceptable to the readers of the book. As will be seen later, this was a little different for Marianne, who gave the impression of comfortably holding together ideas and values that some would consider contradictory: a genuine belief in the importance of the domestic in women's lives, with an enthusiasm for women to earn their own living, and to fulfil their potential, even at the cost of crossing conventional boundaries. Her remarkable autobiography marks her out as a

---

[48] W.T. Hearne, 'Mary Ann Hearn', *Brief History and Genealogy of the Hearne Family* (Independence, Missouri: Examiner Printing Company ,1907). Marianne's branch of the family spelt their surname differently from the majority of those described in this history.

[49] Winston, 'The Autobiographer', p. 95, p. 111.

[50] Winston, 'The Autobiographer', p. 111.

woman of courage and independent thought who had moved beyond the nineteenth-century need for women to apologise for going into print, especially with accounts of their own lives.

The Book

The various themes and issues introduced above are explored further in the chapters that follow. The next chapter outlines Marianne's life, indicating her development from country girl to nationally-known Christian writer. This provides the backdrop for further chapters discussing specific aspects of her life and work. Chapter 3 investigates her attitudes towards the changing role of women and the nature of women's work. Chapter 4 then explores the role she herself played within the Sunday school movement, focusing on her involvement as a class teacher. This is followed by a chapter specifically addressing the issue of women in public roles in the later nineteenth century, and Marianne's experience as writer, editor, lecturer and member of a School Board. Chapter 6 draws the various threads of her life together in exploring the spirituality which was the foundation for all Marianne's action and writings. In all of these aspects, her life intertwined with contemporary evangelicalism and reflected its changes, uncertainties, and divisions. Marianne's life and work provide us with a significant window not only onto the life of one individual woman, but of the nature of popular Nonconformity, especially for Baptists, and onto changing attitudes to women within evangelical culture. In studying her life, however, her personality, enthusiasm and faith were communicated to me, and I began to feel that in some sense I knew Marianne as an individual. This book is also, therefore, concerned with Marianne as a person, in so far as she can be known, and thus is also a study of 'a plain woman worker'.

Chapter 2

Marianne's Life Journey

I have a past to think of, too, and though there is nothing very remarkable to make it worth the telling, every life is interesting.[1]

Beginnings

Looking back from the early twentieth century, the influential Baptist minister John Carlile commented that 'the dreamy, drowsy little village of Farningham in Kent in 1834 when Marianne Farningham was born, was further away in spirit from modern England than the land of the Rising Sun is'.[2] Such sentiments express the sense of distance felt by early twentieth-century town-dwellers from the rural lifestyle of seventy years previously, and indicate the extent of the changes that Marianne experienced during her lifetime. These developments profoundly affected the evangelical community she wrote for and to which she belonged. She became a comforting, familiar presence for her readers, mediating faith in the midst of changes as she commented on contemporary life in her everyday style. All this lay in the future, however, for the child born into the Hearn family shortly before Victoria came to the throne.

Marianne's home village of Farningham had a population of around seven hundred people: a mixture of agricultural labourers, shopkeepers and craftsmen, as well as those who manned the well-used turnpike on the London to Maidstone road.[3] Most of the houses were built along this road, giving the village a long and thin appearance. The river Darent ran at right angles to the main street, and two of the four inns in the village stood alongside it. One, the Lion, had grounds running down to the river, as it still has today. The coach, Marianne recalled, changed horses at an inn opposite her house.[4] With several

---

[1] M. Farningham, *A Working Woman's Life* (London: James Clarke, 1907).
[2] *Freeman and Baptist Times* 19 March 1909.
[3] S.B. Black, *A Farningham Childhood* (Sevenoaks: Darenth Valley Publications, 1988), pp. 7-9. These early years of her life have been helpfully set in context by Shirley Burgoyne Black, in a little volume which also reproduces the first four chapters of Marianne's autobiography.
[4] Farningham, *Life*, p. 38.

coaches a day stopping in its heart, the village probably did not seem dreamy or drowsy to those who lived in it.

Joseph and Rebecca Hearn, Marianne's parents, were married on Christmas Day 1833, and so had been man and wife for just under a year when their daughter was born on 17 December 1834. Joseph, a shoemaker and the village postmaster, was the son of Ann and Thomas Hearn. This appears to have been Ann's second marriage.[5] Thomas died in 1816, but unusually for the time, Ann survived into old age, living with her son and his family.[6] The cottage had initially belonged to Ann, but at some stage Joseph seems to have taken over the tenancy from his mother. Although Marianne was not quite five when her grandmother died, at the age of 70, in November 1839, she remembered her as 'a dear old lady'. Ann wrote poetry, and her prayers made an impression on her young granddaughter who later recalled that they 'always seemed to take me into heaven'.[7] Marianne's facility with words might well have been inherited from her paternal grandmother, and the latter's spirituality clearly made an indelible impression.

Joseph's wife Rebecca was also locally born, the daughter of George and Mary Bowers. George earned his living as a paper-maker,[8] and Shirley Burgoyne Black comments that he was a man 'of ability and intelligence', and a popular 'workingman preacher of considerable force and originality'.[9] In her autobiography, Marianne recalled that some of her earliest memories were of her maternal grandfather preaching to a full chapel and making people both laugh and cry. It is interesting that humour was an accepted part of his sermons, as it was later of her lectures. She was a little afraid of him when he sat in their kitchen with his friends, 'each smoking a long clay pipe, and with a glass of home-brewed beer on the table'. The men discussed 'Calvinistic doctrine and the heresies of Arminianism, and sometimes they lapsed into village gossip'.[10] Such comments are typical of Marianne's colloquial style which gives the reader the impression of a conversation with a friend. The scenes she described appear fresh and lively, and her memories of childhood, although written through the lens of old age and with all the complications of autobiography discussed in the introductory chapter, do provide a first-hand account of village life in Kent in the early years of Victoria's reign.

---

[5] For this and other information on the Hearn family, see Black, *Farningham Childhood*, pp. 22-31.
[6] E. Hopkins, *Childhood Transformed: Working-class Children in Nineteenth-century England* (Manchester: Manchester University Press, 1994), p. 102.
[7] Farningham, *Life*, p. 13.
[8] W.T. Hearne, 'Mary Ann Hearn', *Brief History and Genealogy of the Hearne Family* (Independence, Missouri: Examiner Printing Company, 1907), http://www.cragun.com/brian/hearne/history/hh800m.html accessed 12/02/2006.
[9] Quoted in Hearne, 'Mary Ann Hearn', *Brief History*.
[10] Farningham, *Life*, p. 12.

Early Childhood Memories

Marianne was not the only child for very long, as 'in the course of time other children came to keep me company'.[11] Joseph and Rebecca had four other children, giving Marianne two sisters and two brothers: Rebecca 'Heppie' or Hephzibah Alfred, and finally Tom Various childhood cameos are sketched in Marianne's autobiography, in her conversational style. She recalled rocking her baby brother whilst reading, day-dreaming whilst doing chores, and going hop-picking to earn some extra income.[12] Marianne described herself as a 'rollicking, mischievous child, often getting into trouble', preferring to stare at the sunset rather than helping her mother with her brothers and sisters, and choosing to read a book rather than working at needlework, daydreaming even when she was working. As an adult she still tended to be disorganised at times, confessing in a letter to a friend that her writing had been delayed (possibly weeks) because she had been unable to find the original to reply to: she had 'hunted for it everywhere again and again but have only just succeeded in finding it'.[13] Rather than feeling guilty about childhood day-dreaming, which Deborah Nord has suggested was a characteristic of Victorian women,[14] Marianne seemed to relish this memory, using it to demonstrate that she had different inclinations to her siblings. She often got her clothes dirty and torn, remembering one particular occasion when she ripped a new pinafore when scrambling through a hedge. Finding her mother was out that evening, she put herself to bed, first praying earnestly at the side of her bed that the hole would be mended, then lying eagerly in bed to see if it was. 'Several times I got out (of bed) to pray again and examine the hole... but after a time the disappointing conviction was forced upon me that the hole remained exactly the same, and I lay in my bed softly sobbing for unanswered prayer – not knowing how many thousands had done so before me.' The little tale had a happy ending, as her aunt Mary came in, heard the whole account, and took the pinafore away to be mended, saying that perhaps God's answer to the prayer had been to send her to the house that evening to help out.[15] Retold in old age, this story gained a spiritual purpose, becoming more than merely an amusing tale of the misunderstandings of a child. The choice of this, and other stories to do with

---

[11] Farningham, *Life,* p. 17.

[12] Farningham, *Life,* p. 20, p. 18, pp. 35-38. Hopkins comments that children were expected to do chores from an early age in working-class families. Hopkins, *Childhood,* p. 118, whilst Thompson notes that older sisters usually minded the baby: F.M.L. Thompson, *The Rise of Respectable Society: A Social History of Victorian Britain 1830-1900* (London: Fontana, 1988), p. 130.

[13] Letters to Pollie, (2) 1864.

[14] D. E. Nord, *The Apprenticeship of Beatrice Webb* (London: Macmillan, 1985), pp. 61-65. Her study indicated that Victorian women regarded daydreaming as 'an illness to be purged', which is not how Marianne thought of it.

[15] Farningham, *Life,* pp. 23-24.

religion or church, is an indication that faith and of prayer remained important to Marianne at the end of her life. As she retold and re-imagined her own past, Christian belief and practice held a central role, and there is every indication that, for her, this had always been the case.

Marianne also developed a love of nature at an early age, describing how she spent hours leaning against the wall at the bottom of their garden and looking at the meadows, lime trees, meadow with watercress and forget-me-nots, the river, and in the distance hills, woods and villages. Often, she recalled, she 'stood with tears in my eyes, and my heart throbbing with love and gladness' as she watched sunsets from this vantage point.[16] Burnett identifies this as one of two key 'awakenings' in her early life, the other being her discovery of a poem by Felicia Hemans. He notes that several working-class autobiographers identify such key moments in their childhood.[17] This love of nature remained with her all her life, and she took every opportunity to spend time in a natural environment. She believed that everyone who had been brought up in the country started life with a great advantage: the Northumberland heroine Grace Darling, subject of Marianne's first biography, and the well-known Baptist preacher Charles Haddon Spurgeon, were amongst those she admired who, like herself, fell into this category. This appreciation was later threaded into poems, prose pieces and biographies.

The death of her brother Alfred was Marianne's 'first real sorrow'. He was only a young child, and she remembered his death only as 'a faint memory', but it nevertheless affected her. She recalled how she and her sisters were dressed for the funeral in 'black frocks and white diaper pinafores' with white socks and patent shoes.[18] The event was as notable in her memory for the distinctive clothes she wore as for the death itself. For the most part 'Polly' herself, as she was known, was a healthy child, and it was expected that she would grow to adulthood.[19] She did, however, have one serious illness when she was very young, smallpox 'with complications', a dangerous illness which she barely remembered. Delirious at times, her life was in danger, and she needed a 'long and weary period of convalescence'.[20] Not long afterwards, vaccination made smallpox a less threatening illness.[21] She also had an underlying weakness of the heart, which was identified in adulthood when she tried to have her life insured.[22] Yet Marianne generally 'enjoyed excellent health'[23] during her

---

[16] Farningham, *Life*, pp. 21-22.
[17] J. Burnett, *Destiny Obscure: Autobiographies of childhood, education and family from the 1820s to the 1920s* (London: Routledge, 1982, reprinted 1994), pp. 9-10. Burnett does not choose Marianne's account as one of his main examples, but does refer to it in the introduction to the first section of his book, on childhood.
[18] Farningham, *Life*, p. 25.
[19] It was common at the time for girls called Mary Ann to be known as Polly.
[20] Farningham, *Life*, p. 18.
[21] Hopkins, *Childhood*, p. 114.
[22] Farningham, *Life*, pp. 228-29.

working life, outliving all of her siblings, and in old age was keenly aware of being the last living member of her family from her generation, despite being the firstborn.[24] She gleefully remarked that it was the insurance company which lost out by rejecting her custom.[25]

In appearance Marianne was not particularly attractive. She regarded herself as 'much more plain looking and uninteresting than my brothers and sisters',[26] commenting that as a child she had 'neither face nor manners'.[27] A portrait in middle age makes her look quite a formidable woman, yet her own writing, and the comments of others, give the lie to that. She was aware of her dour appearance, however. When contemplating giving a series of lectures, she was concerned that once people saw 'the plain little woman', they would no longer want to read her work.[28] Later, on becoming editor of the *Sunday School Times* in 1885, her picture was included in the first number she was responsible for, and she jokingly commented she was surprised that it 'did not frighten away half the subscribers at one fell blow'.[29] There is more to attractiveness than physical appearance, however, and her enthusiastic, sympathetic and at times mischievous personality was communicated both in person and in words, despite her looks. Her friendly reputation has survived. In conversation a few years ago, the caretaker of College Street Baptist commented that 'She looked very stern, but apparently she wasn't like that at all.'[30] One friend, Jennie Street, insisted that she was anything but plain in appearance, because of her 'soul-beauty',[31] whilst Glandwr-Morgan similarly noted that 'her countenance radiated light and sweetness', despite a 'momentary disappointment' when he first saw her.[32] Such comments indicate that her personality affected her appearance.

It appears too that Marianne had an innate sense of fun, which she never lost. She remembered being rebuked as a young teenager by one of the church deacons for laughing in the Sunday morning service,[33] and although her humour became more appropriate, it was a consistent feature of her life. Marianne's explanation for the friendship she received, given on more than one occasion, was a prayer her father frequently prayed for her when she was

---

[23] Farningham, *Life*, p. 228.
[24] Hearne, 'Mary Ann Hearn', *Brief History*.
[25] Farningham, *Life*, pp. 229.
[26] Farningham, *Life*, p. 34.
[27] M. Farningham, *Homely Talks about Homely Things* (London: James Clarke, 1878), p. 49.
[28] Farningham, *Life*, p. 156
[29] Farningham, *Life*, p. 192.
[30] personal conversation
[31] *SST* 26 March 1909.
[32] W. Glandwr-Morgan, *Marianne Farningham in her Welsh Home* (Birmingham: Ellesmere Press 1923 [first edition James Clarke 1909]), Chapter 2.
[33] Farningham, *Life*, p. 54.

young, knowing that her physical appearance, 'plain-looking and uninteresting' might not endear her to others: 'Bless dear Polly, and grant that she may find favour with thee, and with the people with whom she may come in contact.'[34] Elsewhere she explained that she did not understand the prayer at the time, but that in later years she received an 'abundant answer' in the form of many friends.[35] Rogers regards this as a put-down, and suggests that Marianne internalised this comment on her appearance which then contributed to her spinsterhood, but this is not entirely convincing.[36] It is more likely that circumstances combined with a desire to continue working were the main reason for her single state, and it is possible that, as she claimed, she genuinely appreciated her father's prayer. This capacity for friendship became one of Marianne's strengths.

Eynsford Chapel

The whole family was involved in a little Baptist chapel at the nearby village of Eynsford whose pastor, John Rogers, was related to them by marriage, his wife being the sister of Marianne's paternal grandmother. Eynsford was only a mile or so away, and the chapel was the focus of much of Hearn family life. She said of her parents that 'indeed, the life of the chapel was their life, and it became mine'.[37] Her father Joseph was a deacon in the church, and both her parents taught in the Sunday school, which is interesting as women frequently gave up such a role once they had a family.[38] Marianne was told by her parents of her first visit to the chapel, at one month old, when after tea in the vestry she lay on a table in the chapel while friends held a prayer-meeting for her, which she regarded as a 'real consecration', more so than an infant baptism could have been.[39] There was a strong sense of belonging amongst chapel goers, no doubt forged in part by the difficulties the older generation had faced because of their allegiance. Almost all the people mentioned by Marianne who impinged on her childhood world were part of that gathered community.

The Baptist congregation at Eynsford had started meeting together in 1775. For the first few years it met in an assortment of rented buildings. John Rogers, who became pastor in 1802, was an energetic man, and barely two years after

---

[34] Farningham, *Life*, p. 34.
[35] Farningham, *Homely Talks*, p. 49.
[36] H. Rogers, ' "First in the House": Daughters on Working-Class Fathers and Fatherhood', in T. L. Broughton and H. Rogers (eds.) *Gender and Fatherhood in the Nineteenth Century* (Basingstoke: Palgrave, 2007), p. 133.
[37] Farningham, *Life*, p.14.
[38] L. Wilson, *Constrained by Zeal: Female Spirituality amongst Nonconformists 1825-75* (Carlisle: Paternoster Press, 2000), p. 143.
[39] Farningham, *Life*, p. 14.

he took up the pastorate, in 1804, a meeting house with a vestry was opened.[40] The church expanded under his capable leadership, and he remained there until his death in 1840. Some sources give the impression that life was very difficult for dissenters in Eynsford and Farningham in the early years of the church. Marianne suggested that 'our people were pretty abundantly persecuted', citing as an example the experience of her own grandmother, Ann Hearn, who was attacked after being baptised in the river Darent. On her way home she was followed 'by a mob of rough village folk' who threw stones, and seriously injured her.[41] Marianne also recounted a later baptism, in the chapel, when a woman was baptised whilst her husband sat in a pew with a loaded gun, waiting to shoot her when she came out of the water. There is no mention of how this tragedy was averted. Black, however, dismisses these as 'occasional acts of hooliganism',[42] arguing that there is little evidence of the persecution of these early dissenters, and that several of them were tradesmen who depended on the custom of the local people, whilst the local paper mill owner was a strong patron, although not a member.[43] The stories that Marianne told had become part of the story and identity of Eynsford Chapel, but the chapel-goers had possibly not been as oppressed as they were inclined to believe.

Rogers was followed as pastor by the less than satisfactory George Whitbread, whose capacity for pastoral work was limited, and then in 1846 by William Reynolds, who left in 1851 owing to the low income of the position.[44] The following year Jonathan Whittemore, whose living was partly derived from other sources, took his place. He spent part of the week in London pursuing his publishing interests, and the rest of the time based in Farningham, which was convenient for travel to London.[45] In the few years he pastored the church, until his sudden death in November 1860, he stirred up some controversy, as his faith was of a broader kind that Eynsford Chapel was used to, but he was a breath of fresh air for Marianne.[46]

Chapel Life

Chapels have been called 'something of a home from home' for their members during this period, and this was certainly true for the Hearn family.[47] They regularly spent their Sundays at the chapel, taking a packed lunch which they

---

[40] *A Short History of Eynsford Baptist Church 1775-1906* (1906). pages.ukonline.co.uk/Eynsfordbaptist/hist1.htm, accessed 16 June 2004.

[41] Farningham, *Life*, p. 33.

[42] Black, *Childhood*, p. 39.

[43] Black, *Childhood*, p. 39 and p. 37.

[44] Black, *Farningham Childhood*, p. 35

[45] Farningham, *Life*, p. 80.

[46] Whittemore's obituary in *CW*, 9 November 1860, gives details of his life as a publisher.

[47] Hopkins, *Childhood*, p. 149.

consumed in their own pew, then sharing tea in the vestry with other members following the afternoon service. The Sunday programme was 'Seven o'clock prayer meeting, nine o'clock Sunday School, half-past ten public worship, two o'clock Sunday School, three o'clock service, half-past five o'clock prayer meeting, six-o'clock service'. After this, they would go home and have further lessons and family worship! Despite this rigorous schedule, it appears that Sundays were eagerly anticipated, at least by some members. The picture Marianne paints of the chapel is of a strong community who enjoyed spending time together. She later described chapel life as 'full of joy and gladness' so that when she left she 'missed the companionship of those who were dear to me in Farningham and Eynsford more than words can say'.[48] When she did attend school, her friends there were also Baptists: the little dissenting community had a distinct identity even amongst the children.[49] Her experience of God and of church were very closely connected, and the church family was of great importance to her in her spiritual development. When she returned to live in Farningham as an adult, after a spell in Bristol, she enjoyed further aspects of this community, such as visiting friends, going for walks together and borrowing books. In old age she looked back nostalgically to the time when she belonged to that congregation, and to the joys of walking along the road with her friends to chapel, singing as they went, and wondered if those who were going there 'now' were as fond of them as she and her friends used to be.[50] Clearly those early days still held a special place in her memory, perhaps all the more so as she neared the end of her life. The close network of relationships she later developed with her girls' class was probably based on the example of this closely-knit chapel community.

Doctrinally, however, it was a rather narrow upbringing. Eynsford Chapel was 'Strict and Particular', in other words, Calvinist and practising closed communion. It became largely teetotal when Marianne was a child, and she herself remained a staunch opponent of drink all her life. A journalist writing in the *Northampton Independent* following Marianne's death in March 1909, commented that in this environment 'she was subject to such strict Calvinistic training that the wonder is her poetic fire was not stifled at the outset'.[51] Indeed, she recalls some older church members being horrified when she was given a present of an edition of Shakespeare. Marianne recalled that 'One anxious lady begged me to let her burn it, as she was sure it was an offence in the sight of God, and several who heard of it advised me not to read it'.[52] Such narrowness of understanding, however, was balanced by the positive influence of a strong, affectionate, and joyful community. Marianne herself wrote about the contrast

---

[48] Farningham, *Life*, p. 88.
[49] Farningham, *Life*, p. 26.
[50] Farningham, *Life*, p. 70.
[51] *Northampton Independent* 20 March 1909.
[52] Farningham, *Life*, p. 71.

between Christianity which was 'of a healthy, gladsome sort', compared to that found 'among rigid Calvinists or Unitarians',[53] but it seems that she considered Eynsford to be in the former camp, although perhaps it was unusual in this respect. Certainly, Marianne's recollections of her childhood experience of chapel were largely positive,[54] in contrast with other writers such as Edmund Gosse, who discarded strict evangelicalism as they grew up.[55] Although in due course she left much of its narrow doctrine behind, this early experience of church as gathered community shaped her thinking, her expectations and her practice in the years ahead. In addition she had the support and encouragement of her pastor, who was himself a man of wider sympathies, being the person who had given her the Shakespeare. Even rural congregations were not immune to the cultural trends in the country as a whole, especially with a well-read pastor.

Her religious involvement also led, not surprisingly, to childhood games which were connected to chapel life. There is an amusing account in her autobiography of a group of children playing at baptisms in the river Darent which ran near the school playground. A bucket played the person to be baptised, with some boys as the deacons passing it along, and Marianne as the pastor dipping it in the water. When the bucket was lost and the children got into trouble as a result, she was rightly accused of being the ring-leader.[56] Marianne was clearly a leader and initiator even as a child and she had no difficulty stressing that role as she composed her account in old age. It might be too much to read into this an aspiration to be a pastor, but clearly she felt no need to portray herself as some idealised, demure Victorian woman, and was comfortable discussing her rural background and her tomboy characteristics, giving the impression of someone who was comfortable with herself and confident in her own identity. This supports the suggestion made by Carole Jenkins, writing about female autobiographies, that women became confident as the nineteenth century progressed, 'writing with pride of their own lives and work'.[57] Marianne provides a good illustration of this development.

Rebecca Hearn's Death

Social historians have noted that in Victorian times many children lost at least

---

[53] E. Hope, *Great Modern Women* (London: Walter Scott, 1886), p. 204.
[54] Farningham, *Life,* p. 55. For further exploration of joy and spirituality see Chapter 7, p. 177.
[55] E. Gosse, *Father and Son* (London: William Heinemann, 1907) but note the alternative description of Philip Gosse in A. Thwaite, *Glimpses of the Wonderful: The Life of Philip Henry Gosse 1810-1888* (London: Faber, 2002).
[56] Farningham, *Life,* p. 27.
[57] C. Jenkins, 'The major silence: autobiographies of working women in the nineteenth century', in J.B. Bullen, ed, *Writing and Victorianism* (Harlow: Addison Wesley Longman, 1997), p. 45.

one parent in their early childhood, and this was Marianne's experience.[58] Rebecca Hearn died of tuberculosis when her daughter was only twelve years old, and Marianne later recalled that her father said many times that she 'never had a girlhood, but grew at once from a child to a woman'.[59] She describes movingly in her autobiography how her mother had to stop suddenly while showing the children how to skip, and blood came to her lips; how she lay ill in bed for many months while Marianne read to her from a book called 'The Dying Christian', and talked with her; how Marianne prayed that her father would die instead of her mother. As Rogers has highlighted, Marianne suggested that their home life was happy because her mother 'was the presiding influence in the house', ruling with love whilst her father's authority was more firmly enforced.[60] When, after many months, Rebecca died, early on Christmas day, the young girl was devastated. In her autobiography she wrote vividly of her mother being near death on Christmas Eve, and how as the bells were ringing in the evening 'I shrank from their sounds as if they were blows'. When she heard the carol singers she recalled how 'I felt as if all the light of my life went out, and that the Babe of Bethlehem could never be anything more to me again'.[61] Even as an elderly woman, she found Christmas a difficult time, confessing 'I do not know how to bear the sounds of Christmas bells and carol-singers'.[62] This grief was not clearly portrayed in her writing prior to the autobiography, although it was hinted at in various ways in her sympathy to those who were suffering. The anguish of such early bereavement is movingly communicated in this account, despite being written many decades later. Whilst she was composing the chapters about her childhood, she was often in tears, as she vividly recalled emotions as well as incidents from years before.[63] Marianne noted that most of the villagers from Farningham and Eynsford attended the funeral, an interesting comment on the place her parents held within the community, and the acceptance of Baptists at that time. No doubt her father's role of local postmaster meant the family was known to everyone, but it is evident that they were regarded as fully a part of the village, despite their dissenting allegiance.

Rebecca's death led to a difficult time for the whole family, but particularly for Marianne as the eldest girl. For a few months, her mother's unmarried sister, Mary Bowers, who had nursed her in her last illness, and was presumably the one who had mended Marianne's pinafore, lived with them and helped to look after them, but she also died within a year. Marianne, who had loved school, had to abandon her education to run the house, which she was

---

[58] E. Hopkins, *Childhood*, p. 102.
[59] Farningham, *Life*, p. 43.
[60] Rogers, 'Daughters', p 133.
[61] Farningham, *Life*, p. 41.
[62] Farningham, *Life*, p. 41.
[63] Glandwr-Morgan, *Welsh Home*, Chapter 3.

sure 'was done very badly'.⁶⁴ It has been suggested that her father withdrew her from school because he believed 'all secular knowledge was useless', but it is clear that the reason was practical and financial necessity following Rebecca Hearn's death.⁶⁵ A cousin stayed briefly to help, but she was only the same age as Marianne, who commented that after the cousin left she and her sisters 'had everything to do, washing, mending, scrubbing, cooking'.⁶⁶ During these months after the death of her aunt, Marianne longed for a step-mother, even an 'unsympathetic' one, but none appeared, although when her father finally did remarry, she made no comment about his wife.⁶⁷ It was, she asserted, in a considerable understatement, 'a bad time for a girl to pass through'.⁶⁸ The loss of her mother at such an early stage, combined with the elevation of motherhood in contemporary culture, led to a romantic, idealised view of mothers in Marianne's writing.⁶⁹ Her mother's death, not surprisingly, was a watershed in her experience.

Marianne's portrait of her father is sympathetic, yet there are hints that he was not the easiest man to live with. Rogers notes that the relationship revealed by her autobiography was more 'complicated and troubled' than her portrayal of fatherhood in her early writings suggested.⁷⁰ She clearly wanted to speak well of her father, suggesting that his 'was the hardest lot', and remembering how he always cleaned the girls' shoes, and lit the fire, explaining that 'on cold winter mornings we never came downstairs without finding a cheery fire burning in the grate ready for us', and recalling that they were always welcome to bring friends home for tea. He was also 'full of fun and jokes'. ⁷¹ Both the hospitality, and the sense of fun, which so marked Marianne's adult life, were learnt partly from her father during those difficult years of girlhood. It is also significant that, once he really understood how much education mattered to her, he found a way of letting her pursue it despite the family's hardship and the need for her earnings to help sustain them.⁷² Yet she also commented that 'parental authority was no dream in those days', and there was strong discipline in the house, with the proverb 'spare the rod and spoil the child' being frequently quoted.⁷³ Marianne makes no judgement about this treatment, not

---

⁶⁴ Farningham, *Life*, p. 44.
⁶⁵ T.W. Laqueur, *Religion and Respectability: Sunday Schools and Working Class Culture 1780-1850* (New Haven and London: Yale University Press, 1976), p. 153.
⁶⁶ Farningham, *Life*, p. 45.
⁶⁷ Rogers, 'Daughters', p. 133.
⁶⁸ Farningham, *Life*, p. 44.
⁶⁹ See Chapter 3, pp. 76-80.
⁷⁰ Rogers, 'Daughters', p. 133.
⁷¹ Farningham, *Life*, pp. 45-47.
⁷² Farningham, *Life*, p. 50.
⁷³ Farningham, *Life*, p. 34. Hopkins discusses the issue of differing perspectives on the treatment of children in the first half of the nineteenth century in Hopkins, *Childhood*,

clearly indicating if she regretted the passing of that attitude, or if she now considered it old-fashioned. She was, however, much more likely to talk about encouragement than discipline when discussing the training of Sunday school children. Joseph liked to be busy. Later in life Marianne mentioned that her father 'could not be quite happy to have no occupation' which also described his daughter, but must have made him a difficult house guest when he was elderly and infirm.[74] Her relationship with her father was a complex one.

Early Christian Experience

In old age Marianne recounted that she went through a period of rebellion and bitterness towards God following her mother's death, when she did not pray, 'and was not anxious to be good', but 'very bitter and naughty'.[75] Laqueur links this phase to the lack of female role models in her reading material, but in Marianne's understanding of her own experience this was a symptom of her rejection of God after her bereavement rather than the primary issue.[76] This period did not last very long, however. She had a few people who were concerned about her, one of whom was her Sunday school teacher, one Miss Eliza Hearn, who was also in charge of the Nonconformist British School. According to Marianne, Eliza was unrelated to her, although Black suggests it is more likely that she was a distant relative.[77] One Sunday morning when Marianne was 'burning with indignation and anger', Eliza encouraged her to sit next to her, and held her hand. As she sat there, and felt the compassion of her teacher 'all bitterness died out of my heart... and I was quite another child when the service came to an end'.[78] This little episode was the closest Marianne came to a conversion experience, for in common with many who have been brought up in Christian homes, she 'could not remember when I was converted or if I had ever been... All I knew was that I loved and trusted the Saviour.'[79]

A strong emphasis was put on conversion within evangelicalism, such that it has been highlighted by Bebbington as one side of his famous 'evangelical quadrilateral'.[80] Marianne's explanation portrayed coming to faith as more of an awareness that had been developing for much of her life, although her

---

pp. 116-17. See also L.A. Pollock, *Forgotten Children: Parent-Child Relationships from 1500 to 1900* (Cambridge: Cambridge University Press, 1983).

[74] Farningham, *Life,* p. 151.

[75] Farningham, *Life,* p. 44.

[76] Laqueur, *Religion and Respectability,* p. 153.

[77] Black, *Farningham Childhood,* p. 26.

[78] Farningham, *Life,* pp. 44-45.

[79] Farningham, *Life,* p. 55. Rogers, 'Daughters' p. 134 suggests that her conversion took place through a Sunday school teacher, but I think this is a misinterpretation of the account.

[80] D.W. Bebbington, *Evangelicalism in Modern Britain* (London: Unwin Hyman, 1989), p. 3. See also Chapter 4, pp. 110-113 and Chapter 6, pp.178-182

inability to 'name.. a definite experience or time that marked my passing from carelessness to earnestness' was by no means as unusual as she seems to have thought.[81] Being certain of her faith, she applied for church membership at an unusually early age, and was questioned concerning her experience and beliefs by the minister, Rev William Reynolds,[82] and deacons, in front of the other church members, quite an ordeal for a fourteen year old. She remembered giving them the answers they wanted, but once again, as she was writing so long afterwards, it is hard to be sure that she really had the consciousness of giving such contrived answers.[83] She wrote little about her actual baptism, an event that many Baptists regarded as a significant rite of passage, except to comment that it was a 'lovely Sunday evening in June'.[84] So Marianne joined the church, becoming fully a part of the community to which she had always belonged.

Education

In common with many working-class children of the time, especially girls, Marianne had a sporadic education.[85] The options were limited: a local girl's boarding school which was far too expensive, or a National School which was out of the question as it was connected with the Church of England. Attendance there would have meant learning the Anglican catechism which was considered totally inappropriate for Nonconformist children. Marianne was eager to study, however, and made the most of the few opportunities which came her way. Her grandmother, Ann Hearn, taught her to read, and Marianne claimed that by the age of six she 'could read any chapter in the Bible', which was her only text book. At some stage she also attended a local dame school, but gave no impression of having learnt much there. She was eager to write, too, being frustrated because many of her contemporaries could already do so. She recalled 'in the matter of writing I was quite behind the other children of my age. My ignorance in this respect was a sore trouble to me, and I made the lives of my parents a burden to them with my continual cry "Teach me to write".' [86] Her first attempt at poetry was an epitaph on a toad, which remained unrecorded because of her inability to write. This episode has led to a few citations of Marianne in contemporary writing, for instance she is referenced on

---

[81] Farningham, *Life,* p. 55; Wilson, *Zeal,* pp. 85-88.
[82] http://pages.ukonline.co.uk/enysfordbaptist/hist1.htm accessed 16 June 2004.
[83] Farningham, *Life,* p. 55.
[84] Farningham, *Life,* p. 58. For baptism as a significant event see M. Watts, *The Dissenters Vol 2,* (Oxford: Clarendon Press, 1995) p. 191, and Wilson, *Zeal,* p. 46-47.
[85] Hopkins, *Childhood,* p. 133 and p 138-39.
[86] Farningham, *Life,* p. 20.

websites discussing literacy in the nineteenth century.[87] Finally an appropriate solution was found, and she was taught by a neighbour, Isabella, the youngest daughter of the pastor of Eynsford, John Rogers, who lived two doors away. Marianne's father spent a considerable time making her a little box shaped like a book for her to keep everything she needed for writing, and she went next door but one for her lessons.[88] Only Marianne's persistence led to her acquiring the skills she would need for her future career.

When Marianne was nine there was an exciting new development: a British School opened at Eynsford, and she was able to spend a few years there.[89] Here she was 'passionately eager to learn', despite frequently getting into trouble. Levine has highlighted the fact that many intelligent women in this period were largely self-educated. In Marianne's case, though, this was due to the lack of a suitable school in the early years, and the consequences of her mother's death later, rather than to any parental belief that education was unsuitable for girls.[90] She continued to seek every possible means to extend her education. After her mother's death she helped her father sort the village letters, and she took the opportunity to copy the handwriting for practice. One summer, she got up at five o'clock, whilst at another time she 'burned the midnight tallow' (as they could not afford oil) in order to read, keeping herself awake with strong tea surreptitiously sneaked out of the kitchen.[91] On one such occasion she set her bedroom on fire. After this incident her father arranged for her to return to school for part of the day, but as he could not afford to lose her labour completely, at the same time she contributed to the family income by shoe-binding. Joseph Hearn, it seems, was willing to enable Marianne to continue her education, even part-time, at an age at which many working-class children were already contributing to the family income.[92] She and her sisters all went, as she described it, 'in fits and starts', as between them they also had to maintain all the house management.[93] In old age Marianne still regretted her lack of education, writing in her autobiography that 'One of my greatest regrets, even now, is that my attendance at the Eynsford British School was so

---

[87] For example http://www.nrdc.org.uk/content.asp?CategoryID=546, accessed 13 September 2005.

[88] Farningham, *Life*, p. 20.

[89] Farningham, *Life*, p. 26, p. 46. The British and Foreign School Society, founded in 1808, was anti-establishment and Nonconformist. It was in a minority compared to its rival, the schools of the Church of England National Society for Promoting the Education of the Poor, established 1811.

[90] P. Levine, *Feminist Lives in Victorian England: private roles and public commitment* (Oxford: Blackwell, 1990), p. 54.

[91] Farningham, *Life*, p. 48.

[92] F. Thompson, *Lark Rise to Candleford*, (London: Oxford University Press, 1945), p. 131.

[93] Farningham, *Life*, p. 45.

perfunctory and intermittent'.[94] There is some suggestion that her education was completed by a few weeks' training at The Home and Colonial College in Grays Inn Road, London, which was founded in 1836 to provide training for infant teachers. If it had taken place, even such a short period of training would have given her an advantage, as many teachers had no training at this time.[95] Marianne exploited her limited education to the full. She clearly believed that it had made it hard for her to pursue her career: but it may well be that the self-motivation she developed was not equalled by later children who had to attend school whether they were eager for it or not. She was an example of someone from the working class who was determined to make her mark on the world, taking hold of any suitable opportunities that came her way.

These formative years were thus influenced by a variety of factors: by family and village, by the rural environment, and by the traditional rural Baptist church. Themes that echoed through her writing were rooted in her childhood experience; women, work and faith, and also others, such as the importance of a secure family base, the nature of church, and a love of nature.

Bristol

In 1852, aged 17, Marianne moved to Bristol to be an assistant to Miss Bamford, who was running a school on Durdham Down.[96] Many years later, she wrote eloquently of the city, of seeing ships for the first time, sharing a picnic in Leigh Woods, and of the West Country people she met.[97] In the previous century, Bristol had been the second city in the nation, with its riches founded on commerce based on the slave trade and goods such as tobacco. By the time Marianne lived there, it was no longer at its peak, but was still a bustling city and an important centre for trade. Much of medieval Bristol was still preserved and Marianne recalled finding this a delight: 'A walk down the "Steps" and through the streets was a holiday'.[98] These would have been the Christmas Steps, one of the few parts of the old city still in existence today. Not all of Bristol would have been so pleasant: Whiteladies Road, which leads from Durdham Down into the centre of Bristol, still had an open sewer running alongside it when Marianne was there.[99] In the school, she taught the top girls' class, learning herself as she went along. Although she 'could not have passed an examination', standards were lower in those days, and she was able to pass

---

[94] Farningham, *Life*, p. 46.
[95] Black, *Childhood*, pp. 46-47.
[96] Details of this establishment have been impossible to discover, as not even the name is given.
[97] Farningham, *Life*, p. 63.
[98] Farningham, *Life*, p. 63.
[99] J. Latimer, *Annals of Bristol in the Nineteenth Century*, 1887 (Bath: Kingsmead Reprints, 1970), p. 314.

on everything she knew.[100] It appears that she thoroughly enjoyed this first venture away from home, despite the move from a small village to a bustling city of nearly 140,000 people.[101] With hindsight, at least, her time in the West Country was a welcome adventure.

During this year Marianne often attended Counterslip Baptist church, a thriving chapel of around 600 people,[102] on the recommendation of another teacher, Matilda Lewis, who befriended her and who sang in the choir.[103] This friendship, she commented, lasted for 50 years, an indication of the importance of friends to Marianne, and of her ability to maintain such relationships over a long period despite living at a distance from the other person. She mentioned the minister who was known affectionately as 'Father' Winter. Thomas Winter pastored the chapel from 1823 to 1860. Marianne sometimes attended other churches and occasionally visited Bristol Cathedral, for instance for a memorial service for the Duke of Wellington. In Bristol she also claimed to have become acquainted with George Muller, who apparently gave her a copy of his life which had been published a few years previously. She remembered that she was influenced by his prayers and his preaching.[104] Bristol was a lively and interesting place for a young Christian woman.

A few comments she made about herself as a young woman highlight the contradictory influences Marianne was subject to in portraying her own character. Referring to her arrival in Bristol to teach, aged seventeen, she described herself as 'the plainly dressed, timid little stranger from Kent'. Here she demonstrated not only her poor origins, but a shyness which she spoke about later, too. Yet on the next page she wrote that when attending the memorial service for the Duke of Wellington, although the cathedral was very crowded, 'being small and resolute, I managed to push my way up to the very front'.[105] There seems to be a contradiction here: was she 'timid' or 'resolute'? One explanation is that although she was always a very determined woman, with strong ideas, in public speaking, or even in personal relationships, she developed from shyness to confidence. But the way she highlighted both aspects might indicate a conflict in her mind as to the nature of womanhood and the desirable characteristics of a woman which was still not completely resolved at the time of writing.

The Start of Marianne's Writing Career

This enjoyable time lasted only a year before the sad news arrived that

---

[100] Farningham, *Life*, p. 66.
[101] Latimer, *Annals of Bristol*, p. 324.
[102] *Counterslip Baptist Church: A Brief History 1804-2004*, p. 30.
[103] Farningham, *Life*, p. 63.
[104] Farningham, *Life*, pp. 63-66.
[105] Farningham, *Life*, pp. 63-64.

Marianne's younger sister Rebecca was dying of consumption, 'that scourge of young people' during this period as Davidoff and Hall call it.[106] Her father wanted her to return home and nurse her sister.[107] A doctor had advised them that the only hope for Rebecca was to take her to a different climate in the south of France. 'Of course,' Marianne commented, 'that was utterly impossible, and so we had that very common experience of the poor. We watched our dear one get worse and weaker day by day...'.[108] It is significant that, whilst realising that if they had been richer, they might have been able to save Rebecca's life, there was no bitterness in her tone, but rather she then described the next few months as a 'sacred time' when her sister, who was recently converted, apparently had a strong sense of the presence of Christ with her.[109] During these weeks, as she watched over her sister, she wrote poems, and later discreetly sent them to magazines such as the *Christian Cabinet* under the name of 'Echo'.[110] She claimed never to have had one returned. So her published career began, made possible because Marianne remained at home for some time after Rebecca's death. During this period her sister Hephzibah who 'was more sensible and domesticated', despite having had no-one to teach her as she had been only six when their mother died, took the responsibility of running the house, allowing Marianne time to write and study. Although she was the younger sister, Heppie almost mothered Marianne: 'She cared for me with almost more than a sister's love', was the writer's comment concerning this phase of her life.[111] With this exception, however, and despite Marianne's close relationship with her family, they did not particularly understand or encourage her enthusiasm for learning and talent for writing.

Rather than her family, it was Jonathan Whittemore, her pastor, from whom Marianne received encouragement. After she had been publishing material for a little while, it came to his attention, and he talked with her about her writing. In the past, she says, he had always been critical of her work and sarcastic, so she had avoided sending him any of her later verses. Now, however, he encouraged her to send contributions to the *Baptist Messenger* which he was editing at the time, and to write some hymns for a collection he was publishing. According to her account, 'he took me into his confidence' with regard to his future plans, including the idea of a weekly religious paper. This became the *Christian World*, and she was involved in its development prior to publication, and then contributed to it for all her life.[112] At this time there was a rapid expansion of

---

[106] L. Davidoff and C. Hall, *Family Fortunes: Men and Women of the English Middle Class 1780-1850* (London: Routledge, 1992 edition) p. 65.
[107] Farningham, *Life*, p. 46.
[108] Farningham, *Life*, p. 67.
[109] Farningham, *Life*, p. 67.
[110] See for instance *The Christian Cabinet* 1 November 1856.
[111] Farningham, *Life*, p. 69.
[112] Farningham, *Life*, pp. 68-69.

the popular press facilitated by developments in printing, economics and transport, and Whittemore took advantage of the situation.[113] The idea of a non-denominational weekly Christian newspaper was a new one, and the aim of it, according to Marianne, one of its strongest advocates, was to help Christians from different traditions understand each other, fostering the idea that friendship between people of differing religious views was not automatically a betrayal of their own denomination. Its motto was 'In things essential, unity; in things doubtful, liberty; in all things, charity.' The fact that it also contained the week's news was an added advantage, she believed, making it popular in villages and small towns.[114] She commented on the incongruity of such a paper coming from a minister of a church with a narrow view of salvation and communion, suggesting that 'Extremes provoke revolt'.[115] Whittemore was an unusual man, and Marianne was fortunate to have him as a mentor.

Gravesend

After some time back at Eynsford, it became apparent that Marianne would need to earn her own living again, as it was 'difficult to make both ends meet' whilst staying with her father. So in 1867 she applied for a teaching post advertised in the *Christian World*. The advert was for 'a young pious female of dissenting principles' to take charge of young children in a local British School.[116] Given the job, Marianne found herself teaching in nearby Gravesend, a town which had grown rapidly during the nineteenth century mainly through tourism which brought people from London via the Thames to the beach and pleasure garden.[117] This was a very different experience from her year in Bristol. Writing about the latter, Marianne had given no hint of having felt homesick or lonely, although she might have been looking back at that time with rose-tinted spectacles. Bristol had delighted her with new sights, and she seemed never to have been short of friends there. Gravesend was a very different place and here she did recall feeling lonely and miserable. It is possible that she was suffering from some type of depression following the recent death of her sister, which affected her usually positive outlook on life, but this is pure conjecture. Very little is said in her autobiography about this part of her life, perhaps because she never settled there. She formed few lasting

---

[113] A. Lee, 'The structure, ownership and control of the press, 1855-1914', G. Boyce, J. Curran and P. Wingate, eds, *Newspaper History from the Seventeenth Century to the Present Day* (London: Constable, 1978), pp. 117-129.

[114] Farningham, *Life,* pp. 73-74.

[115] Farningham, *Life,* p. 74.

[116] *CW*, 27 November, 1857. The advertisement was noted by B.M.A. Evans, 'Marianne Farningham (1834-1909) 'Aspects of the Life of a Victorian Woman', (unpublished MA dissertation, University of Leicester, 1994), p. 9.

[117] Farningham, *Life,* p. 88.

friendships in this period, although one, with Miss Gordge, a headmistress in the town, proved to be life-long. There is a clear contrast in her account between her experiences in Bristol and this new job, even though it was within easy reach of her home. She took every opportunity to walk the eight miles home to Farningham to visit family and friends. In her typical way of making the best of every situation, however, Marianne did try to draw something positive from her rather bleak time in Gravesend, writing that she was 'glad to have had that experience, because I have ever since known how to sympathise with lonely girls'.[118] This is an example of how Marianne developed the knack of weaving every experience she chose to recount into a purposeful whole. No doubt much of this was with hindsight, but it also indicates her belief in that her whole life was lived under the hand of a Divine purpose.

The Move to Northampton

Marianne moved to Northampton in 1859, not expecting to stay very long, yet she remained there the rest of her life. There was a sense in which Northampton considered her its own: by the end of her life she had practically become a Northampton institution. After her death, the *Northampton Independent* regretted the loss of 'its most notable woman' and enthused about 'the persistence with which she praised the town and people in her widely-read writings'.[119] Her girls' class, too, was well known in the town.[120] The move from Gravesend came about because of Miss Gordge, who had had to leave her previous post because of ill-health, possibly stress. The two women had developed a strong friendship, planning that when she gained a new position, if at all possible, Marianne would join her. So when Miss Gordge became head of the British School in Northampton, she approached Marianne and invited her to take up the headship of the infant department. Marianne remembered this being a difficult decision, primarily because it took her further away from her family and friends in Kent, without a compensating increase in salary. 'As far as I knew, the only gain would be the companionship of my friend, which, however, was one which I most highly valued.'[121] As at many crucial junctures, she sought male advice, consulting Jonathan Whittemore, who encouraged her to make the move as it would broaden her horizons. Friendship was the motivation behind this change, indicating relationships were very important for Marianne and could be a determining factor in her decisions.

---

[118] Farningham, *Life*, p. 88.
[119] *Northampton Independent* 20 March 1909.
[120] *Northampton Independent* 20 April 1907.
[121] Farningham, *Life*, p. 89.

Northampton in the Later Nineteenth Century

Like other industrial towns, Northampton experienced a rapid population increase during the nineteenth century, as manufacturing businesses developed. It was the centre of a large boot and shoe industry, which provided much of the employment. The major shoe factories attracted workers who had previously been based at home, and the numbers were rising overall. Many of the girls in Marianne's Sunday school class worked in these factories. Whereas in 1831, 1,322 men, one third of the town's total, were shoemakers, by 1871 following the introduction of mass-production methods, such as sewing machines, that number had risen to 4,641, representing two-fifths of the town's total male population at that stage. Other industries in the town included breweries, iron foundries, flour mills, and coach works. In the middle of the century many new houses, schools and factories were being built. Some manufacturers erected terraced houses to house their workforce. The town's economy also benefited from good rail connections. The first station opened in 1845, and when in 1872 St John's Street Station was built it became the third one.[122] The transport situation made it possible for Marianne to live in the town yet edit a weekly newspaper based in London.

The town was also a stronghold of Dissent, having had several Nonconformist congregations since the late seventeenth century.[123] One of these was College Street Baptist, which was certainly meeting earlier than 1697, and completed its first meeting house in 1714.[124] Nonconformity became increasingly influential in the town during the eighteenth century, with Rev Phillip Dodderidge pastoring at Castle Hill, as well as running his famous Dissenting Academy, from 1729 to 1751. As the author of various works including *The Rise and Progress of Religion in the Soul*, and *Evidences of Christianity* he ensured that Northampton Nonconformity would have an influence over not only Dissent, but within the evangelical wing of the Church of England. College Lane, as it was then known, flourished under the ministry of John Collett Ryland and his son, also John Ryland, its ministers between 1759 and 1792. In the early years of the nineteenth century, it established several congregations in surrounding villages, although there was also a division in the mother congregation. Nonconformity was vigorous in the town during the nineteenth century:[125] Marianne believed that in the 1880s, the town had 'a larger average of church-going people than almost any other'.[126] The Unitarians were also strong in the town, with many leaders of the Liberal party being Unitarians.[127] Northampton was significant for its Dissent and its

---

[122] www.Northampton.org.uk, accessed 5 July 2005.
[123] Christianity in Northamptonshire, p. 41.
[124] Christianity in Northamptonshire, p. 43.
[125] Christianity in Northamptonshire, p. 60.
[126] Farningham, *Life* p. 92.
[127] Farningham, *Life,* pp. 46–48.

independent spirit.

The town was also politically famous, if not notorious, during the time Marianne lived there, returning the first atheist MP, Charles Bradlaugh, to parliament. The founder of the National Secular Society, and an advocate of contraception, Bradlaugh was elected MP for Northampton in 1880, at the fourth attempt. There followed a controversy over whether he could take his seat, during which he was forced to contest it successfully several more times before the issue was settled. He was finally permitted to sit in Parliament in 1886. Several years later, in 1894, the town erected a statue of Bradlaugh, an indication of the strength of his local support. To many people elsewhere in the country, however, including some Nonconformist Liberals, the MP was the epitome of atheism and republicanism, and Northampton was perceived 'as a town of secularist unbelievers'.[128] Marianne even came across Christians who were surprised that she came from Northampton, believing that nothing good could come out of it. As a Northampton resident with Liberal sympathies, however, she took a different view, arguing that the town 'insisted on sending Mr Bradlaugh to Parliament, not because it was less religious, but because it cared more strongly for liberty than most'.[129] The Dissenting mindset which encouraged diversity and freedom of conscience extended in this case, it seems, even to those whose ideas were opposed to its own. This atmosphere of Liberalism and Nonconformity was one in which Marianne came to feel very much at home. Although she insisted it was her girls' class that kept her in the town, her beliefs and values were in sympathy with its prevailing ethos.

College Street Chapel

Marianne was advised to attend College Street because of the minister, John Turland Brown, whom Jonathan Whittemore asserted 'preached like a prophet and prayed like a seraph'.[130] He was in ministry there from 1843 to 1894, was in sympathy with the Chartists, was involved with Anti-State Church Association founded in 1844, and, like many Nonconformists, was also a strong Liberal supporter.[131] Marianne's first impression of the chapel, built in 1714, was of 'a very tumble-down old place, with worn brick floor, and pews awry through their great age. I did not like it, and was glad to hear that a new chapel was soon to be built.'[132] For a while she and her friend, presumably Miss Gordge, attended a Congregational church instead, singing in the choir, and

---

[128] E. Royle, 'Bradlaugh, Charles, (1833-1891) *Oxford Dictionary of National Biography*, (Oxford: Oxford University Press, 2004), www.oxforddnb.com/view/article/3183, accessed 12 July 2005.
[129] Farningham, *Life*, p. 92.
[130] Farningham, *Life*, p.90.
[131] Christianity in Northamptonshire, p. 61.
[132] Farningham, *Life*, p. 91.

were befriended by the pastor and his wife, Rev and Mrs Prust. It was during this time Marianne gradually discovered that the people of Northampton were welcoming.[133] She eventually settled at College Street, and obtained a seat in the new chapel, in pew number 80,[134] although she confessed to 'a sense of loneliness' which 'oppressed me at College Street for some years'.[135] Reading between the lines, it seems that the sense of community and friendship which marked her youth in Eynsford, was not repeated for her within the chapel community. Later, this gap was filled to some extent through the girls' class which she began to teach in 1867. Over time, however, she did find some friendship and support in the church itself, especially from the minister Rev Brown and the deacons. John Whittemore's recommendation of Brown proved to have some worth, for Marianne wrote after his death that 'What his prayers and sermons did for me I could never adequately tell.' She drew spiritual strength and sustenance from Brown's sermons and prayers, and not infrequently used their subject as the topic for that week's contribution to the *Christian World* or the *Sunday School Times*, estimating that nearly a third of her contributions to those papers were taken from his Sunday sermons.[136] When he died in 1899, after fifty years of pastoring the chapel, it was a great loss to Marianne, as to all the members.

In April of the same year, when College Street held its first ever Bazaar to raise funds for improvements to the chapel, Marianne was heavily involved. Bazaars had become popular much earlier in the century as a means of fund-raising for both religious and charitable causes, and women were often involved in their organisation.[137] Prochaska suggests that evangelicals had less difficulty with using these as a fund-raising tool than did Anglo-Catholics, but many Nonconformists were suspicious of them, including in the mid-century, John Angell James, minister of a leading Congregational church in Birmingham and a central figure in the Evangelical Alliance, and the influential Baptist pastor William Landels.[138] It is instructive that it was nearly the twentieth century before this Northampton Baptist chapel held its first bazaar, which suggests that these fund-raisers were more problematic for evangelicals than Prochaska has suggested.[139] Appropriately, Marianne was in charge of the bookstall, with help from her friend Agnes Groves, and three of her nieces. On the third day she opened the Bazaar. The handbook contained a photograph of

---

[133] Farningham, *Life*, p. 91.
[134] *Baptist Monthly* September 1899.
[135] Farningham, *Life*, p. 91.
[136] Farningham, *Life*, p. 257.
[137] F. Prochaska, *Women and Philanthropy in Nineteenth Century England* (Oxford: Oxford University Press, 1980) pp. 47-72.
[138] J. James, *Female Piety*, (London: Hamilton, Adams, 1852), p. 127; W. Landels, *Women's Sphere and Work considered in the light of Scripture: a book for young women* (London: 1859), p. 224.
[139] Prochaska, *Women and Philanthropy*, p. 68.

her and a rather sentimental quotation about her 'dear grey head', and 'sympathy with those who mourn'.[140] Her involvement in this event is evidence that despite the uncertain start, College Street retained not merely her allegiance, but her active involvement, for the rest of her life.

Teaching in Northampton

Initially, Marianne disliked Northampton as she had done Gravesend. Again, she felt lonely, even though this time she was living with a friend but this initial phase only lasted a few months, and she was able to describe the people as being 'friendly and hospitable'.[141] It seems that her first home in Northampton was a shared house, with Miss Gordge and two young Quaker women. She lived for some years with Miss Gordge when they were both teaching, later reminiscing that 'I suppose that they were strenuous years, but they were delightful ones'.[142] The friends worked together, and indulged their shared love of nature by often walking to nearby villages. At one stage, there was a pupil teacher, Mary Ann Constable, training in the school, to whom she later wrote some letters.[143] Although Marianne was not directly responsible for Mary, they worked closely together and developed a friendship. Towards the end of 1865 she was looking back wistfully on her earlier teaching days, writing to 'Pollie', as she was known, 'I am glad you don't forget the good old times. I often think I should like to have them back. I feel very lonely sometimes, now you are all gone.'[144] It seems that after an initial period of settling down, Marianne thoroughly enjoyed her teaching for a time, but once various teachers had left, and she was carrying more responsibility, some of the pleasure went out of the work for her, possibly at the time her friend Miss Gordge left to marry and was replaced by a Miss Roe. All the time she was teaching, she still spent all her holidays in Farningham with her family, which shows again how strong those relationships were. The evidence seems to be that she only really found the lifestyle that she enjoyed and which most suited her once she had the girls in her class to care for, her family near at hand, and was able to write rather than teach. Marianne had a large capacity for friendship, and needed a sense of connection to many people, and a sense of belonging in a church family, which took time to develop.

---

[140] Official Handbook to a Grand Bazaar in aid of College Street Bi-Centennial Commemorative Fund, 1899.
[141] Farningham, *Life*, p. 91.
[142] Farningham, *Life*, p. 92.
[143] Barbara Evans has argued that Pollie was Mary Ann Constable and this seems a reasonable conclusion. See Evans, 'Marianne Farningham' p. 51.
[144] Letters to Pollie (3) 1865.

Engagement

During her early years in Northampton, when sharing with Miss Gordge and two others, there appears to have been a time when Marianne came close to marriage. All of the women were engaged, as in her autobiography Marianne commented that 'we had fun in arranging for our visitors, and in talking over prospects'.[145] She, however, was the only one of the four who did not eventually marry. The end of her engagement was dismissed with frustrating brevity in her autobiography by the phrase 'I was made to know that the sheltered life of a married woman was not God's will concerning me'.[146] It is not easy to reconstruct the actual events, especially as the name of her fiancé is never given: possibly the engagement was broken off. Evans favours this conclusion, speculating that this fiancé was the same man who once proposed marriage with the argument that she needed someone to take care of her finances.[147] It seems more likely, however, that the latter proposal was never treated seriously, but that her actual fiancé died. One wonders if this was one of the aspects of her life which she was thinking of in her old age when she wrote 'I have had sorrows, some even verging upon tragedies, especially in my early days, which I could not now describe, and which would do no good if I could'.[148] As she did include the deaths of her mother and younger brother and sister, this must have referred to other events, and it is possible that the loss of her fiancé was one of those sorrows.

There are also various references to death and loss in her prose and poetry which might indicate she had experienced the death of a fiancé. The most obvious was in her first published prose collection, *Life Sketches*, which dates from 1861, and was thus written very close to the time when she was engaged. In one short piece, 'Whatever is, is Best', she wrote that sometimes 'everything appears to be happening for the very worst', yet she affirmed her belief that disappointments are 'blessings in disguise' and that God, who can see the end from the beginning, knows best. 'Dreams fade, and hopes are blighted... But as days pass, we see that had our wishes been granted, they must have brought distress and unhappiness.' Even bereavement, she suggested, has a positive side, as through it we learn to depend on God. 'It is at the open grave we often learn to love the risen Lord.' In this short piece, there is an acknowledgement that at times everything in life can seem to be going wrong, an affirmation of trust in God, whatever the circumstances, and an innocent belief that good can always come out of tragic situations for those who do exercise such trust. She urged her readers to 'Yield thy wishes to him – his mind is infinite, and he cannot do wrong', encouraging them to be cheerful even if life did not work out

---

[145] Farningham, *Life*, p. 92.
[146] Farningham, *Life*, p. 93.
[147] Evans, 'Marianne Farningham', p. 15, Farningham, *Life*, p. 275.
[148] Farningham, *Life*, p. 278.

in the way they would have chosen. [149] These sentiments, however, whilst indicating that she had experienced the death of people close to her, are not conclusive proof that she was bereaved at this precise time. They could be references to the death of her sister.

What this passage and others do indicate, however, is that in retrospect, and possibly at the time, Marianne interpreted the breaking of her engagement not as betrayal or tragedy but as the will of God. Looking back after many years she explained that, before long, she discovered that there were advantages to being single, primarily in the areas of friendship and of intellectual satisfaction. She recalled, 'I accepted His decision, and soon began to learn something of the law of compensation'. [150] Deborah Nord has suggested that Victorian women who remained single 'concluded that matrimony and the exercise of an independent mind were incompatible experiences' and there is a hint that Marianne would have had some sympathy with this view. [151] In due course school work, the development of her journalism, along with 'new interests and new friends' kept her busy and brought her fulfilment, so she could declare that her 'time of loneliness was quite lost and forgotten'.[152] This experience of finding satisfaction in a single state she had not chosen is in contrast both with women who made a conscious decision to stay single, and others who found singleness a depressing state. Dora Greenwell who was a contemporary of Marianne, had a very different experience, writing of 'the lonely and sensitive single woman' who experiences 'life's narrowness and poverty' more strongly than others. According to Greenwell, the friends of a single woman 'give her their kindness rather than their affection', telling her of their sorrows but not asking about her own.[153] But Greenwell had a subdued, if not depressive, temperament, and living as she did under the shadow of a domineering mother, she had restrictive circumstances. Marianne's experience appears to have been quite different, with many close friends and family and a rich social life.

As well as women who had singleness forced upon them, there were others such as the headmistress Dorothea Beale who, as Levine has highlighted, actively chose to avoid the distraction of marriage in order to further their careers.[154] The implication of Marianne's narrative is that neither of these extremes applied to her, but rather that she was making the best of an apparently unfortunate situation which she came to understand and appreciate as God's plan for her life. The single life appears to have suited Marianne, but she wrote about it only infrequently and made few observations which might

---

[149] M. Farningham, *Life Sketches and Echoes from the Valley* (London: James Clarke, 1861), pp. 73-74.
[150] Farningham, *Life,* pp. 92-93.
[151] Nord, *The Apprenticeship of Beatrice Webb,* p. 68.
[152] Farningham, *Life,* p. 93.
[153] *North British Review* (February-May 1862), xxxvi, p. 62.
[154] Levine, *Feminist Lives,* p.46.

also apply to other women. A rare mention is found in one of her novels, *Nineteen Hundred*, written quite late in life, when one of the main characters, Mary, rejects a proposal of marriage with the declaration that 'It is not every woman who desires to be married, or who ought to take upon herself the responsibilities of a home. I have chosen a different lot from many.'[155] Her suitor regards this as 'unnatural', and there is a hint that she does love someone else, yet when the novel ends Mary is still unattached. The placing of that declaration in the mouth of a woman, whilst not necessarily indicating that Marianne felt strongly that a single life could be chosen as a preferred option, suggests that she was at least aware of that argument, which was current within feminist circles at the time. Yet another comment in the same novel, concerning a different character, was probably closer to Marianne's own heart. Thomasine had one man whom she could have loved, but it took until the end of the novel for the relationship to develop. In the meantime she led a fulfilled life:

> which contained great joy, if not the bliss of which every woman dreams, and the larger ministry of love which embraces many instead of one. And Tom deliberately chose it for herself now. There was only one possible person for her; and if he did not wish to share her life, no one else could.

She was also 'too sensible, perhaps, to waste time and shed tears in useless regrets'.[156] It seems to me that this was Marianne's own attitude: having lost her fiancé, she too chose to make the most of 'the larger ministry of love'.

Little is said in Marianne's autobiography of the seven years she spent teaching in Northampton. She gives the impression that her real life work was twofold: her writing, along with her girls' class, and that in many ways her mature life started only when she gave up teaching. Yet seven years is a considerable period for someone in her twenties, and she did describe those years as 'a good time'.

A few glimpses of that period of her life can be found in her letters to 'Pollie'. In the autumn of 1865 Marianne felt under a great deal of pressure as she was preparing her own pupil teachers for their examination. A letter started on 2 October was not completed until 9 December, because she was 'so worried with the examination that I have been driven as you would say almost "cranky" '.[157] She had heard that in 'nearly all the church schools of the town' some of the pupil teachers had failed their exam, and was concerned for her own pupils. This letter sheds an interesting light on this time, indicating that it was more difficult than she later recalled.

---

[155] M. Farningham, *Nineteen Hundred? A forecast and a story* (London: James Clarke, 1892), p. 248.
[156] Farningham, *Nineteen Hundred*, p. 284.
[157] Letters to Pollie, 3, Northampton City Library.

Full-time Writing Career

In 1867, after several years of teaching full time whilst also contributing to the *Christian World* and the *Sunday School Times*, Marianne was offered a full-time post as a journalist on the staff of the *Christian World*. Although she enjoyed teaching, she had obviously felt under pressure sustaining two jobs. She commented that the work was 'sometimes badly done' because of a shortage of time, and there is an evident sense of relief in the way she wrote about leaving teaching as 'being set free'.[158] Teaching could be exhausting work.[159] Marianne's father, however, needed convincing that she had made the best decision. She recalled him questioning whether her work would be ' "worth a hundred or so a year to him?" There was a very uncomplimentary doubt in my father's voice.' [160] He was not the best source of encouragement in the early stages of her career, but it is significant that Marianne felt able to take up this invitation regardless of his opinion, demonstrating a measure of independence from family control. Attitudes towards women earning their living through the pen gradually changed throughout the Victorian period. In the middle of the century the Bronte sisters felt the need to use male pseudonyms when attempting publication of their novels, but only a few years later there were many female writers, such as Mrs Oliphant and Emma Worboise, who from the beginning of their careers freely used their own names. There was certainly a difference between sending in a few verses or short prose pieces on a regular basis to a magazine or paper, and becoming solely dependent on the pen for one's income, as Marianne did when she became a full-time paid staff member of the *Christian World*. There is a defensive pride in Marianne's self-identification as a 'working woman'.

Once she had become a full-time journalist and writer in 1867, this work dominated the remainder of Marianne's life. She produced regular copy for the *Christian World* and the *Sunday School Times,* and thoroughly enjoyed the work, despite at times running perilously close to the weekly deadlines. It is evident that she found a great deal of fulfilment through her writing, and in all that was associated with it. She enjoyed finding new subjects for her writing, including travelling – she considered herself a born traveller as it never tired her – not only in Britain but to Europe and even as far as Israel. Many of Marianne's published works were merely collections of poetry or prose pieces that had previously appeared in the two papers. It appears that she did not receive payment from James Clarke for such works, as she had been paid for the original contributions. Her life became extremely productive once she was

---

[158] Farningham, *Life,* p. 93.

[159] In an article in the *Sunday School Times* in 1891 written as if by a young female teacher, the author commented 'I often come home with aching back and throbbing head, and too weary to do anything'. It is extremely likely that this article was written by Marianne, but if not, as editor she would have supported it.

[160] Farningham, *Life,* p. 144.

able to focus on writing. Having only produced two collections while she was teaching, one of poetry: *Lays and Lyrics* in 1860 and the second, short prose pieces, *Life Sketches,* in 1861, the years that followed saw a wealth of publications, reflecting the increased contributions to both the *Christian World* and the *Sunday School Times.* During the ten years from 1868 to 1878, sixteen books were published under Marianne's name, including poetry, prose, two novels which had previously been serialised, and some pieces for children, as well as one on the subject of Sunday schools, first given as a paper to an audience of Sunday school teachers.[161] The apparently slower rate of publication in the years after that partly reflects the fact that by that stage she was also writing under another name, that of Eva Hope.

Eva Hope

According to her autobiography, this new opportunity occurred when in 1876 Marianne was approached by a Mr McAllum with an invitation to write a biography of the Northumberland heroine Grace Darling. She was eager to attempt the work, but did not feel that she could use the name of Marianne Farningham when writing for a publisher other than James Clarke, so a different name was agreed. Marianne remarked that after some discussion concerning a name, they 'selected about the weakest we could have found', Eva Hope.[162] She duly produced her work on Grace Darling for the Walter Scott Publishing Company, and it was followed by several others, mostly biographies, under the same name. These included a *Life of General Gordon*, one of *Stanley in Africa*, *New World Heroes* which contained biographies of Presidents Lincoln and Garfield and *Queens of Literature*, reprinted as *Great Modern Women*. This latter covered several prominent women including Mary Somerville and Harriet Martineau as well as the more pious Felicia Hemans, and is an indication that Marianne had sympathies with the movement for women's rights. Also under this pseudonym Marianne edited several books of poetry including volumes of Longfellow and Cowper, indicating her own love of poetry. The quality of her compositions was variable, but Marianne was a prolific writer.

Until quite late in her life Marianne seemed determined to protect the existence of her alter ego 'Eva Hope', insisting for instance as late as 1897 that she had 'remained faithful to the firm of Messrs James Clarke & Sons (sic)... and all my books have been published by them'.[163] This was, of course, an untruth, as she must have been aware. Possibly she had not told her first publishers about this venture. When she did reveal the truth, in her autobiography, there is no indication why she had kept it hidden, although there

---

[161] For a full list of Marianne's published works, see the bibliography on pp. 235-241.
[162] Farningham, *Life,* p. 131.
[163] Hearne, 'Mary Ann Hearn', *Brief History.*

are some hints within the books themselves. In these works she was more forthright on the subject of the role of women, as the following chapter demonstrates, and she was also eager to appear faithful to her original publisher. Even at this late stage her own list of her writings did not include those by Eva Hope, as if she still thought of Eva's work as separate.[164]

Marianne's Girls' Class

After giving up professional teaching to develop her writing career, Marianne immediately took a holiday in Hastings to consider what to do next, returning from her break determined to move away from Northampton.[165] This plan, however, was never put into action, because shortly afterwards, in the spring of 1867, Marianne was asked to take a Sunday school class of young women on what intended to be a temporary basis. She remained involved with the class for over thirty years, during which time it developed from a group of around sixteen young women to a gathering of well over a hundred, probably closer to two hundred at times.[166] The group consisted of quite a cross-section of women, but all, like Marianne, needed to earn a living, although none were extremely poor. This was why she never left Northampton, a decision which she later considered a mistake, at least in career terms. The influence she exerted through her class was recognised locally. In 1907, for instance, an article in a local paper suggested that there were old scholars from the class all over the world, and commented that Marianne 'rarely if ever visits a town without meeting some of them, who come forward to renew their acquaintance with their revered teacher'.[167] This class came to play a large part in Marianne's life, as Chapter 4 explores in more detail.

Further Developments

Given the close relationships within the Hearn family, it must have been a source of pleasure to Marianne that in 1871, after she had been in Northampton over ten years, her sister Hephzibah and her husband and family joined her in the town, and Marianne moved in with them. Previously she had lived in several different locations, including Princes Street, Adelaide Terrace and St George's Terrace.[168] Heppie had married Thomas Sharwood, and they eventually had nine children, of whom two died very young. Five of them were girls: Elizabeth, Alice, Minnie, Marie and Patty, and there were two boys, Herbert and Frank. (Her brother Thomas, married to Elizabeth, had only two

---

[164] Farningham, *Life*, p. 276-77.
[165] Farningham, *Life*, p. 93.
[166] See Chapter 4, p. 99.
[167] *Northampton Independent* 20 April 1907.
[168] Letters to Pollie, 1863, 1864, 1865

children: Geoffrey and Margaret.) Marianne became very close to her sisters' children, later having several of her nieces to live with her. No doubt this close relationship with her nieces, which lasted the whole of her life, was first developed when they were sharing a house in the 1870s. Here Marianne had her own sitting room as well as bedroom, giving her more freedom and independence. This was her home for many years, and as far as one can tell the arrangement seems to have been amicable and satisfactory.

A few years later, in the winter of 1877-8, Marianne also embarked on a lecturing career. The initial inspiration for this was a sense that she had something to say on the subject of women's rights, and for several years she chose a different topic each winter and travelled around the country, usually with a friend, giving the lecture in a variety of locations. This proved to be a popular enterprise, and one which boosted her earnings helpfully, enabling her to rent on a long-term basis a little cottage in Barmouth, North Wales. It is possible that for some of those tours, at least the later ones, Emily Cotching was her travelling partner, as in 1881 she was living with Marianne in the capacity of companion.[169] In 1885, she added to her responsibilities the not inconsiderable one of editing the *Sunday School Times*, still working from her base in Northampton, although at this stage she considered once again moving to London. The following year she was elected to the Northampton School Board, adding another responsibility to her already busy portfolio. This involved not only a regular monthly Board meeting, but sitting on various committees concerned with specific schools and other matters. Add to this her responsibility for her girls' class, and it will be seen that she was probably working at full capacity, if not beyond it.

12 Watkin Terrace

In 1879, after eight years living with her sister and her family, Marianne bought her own house. This development was triggered by the death of her father's second wife whilst the couple were staying with Hepzibah and her extended family one Christmas. As Marianne was by now increasingly financially secure, she decided to buy a house which her father could share. All her immediate family had now left Farningham. Despite having lived all his life in a village, her father, who had helped to choose the house, enjoyed the new experience of living near a town.[170] It is significant that, because of her need to earn a living, Marianne was never faced with the need to sacrifice her own independence and career for the sake of caring for him, unlike many middle-class single women. Their relationship was thus on a different footing from that experienced by some of her contemporaries who faced a choice between family

---

[169] 1881 census, www.nationalarchives.gov.uk/census.

[170] Farningham, *Life,* p. 151.

and their own needs.[171] Her new home was in Watkin Terrace, a road on the edge of the common, looking over the country, but within walking distance of the town. One of her 'girls' later described it as 'a good-sized house, two sitting rooms, study, and kitchen'.[172] The house still stands on the edge of a green area, and one can see that the row was once rather imposing.

Having grown up in a noisy family, Marianne always preferred to share her house, commenting at one stage that 'a home needs to have at least one other person in it or it becomes lonely. If the talk is not wise then at least it is familiar.'[173] In the years that followed, a succession of friends and relatives helped to provide that talk. As well as her father, at least one companion and several of her nieces lived with her at various times.[174] At the time of the 1881 Census, Emily Cotching, then aged 27, was listed as a companion. This might have been a paid position, but it is hard to tell. Ten years later, on census night, Emily was staying as a visitor. The friendship continued even though the nature of the relationship had changed.[175] At that stage, as well as a young servant, she also had three nieces staying with her: Rebecca E. Sharwood (sometimes, confusingly, known as Elizabeth), by then the headmistress of a local Board School, and two of her sisters, Minnie Duffield, who at 23 was already a widow and working as a hospital nurse, and a younger woman, probably Marie, a pupil teacher. Marianne enjoyed the company of her nieces.

Her father suffered from chronic asthma, and was unwell during the time he stayed with her, although he soon married for the third time. It is probable that his new wife was also living in the house, as the indications are that her father continued to live there after this marriage. Marianne wrote of him sleeping in an easy chair in her study when he could not sleep in bed, and he died in that chair on 7 April 1889. There is no indication of what became of his third wife. Marianne does not indicate whether she was present when her father died, but if her dates are correct, she was in fact in Italy at that time, as part of her continental holiday which followed her breakdown. If this is correct, it is strange that there is no mention of this, or expressions of regret at not being present. Yet the dates of her time away are accurate: in her autobiography she includes a dated letter sent from abroad, and it correlates with dates when she was absent from the Northampton School Board. Presumably someone else was with her father in her house when he died, and she chose not to draw attention to her absence, perhaps because of a sense of regret or even guilt at the timing

---

[171] Nord, *Apprenticeship*, p. 68.
[172] Farningham, *Life*, p. 128.
[173] M. Farningham, *Homely Talks*, p. 26.
[174] Farningham, *Life*, p. 157, p. 256.
[175] 1881 census, www.nationalarchives.gov.uk/census/ and 1891 census http://content.ancestry.co.uk.

of his death.[176]

It is possible to catch only a few glimpses of the other people who lived with her. In 1881 and again in 1901 Marianne had a resident servant. The first was a twenty-two year old woman, Emily Judge, the second Rebecca Webb, who was thirty-one at the time of the census.[177] Presumably, given Marianne's busy lifestyle and the fact that many households, even quite small ones, employed at least one servant, she would often have had domestic help, particularly when her nieces were not living with her.[178] These young women played a large part in her life, and she commented that they had 'made my home life happy for many years'.[179] In 1897, she wrote to William Hearne of Missouri, who was researching a family history, that her sister Hephzibah 'married Thomas Macgregor Sherwood. She died four years ago, leaving nine children, and four of her girls live with me and are of great comfort to their aunt.'[180] No doubt the appreciation was mutual. Marianne genuinely appreciated the contribution younger people made to her home life, and the different perspectives they brought.

Marianne believed that home should be a place where one could relax with friends, and enjoy good conversations. In one's own home, she suggested, it was possible to invite people who held different points of view, in order to 'learn from those who disagree with us'. She particularly had politics in mind, complaining in *Homely Talks about Homely Things* that conservatives and radicals had become polarised, unwilling to listen to each other, whilst she was interested to discuss issues with people of various opinions.[181] This, incidentally, demonstrates that Marianne was always open to hearing a different point of view, and although she had strong opinions, was willing to have them challenged and even changed. The evidence suggests that it was a welcoming home, open to many friends as well as to those she shared the house with. A close friend, Jennie Street, commented that she was at her best 'talking to a friend alone' and that friends 'timed their visits so as to find her free; they waited for their turn when other visitors were there, and the fortunate person who… had a long hour with her was envied by all the rest'.[182] Girls from her class visited frequently. The author of an article in the *Baptist Monthly* for 1899 suggested that friends visited every day, and he commented that he personally received 'the heartiest of welcomes to the happiest of homes', suggesting that

---

[176] Farningham, *Life*, p. 227. It has proved impossible to track down external evidence of the date of his death.
[177] 1881 census, www.nationalarchives.gov.uk/census/.
[178] www.1901census.nationalarchives.gov.uk.
[179] Farningham, *Life*, p. 256.
[180] Hearne, 'Mary Ann Hearn', *Brief History*.
[181] Farningham, *Homely Talks*, pp. 12-14.
[182] M.J. Street, *SST*, 26 March 1909.

'a visit to 12 Watkin Terrace, Northampton, is a thing to be remembered'.[183] In her own house, Marianne was able to give full expression to her love of friendship and hospitality.

The Hearn Family

As the record of those who shared her house shows, despite the early loss of her mother, Marianne's experience of family was a positive one, and she retained a strong sense of family belonging. Her loneliness in Gravesend and in the early years in Northampton was largely due to separation from her family and especially her sister who was 'full of fun'.[184] In September 1864 she wrote that her brother's intention of moving to the Northampton for a while 'brightened' the prospect of the 'long winter' which faced her. Her close relationship with her sister was worked out in practice when, as indicated above, Marianne lived with Hephzibah and her family for some years after they moved to Northampton, and it continued once she had her own house. She also had an affectionate relationship with her nieces. The eldest of her sister's children, Elizabeth (Rebecca) Sharwood, seems to have been especially close to Marianne, and probably lived with her for longer than the other nieces. She was still resident at the time of the 1901 census, being described as the 'head' of the household, presumably because Marianne was travelling at the time. She, too, was both a teacher and a writer. Under the name of 'REST' she contributed to the *Sunday School Times*, even editing it briefly at one stage.[185] In the long term, however, Elizabeth remained in teaching, making a different choice to Marianne. In the 1901 census she is listed as an 'elementary schoolmistress'.[186] By the time Marianne drew up her final will, on 17 February 1908, Elizabeth was living next door, at 14 Watkin Terrace, in her own home but still living close enough to her beloved aunt to share much of her life, and no doubt to help in providing care for her in her old age.[187] Another niece, Elizabeth's youngest sister Patty also had a special relationship with her aunt. As 'Aunt Patty' she contributed to the *Sunday School Times*. When the younger woman was planning to leave for South Africa, Marianne commented to a friend that she would 'miss Patty more than I can express. She understands me so thoroughly and is such a help to me in every way, but she has promised to return to me whenever I really want her.' Patty kept her promise, returning to care for her aunt in Marianne's final months.[188] Marianne naturally involved her close

---

[183] P. Morton, 'Marianne Farningham and her Work' in the *Baptist Monthly* 1899, pp. 6-7.
[184] Farningham, *Life*, p. 88
[185] Farningham, *Life*, p. 214.
[186] www.1901census.nationalarchives.gov.uk
[187] Northampton County Record Office, Wills, p. 138, no. 132.
[188] Glandwr-Morgan *Welsh Home*, Chapter 3.

family in aspects of her own life.

Marianne's will also indicates that she regarded her family as of first importance. One of her two executors was her niece Elizabeth Sharwood, the other being a friend, George Petit. Most of Marianne's bequests were to her nephews and nieces and her bereaved sister-in-law Elizabeth Hearn. Whilst all of these received gifts of various kinds, it is instructive that the bulk of her estate was divided between her widowed sister-in-law and her six nieces.[189] She did not discriminate, as one might have supposed, between her single or married nieces, but left them all a share. No doubt she considered that all women needed some practical help, and she had been very close to her nieces. Only items of sentimental value were left to her three nephews, Geoffrey Hearn and Frank and Herbert Sharwood. This difference is a clear indication of her attitudes to women and the importance to her of female financial independence.[190] Marianne appears, however, to have been fond of her nephews too, as she made specific bequests to them, which appear to have been carefully chosen so as to be suitable for their recipients. This indicates a close familiarity with those she left gifts to, and a thoughtful consideration of their preferences.[191] To one nephew, Herbert, she gave 'my silver Barmouth trowel' (no doubt used to lay the foundation stone of the new Congregational chapel in 1896),[192] a Sunday school worker's certificate, and any picture he chose, whereas Frank Sharwood, who was similarly left a silver trowel, this time from a church in Northampton, and a testimonial from the Sunday School Union, was given the right to choose any books he liked. It is quite probable that Frank was a keen reader, but Herbert was not, as otherwise she might have given Herbert the second choice of books, as she did one of her nieces, Margaret Hearn, along with household articles.

Although throughout her life she had many friendships which she valued deeply, it was her family connections which she spoke of as the most significant relationships. This belief of the centrality of family relationships is seen for instance in her poem 'Mine own people', published in 1903:

> 'What are my people more than are others?'
> How can you ask who have some of your own?
> Full is the world; but one's sisters and brothers
> Dwell at the heart of things, safe and alone....

---

[189] Wills, p 138 no 132, Northampton County Record Office.
[190] M. Farningham, *Girlhood* (London: James Clarke, 1869), p. 34. See also discussion of women and work in Chapter 3, p. 80-88.
[191] Northampton County Record Office, Wills, p. 138. no 132.
[192] Glandwr-Morgan, *Welsh Home*, Chapter 5.

And they will be true when all else have forsaken
For the love of one's own is the love that is best.[193]

Marianne shared with many of her contemporaries a view of family and home that was rather sentimental, but her own experience was on the whole a positive one. [194]

Friendship

Although family held first place in her heart, throughout her life Marianne also valued friendship highly and it was at times the motivation for major decisions. Used to being surrounded by friends and family, she looked for that same companionship once she was settled in a new situation. It was because of her friendship with Miss Gordge that she moved to a new job in Northampton, and it was because of friendship with the girls in her class that she later did not move to London when it would have been an astute career move. Her admitted addiction to work did not prevent her from making friendships. Although she rarely elaborated on these relationships they were clearly important to her. So she took the trouble to thank her friend Pollie for a gift of grapes, noting that 'it touched me more than I can tell you' whilst in an earlier letter she was eager to have first-hand news of her friend, 'how you are getting on... and whether you are any happier', pleading at the end 'Pollie darling could you let me have a line to tell me that you haven't forgotten me'. She had a strong need to love and be loved. She was also sensitive to others, including in the letters concern for some children recently orphaned and encouragement to Pollie to write to a mutual friend, Georgie, who was unwell.[195] The networking ability and care for others which reached a fuller and more settled expression in later years, were already evident when she was teaching.

Marianne insisted that apart from her first weeks in Gravesend, and later in Northampton, she was never lonely, and appears to have found it comparatively easy to make friends. Perhaps with hindsight she had forgotten that she also confessed to loneliness at a later stage of her teaching career,[196] but it is certain that in Northampton she made many friends, including a few who she described as 'intellectual friends' whose conversation helped to provide her with topics for her writing.[197] She also had a wide range of friends in different parts of the country, listing in her autobiography various people who she stayed with while lecturing, including 'my lifelong friend, Mrs Wilshire' who lived in Derby, and

---

[193] M. Farningham, *Harvest Gleanings and Gathered Fragments* (London: James Clarke, 1903), p. 53.
[194] Marianne's attitude towards home is further explored in Chapter 3.
[195] Letters to Pollie (3) 1865 and (2) 1864
[196] See p. 46 above, Letters to Pollie (3) 1865.
[197] Farningham, *Life*, p. 172.

prominent Nonconformists such as Mr & Mrs Cadbury of Birmingham.[198] She took most of her continental holidays with Mr & Mrs Bramwell of Sheffield,[199] whilst another friend, Miss Kirkpatrick, paid for them both to travel to the Holy Land with Thomas Cook. Unfortunately, the sponsor of the trip became ill while they were away, only just surviving to die at home.[200] Interestingly, they were able to return home quickly because Thomas Cook, himself an evangelical, had given Marianne a note addressed to all his agents, 'directing them to come to my aid in any way I required', yet another indication of the respect in which she was held within the evangelical community.[201]

In her writing, Marianne sometimes reflected on the importance of having good friends. As early as 1861 she highlighted the importance of forgiveness within a friendship,[202] whilst in *Homely Talks about Homely Things,* published in 1886, she demonstrated her affinity with young people when she commented that the companionship of young intelligent people can be the best kind, because in conversation with them, our ideas are challenged and corrected, which should be seen as an advantage rather than an annoyance.[203] An interesting comment made late in life is found in the book *Women and their Saviour*, which consists of short meditations on Bible passages. Discussing the friendship between Elizabeth, the mother of John the Baptist, and Mary the mother of Jesus, Marianne stressed the importance of female friendships, insisting that women need friendships with other women.[204] Highlighted by Levine as important for feminists, friendship networks were equally valuable to Marianne Farningham.[205]

It does appear, however, that some of her friendships were more significant for her than for the other party. Thus, although Marianne referred to Spurgeon as a life-long friend, one searches in vain in his papers or published works for any indication of this friendship.[206] Similarly, she had a strong admiration for Frances Power Cobbe, who lived in Hengwrt, a substantial house close to Barmouth. Marianne recalled that Cobbe 'used to congratulate me because I was still a journalist', presumably because Cobbe had stopped writing leaders for the *Echo* some years before their friendship. When Cobbe died in 1904, Marianne was one of a group of directors appointed to take care of her library, which she bequeathed to Barmouth. On 7 July the same year there was an opening ceremony for the room set aside for her books at the library, at which

---

[198] Farningham, *Life,* p. 155 and p. 158.
[199] Farningham, *Life,* p. 158.
[200] Farningham, *Life* pp. 179-186.
[201] Farningham, *Life,* p. 185. For Cook, see T. Larsen, 'Thomas Cook' in T. Larsen ed, *Biographical Dictionary of Evangelicals* (Leicester: IVP, 2003), p. 155-56.
[202] Farningham, *Life Sketches,* p. 33.
[203] Farningham, *Homely Talks,* pp. 26-28.
[204] M. Farningham, *Women and their Saviour* (London: James Clarke, 1904), pp. 8-10.
[205] Levine, *Feminist Lives,* p.46.
[206] Farningham, *Life,* p. 148.

various people made speeches, including Marianne.[207] There is, however, no evidence in Cobbe's writing of reciprocal affection, although this could be because it began late in life.[208] The evidence for some friendships is frustratingly absent.

Appreciation, however, was more usually mutual. People who knew her well wrote of Marianne with warmth and affection. Jennie Street, a widely-read journalist who was a fellow-worker on behalf of Sunday schools, called her 'my dear friend', and enthused about her capacity for friendship: 'I found she had a genius for friendship, a wonderful loyalty in her friendships, a rare gift of sympathy. Many a time I have gone to her for counsel or consolation, and she never failed me, and I am only one of very many who will say the same.' These conversations, Jennie noted, took place not only in the house in Northampton or her cottage in Barmouth, but 'in railway carriages and vestries and waiting rooms, and under the sunshine' outdoors.[209] Marianne was a lover of conversation at all times and in all places. She had friends in many walks of life. One Baptist leader and writer, John Carlile, regarded her as an 'elder sister', whilst the Congregational minister at Barmouth, Rev. Glandwr-Morgan, enjoyed 'many pleasant afternoons' in Marianne's cottage in the last few years of her life. Her conversation, he recalled, was 'full of inspiration' and he valued her 'kind words' and constructive criticism of his sermons. On other occasions she read out to him freshly-written portions of her autobiography.[210] Even some who only met her briefly were struck by her capacity for friendship. Philip Morton, a journalist who interviewed her in 1899, commented on this ability: 'Good-natured and humorous, she makes a host of friends, but never an enemy.'[211] It is evident that Marianne had a great facility in friendship.

One way this was demonstrated was that when she travelled, which she did to find fresh material for her journalism, for a holiday, or to lecture, she often took a travelling companion. This was a common practice, but Marianne seems to have had a particular affection for these women. For instance, when she first embarked on a series of lectures, she took with her 'a kind, good friend and companion', whose name is unknown, who was living with her at the time, and who also enjoyed 'seeing fresh places'. Marianne was a good traveller who was not easily tired but despite the careful arrangements the pressure of so much travelling 'was rather hard on my friend'.[212] It is significant that she is eager to preserve the anonymity of this friend. Others are mentioned by name in her account, but presumably this particular companion did not welcome publicity

---

[207] E.R. Jones, *History of Barmouth and its Vicinity* (Barmouth: John Evans and nephew, 1909), p. 85.
[208] Farningham, *Life*, pp. 237-39.
[209] *CW*, 18 March 1909 (supplement)., Glandwr-Morgan, *Welsh Home*, Chapter 3.
[210] J.C. Carlile, *SST*, 26 March 1909.
[211] *Baptist Monthly* September 1899.
[212] Farningham, *Life*, p. 157.

and Marianne was respecting that preference and at the same time fitting in with the convention that people still living should only be discussed in print with circumspection.

Marianne's gift for friendship is also evident from her will. Although by this stage many of her contemporaries had died, this document demonstrates that she still had a number of good friends. Some of these are listed by name as the recipients of specific gifts. One friend, Emily Cotching, was given permission to choose any article of Marianne's personal property, whilst another, Agnes Groves, was to receive 'the low chair presented by my girls' class' and a bible which had been promised to her. Agnes was, like Marianne, a single woman who was earning her own living, in her case as a schoolmistress. Recorded in the census of 1901 as being 42, and living with her father, she was a good twenty-five years younger than her friend. She had been born in Northampton, and was one of Marianne's 'girls' and the friendship had continued due to similar circumstances and continued geographical proximity.[213] The will contains an indication that these were just two of the closest of many friends, as there is a general mention of mementos to be given at the executors discretion 'to such of my close personal friends as they may think fit', indicating that there were other unnamed people who fell into that category.

Nor were Marianne's friends only women: her executor George Petit, a tanner and leather dresser who ran his own business, twenty years her junior, is also referred to as 'my friend'. He was a neighbour, who had lived at 46, Watkin Terrace, although by 1908 he and his wife had moved to St George's Avenue. Marianne left him her reading stand, indicating that he was a keen reader or at least that she wished to encourage his reading![214] In her old age, Marianne retained her capacity for nurturing friendship, including friendship with both men and women, some of whom were considerably younger than herself. Certainly, as with several feminist contemporaries, but in contrast to Dora Greenwell, her network of friends and family appears to have supplied a comprehensive emotional alternative to marriage.

Breakdown

In 1889, Marianne experienced what she described as 'a rather serious breakdown', the result of a mixture of family problems and overwork. Her brother Tom and her sister's husband were working in South Africa, and towards the end of 1888 news came that her brother Tom had died there. Meanwhile, her sister had also gone out, leaving some of her older children in England, one of whom became seriously ill with typhoid fever just after his mother had left. These difficulties put a strain on Marianne in addition to the excessive amount of work she was doing, and whilst giving a lecture the following February she

---

[213] www.1901census.nationalarchives.gov.uk.
[214] Northampton County Record Office, Wills, p. 138 no 132.

became very ill. Her doctor explained that she was 'suffering from overwork and brain fag', and that if she took some rest immediately she would be able to work for many more years, but if she did not, she could consider her career at an end.[215] He wrote to the *Christian World*, and Percy Clarke told her in no uncertain terms not to send in any work for three months as they would not publish it if she did. Her niece, (Rebecca) Elizabeth Sharwood, stepped in and took over the editorship of the *Sunday School Times* for a short time, whilst Marianne took the opportunity to spend some weeks touring Italy with a friend. Marianne explained that she had been working almost without a break for thirty years, and that her work had increased as the years went on, yet she 'had not realised how hard I was working, because the work to me was so intensely interesting, and I loved it so much'.[216] Whilst it has been suggested that some women suffered breakdowns because of the conflict between the traditional role expected of them and their own desires, in Marianne's case the cause was clearly a mixture of overwork and family tragedy.[217]

This little episode is particularly interesting, as a similar pattern can be seen in male biographies in the nineteenth century. Whilst biographies written in the nineteenth century often leave out many private aspects of their subjects' lives, breakdowns due to overwork do not seem to come into this category. For instance, John Bright was taken ill in 1856 as a result of overwork, and spent nearly two years in the highlands of Scotland, and then travelling in Algiers and on the continent, to France and Italy.[218] A range of other public or religious figures, such as John Angell James, R.W. Dale, Richard Hamilton, and Aldous Huxley, all had similar experiences, also carefully explained in their biographies.[219] It seems as though such an episode was an extra confirmation of the worth of the person: to have worked so hard in their particular cause that they had a breakdown of health was an authentication of having been engaged in serious and important work. A few weeks or months of travel on the continent was the accepted cure for such a state.[220] Whether consciously or unconsciously, the inclusion of this episode amounts to a claim by Marianne that her work was of equal importance to that of ministers of religion or political figures. In recounting her experience, Marianne was affirming her identity as a worker, and transcending gender boundaries.

Working both for James Clarke, and as Eva Hope, and in addition lecturing

---

[215] Farningham, *Life* p. 213.

[216] Farningham, *Life,* pp. 214-15.

[217] Nord, *Apprenticeship*, pp. 69-70, suggests that such conflict and 'the impossibility of achieving an integration of self' was at the root of the breakdowns suffered by women such as Florence Nightingale.

[218] G.M. Trevelyan, *The Life of John Bright*, (London: Constable, 1913), pp. 254-55.

[219] A. Desmond, *Huxley: From Devil's Disciple to Evolution's High Priest* (London: Penguin); R.W. Dale, *The Life and Letters of John Angell James* (London: James Nisbett, 1861).

[220] I am grateful to Timothy Larsen for pointing this pattern out to me.

for several years, meant that Marianne would have had a reasonable income. However, she never appears to have been rich. This was illustrated when, towards the end of her life, a testimonial fund was opened for her which readers of the *Christian World* and local people in Northampton contributed to, and this was presented to her on November 6, 1907. The *Northampton Independent* noted that when the fund closed £422. 16s 10d had been collected 'by the admirers of the life and work of this christian woman'.[221] In her speech of thanks, Marianne commented that 'the gift would be welcome to her, for she had never known how to save money – there were so many pleasant ways of spending it'.[222] This attitude to finance is an intriguing departure from Victorian values and from the financial prudence which had been part and parcel of evangelicalism for many years. John Wesley had famously advised his followers to 'earn all you can, save all you can, give all you can', and many evangelicals had followed this advice and lived frugal lives.[223] Marianne, however, was part of the affluent middle-class and enjoyed the proceeds of her earnings, having a much more relaxed attitude to money and possessions. She was, it seems, a spender rather than a saver. Perhaps the poverty of her childhood meant that she was only too glad to enjoy the material blessings she received. On the question of giving she was silent, but given her generous character, this was probably because she believed giving should be secret, rather than because she did not practice charity. Her confessed inability to save is probably the explanation for the lack of wealth at her death, although it should also be remembered that she received no extra payment for many of the collections of articles published by James Clarke & Co. Probate was granted on 22 May 1909, and her wealth amounted to £602 18s. 11d,[224] not a very great amount for a woman who had worked so hard and had so much published.

A Cottage in Barmouth

Once she could afford it, Marianne permanently rented a holiday cottage in Barmouth. This cottage merited a whole chapter in her autobiography, indicating how important it was to her. For years she had dreamed of having a little cottage by the sea which would be 'like a second home' and which she could use as a kind of retreat. Barmouth in the later nineteenth century was a small town and port, popular in the season as a health resort, which by 1871 had a population of 1,733.[225] It was described by an observer as having 'an

---

[221] *Northampton Independent* 2 November 1907.

[222] Farningham, *Life*, pp. 283-84.

[223] J. Wesley, Sermon 50, in A.C. Outler, 'The Works of John Wesley Vol 2: Sermons 2 34-70' (Nashville: Abingdon Press, 1985), p. 277. The original comment here reads 'Having first gained all you can, and secondly saved all you can, then give all you can.'

[224] http://www.oxforddnb.com.

[225] Lloyd, *Maritime Merioneth*, p. 32.

exceptionally fine sand beach, mountain and river walks,' with Cardigan Bay on the west, and the Cader range of mountains to the south. It was said to resemble Gibraltar, with 'narrow ledges, rising in successive tiers from the base nearly to the summit, with steep steps and winding paths leading from one ledge to another. Set on these ridges are the stone cottages of "Old Barmouth".'[226] Another writer described these cottages on the hill as being 'placed on the steep sides, one above another, in such a manner as to give the upper an opportunity of seeing down the Chimneys of their next subjacent neighbours'.[227] Marianne's home, two thirds of a building, was quite high up the hill, close to the home of Fanny Talbot, who owned the land, and who Marianne apparently regarded as 'one of the most Christlike women she had been privileged to meet'.[228] The house enjoyed magnificent views, which she delighted in pointing out to visitors.[229] These cottages remain much the same today. When the present owner first moved in as a child, the house was still known locally as 'Marianne Farningham's cottage'.[230] Remembrance of her lingered into the middle decades of the twentieth century.

In the 1860s the new railway made Barmouth much more accessible, indeed made it possible for Marianne to have her retreat here, travelling to it with comparative ease. She would have been at home in the religious environment for, as in Wales generally, Nonconformity was strong in Barmouth, with several different chapels. The Baptists established a congregation there only as late as 1877, but by 1909 it could be said that 'the Baptist denomination wields great power and influence for good, and its members are steadily increasing'.[231] In the summer they held English services, but at other times of year Marianne would have needed to go to one of the two English chapels, either Congregational or Presbyterian, to worship in her own language, and she chose to join with the Congregationalists.[232] Intriguingly, there was also a strong connection between Barmouth and the well-known author and art critic John Ruskin. Concerned about possible revolution, Ruskin had established the Guild of St George with the aim of giving practical help to poor people and some Barmouth cottages were given to this guild in 1875 by a local woman.[233]

---

[226] Jones, History of Barmouth, p. 1.

[227] T. Pennant and J. Rhys, *Tours in Wales* (Carnarvon: Humphries, 1883), vol 2, p. 253, quoted in Dr Lewis William Lloyd, *Maritime Merioneth - the town and port of Barmouth 1565-1973* Porthmadog Gwynedd, Wales: Snowdonia Press, 1975) pp. 24-25.

[228] Glandwr-Morgan, *Welsh Home*, Chapter 3.

[229] Glandwr-Morgan, *Welsh Home*, Chapter 3.

[230] Personal conversations, Barmouth, 19 June 2006.

[231] Jones, *History of Barmouth*, pp. 121-22.

[232] Jones, *History of Barmouth*, pp. 119-20; Glandwr-Morgan, *Welsh Home*, Chapter 2.

[233] B. Atkinson, *Ruskin's Social Experiment at Barmouth*, (London: James Clarke, 1900). A further interesting connection is that James Clarke, Marianne's employers, were the publishers for this pamphlet.

Although there is no specific indication that this played a part in Marianne's fondness for the place, and the date of her first renting the cottage means no clear conclusions can be drawn, her high opinion of Ruskin must make that a possibility.[234]

Although she talked about Barmouth as a place to get away from everything, this did not mean isolation, as she practised hospitality there. Before she even visited it herself, her sister took an invalid son there who subsequently recovered. 'What my cottage was to him, and has since been to many, I could not tell; and what it has been to me cannot be put into words,' she wrote.[235] At times, some of her 'girls' from Northampton also stayed in the house, whilst admirers who wanted to visit were welcomed.[236] Having eulogised on the benefits of getting away to a place regularly she commented that she could not understand why more people did not do the same.[237] The Baptist minister John Carlile, who wrote an appreciation of her after her death in the *Baptist Times and Freeman*, recalled 'visits to her little cottage away on the mountain-side at Barmouth: perched high above the sea, like an eagle's nest, it was as the Kingdom of Heaven, difficult to attain, but blessed when one had arrived'. He was expressing a sentiment that others had commented on in Northampton: that Marianne's hospitality was warm and friendly. In the same article Carlile recounted an occasion in Barmouth when Marianne's impish sense of fun was expressed. A planned outing for a party of ministers involved climbing nearby then returning for tea at her cottage. Marianne gave them directions, which some of the party followed, whilst two others discovered a short cut.[238] 'When we returned', Carlile explained, 'they badly needed a wash and brush-up. They were black indeed. The near cut was a cinder track. Our hostess laughed heartily. "Ah", she said, "now you know that an old woman may be a truer guide than a doctor of divinity." Carlile obviously relished her humour, recalling that 'she was always a girl. The last words I heard from her were young enough to be counted frivolous by the solemn-faced people who do not understand that the disciple of Jesus Christ is always a *child* of God.'[239] Similarly, Glandwr-Morgan recalled that she was 'brimful of humour', a characteristic he clearly appreciated.[240] There was a shared belief between Carlile, Glandwr-Morgan and Marianne, that enjoyment of life is synonymous with, not excluded by, being a Christian. Yet Barmouth did allow her comparative peace. In the early twentieth century a friend commented that her

---

[234] For instance, in *Harvest*, p. 138, she refers to herself as a disciple of Ruskin, and writes that 'He gave to us new sight, new love/ He made all life shine brave and clear...'
[235] Farningham, *Life*, p. 232.
[236] Glandwr-Morgan, *Home Life*, Chapter 3., Chapter 4.
[237] Farningham, *Life*, p. 234.
[238] *Baptist Times and Freeman* 26 March 1909.
[239] John Carlile writing in the *Baptist Times and Freeman* 26 March 1909.
[240] Glandwr-Morgan, *Welsh Home*, Chapter 3.

neighbours allowed her to be quiet. She said to him that she 'was able here to do a great deal of work'. She either wrote outside 'amongst the gorse and bracken' or sitting up in bed in the early morning, looking out at the view across the bay to Cader Idris.[241] Much of her autobiography, it appears was completed in this way.

Marianne also became involved in local Barmouth affairs: her love of people and her interest in community life meant that this retreat was far from isolated. She was regularly involved in the prize day at the County School, and was for some years after its opening in 1901, the Vice-President of Barmouth library and was apparently active in that role, working with Frances Power Cobbe. When Cobbe died, leaving her personal book collection to the town library, Marianne was one of the Trustees of the collection, and 'with her own hands helped to unpack, classify and shelve' the donated books.[242] Towards the end of her life, in October 1907, the inhabitants of Barmouth presented her with a purse filled with gold 'in acknowledgement of her valuable services to the town by the way she has praised the town and its people in the press'.[243] The meeting was, appropriately enough, held in the Frances Power Cobbe room in the library. Various speeches were made, including one by William George, solicitor and brother of David Lloyd George, and another from Edmund Jones, the Headmaster of the County School, with everyone expressing their appreciation of her local involvement.[244] Marianne had become as much a part of Barmouth as she was of Northampton.

End of Marianne's Life

A final chapter was added to the later editions of *A Working Woman's Life*, summarising the last two years of Marianne's life and in particular, giving an account of her final illness. She became ill towards the end of 1907, not long after the Barmouth presentation, and in the early weeks of 1908 'lay for many weeks in a very critical condition'.[245] As spring arrived the invalid improved, and was able to travel to Barmouth, where she stayed not in her own cottage but in a house on the level 'where she could be wheeled about in a bath-chair'. By June she was back in her own cottage and wrote to the editor of the *Christian World* that she was surprised to still be alive 'but God's will be done! I find there are many people glad to have me still in the world with them, and perhaps he will give me some message to them. However, I am thankful to see the beautiful world once more.'[246] In due course she returned to Northampton.

---

[241] Glandwr-Morgan, *Welsh Home*, Chapter 3.
[242] Glandwr-Morgan, *Welsh Home,* Chapter 5.
[243] The *Northampton Independent* 1 November 1907.
[244] Glandwr-Morgan, *Welsh Home,* Chapter 5.
[245] Farningham, *Life,* p. 284.
[246] Farningham, *Life,* p. 284.

Here once again are some of the key themes of Marianne's writings, lived out as her life was coming to an end: love for God, a belief that all events are in his hands, an appreciation of friends, a love for nature and an eagerness to fulfil a role through her writing. Work, as always, provided both motivation and fulfilment, and she began once again to write occasional contributions for the *Christian World* and sporadic editorials in the *Sunday School Times*. In February 1909, however, her final poem appeared in the *Christian World*, and in the middle of that month she became ill for the last time. She longed to see Barmouth one more time, and did manage to travel there shortly before her death, although she was not able to make the climb to her own little cottage, so spent her last few days in Bronwynedd, the cottage of a friend.

Just as Marianne's autobiography bore little relation to the conversion narratives which served as obituaries in the denominational magazines of the nineteenth century, and in some early spiritual autobiographies, so the account of her death was very different from the Victorian 'good death' found in those earlier narratives.[247] The unknown writer of this final chapter devoted less than a page to her final illness. Apparently she became unconscious a day or two after arriving in the town, and died peacefully in her sleep in the early morning of Tuesday 16 March. Her final words, to her nephew Frank, were 'It is the end, Frank. It has been a long day, and a beautiful one, but it is over.' Three verses of a hymn which she asked for were also given.[248] There is no indication of insistent questioning of the dying which is recorded in some earlier death-bed scenes, and no need to extract an assurance that Marianne was trusting in God as she died. Rather it was her life and writing which demonstrated her faith, and her actual death was recorded in a simple, understated manner, in a style of which she would surely have approved.

On the following day, early in the morning, Marianne's body was taken to the station for the journey back to Northampton. Rev Glandwr-Morgan was one of the few people accompanying her to the station, as it was thought better for her 'relatives and nurses' to avoid the strain of a crowd. He commented that although this was a wise decision, it caused 'much disappointment' to friends who would have liked to be present.[249] Marianne's death was marked by a special service in Barmouth, whilst her actual funeral took place in Northampton three days after her death, on Friday 19 March, at Northampton General Cemetery. This event was reported on the front page of the *Northampton Daily Chronicle*.[250] The funeral service was led by Rev Charles Brown, the President of the Baptist Union, an indication of her significant role within Baptist circles. An observer recorded that there were 'remarkable

---

[247] See P. Jalland, *Death in the Victorian Family* (Oxford, Oxford University Press, 1996).

[248] Farningham, *Life,* pp. 286-87.

[249] Glandwr-Morgan, *Welsh Home*, Chapter 1.

[250] *Northampton Daily Chronicle* 20 March 1909.

demonstrations of public sorrow' at this service, 'mingled with expressions of thanksgiving'.[251] The simple pamphlet, with its black border, prepared for the occasion, reveals very little of who she was or what her friendship meant to many people. She had become known as 'Marianne Farningham Hearn' and that is how the funeral pamphlet, the local papers, and eventually a memorial plaque in College Street chapel, named her. The names of the opening and closing organ voluntaries, and the titles of the hymns, were inside, and on the back a few short verses of her own. An indication of the pervasive influence of Marianne can be seen from the large number of people who attended the funeral, including the Mayor and Mayoress of Northampton. The street outside the chapel 'thronged with sorrowful sympathisers'. The Mayor, Councillor Brown, had been in Marianne's infant class when she first taught in the town, whilst his wife had been one of her 'old girls'. According to the *Sunday School Times*, many of these 'old girls' were present, some of them being women with married daughters who had also been in Marianne's class.[252] Her extensive influence, networking ability, and the respect in which she was held especially in Northampton where she was best known, was evident in this commemoration of her life.

Her influence lasted for a few years after she died. Some of her hymns continued to be printed in collection for some years after her death and people still gave each other gifts of her books.[253] For instance, my copy of Marianne's autobiography is inscribed 'To Winnie, with grandmother's love, April 23rd 1929'. In 1923, introducing the third reprint of his little book *Marianne Farningham in her Welsh Home*, Rev Glandwr-Morgan commented that 'Repeated requests have been made for another edition' from her 'many admirers'.[254] However, this edition was only a local, not a national publication. It was in the places she had had the most influence that she was remembered the longest, whilst today she is almost completely neglected.

Marianne portrayed herself as being 'not very remarkable', yet in the journey from poor village girl to affluent, capable and well-known woman, Marianne developed in a way that could indeed be called remarkable. In her childhood she had longed to read about 'some poor ignorant *girl*' who, starting from similar beginnings to hers, had 'yet been able by her own efforts and the blessing of God upon them to live a life of usefulness, if not of greatness'.[255] She found no such inspiration, but she lived it out despite that, finding a place not only in the hearts of many friends and readers, but in the public world. Central to her developing writing career, and her mentoring of 'her girls' in Northampton, was her understanding of the role of women, and the importance

---

[251] *SST* 26 March 1909.
[252] *SST* 26 March 1909.
[253] See Chapter 5.
[254] Glandwr-Morgan *Welsh Home,* Preface to Third Edition.
[255] Farningham, *Life*, p. 44. Her italics.

of on the one hand, the female domestic role and on the other, the freedom to develop whatever gifts a woman was born with. How that combination and tension, rooted in popular evangelical spirituality, was worked out in her attitudes to women, her girls' class and her public life, is the subject of the following chapters.

Chapter 3

Afraid to be Singular?
Marianne and the Role of Women

> Many women, simply because they are not courageous enough to brave the adverse opinions of those by whom they are surrounded, lose golden opportunities of distinguishing themselves. They are afraid to be singular.[1]

When Marianne Farningham published her autobiography in 1907, towards the end of her long career as a journalist and author, she gave it the forthright title *A Working Woman's Life*. She was indicating by this that in her old age she constructed her identity both as 'woman' and 'worker', closely bound up with her gender as well as with the type of life she had lived, and identifying with the working masses. Looking back from the perspective of the early twentieth century, she gave the impression that she had always had a strongly gendered understanding of the world. It is certainly true that many of the pieces Marianne composed during her years of writing focused on women's lives. Various aspects of her beliefs are to be found in her regular newspaper columns, and in the collections of these contributions such as *Girlhood* (1869) and *Homely Talks about Homely Things* (1886). Over many years she made observations about a wide range of female experience: the domestic role of women; their working lives, whether paid or unpaid as well as wider issues such as education and the vote. Writing when 'the woman question' was of major public interest, she used prose pieces, poetry, fiction and biography as the means of conveying her opinions concerning the role of women and as an encouragement to women to find focus and purpose in their lives. Whilst some of her ideas remained unchanged, others developed over the years, and in this it is possible to see a reflection, even an influencing, of popular evangelical opinion. It is significant that, for Marianne, the belief that women had a place in the public sphere was entirely compatible with extremely conventional, even sentimental, beliefs about the home and the role of women within it. Both were the logical consequence of her popular ideals of duty and service and of her evangelical faith.

---

[1] E. Hope, *Grace Darling, Heroine of the Farne Islands* (London: Walter Scott, 1875), p. 11.

Grace Darling – A Role Model

The clearest expression of Marianne's views on the place of women at home and in society is to be found in the first book she produced under the pseudonym of 'Eva Hope'. According to her autobiography, in 1876 Marianne was asked to write a biography of Grace Darling, the 'heroine of the Farne Islands', a suggestion which greatly appealed to her. By her own admission she knew very little about the subject, so the publisher provided her with letters and newspaper cuttings which formed the basis of her account.[2] The original event which made Darling famous was well known: on the night of 5 September, 1838, the Forfarshire had gone aground on rocks near the Longstone lighthouse on the Farne Islands, off the Northumberland coast. Grace Darling and her parents were manning the lighthouse by themselves, her brothers being on the mainland at the time. She and her father launched the lifeboat, with some help from her mother, who had initially objected to the attempt, and the two of them rowed across the rough sea and managed to rescue several survivors stranded on a rock. Out of this simple incident, Marianne constructed a book of over 300 pages without, it seems, ever visiting the area or doing any first-hand research. This unsophisticated approach is reflected in her style. Her account of the actual rescue, for instance, put words into the mouths of the participants as if she were composing a work of fiction. These words, however, are extremely revealing. As the survivors watched the boat approaching, a sailor, 'with moisture in his eyes' is recorded as saying: 'One is a woman... God bless her; she is an angel sent from Heaven to succour us.' Thus the popular image of Grace Darling in her rowing boat was linked in Farningham's account with the whole ideology of women as angels, and by implication with the idealisation of a certain kind of femininity that was found in such writers as John Ruskin and Coventry Patmore.

Marianne intended that others should imitate her heroine, suggesting that there were many women like Grace Darling,

> women who fear God and love the right, and delight in nothing so much as self-abnegation, if only they can serve those who are needy or sad. Let the girls of England resolve to join their ranks.[3]

Denial of self is thus seen as a virtue. Whatever women's work involves, within the home or elsewhere, it is primarily for the benefit of others. Here, too, we see the conventional stereotype of womankind reinforced. It is likely that this story was influential in forming the self-image of many readers, as the account which became, according to Richard Armstrong, accepted by the world 'as the last word, authoritative and indisputable, on the "girl with the wind-

---

[2] M. Farningham, *A Working Woman's Life* (London: James Clarke, 1907), pp. 131–32.
[3] Hope, *Grace Darling*, p. 59.

blown hair" ',[4] went into many reprints and was a major contributing factor to the common view of Darling as the archetypal Victorian heroine.

This *Life of Grace Darling* is thus an excellent source for Marianne's beliefs about womanhood. The whole of the first chapter was given over to 'one of the vexed questions' of the time: a discussion about the nature of women's work.[5] After outlining two types of answers given by contemporaries, both male and female, either that women should only run their homes and that there are some occupations not suitable for them, or conversely that they are capable of doing anything that men can do, Marianne suggested that some women simply dealt with the controversy by getting on with whatever work was at hand: a pragmatic, rather than a theoretical approach, and one of which she clearly approved. She also argued that the line between right and wrong, between instructing one's own children in the Bible and teaching a small congregation, or between being a doctor to one's own children and entering the medical profession, was not as straightforward as some critics implied.[6] If there were people to be helped, or income was needed to provide for the family, then a woman should do 'what she can'. Marianne outlined the passage from the Bible where this little phrase originated. When Jesus was at the house of Simon the leper, Mary poured ointment on Jesus' feet. Jesus commended her action in the face of criticism from the other guests, and in one of the gospel accounts of this incident, he is recorded as saying 'She did what she could'.[7] Marianne used this conventional evangelical phrase to justify the involvement of women in professional life, which to her was acceptable provided that the women concerned did not 'neglect homely duties'.[8] Marianne's beliefs were clearly identified in these pages: the primary responsibility of a woman was in the domestic arena, to her own family and home, but also 'if she have leisure, strength and ability' she could and should take hold of other opportunities that arose.[9] This was not an unusual suggestion: involvement outside the home, especially in charitable enterprises, was a generally accepted extension of women's role and ability. Frank Prochaska has documented this role of women in philanthropy, which was common enough to be satirised by Dickens in *Bleak House* in the person of Mrs Jellyby.[10] The distinctive aspect of Marianne's attitude was her assertion that paid work was as valid as voluntary service or domestic duties. The suggestion that such a contribution on the part of women

---

[4] R. Armstrong, *Grace Darling: Maid and Myth* (London, J. M. Dent & Sons, 1965), p. 10.
[5] Hope, *Grace Darling*, p. 2.
[6] Hope, *Grace Darling*, p. 3.
[7] Hope, *Grace Darling*, p. 1; Mark 14·8.
[8] Hope, *Grace Darling*, pp. 3–4.
[9] Hope, *Grace Darling*, p. 4.
[10] F. Prochaska, *Women and Philanthropy in Nineteenth Century England* (Oxford: Clarendon Press, 1980); Charles Dickens, *Bleak House* (London: Penguin, 1985 [1853]), for example pp. 84–86.

might be desirable moved beyond a simple voluntary contribution to the public sphere and into the territory of feminism and equal rights. It gives us a hint of the apparent contradictions inherent in Marianne's understanding of the role of women.

Afraid to be Singular

This is spelt out more clearly further on in the first chapter of 'Grace Darling', where Marianne enthusiastically argued that the lives of pioneers such as Florence Nightingale and Elizabeth Fry exemplified this motto of 'doing what they could'. Such women, who were 'speakers and preachers, scientific women and teachers' were in her eyes positive role models, and she encouraged others to emulate them. Indicating the opposition which such women had encountered, she suggested that

> Many women, simply because they are not courageous enough to brave the adverse opinions of those by whom they are surrounded, lose golden opportunities of distinguishing themselves. They are afraid to be singular. But this fear is no honour to the sex. A woman should be so far free and independent as to do that which she feels to be right, no matter though the right seem to call her to heights which she had not occupied before... what does matter is, that she should gain the high praise of Him who sees not as man sees.[11]

This passage provides a vivid insight into Marianne's understanding of the role of women. She believed that the fear of what others might think deterred women from grasping important opportunities. This obstacle could be overcome, however, if they understood that pleasing God was more important than satisfying the expectations of other individuals or of society. There was, however, an unspoken assumption that what 'she feels to be right' was always in the context of acceptable Christian behaviour and morality.

It is interesting to note that this assertion that some women were afraid to be different, like some of Marianne's other more outspoken comments on the lives of women, was not published under her own name. Possibly this was because writing a whole book afforded her the opportunity to outline her beliefs in a way that short contributions to a paper did not, and the pseudonym was incidental. Alternatively, and perhaps more likely, she may have felt freer to express strong opinions about women under another name than she did under her own name in the pages of the *Christian World* for fear of causing problems for the newspaper's proprietors, or of alienating some of her readership. By 1880, however, she was willing to be known as a supporter of the vote for women, even if she was hesitant to write directly about it. In February 1880 a demonstration was held at the Free Trade Hall in Manchester in support of the franchise for female householders. The *Christian World* reported that from all

---

[11] Hope, *Grace Darling*, p. 11.

over Great Britain 'women of all ranks, and occupations, many of them delegates from large associations, were assembled there for the sole purpose of testifying by their presence to their interest in the cause'.[12] The hall was packed and an overflow meeting had to be hastily arranged. Messages and telegrams of sympathy were read out from two hundred women 'many of them women of rank, or distinguished in literature, art, science, or philanthropy' who were unable to be present, but wished to publicly state their support for the cause. The only person the reporter mentioned by name was Marianne, indicating that she was happy to be known as a supporter of women's rights by this stage, even if she rarely wrote about the matter. She was amongst the pioneers of the cause of votes for women.

If she was, at this stage, still a little wary of committing herself so definitely to print on behalf of women's rights under her 'own' name, many years later, when her autobiography was completed, she freely expressed similar opinions in print as Marianne Farningham. She probably no longer had any concern that either her own career or the circulation of the paper would be affected, as both were now well established. What is more, voices in the evangelical press other than her own were by that later stage articulating support for a wider role for women in society. For instance, in February 1907, the *Freeman and Baptist Times* carried a report of a women's procession led by the moderate suffrage campaigner Mrs Fawcett, with the comment that 'nothing marred the perfect order and good taste of the whole demonstration from beginning to end. Saturday was a complete answer to those who still maintain that women do not desire or deserve a vote.'[13] A few months later, a minister writing in the same paper claimed to have always been in favour of the vote for independent female householders aged twenty-one or over.

> I have always felt that it is impossible logically to argue against woman suffrage. Why should an educated and property-owning woman – whether spinster or widow – be deprived because of her sex of the privilege of voting for a representative in Parliament, that right being freely granted to her gardener or coachman?[14]

Once women have the vote, he continued to argue, there would be more 'peaceful and progressive measures'. He even suggested that such a development would bring the millennium closer. Such views would probably have also become more acceptable to the evangelical readership of the *Christian World* by this stage. It is possible that Marianne waited until her opinions were no longer controversial in the eyes of many of her readers before expressing them freely under her own name.

The question then arises as to whether Marianne herself was, to some extent,

---

[12] *CW*, 12 February 1880.

[13] *Freeman and Baptist Times* 15 February 1907.

[14] *Freeman* 24 May 1907.

'afraid to be singular', not in her lifestyle, but in the degree of force with which she expressed certain opinions in writing. Although that is a possibility, it is probably an unfair suggestion, for, as was mentioned earlier, she explicitly asserted that ideally the opinions of others should not affect women's behaviour.[15] Perhaps the real explanation can be found in her desire to avoid controversy wherever possible. Marianne disliked disagreement: she went out of her way to work with people from different sections of evangelicalism and to express appreciation of those she disagreed with, and of those who did not let opinion stand in the way of friendship. There are several examples of this attitude in her writing. In her autobiography, for instance, she recalls her delight at seeing her editor, James Clarke, and the well-known Baptist minister, Charles Spurgeon, greet each other as old friends at a time when they were at loggerheads theologically.[16] Putting aside doctrinal disagreements for the sake of unity was also a major theme in her novel *Nineteen Hundred*. At one stage in the novel, a group of Nonconformist ministers and an Anglican clergyman joined together to work for the good of their village. Marianne portrayed them as 'brothers, who respected the good that they saw in each other, and carried together the burden of the souls of the people',[17] despite their differences of opinion. She believed that Christians should work together for the good of the communities in which they lived. This characteristic would suggest that, because Marianne so valued understanding between those of different opinions, she was herself hesitant to give any cause for misunderstanding or disagreement. The reality is that Marianne was gradually challenging some conventional attitudes, especially towards women who earned their own living, whilst at the same time reinforcing others, in particular the significance of domesticity. Her comments reflected the thoughts of someone who was grappling with the complex issues of what it meant to live out one's life as a woman and a Christian, in the context of Victorian society.

The Fear of Wasted Lives

One aspect of Marianne's awareness as both Christian and a woman, was her keen sense that many women wasted their lives because they lacked purpose and direction, which faith, combined with work, could supply.[18] People who did not work, or had a negative attitude to work, were in her eyes leading purposeless and futile lives, whilst those who did work were contributing to society as well as finding personal fulfilment. In her writing she contrasted the satisfaction of work with the bored and useless life of a lady of leisure. Like

---

[15] Hope, *Grace Darling*, p. 11.
[16] Farningham, *Life*, pp. 209–10.
[17] M. Farningham, *Nineteen Hundred: a forecast and a story* (London: James Clarke, 1892), p.73
[18] M. Farningham *Life Sketches* (1st series, London: James Clarke, 1861), p. 66.

Sarah Ellis before her, Marianne had little sympathy with the increasingly leisured middle classes, and her comments are loaded with social criticism. She expressed this opinion consistently, and under both her pseudonyms. It can be found, for instance, in a little volume of prose pieces *Girlhood* published as early as 1869, as well as in her biography of Grace Darling written as Eva Hope many years later. In the introduction to *Girlhood*, Marianne criticised young women whose 'whole thoughts are given up to pleasure. They have no reflection, no thought, no depth.'[19] Those girls who spent their time in 'giddy mirth and idleness' would never find happiness through 'pleasure-making', she asserted. Rather, it was the 'thoughtful, earnest girls' who would find happiness, through taking responsibilities seriously, and keeping an appropriate balance of work and leisure.[20] Later in the collection she contrasted an imaginary girl, 'Clarissa Montague' who had no occupation, with an equally imaginary reader who was hardworking. Clarissa rose late, was always tired, and was constantly dissatisfied with life, and the round of social activity she endured, whilst her 'reader' worked hard, enjoyed her leisure, and slept well.[21] The message is clear and simple: satisfaction is found in work, whether paid or unpaid, whilst the woman who spends her time in pleasure is always disappointed.

A similar message is conveyed in *Grace Darling*. Here Marianne claims that women of Grace's quality 'are not the produce of ballrooms, where the air is poisoned by gases, and where women spend nights in scenes of excitement and gaiety' and are prone to 'sickly sentimentalism'.[22] Such a life, according to Marianne, carries the seeds of its own frustration. To be free from these dangers, girls should be partially educated in the fresh air, and taught to despise frivolities. This is a direct criticism of the upper classes, and those of the middle classes who aspired to a life similarly consisting merely of pleasure and social activities. Whilst she is careful to say that it is not having money that is the problem, there is an implicit social comment that those women who do have riches are more likely to be indolent and make little useful contribution to society. Marianne was not afraid to criticise those above her in the social hierarchy. She was not alone in this. At first sight such ideas as the disapproval of idleness, and careful husbandry of time, might seem to be purely evangelical attributes, rooted in concepts of duty and service. Yet the reality was more complex. Marianne's working-class background, as well as her need to earn her own living, probably contributed to her attitude towards such time-wasting. Also, as Philippa Levine has pointed out, a similar view was expressed by many feminists, including Frances Power Cobbe, who later became a friend of Marianne.[23] Marianne's views on idleness could as easily be understood as

---

[19] M. Farningham, *Girlhood* (London: James Clarke, 1869), p. 8.

[20] Farningham, *Girlhood*, pp. 1–3.

[21] Farningham, *Girlhood*, pp. 30–32.

[22] Hope, *Grace Darling*, p. 14.

[23] P. Levine, *Feminist Lives in Victorian England* (Oxford: Blackwell, 1990), p.126.

representing a feminist viewpoint as an evangelical one.

Further evidence of this is found in the way Marianne portrayed Darling as having physical strength, and as demonstrating a certain independence of spirit, and willingness to take initiative. She wrote that 'strong women are needed for the work of these days, and let all who would not be mere logs floating down the stream, listen to the injunction, and gird her loins with strength, and strengthen her arms'.[24] Thus Darling, who was used to the outdoors, could row a boat and was willing to take initiative to rescue the sailors in the face of her mother's disapproval, was a role model to be emulated. She demonstrated a mixture of strength and weakness which made up Farningham's ideal of womanly behaviour and which to her was not inconsistent, as it all derived from faith and which expressed itself either in quiet obedience or strong-willed action as the occasion demanded.

Closely related to this dislike of idleness was a sense of duty. In 1861 Marianne declared 'we live for work, for service, for some good end, and not for self-gratification merely'.[25] Duty was still an important concept to her some years later, as she referred to it several times in her biography of Grace Darling. Grace, she suggested, was motivated in her daily life 'by the one desire, to do her duty'.[26] Duty, like a dislike of frivolity, is often thought of as a particularly evangelical characteristic. Yet, as Bebbington has pointed out, this perspective on life was shared by many contemporaries in the 1850s and 60s, the decades which shaped Marianne's ideas.[27] Concepts such as duty, which originated within evangelicalism, had by this stage filtered through to the mainstream of mid-Victorian belief and practice, and as they fitted with her concept of Christian behaviour she reflected these opinions. Whilst her understanding widened to include not only philanthropic involvement outside the home, but paid work of various kinds, all of which might be construed as part of a woman's 'duty', the obligations of domesticity were given the primary place in her writings.

Women and Domesticity

In *Homely Talks*, compiled as late as 1886, Marianne stated her belief that 'probably all life that is worth anything begins in the home'.[28] This sentence summed up the importance of home to the author, both in her own life and in her writings. Her opinions on this topic never wavered. During more than fifty

---

[24] Hope, *Grace Darling*, pp. 296–97.
[25] Farningham, *Sketches*, (1861) p. 66.
[26] Hope, *Grace Darling*, p. 294.
[27] D.W. Bebbington, *Evangelicalism in Modern Britain* (London: Unwin Hyman, 1989), p. 105.
[28] M. Farningham, *Homely Talks about Homely Things* (London: James Clarke, 1886), p. 66.

years of writing about the home, she maintained a consistency of attitude and approach, remaining clearly committed to the Victorian ideal of domesticity and a particular understanding of feminine characteristics. Whether writing as Marianne Farningham, or as Eva Hope, her comments about women's work and role were embedded in a discourse which regarded the home as the primary locus of womanly accomplishments. She consistently taught that domestic responsibilities were the most important duties for women, and that affairs should be running smoothly at home before a woman even considered venturing out into the wider world.

Marianne's tendency to idealise the home and its inhabitants can be detected as early as 1869, in *Home Life,* one of the first collections of her regular prose writing. In one piece in the collection, she asserted that 'the true life is that which is lived in a well-conducted Christian Home', declaring that 'home should be the first place in our affection'.[29] Earlier, in 1861, she had similarly described a wife's life at home as being 'the happiest and holiest' way to live, whilst the husband should be 'the very sun and centre, the light, and joy, and warmth of the little, earnest, loving, loyal band at home'.[30] Those words were directed to both sexes, but in Marianne's thinking, as in much contemporary teaching, there was a particular application for women. She encouraged her female readers to value home highly. Following Sarah Ellis, the writer of advice books including *Women of England*,[31] Marianne believed in the power of the home and the hearth to keep men (it was usually men) from straying from the straight and narrow. The first duty of women was to maintain that unsullied home.

In Marianne's novel *What of the Night?* published in 1876, the heroine Edith Knelston, married to an errant pastor, became the means of his rescue. She 'took the greatest care not to neglect her home' so that when he returned after a meeting 'his bright little rooms were always ready for him, and what was best of all, his wife's smile and loving caress waiting to welcome him'.[32] Such comments could indicate that Marianne subscribed to conventional beliefs concerning the role of women and in particular their domestic obligations, accepting a version of the domestic ideology as suggested by Leonore Davidoff and Catherine Hall, in which the main area and focus of women's lives was the home.[33] According to their thesis, between 1780 and about 1850, the formation of the middle classes and the process of industrialisation were linked with the fragmentation of men's and women's lives into separate areas. The development of this sexual division of labour into public and private spheres

---

[29] M. Farningham, *Home Life* (London: James Clarke, 1869), pp. 1, 8.
[30] Farningham, *Sketches* (1861), pp. 4–5.
[31] S. Ellis, *Women of England* (London: Fisher, & Son, 1839).
[32] M. Farningham, *What of the Night? A Temperance Tale* (London: James Clarke, 1876), p. 104.
[33] L. Davidoff and C. Hall, *Family Fortunes* (London: Routledge, 1987), p. 74.

was accompanied by a discourse which appeared to give women an elevated status, but actually limited their involvement in society. Certainly, to some extent at least, Marianne thought in terms of a binary reality of private and public aspects of life, supporting the assertion that separate spheres had become 'the common sense of the middle class' in this period.[34]

For Davidoff and Hall, this development was an essential component in the development of capitalism, and was inextricably connected to evangelicalism.[35] Their thesis has been questioned, for instance by Amanda Vickery who challenged its premises, doubting that the development of separate spheres was essential to the rise of the middle classes, and also whether the latter were formed between 1780 and 1850 as Davidoff and Hall assumed.[36] More recently, Robert Shoemaker has argued that the same division of spheres was apparent in the early modern period, and was not a new construct in the nineteenth century.[37] In the preface to the second edition of their book, Davidoff and Hall have acknowledged the ongoing debate, including this continuity with the past, but still argue that their basic premise is valid.[38] Separate spheres have become a little fuzzy at the edges, but the construct can still make a useful contribution in illuminating nineteenth century gender roles.

There was certainly much sentimental and idealised writing about women and domesticity during the Victorian era, especially around the time when Marianne's beliefs would have been formed. The poet Coventry Patmore and the art critic and writer John Ruskin are often regarded as the main proponents of this stereotype, and Marianne referred to Ruskin with admiration.[39] Sarah Ellis also helped to influence and shape the ideal of the home as the place where women primarily lived out their obligation to influence the nation's morality. Their sphere, she argued, 'is the minor morals of domestic life'.[40] Much of Marianne's writing about the home seems close to that of Ellis, although there is no direct reference to the latter in her work. This similarity

---

[34] L. Davidoff and C. Hall, *Family Fortunes* (London: Routledge, 2nd ed. 2002), p. xvi.

[35] Davidoff and Hall, *Family Fortunes* (1987) p. 13.

[36] A. Vickery, 'Golden Age to Separate Spheres? A Review of the Categories and Chronology of Women's History', *Historical Journal*, Vol 36, No 2, (1993), pp. 383–414.

[37] R. Shoemaker, *Gender in English Society, 1650-1850: The Emergence of Separate Spheres?* (London/New York: Longman, 1998).

[38] Davidoff and Hall, *Family Fortunes* (2002), pp. xiii–xl.

[39] C. Patmore, 'The Angel in the House', ed. Frederick Page (London: Oxford University Press, 1949), p. 89, and J. Ruskin, 'Of Queens' Gardens' in *Sesame and Lilies* (London: Collins 1864–69), pp. 95–158. For Marianne's opinion of Ruskin, see for instance 'Ruskin', in M. Farningham, *Harvest Gleanings and Gathered Fragments* (London: James Clarke, 1903), p. 138.

[40] Ellis, *Women of England*, pp. 38 and 58. See also L. Wilson, *Constrained by Zeal: Female Spirituality amongst Nonconformists 1825-75* (Carlisle: Paternoster Press, 2000), pp. 136-44.

can be seen, for instance, in her book about Grace Darling. Strange as it might seem, despite stating categorically in the first chapter that women should be free and independent, this work also contains some classic formulations of domestic ideology. Grace is made to say that, even after being the guest of the Duchess of Northumberland at Alnwick Castle, she loved her home the most of all: 'No indeed, it is the dearest and sweetest spot on all the earth to me, because it is home'.[41] Marianne uses this attachment as an opportunity to sermonise about the value of women loving their homes.

> Let the women of England remember ... that the homes they know shall surely be bright or dark, sad or happy, as they shall make them, by their meek or gentle spirit, and unselfish devoted affection... Women should understand that their home-life is the most important, and give to it their devotion and love.[42]

This was a constant theme in her writings, reinforced in many ways. Her perspective reflected that of her readers, and her sentimentality would have found an answering echo in their hearts. Marianne held conventional beliefs regarding the priority of the home.

It is not surprising, given the quasi-religious nature of the contemporary discourse about home, that it was also regarded by Marianne as a place of peace and spiritual tranquillity. 'Home', wrote Marianne Farningham in *Homely Talks*, is 'a haven in which we can hide from the sea of troubles and forget our tossings.'[43] Her language concerning the home was not that far-distant from her language about Christ, and especially about heaven, often understood by the late Victorian period in domestic terms.[44] Towards the end of her life, she was still expressing similar sentiments, for instance in the poem 'God Bless Our Home' from *Harvest Gleanings,* published in 1903.

> O snug little nest in a shelter so cheery,
> O place of sweet rest for the troubled and weary...
> No spot is so dear to the heart, nor is any
> Ignored by so few, or beloved by so many.[45]

This piece of sentimental doggerel appropriately highlights simultaneously Marianne's rather variable talent and her appeal to contemporaries who shared her beliefs concerning the sacredness of the home.

An important aspect of this domestic discourse stressed by Marianne was the role of the home as a bulwark against the temptations of the world. For instance, in an early poem, 'Fireside poetry', she painted a scene of a family around the fire listening to Bible stories and praying together. In the second

---

[41] Hope, *Grace Darling*, p. 275.
[42] Hope, *Grace Darling*, p. 279.
[43] Farningham, *Homely Talks*, p. 3.
[44] See Chapter 6, p. 205.
[45] Farningham, *Harvest*, p. 45.

verse it was asserted that a youth leaving home would be helped by recalling these memories.

> Life's busy din was calling him 'mid sterner scenes to roam;
> But O! those clinging arms, those eyes lit with such pleading love,
> Will be to him as well-trimmed lamps, lighting his steps above.
> The tempter's voice may tell him that the paths of sin are fair
> But in his heart will ever be thoughts of that fireside prayer.[46]

The mere memory of home and family, it was suggested here, would be enough to deal with the 'tempter' and prevent the young man from falling into sin, the nature of which is never made explicit. Home, rather than church, was where the sacred is located, in opposition to 'the world'.

This theme is also found in Marianne's fiction. As noted above, in *What of the Night?* the wife, Edith, does her best to keep her straying pastor husband, Edwin Knelston, away from drink by taking the greatest care not to neglect her home.[47] Edith's priority was clearly this role of providing a safe and loving home environment for Edwin, rather than, for example, working alongside him. There are no examples of straying wives or young women: Marianne's expectation was clearly the conventional one that the women would act as the means of redemption and not be the recipients of rescue attempts. There is little recognition in her writing of the fallen woman, despite the large numbers of prostitutes in Victorian England.[48]

The task of providing such a homely refuge was not in Marianne's eyes, however, confined to wives and mothers. She believed that sisters could also fulfil this function for their siblings. An example of this is found in 'Carrie's Resolution', a story serialised in the weekly *Christian World Magazine* in 1870. This tale contained stereotypes of the home-based pious woman and the errant male in which the woman is a sister, rather than a wife or mother. Carrie's brother was bringing distress to his parents, and it is her prayers and persistence which in the end achieve the aim, although with typical womanly modestly she says it was all due to God. It is significant that his salvation involves staying within the home: the world is far too dangerous a place for him.[49] Thus the redemption of a wandering male is brought about by a faithful woman, and the gender expectations of Victorian evangelicalism are upheld. Marianne's evangelical readers would have felt comfortable with these sentiments, and felt able to trust her. This role of a sister reflected her own experience following her mother's death, when for some time she helped her father with the housework and cared for her younger siblings. A significant difference is that she also

---

[46] M. Farningham, *Lays and Lyrics of the Blessed Life* (London: James Clarke & Co: 1864 [1861]), p. 100.
[47] Farningham, *What of the Night?*, p. 104.
[48] L.S. Nolland, *A Victorian Feminist Christian: Josephine Butler, the Prostitutes and God* (Carlisle: Paternoster, 2004), pp. 2–4.
[49] *Christian World Magazine* 1870 January – June.

helped him in his work as the local postmaster and later cobbler, taking shoes to school to mend during the lunch hour.[50] Later in Northampton she fulfilled a similar role as the single head of a household which at one stage included several of her nieces. Single women could also, in Marianne's experience, create a significant home base for their relatives, as the leader not just the supporter, an extension of the classic formulation of women's role. These largely conventional views on women and home reflected and reinforced the evangelical view of domesticity and the role of women within that setting

In common with many of her contemporaries, Marianne appears to have been simply unaware that not all homes were havens of peace, and that cruelty and abuse frequently occurred in some of them. This is evident in *Home Life* and elsewhere. There was little or no understanding that the home could be a place of tyranny and misunderstanding. At the very least, there was an assumption that any difficulties were resolvable by a faithful or loving mother or sister. Occasionally there were indications that Marianne was aware that not everyone treated their homes with respect, but rarely is there any suggestion that a Christian home could be other than a place of redemption. Marianne believed that in a truly Christian home, 'vice dare not lift its head',[51] displaying a naiveté about the nature of some domestic situations. Drunkenness and loss of faith seem to have been the worst sins a man could commit, and whilst there was much mention of 'thoughtless' girls who preferred their own freedom to a selfless service of others, there was a lack of appreciation of the reality of some homes. This is possibly why, when the founder of the Society for the Prevention of Cruelty to Children, the Congregationalist minister Benjamin Waugh, insisted that 'the worst and most cruel offenders' in the ill-treatment of children were parents, Marianne found this 'at first incredible'. The discovery of the frequency with which ill-treatment was occurring within families came as a shock to her compassionate nature. She declared: 'I knew that there were a few inhuman monsters, but I did not believe they could be many.' With typical journalistic curiosity, however, she attended a meeting where Waugh was speaking. Arriving late, she met a friend leaving, 'looking very white and faint', who tried to persuade her not to go in, insisting that the speaker must be exaggerating, and that it would make her ill to hear him. Marianne was determined to listen, but commented that it did, make her ill, indeed, near to despair about the country, believing that 'it was a national disgrace' that the society was needed.[52] This is, perhaps, an indication that her outlook was basically optimistic, shaped more by Enlightenment ideas of the progress of humanity, and Romantic beliefs in the essential goodness of humanity, than by the evangelical tenet of original sin, or the doctrine of total depravity which she would have heard preached in her youth at the Calvinistic chapel of Eynsford.

---

[50] Farningham, *Life*, p. 50.
[51] Farningham, *Home Life*, p. 5.
[52] Farningham, *Life*, p. 251.

Her interest in contemporary issues, and her honest integrity, however, meant that she was able to absorb new information and integrate it, albeit with some difficulty at times, into her world view.

Some observers of Marianne's writing have misunderstood her because of her conventional attitude to domesticity. Thus Armstrong complained that her account of Grace was 'clouded with romantic moonshine'.[53] Similarly, although in a more polite fashion, Brian Knight has suggested that Marianne's intention in *Girlhood* and other works was to reinforce 'the concept of female subordination'.[54] He has wrongly deduced that her traditional beliefs concerning the home were echoed in a conservative attitude towards women's role in society at large. It is easy to understand how such misunderstandings could have arisen, as both orthodox and unorthodox constructions of femininity co-existed within Marianne's writings. Her readers were enthusiastically urged to be good Victorian wives and daughters, as well as to take initiative in new areas. In her biography of Grace Darling there is a considerable amount written about the wider role of women. Yet, probably because he was writing before the development of feminist history, Armstrong completely failed to notice the significance of much of this discussion. He dismissed the first chapter as 'totally irrelevant', failing to see that in its advocacy of an extension of women's role, it illuminates the whole account, putting the rest of the biography in context.[55] What is more, Marianne's emphasis on the home needs to be seen in relation to her emphatic enthusiasm for women's involvement with work, of which the domestic arena is only one manifestation.

In her beliefs about the priority of home, Marianne was also in tune with some moderate feminists of her time. Frances Power Cobbe, for instance, labelled by Levine as 'an important figure'[56] in the early feminist movement, who, like Marianne, was a journalist and a lecturer, asserted that that 'the private and home duties of *such women as have them* are, beyond all doubt, their first concern'.[57] Like Marianne, Cobbe believed passionately that women should be involved in the public sphere, but not at the expense of their private duties, taking a positive delight in 'a well-ordered house and table, rooms pleasantly arranged and lighted, and decorated with flowers, a hospitable attentions to guests, and all the other pleasant cares of the mistress of a family'.[58] Cobbe, however, held this mixture of beliefs without the unifying

---

[53] Armstrong, *Maid and Myth*, pp. 7–9.
[54] B. Knight, 'Strategy, mission and people in a rural diocese in a critical examination of the diocese of Gloucester' (PhD thesis, University of Gloucestershire, 2002), p. 230.
[55] Armstrong, *Maid and Myth*, p. 8.
[56] P. Levine, *Victorian Feminism 1850-1900* (London: Hutchinson, 1987), p. 18.
[57] Quoted in M. Vicinus, *Independent Women: Work and Community for Single Women 1850-1920* (London: Virago, 1985), p. 15.
[58] F. P. Cobbe, *Life of Frances Power Cobbe* (London: Richard Bentley & Sons, 1894), p. 75.

religious foundation expressed by Marianne. By her own account, Cobbe had experienced an evangelical conversion, but moving away from what she perceived as restrictive beliefs, she toyed with Deism before settling on a form of theistic belief which was some distance removed from her theological origins.[59] Her attitude to the home was still shaped, however, by middle-class assumptions concerning the virtue of domesticity. Although she herself had moved beyond personal spiritual allegiance, she did not question the basic tenets of the discourse of domesticity, which still dominated understanding of the feminine role both within and beyond evangelicalism. Marianne was therefore not as unusual as might first appear in her advocacy of a woman's primary domestic role being combined where appropriate with a public function.

Evangelicalism and Feminism

This discussion highlights the fact that the relationship between evangelicalism and the development of feminism is a complex one. Various opinions have been expressed on the matter. Some historians have focused on the limitations evangelicalism imposed, whilst others have stressed the opportunities which religion opened up to women during the nineteenth century. Martha Vicinus has shown how belonging to an evangelical sisterhood both restricted freedom and enabled the growth of 'self-development and self-knowledge'.[60] Similarly, but in a wider sense, Levine has suggested that women 'were granted a role in spiritual life which at one and the same time empowered and confined them,'[61] and as discussed earlier, Davidoff and Hall have famously argued that evangelicalism was complicit in the development of separate spheres and thus in the creation of an ideology which suggested that, ideally, women should be confined to domestic roles. There is an assumption in much of this discussion that evangelicalism and feminism were mutually exclusive. No doubt this is in part due to the lack of work that has been done on the 'role and dimension of religion in women's lives' as Sue Morgan has pointed out. She has also highlighted the involvement of evangelical women in feminist campaigns, arguing for a wider definition of feminism than has sometimes been used.[62] Aspects of Marianne's beliefs and behaviour are decidedly feminist: others are less so. To some present-day observers the contrast between her attitudes to work and to home sets up a tension: to her, there was no such tension. The question was of priorities, rather than conflict, and in her belief system the home always took first place. All that she did, and advocated, stemmed from a

---

[59] Cobbe, *Life*, p. 83.
[60] Vicinus, *Independent Women*, p. 61.
[61] Levine, *Victorian Feminism*, p. 12.
[62] S. Morgan, 'Women, Religion and Feminism: Past, Present and Future Perspectives' in *Women, Religion and Feminism in Britain, 1750-1900*, S. Morgan, ed. (Basingstoke: Palgrave Macmillan, 2002), pp. 1–3.

mixture of her background and her evangelical faith, which to her had a logical consistency.

Home was, to Marianne, a place of belonging, and of refuge, and caring for it was the first duty and responsibility of a woman, whether married or unmarried. No doubt in this belief she was also reflecting, and reinforcing, the conventional views of the majority of her readers, both male and female. She also assumed, as indeed did Sarah Ellis and many others, that this domestic role equipped women to become involved in philanthropic work, which in many ways was an extension of the same mothering gifts and abilities applied to a wider society. Also in line with convention, she taught that such an extension of the female role should only be undertaken if everything was in order in the domestic world. A woman, she insisted, should not 'neglect homely duties, for those which call her away from friends and kindred who need her. She is not to stretch out her hands beseechingly for higher service, if they are already full of lowly tasks not yet accomplished.'[63] Home had first place in her thinking and writing.

With those criteria fulfilled, however, a woman should 'do with her might whatever her hands find to do'.[64] This is the point at which Marianne ventured over a boundary that many people never crossed, because she made no distinction here between offering care or engaging in preaching, between helping a neighbour's children when they were ill or becoming a doctor in paid employment.[65] A woman's response to the needs around her could lead her far beyond the home. Marianne rather naively assumed that women she admired, such as Elizabeth Fry, had their homes and families appropriately in order before venturing out to engage in more public occupations. She wrote of her admiration for Fry, who became involved in a variety of causes, of which the best known is her involvement with women prisoners and prison reform, asking 'Was Mrs Fry less a good wife and able mother, because she visited prisons, and saved many of her sex from desolation and death? She had eight children, and no-one doubts that each one had every care that a devoted mother could bestow upon him.'[66] This assumption that Fry's home duties were all in order does seem to have been a rather generous one, demonstrating Marianne's tendency to make uncritical assumptions about people. In reality, Fry made a choice between motherhood and her calling. Her involvement in various causes actually led to accusations from fellow Quakers that she was neglecting her home and children,[67] and there is evidence that when her many children were young she considered them a distraction from what she believed was her real purpose in life, farming them out to relatives from time to time so she could

---

[63] Hope, *Grace Darling*, p. 5
[64] Hope, *Grace Darling*, p. 5.
[65] Hope, *Grace Darling*, p. 3.
[66] Hope, *Grace Darling*, p. 13.
[67] J. Rose, *Elizabeth Fry* (London: Macmillan, 1980), see for instance pp. 101–102.

continue her work.⁶⁸ As adults, some of them were critical of their mother's continual involvement with prison work and other causes.⁶⁹ Elizabeth Fry was not as Marianne imagined her. Her understanding of Fry, and the other women she held up as heroines, was thus sentimental and incomplete. She constructed these women as she wished and imagined them to be, unaware of conflicts in their lives between public and private roles which would have made her uncomfortable. Yet the fact remains that she was celebrating women who took initiative outside the home in both philanthropy and paid work.

Motherhood

Closely linked to the role of women in the home was the whole ideology surrounding motherhood. Mothers featured strongly in Marianne's writing, and in this area, just as in her conventional attitude to domesticity, there was an unquestioning reflection of contemporary idealisations and priorities. For instance, in a book of daily readings published in 1904, entitled *Women and their Saviour*, she commented on the passage in the gospels where mothers brought their children to Jesus to be blessed, claiming that these mothers of Salem personified the mothers 'of all the ages. Motherhood is a sacred thing with solemn responsibilities.' Ever since then, she suggested, mothers have been bringing little ones to Jesus: 'The mothers of Salem showed the mothers of the world the way'.⁷⁰ This concept of the responsibilities of motherhood especially, but not exclusively, focused on spiritual training, recurred several times in Marianne's writing. Commenting in a short piece from *Women and their Work*, published in 1906, on the story of Jacob and Esau, she highlighted the mistakes of Rachel, stressing that mothers have 'a great responsibility. They can, to a large extent, make or mar the lives of those whom they love.'⁷¹ In this emphasis on the responsibility and the influence that mothers possessed, Marianne was once again echoing the teaching of Sarah Ellis in her emphasis on the role of women in training up the next generation.⁷²

Perhaps the story which best illustrates this conventional attitude to motherhood is another one drawn from the same collection. The date of writing indicates that, as with domesticity, Marianne's understanding of motherhood did not significantly alter during her writing career. In three episodes, she recounted and commented on the biblical account of Hannah and Samuel. Hannah prays in the temple in desperation for a child, promising to give him to God if her prayer is answered. Samuel, the result of the prayer, is accordingly sent to be a temple assistant to Eli once he is weaned, and Hannah sees him

---

[68] Rose, *Elizabeth Fry*, p. 58.
[69] Rose, *Elizabeth Fry*, p. 164.
[70] M. Farningham, *Women and their Saviour: Thoughts of a minute for a month of mornings* (London: James Clarke, 1904), pp. 40–41.
[71] M. Farningham, *Women and their Work* (London: James Clark, 1906), p. 23.
[72] See for instance Ellis, *Women of England*, p. 54.

only once a year when the family visits the temple and she takes him a new coat she has made for him. Marianne attributed thoughts and attitudes to Hannah with a story-teller's imagination and typical sentimentality. She drew a picture of the mother thinking of her son whilst she sewed his new coat each year.

> The next best thing to seeing her boy was to be doing something for him; and we can imagine this woman, with her thought and heart full of the darling whom she had given to God, while her hands were busy with stitches and embroidery. Mothers' prayers often sanctify the little garments they make. Ah! If their boys only knew the dreams and hopes that occupy the mothers' brains while their hands are occupied in ways that seem commonplace.[73]

In this one story, practical care, deep love, and prayer were all highlighted as important aspects of motherhood, an emphasis found in many authors, in obituaries, biographies, and autobiographies of nineteenth-century women, as well as in sermons and advice books. When Marianne further suggested that his ephod and coat would have helped him remember he was set apart for God, she emphasised the role of a mother's prayer. 'In any temptation there is nothing which so helps a boy as to know that his mother is praying that he may be true and strong. Samuel's life, so great in greatest ways, was as much an answer to his mother's prayers as his birth.'[74] Here she adds to the Old Testament account her own presuppositions about the role of mothers and prayer. This use of the imagination was rather typical of Marianne. These assumptions are not in the text, but read into it, and they reflect her cultural preconceptions. Mothers are, in her mind, almost obsessive in the way their own lives are based on their hopes and longings for their children.

Marianne could also be rather sentimental about motherhood, especially in her poetry, as the following verse demonstrates. It is taken from a poem entitled 'The Wind of Spring' published in *Christian World Magazine* in May 1867. Marianne invites the wind to blow from the south, chasing winter away and bringing new hope along with fresh scents.

> And touch the aching head
> Of every care-worn mother, bowed with care
> And whisper to her that the angels tread
> About her place of prayer.[75]

A similar sentimental picture of the troubled mother is created in *Boyhood* where Marianne gave advice to boys about how to treat their mothers. She insisted that they needed to be treated with respect by their sons who would never find such a good friend again after leaving home. So they should be careful of their action, because 'if you sneer at goodness, and mock at that

---

[73] Farningham, *Women and Work*, p. 85.

[74] Farningham, *Women and Work*, p. 86.

[75] *Christian World Magazine* 1867, p. 400.

which is right, be very certain that tears are often mingled with your mother's prayers'.[76] Her words, however, would have chimed with readers used to sentimentality. In this characteristic, Marianne was in tune with the popular culture of her time.

Whilst Marianne often refers to mothers in the context of home and children, she mentions fathers only occasionally, indicating that she believed that in reality it is the mothers who shaped the nature of a home. In the early collection, *Home Life,* she asserted that the father was the most important person in the house, declaring that 'there can be no doubt of this reality, and none will hesitate to admit it', yet he is portrayed as essentially passive within the home environment.[77] Some years later she expressed the opinion that both parents should be actively involved with their children, with fathers preferring time with them to reading newspapers, but again more of the focus in this work is on other family members.[78] John Tosh has argued that despite the contemporary representations of separate spheres, in the mid-Victorian period men also located much of their identity, especially their spiritual identity, in the home.[79] Marianne would have agreed that the home was an important base for men, but in common with much other Victorian literature, her writing gives centre stage in the home to women, and especially mothers. Only in some of her later fiction are fathers given a larger role, possibly because by this stage she had a wider experience of life. For example, in *Window on Paris,* published in 1898, Mr Clifton, father of the heroine Mary Clifton, has a comparatively full and sympathetic portrayal.[80] However, fathers were never given centre stage in her writing.

Motherhood was not, in Marianne's eyes, reserved only for those who were able to be natural mothers. On one occasion, late in her life, Marianne wrote that

> every woman, whether married or not, is the better and sweeter and more loveable for having some motherliness in her nature. And if she has not quite the joy she longs for, she can have something like it. The world wants mothers almost more than anything else. And many women who have no children of their own can still say 'He maketh the barren women to rejoice'. [81]

It is interesting, although not unexpected, that in this extract there is a strong identification of the female with the mother. It is evident that for Marianne, motherhood was an integral part of being a woman which needed to find its

---

[76] M. Farningham, *Boyhood* (London: James Clarke, 1870), p. 103.
[77] Farningham, *Home Life,* p. 10.
[78] Farningham, *Homely Talks,* p. 33
[79] J. Tosh, *A Man's Place: Masculinity and the Middle-class Home in Victorian England* (New Haven and London: Yale University Press, 1999), pp. 46–50.
[80] M. Farningham, *Window on Paris* (London: James Clarke & Co, 1898).
[81] Farningham, *Women and Work,* p. 86.

expression either in natural children, or in another way with some type of substitute children. This accords with the concept labelled by Helsinger, Sheets and Veeder as the 'Angel out of the House', a role that did not challenge the responsibility of men, but extended the traditional activities of women beyond the home into philanthropy or church work.[82] It was the expression of motherly and home-based instincts in the world for the good of the world, and would have been largely a reflection of the high value that contemporary society put on motherhood, as seen for instance in Sarah Ellis's writing. In this area, too, Marianne was reflecting the culture around her, rather than bringing an alternative voice. Although she affirmed the value of her single life, she did so in terms which acknowledged and accepted the dominant nineteenth-century ideology of women.

Was there a personal element in her emphasis on motherhood, in addition to the reflection of common assumptions? A couple of aspects of her life could have helped to increase the focus on mothers already present in Victorian culture. One is the early death of her own mother.[83] The experience of losing at such a young age a mother who was well-loved and devoted to the family, and its effect in the change to her lifestyle, could have made motherhood seem even more important in Marianne's eyes than it would have been otherwise. This may also explain why, despite her belief in the importance of motherhood, she seemed to have difficulty portraying actual mothers in her fiction, where mothers of adolescents are often shadowy and insubstantial figures. It is the sisters who are the stronger and more pro-active characters. 'Carrie's Resolution' is an early example of this, as the mother in this tale does very little except sometimes give advice.[84] Thus although motherhood is important to Marianne, she was not always successful in its portrayal.

Another contributing factor to her emphasis on motherhood could be the time when she was engaged, and thus came close to potential motherhood.[85] The dashing of her hopes for marriage could easily have increased the importance in her mind of motherhood, and indeed there are indications in her writing that Marianne occasionally regretted her own lack of children. 'It must be a very joyous thing to be a mother', she wrote mournfully in *Home Life*, and to know 'the sense of being of so much consequence in the home place'.[86] She was expressing a longing for a sense of identity different from the one she was experiencing. Many years later, in the account of Hannah and Samuel, Marianne wrote that the story is 'pathetic reading' for 'some of us' as many

---

[82] E.K. Helsinger, R.L. Sheets, and W. Veeder, *The Woman Question*, Vol 1 (Chicago: University of Chicago Press, 1983), pp. xiv–xv.
[83] See Chapter 2, pp. 22-24.
[84] *Christian World Magazine* 1870, assorted pages in January – June numbers.
[85] See Chapter 2, p. 37.
[86] Farningham, *Home Life*, p. 16.

'have the mother-love without the child on whom to bestow it'.[87] She clearly had felt a longing for children at times. This was not peculiar to her: Philippa Levine, in her study of Victorian feminism, has noted that single women expressed more regret at the loss of potential children than the absence of a partner.[88] On another occasion, Marianne recounted a girl's cry: ' "Mother!" exclaimed a motherless girl to a lady who had brought her into the light of the Lord Jesus, and the woman's heart was thrilled with joy'.[89] Almost certainly, this referred to a member of Marianne's girls' class, and it was her own heart that 'thrilled with joy'. Clearly her need to have some kind of identity as a 'mother', found expression in various ways, primarily through her close relationship with her nieces, and through her girls' class.[90] It would thus be a mistake to make too much of Marianne's occasional yearning for motherhood. One is left merely with a lingering suspicion that there was always a slight wistfulness when writing on the subject of children. The personal note of longing, however, was balanced by many indications that she was fulfilled and happy in her single role and in her work.

Women and Work

Work, indeed, was a subject which Marianne always wrote of with enthusiasm, regarding it not only as the main focus of her own life, but of life in general. As a young woman, her ideal was 'a busy bustling day, not a minute to spare: to bed at night tired, but with the satisfaction of having accomplished some good work'.[91] Her evangelical faith was evidently an active one. In *Grace Darling*, for instance, she suggested that 'a woman's work is that which she sees needs doing. It is her duty to put her hand to any occupation that is waiting for workers.'[92] The question of work was linked for Marianne with a belief that women needed to be strong. This, for her, was personified by Grace Darling. Girls should be like the heroine in being 'vigorously healthy, sensible, devoted, self-forgetful'.[93] Similarly she believed that Elizabeth Fry had a strong heart.[94] By strength she partly meant physical health, encouraged by fresh air and exercise, but also strength of mind and purpose and a determination to contribute to the community. Girls can be 'strong in moral courage' she had asserted in 1869.[95] With these attributes, they would be equipped to work.

---

[87] Farningham, *Women and Work*, p. 86.
[88] Levine, *Feminist Lives*, p. 45.
[89] Farningham, *Women and Work*, p. 86.
[90] See Chapter 2, pp. 43-44 and Chapter 4, pp. 99-109
[91] Farningham, *Life Sketches*, (1861) p. 21.
[92] Hope, *Grace Darling*, p. 2. See Chapter. 6 for a longer discussion of activism.
[93] Hope, *Grace Darling*, p. 13.
[94] Hope, *Grace Darling*, p. 8.
[95] Farningham, *Girlhood*, p. 87.

Work is a Blessing

How did Marianne define work? Referring to herself, she primarily meant the paid work of journalism and other writing, although she did describe her voluntary involvement with a girl's class at College Street Baptist as 'this most delightful work'.[96] When addressing her readers she often made no distinction between unpaid and paid work, consistently using a wider understanding of the subject, especially with regard to women. It was not a question of being rich or poor, she insisted, but to do with having a purpose in life, and believing that 'there is dignity in labour'.[97] Work was portrayed by her as a positive aspect of life, definitely a blessing, not a curse, as this emphatic statement demonstrates: 'We should be miserable without it, and perhaps it contributes more to our happiness than anything else'.[98] This was a message which needed to be emphasised, for as Rita McWilliams-Tullberg has pointed out, middle-class women 'had been taught to dread and despise such activity'.[99] Marianne stressed that work could be a pleasure as much as a duty and she certainly regarded her own work in that light, declaring in her autobiography, written in semi-retirement near the end of her life, that 'after fifty years of work, I love it almost as much as ever'.[100] Work was more than the source of provision for Marianne: rather, it was the main purpose of existence, a perception she shared with many of her contemporaries.

Marianne urged this positive view of work onto her readers. For instance, in an item in *Girlhood* entitled 'Work', she insisted that 'very probably it is the greatest good that could happen to you'.[101] The key here is the contrast between usefulness and uselessness, rather than between paid or unpaid work, or between the private or public spheres. Early in her career she quoted John Angel James as saying that 'usefulness is within the reach of us all',[102] and this continued to be an important concept for her. Through the medium of fiction for children, she encouraged both girls and boys to learn at a young age not to have idle hands, in order to 'do good deeds and kind actions'.[103] Similarly, when addressing young women in *Girlhood* she insisted that 'There is not one of you but may be of use in God's world.'[104] Marianne believed such usefulness was the means of achieving fulfilment and happiness.[105]

Marianne's definition of work extended through domestic responsibilities

---

[96] Farningham, *Life*, p. 262.
[97] Farningham, *Girlhood*, pp. 30–35.
[98] Farningham, *Sketches* (1861), p. 66.
[99] R. McWilliams-Tullberg, 'Women and Degrees at Cambridge University, 1862–1897, in M. Vicinus, ed, *A Widening Sphere* (London: Methuen, 1980 [1977]), p. 121.
[100] Farningham, *Life*, p. 273.
[101] Farningham, *Girlhood*, pp. 30–31.
[102] Farningham, *Sketches* (1861), p. 82.
[103] M. Farningham, *Little Tales for Little Readers* (London: James Clarke, 1869), p. 71.
[104] Farningham, *Little Tales*, p. 17.
[105] Farningham, *Little Tales*, p. 102.

and charitable or volunteer work to include a wide variety of paid work. Her working-class realism about the need to earn a living combined with the Victorian and evangelical belief in duty to give her a high view of waged work, for women as well as men. In an early piece, she wrote that it had previously been considered a hardship for girls to have to work, but she insisted that on the contrary that 'if you are obliged to be bread-winners there is no disgrace attached to you for that'.[106] Paid work could be an opportunity and a shaper of character, a positive aspect of life rather than a necessary evil. To some extent this reflects her artisan upbringing: women of her background were expected both to run their homes and contribute financially to the family economy. By the mid-century, however, the middle-classes, which by profession if not inclination she was now a part of, had a complex attitude towards women earning their own living. Marianne was aware that some considered work undesirable, talking about the 'taint of wage earning'[107] but she took issue with that concept. Paid work might have been a necessity for Marianne, but it was also a joyful calling. She suggested late in life that 'we still may remain happy if we are permitted to continue our work' and have 'a firm table, a fountain-pen, a good fire and an easy chair'.[108] Work was essential to Marianne's ability to enjoy life as well as to her sense of personal identity.

Through these comments about work, Marianne was both reflecting and challenging contemporary thinking. In insisting that work is the prime purpose of life, she was reflecting familiar ideas, as work was highly regarded by contemporaries and possibly especially by Nonconformists. But her suggestion that it was appropriate, even godly, for women to be earning their living, was different from the attitudes of many of her fellow-evangelicals, especially when she first raised the issue. Such an emphasis seems more a male than a female trait. She must have been hoping to influence the preconceptions of her readers and subvert the idea of womanly behaviour as consisting only of unpaid work, whether domestic or philanthropic. Paid work, in her eyes, had just the same dignity for men as for women, whether undertaken out of financial necessity, or because a person had skills and abilities which were needed in society, such as caring for others (medicine) or preaching, but it always had to have a selfless motivation of some sort, although she fully expected people to enjoy their work. It has been asserted that women who worked after marriage were by definition challenging the concept of separate spheres,[109] yet Marianne praised such women, whilst maintaining a belief in conventional domesticity. This is another confirmation of the astuteness of Caine's suggestion that categorising

---

[106] Farningham, *Girlhood*, pp. 80–84.
[107] Davidoff and Hall, *Family Fortunes* (2002), p. xxxviii.
[108] Farningham, *Life*, p. 273.
[109] Levine, *Feminist Lives*, p. 44.

nineteenth-century women by later classifications is unhelpful.[110] Yet it is unclear if in taking such an attitude, Marianne was reflecting the views of some of her readers, or whether, in this case, she was propounding an individual perspective which she hoped to influence others to share. Whether in so doing she was looking backwards to a time when work and home were less divided, or forwards to a new era of opportunity for women, is also not self-evident. What is clear is that Marianne did not make a definite distinction between paid and unpaid work: her purpose was to encourage her readers to be workers, and in so doing to find a worthwhile focus for their lives.

Working Women Make Happy Homes

In 1895, over twenty-five years after *Girlhood* was first published, when opportunities for working women were increasing, Marianne expressed her ideas about work in even stronger terms, in an editorial for the *Sunday School Times*:

> it is absurd to write and talk as if the working women were new personages. There are new conditions however, and better ways of earning money than formerly happily exist today. And therefore some of the merriest, happiest homes are those in which women have to be the breadwinners of the family, either because there are no men to fill the post, or they are unable, or perhaps, unwilling, to do it.[111]

This acknowledgement that some women are the main wage earners because their men are too lazy to work, and that in such circumstances the women's lives can be celebrated rather than commiserated with, is an interesting comment, and indicates the way that Marianne's thinking had developed. In the same editorial, she continued to comment that a woman who has such a role then pays taxes and becomes involved in community issues such as lighting, drainage and School Boards, taking 'an intelligent part in all that goes on around her'. No doubt she was partly referring to her own experience here, and using it to make the point that one result of women's greater involvement in the working world was a greater interest and involvement in the public sphere in general, and therefore that female wage-earners contributed to the good of the community they lived in.

Around the same time, Marianne seems to have made some even more extreme comments about the nature of work. In the *Sunday School Times* in 1891, there is a little series about the family, purporting to have been written by different members of an anonymous family. From the way it was introduced, and the style of the contributions, this was almost certainly written by Marianne, and if she did not actually write the pieces, as editor she would

---

[110] B. Caine, *English Feminism 1780-1980* (Oxford: Oxford University Press, 1997), pp. 2–4.

[111] *SST* 25 January 1895.

probably have approved of them. In this series, two interesting suggestions were made. The 'daughter who stays at home' strongly argued that she should be paid wages for her work, just as like the servant, so that she might be in a position to buy small items without always relying on gifts of money from others. The daughter was made to state that 'it would really be a great pleasure if I could feel independent and earn my own money'.[112] In another issue, the 'daughter whose earnings help' made two telling comments. The first was to complain that women's wages are lower than men's, despite their work being equally reliable, arguing that 'ought we not, therefore, be able to earn as much money as they?', whilst the second was a suggestion that if she was expected to help with housework after a hard day's teaching, the same expectation should be made of her brothers: 'my brothers never consider it to be any business of theirs to do housework, yet 'cooking and dusting are like play when contrasted with teaching', surely well within their capabilities.[113] Here we appear to have Marianne advocating three major elements of feminist thinking: wages for housework, equal pay, and equal roles in the home for men and women. It must be stressed that she did not apply this to married men and women, only to adult sons and daughters still living at home, but these are still significant statements to make, and clearly indicate her sympathy with the women's movement.

Writing under her pseudonym of Eva Hope Marianne also spoke highly of women who had been pioneers in various ways, such as Mary Somerville and Harriet Martineau. She was still eager to stress the importance of domestic duties, another indication that this was her own opinion. Thus she portrayed Mary Somerville as being very accomplished in domesticity, not just frustrated by it. 'She was an excellent nurse, and a wonderful cook, and knew how to make jelly better than most women... She never lost sight of her wifely and maternal duties even while most deeply engrossed by her studies.'[114] Similarly, she suggested that Harriet Martineau enjoyed domestic work, and was in fact 'so domesticated that she proved once for all that a clever literary writer can be a not less clever housekeeper',[115] whilst George Eliot ran her father's house 'performing the duties as thoroughly as she afterward did those of authorship'.[116] Whether or not these comments are particularly accurate, they stress that Marianne believed that women both could and should be consistent in their working lives, whether running a home, writing a book or fulfilling a more public role.

Some of her remarks were intended as a criticism of those who argued that women should not be involved in intellectual pursuits, and as proof that women were not less feminine because they attended lectures, wrote great literature,

---

[112] *SST* 9 January 1891.
[113] *SST* 16 January 1891.
[114] Eva Hope, *Great Modern Women* (London: Walter Scott, 1886), p. 14.
[115] Hope, *Modern Women*, p. 71.
[116] Hope, *Modern Women*, p. 195.

grappled with mathematical problems or supported women's rights. Whether making a batch of marmalade for explorers to take to the Arctic, writing about science, or supporting the suffrage campaign, Somerville is still portrayed as feminine. This was, however, redefined femininity, one in which intellectual pursuits were as worthy of a woman's attention as domestic matters. No woman should neglect the latter in order to develop the former, but equally, neither should a gifted woman neglect the development of her intellect to focus only on home duties. Thus Marianne is at pains to stress that when Somerville died, at the age of ninety, still grappling with complex mathematical problems, this is a clear demonstration that 'brain-work, even of a severe kind, does not kill', but on the contrary, 'it seems conducive to longevity'.[117] This was, no doubt, an intentional counter-blast to the opinion sometimes expressed by contemporaries that study could harm a women's health and detract from her femininity.[118] A further redefinition which saw domesticity as socially constructed, and therefore not integral to a woman's nature, nor foreign to a man's, was beyond Marianne's grasp. In this she was similar to many pioneers of the women's movement in the later nineteenth century, regardless of the presence or absence of religious belief.[119]

In old age Marianne reflected that her writing had been a source of great enjoyment to her: she took pleasure in the numbers who read her work, and in the belief that her writing had been an encouragement to her readers in their spiritual lives.[120] Work was a source of both material and spiritual satisfaction. As she wrote of Mary Somerville, she believed that 'honest endeavour is certain to be rewarded by some success',[121] and this was certainly the case in her own life. For Marianne, however, this attitude was also a demonstration of her belief that God had a useful purpose for everyone, if they were bold enough to embrace it. Faith featured as a motivating factor in her writing, combined with personal ambition. Work, Marianne believed, was a gift from the Almighty, and an evangelical experience of God was essential for the process of effective work: without Christ, she believed, people would be poor workers.[122] Thus she described the writing process as one of being 'really helped to write', presumably by God.[123] Work, therefore, should be undertaken in order as service both to others and to God, and that is the criterion by which success should be judged. Near the end of her life, she wrote that she knew she had not been able to do 'any great thing which would impress the world, and

---

[117] Hope, *Modern Women*, p. 29.

[118] See for instance S. Churchill, *Forbidden Fruit for Young Men* (London: J Nisbett, 1887).

[119] Vicinus, *Widening Sphere*, p. x.

[120] Farningham, *Life*, pp. 277–78 and p. 275.

[121] Hope, *Modern Women*, p. 29.

[122] Farningham, *Girlhood*, p. 36.

[123] Farningham, *Life,* p. 141.

cause me to be kept in remembrance, but have hoped that I should be able to do a great many little things which might tell on individuals. My desire has been to "serve my generation, and fall asleep" '.[124] She made no distinction here between small acts of kindness and the work of journalism, by which she reached many thousands, but she was stressing the same view of the primacy of work which she had first highlighted nearly fifty years earlier.

Marianne's idea of a heroine was, it could be argued, a working class version of the Angel in the House, in whom duty, faith, and home-loving obedience are matched with strength and an ability to make decisions, and to take risks when a greater good is involved. Submissive angel and independent, strong-minded worker are not, in Marianne's view, incompatible. Her belief was that everyone, however strong, ultimately needed to submit to God, therefore a strong-minded woman serving her family would not have seemed to her a contradiction in terms. However, serving God had to take first place, even when this conflicted with duty to parents and social norms, as Grace Darling's defiance of her mother makes clear. For she believed Darling to have been worth imitation even without the heroic act that made her famous, because she was dutiful, home-loving, and strong: 'Grace Darling was a working woman' she declares in the conclusion,[125] a phrase which Farningham subsequently drafted into further use in a more prominent role in the title of her own life story.

Single Women and Work

Marianne had particularly strong feelings about the need for single women to take control of their lives. Working could bring the freedom of financial independence, an advantage relished by Marianne. In a collection published in 1861, she commented that it was sad that many young women thought of work as vulgar, and believed that it was a disgrace to earn.[126] Marianne took pleasure in her earning and spending power, as the previous chapter has indicated.[127] Single herself, she valued her own independence, even though it was initially due to the straitened circumstances of her family, and she encouraged a similar attitude in other women. 'Why *should* we', she wrote in *Girlhood*, 'so many of us skilful and quick – gifted by God with power to achieve something noble and good for ourselves – why should *we* be dependent on fathers or brothers? Why not live to some purpose, benefiting ourselves, and thereby all who are dear to us?' [128] She thus demonstrated that for her as a single woman, working was as much a matter of principle as a necessity. Philippa Levine has found similar attitudes in a sample of nineteenth-century feminists, for whom working

---

[124] Farningham, *Life,* p. 275. The Biblical quotation is from Acts 13:36.
[125] Hope, *Grace Darling,* p. 300.
[126] Farningham, *Sketches,* p. 135.
[127] See Chapter 2, p. 53.
[128] Farningham, *Girlhood,* p. 34.

was a statement of beliefs as well as an economic role. One of her sample, Mary Smith, a schoolmistress from Carlisle, is quoted as saying 'I was determined to fight for my own living and be a burden to no-one'. [129] Like Marianne, Mary Smith needed to work but still saw it as a question of principle. This attitude also fits into a pattern suggested by Martha Vicinus in *Independent Women*, that of a single woman with a 'passion for meaningful work, so often underestimated and misunderstood'.[130] For these women, paid work was a vital factor in the self-reliant lifestyle which they relished.

This belief in the importance of financial independence was a tenet which Marianne held consistently throughout her career, from her earliest work. In a piece entitled 'Female Employment', for instance, which was published as early as 1861, she reacted sarcastically to an anonymous writer who suggested it was lamentable that many women had no natural protectors. Surely, she argued, they can work for themselves.

> They may on the whole be vastly inferior in sense, and wisdom, and strength, yet, perhaps, if they tried *very* hard they might be able to pick out type for printing, to copy telegraphic messages, to sell quires of paper, or even skeins of silk and yards of calico. Not so well, *of course*, but well enough, though they *are weak*.[131]

These comments indicate that in reality, she believed women the equal of men, and quite capable of earning their own living. She continued to explain that she liked to see women working in shops, and to read of Female Printing Establishments. (It is interesting to note here that one of her aunts might have been involved in the Metropolitan Female Printing Office in London, where the compositors were all women, and where an early edition of *Lays and Lyrics* was printed.[132]) Marianne hoped that before long no-one would have to sing the 'Song of the Shirt' because the value of working women would have increased, and they would be paid more. This was a reference to an influential poem by Thomas Hood, first published in Punch late in 1843, highlighting the exploitation of needlewomen working for low wages. It was sad, she argued, that many young people thought work was vulgar, and earning a disgrace.[133] At the end of her life, she still held a similar view of work, and her financial independence remained a matter of pride. These attitudes clearly place her in the feminist camp, despite her strong support of domesticity seeming to suggest otherwise. Yet there is no contradiction here, for both attitudes originate in her working-class evangelical roots, and in a disinclination to separate different

---

[129] Levine, *Feminist Lives*, p. 53.

[130] Vicinus, *Independent Women*, p. 1.

[131] Farningham, *Sketches*, p. 134. Her italics.

[132] S. Burgoyne Black, *A Farningham Childhood* (Sevenoaks: Darenth Valley Publications, 1988), p.29.

[133] Farningham, *Sketches*, p. 135. Levine also indicates that for bourgeois women, earning could be an embarrassment. (Levine, *Feminist Lives*, p. 134.)

types of work: all were equally valid. If home and family were in order, then women had the obligation, rather than the privilege, to do other work for the benefit of society at large, and in the process they would find satisfaction.

Women's Rights

Unlike her beliefs in the primacy of home, or in the desirability of financial independence, Marianne's attitude to women's rights developed over the years. In early pieces she dismissed the topics of 'equality of the sexes' and 'women's rights,' as absurdities, answering the question 'Why shouldn't we be as independent and strong as they?' with the assertion that 'it is inexpressibly sweeter to submit than to rule! Because, in our weakness, it is such pleasure to cling to something strong! Because, it has pleased our Maker thus to create us!'[134] In this early writing, her understanding of women's role was, despite her own experience, fixed firmly in the private sphere. This was the period which Davidoff and Hall have argued was the zenith of separate sphere ideology, and Marianne seems to have unquestioningly shared the assumptions of much of evangelicalism and contemporary culture.[135] It is highly likely that these views were shared by almost all her readership. Thus in 1861 she dismissed the question of 'woman's rights' without giving it serious consideration. Yet in her autobiography, written nearly half a century later, she revealed a very different perspective, epitomised by her friendship with Frances Power Cobbe.[136] It is hard to establish when Marianne met Cobbe, but as she explains that the meeting was through a mutual friend in Barmouth, where she rented a cottage, it must have been in the later stages of her career once she had established a second home there. It is an interesting friendship given Cobbe's radical deist religious beliefs.[137] Marianne was enthusiastic about Cobbe's work as a journalist when 'her clever pen sent through the daily press articles which roused enthusiasm for the good, and active antagonism to the wrong'. Attending a meeting at which Cobbe was speaking, she wondered if the audience 'knew all that Miss Cobbe had done for our sex'.[138] She was enthusiastic about the latter's work including her support for the Married Woman's Property Act and tertiary education for women. It seems that consideration of the issues over some years had caused her to revise her first hasty judgement and make her more sympathetic to women's rights issues.

Verbally, although not in print, she explained that this was exactly what had happened, and at a surprisingly early stage. Marianne gave a series of lectures in 1877 on the subject of 'The Women of Today', and one of these, delivered at

---

[134] Farningham, *Life Sketches*, p. 6 and p 29

[135] See Chapter 2, p. 68 for a discussion of separate spheres.

[136] See Chapter 2, p 88 for more details concerning Marianne's friendship with Cobbe.

[137] http://www.oxforddnb.com/view/article/32469, accessed 16 February 2007.

[138] Farningham, *Life,* pp. 237–38. The meeting was the National Union of Women Workers, Birmingham, 1890.

Ebenezer Chapel in Bristol, was reported in the *Western Daily Press* of 13 November, 1877. The reporter recorded the speaker's explanation of her change of mind on the issue. Marianne commented that the phrase 'women's rights' 'had grated on the ears of multitudes and aroused in many hearts of both sexes feelings of bitter hostility'. Although, she explained, she was not there to advocate such rights, she admitted that she had some sympathy with the issues.

> At first, in common with many of her own sex, she was greatly opposed to it, but a little calm thought had convinced her that they (the fair sex) had some wrongs which needed to be righted, and failed, for instance, to see why women, as householders, should not have Parliamentary, as well as municipal, votes.[139]

Whilst the total attendance of these packed lectures would not have approached the readership of her journalism, it is interesting that she was happy to make such comments publicly. Here is an unqualified declaration that women who owned property should be entitled to vote in national elections. Three years later she was willing for her name to be used in public in connection with women's rights. A report of a meeting in the Free Trade Hall, Manchester, in February 1880, mentions that the gathering received at least 200 'messages and telegrams expressive of sympathy' with the cause, many from 'women of rank, or distinguished in literature, art, science or philanthropy'. One of these women was Marianne.[140] Her views, stemming from faith and the need to right a perceived injustice, might well have encouraged and possibly influenced other Christians, both men and women, in their attitude to the vote.

Roughly ten years after these lectures, in one of her many volumes of collected newspaper pieces, *Homely Talks about Homely Things*, Marianne first committed herself more definitely in print to the cause of women's suffrage, although in such a way that those opposed to it would have had little to criticise. The piece was called 'Women and the elections' and is very telling, as she was trying desperately hard to tread a middle line which would affirm some aspects of women's rights whilst in no way threatening their traditional domestic role. She discussed women's differing attitudes to involvement in elections, and suggested that 'even those who have not yet been educated to the Women's Rights point of view' will regret that they can do little to help. There is more than a hint there that she considered support for suffrage a sensible outcome of intelligent thinking. She carefully gave both sides of the argument, however. Some prefer not to be involved, wanting to be 'in the quiet home, out of reach of the turmoil and strife. We do not care for fighting, but cry, "Give peace in our time." ' Whilst this quotation inevitably carries unwelcome connotations for the modern reader, it is hard, given Marianne's stress on the need for women to be strong and take action, to believe that there is not some

---

[139] *Western Daily Press* 13 November 1877.

[140] *CW* 13 February 1880, cited in Evans, thesis p 19.

implicit criticism here. Those she specifically encouraged were those who are 'intensely interested in the struggle', whilst not involved publicly. She stressed the 'power of pleading' and urged them to train up their boys, future voters, well. Here, therefore, Marianne encouraged women to use their influence unashamedly in the private sphere in order that they might influence the public arena in the future through their children.[141] She also explained the frustration that many women feel. 'It is probable', she suggested, 'that all women who are householders and owners of property will feel that either too much or too little has been given them, since they have power to vote at municipal and School Board elections, but are not yet considered worth to be trusted with votes when the contest is a Parliamentary one.'[142] As someone who had served on Northampton School Board for six years as the only woman, and who was herself a householder, her sympathies with the suffrage campaign were evident.

There were occasional indications of that sympathy in the *Sunday School Times*, once her position as editor allowed her freedom to express it, and her writing mediated this important issue to her evangelical readership. In 1890 an account appeared in the paper of a series of meetings in Birmingham which were held under the auspices of the 'Ladies' Union of Workers among Women and Girls'. It was reported that 'the paper by Frances Power Cobbe on "Women's Duties to Women" thrilled all hearts with thankfulness that so much has been done, and with earnest resolve for the future'.[143] Here, her sympathy with female workers is evident. In an editorial written five years later, her feminist sympathies are even clearer. Discussing a strike, she observed that 'It is often said that it would not be safe to grant the franchise to women because they are so easily led; but it would not be so easy to lead us into a strike as it is the men. We think for ourselves too much to belong to the Union.' [144] She evidently disapproved of strikes and unions, but there is a remarkable challenge here to a conventional understanding of women. Marianne referred to the idea that women are easily led, a belief that in part has its roots in the Genesis story, and in essence indicated that she thinks the opposite is true. Far from being easily led, women are less likely to exhibit a herd mentality, and more likely to stick to their own beliefs than are men: this was advanced as an argument in favour of the franchise.

It is perhaps strange that Marianne so rarely wrote about the women's suffrage, given that she developed strong opinions on the topic. She did not often attempt to influence her undoubtedly large audience on the subject. This could have been because she tended to avoid controversy, barely touching on many of the major theological issues of late nineteenth-century evangelicalism.

---

[141] Farningham, *Homely Talks*, pp. 33–36.

[142] Farningham, *Homely Talks*, p. 32. The Municipal Franchise Act 1869 gave women the right to vote in Municipal elections.

[143] *SST* 28 November 1890

[144] *SST* 29 March 1895

Yet she openly supported other feminist causes such as tertiary education for women and the opportunities for women, even married women, to work as doctors, preachers, and workers of all kinds. It is true that she was never actively engaged in any campaigns, but she did use her influence as a journalist to promote some of the causes. Tertiary education and women doctors in particular were regarded by Levine as essentially feminist causes, and Marianne's unequivocal support for Frances Power Cobbe is very suggestive. The strongest assertion of support for some of these causes, however, is found in the biography of Grace Darling which was written under a pseudonym, and in her autobiography, published at the end of her career. One cannot help feeling that she was wary of alienating her readership by being too outspoken on these sensitive issues. Instead she tried to use her influence in many subtle comments. Whilst not an activist, she became a keen supporter of women's rights.

In this she was by no means a lone voice within evangelicalism, particularly with the arrival of the new century. One commentator, arguing in favour of female suffrage, optimistically asserted that

> Woman's instincts are invariably on the right side, and they will support all measures that make for peace, temperance, social purity, and true righteousness. With the advent of woman suffrage we shall be in for peaceful and progressive measures making for the good of the nation and the Empire, and shall get appreciably nearer the millennium than we are today.[145]

The female franchise was thus advocated as a means of hastening the age to come, an attitude with which Marianne would have been sympathetic, as it fitted in with her postmillennial and optimistic views of the future. Marianne's views developed from the support of women in paid employment, enthusiasm for the development of girls' education, and fairer divorce laws, to embrace the even more controversial issue of the vote. Whilst she did not go out of her way to advertise her opinions, she quietly encouraged in her readers a sympathy with the various female causes of education, divorce legislation, opportunities for employment, and limited suffrage for women, and thus helped to develop a climate within the more broad-minded evangelicals towards the widening of women's role. Despite her conventional domestic ideology, Marianne firmly believed that women had a significant part to play in public life, a belief that is evident in her own life, both through her public profile as writer, editor and lecturer, but also through her membership of the Northampton School Board.[146]

---

[145] *Freeman* 24 April 1907.

[146] See Chapter 5 for discussion of Marianne's involvement in public life.

Women and the Church

Given this clear belief, it is surprising that there is so little discussion in Marianne's writing concerning the role of women in the church, or the opportunities that church gave to women. I have argued elsewhere that the church functioned in some ways as a 'third sphere' neither in the public nor the private spheres, where women could not only socialise freely but develop skills and abilities which were beyond those of the home. The church thus served as a potential preparation for the wider public arena. In the secure and bounded environment of Nonconformist church congregations, women learned to pray and to speak in front of those who were neither friends nor family, yet were generally supportive.[147] For Marianne, this development occurred primarily through her involvement with Sunday schools. Chapter 4 will explore the extent to which her role as the teacher of a girl's class furthered her personal development and confidence. Sunday schools also offered the opportunity for young women to be mentored by an older woman whom they might see as a sister or a mother.

Much of what Marianne wrote about women's involvement in the church was either personal reminiscences, or connected with the Sunday school movement. Church had obviously been a vital part of her life, important to her own spirituality, since childhood, and continued to offer times of refreshment and peace in her crowded life.[148] Belonging to a church was clearly important for everyone, in her eyes, and there was no real discussion in her writings of women's belonging as distinct from that of men. Sunday schools, by contrast, were where much of her work was increasingly focused, and from time to time she tried to encourage others, women in particular, also to contribute their energy and ability to the cause.[149] Marianne believed that some women spread themselves too thinly in the roles they undertook in churches. Her admonition to Sunday school teachers to focus only on that role, in order to do it well, indicates that some were involved in many other activities.[150] Indeed, many who are mentioned in the obituaries of denominational magazines as Sunday school teachers or the leaders of Methodist classes for young people, were also listed as being involved in other church-based responsibilities such as delivering tracts, visiting the sick and poor, and collecting for missionary societies.[151] On the other hand, other women, too timid to volunteer for any

---

[147] Wilson, *Zeal*, pp. 200–202.
[148] See Chapter 6, p. 216.
[149] See Chapter 4. for further discussion of Sunday schools.
[150] M. Farningham, *Will you take it? The History of a Young Woman's Class. To which is added a paper on Young Women's Classes in the Provinces read by Marianne Farningham at the Sunday School Union Conference May 1877* (London: James Clarke, 1877), p. 23.
[151] For instance, one Wesleyan woman, Mary Ann Posnet, was involved in tract distribution and missionary collection as well as leading a class for young people. See Wilson, *Zeal*, pp. 174–5.

work, ended up frustrated and unused because no-one asked them to help.[152] Marianne believed that there should be the opportunity for every one, male or female, to serve within the church in some way, but there are few occasions when she wrote about any other such possibilities than those connected to the Sunday schools.

This is illustrated by the regrettable scarcity of comments about women preachers in her writing. When she did mention them, however, it was clear that she approved of their role. In her autobiography, she recalled an incident at a meeting in Northampton where Catherine Booth, who together with her husband General Booth founded the Salvation Army, was due to speak. Someone heckled Catherine while she was speaking, and other people in the audience immediately dealt with the man, causing a disturbance 'which alarmed Mrs Booth'. Marianne, who was also on the platform, recorded that she was able to reassure her that there was no danger.[153] Her eagerness to recount her slight contact with Catherine, and her admiring description of her as 'one of the most saintly and gifted heroines of the century' indicates that Marianne did have sympathy for women preachers, whilst her own presence on the platform indicates the recognition she herself experienced.[154] Although most denominations officially disapproved of women in such a public role, research has shown that there were at least some in most denominations at different stages.[155] Interestingly, Baptist churches were the least likely to have female evangelists or local preachers, so in expressing approval Marianne was swimming against the tide of her own denomination.

As with other issues, the initial chapter in *Grace Darling* is the most explicit with regard to preachers. In discussing Elizabeth Fry, Marianne spoke approvingly of her preaching, asserting that Elizabeth 'preached the gospel both by lips and life' and was an effective preacher.[156]. She was not, Marianne argued, 'an unwomanly woman', but merely one who 'did exceptional work, because she saw it needed doing'.[157] As this phrase was Marianne's equivalent of a sense of calling, such a comment clearly amounts to genuine approval of Elizabeth's actions, despite the fact she is, consciously or unconsciously, echoing John Wesley's rather grudging concession that women could have an 'extraordinary call' to preach. She also praised Miss Marsh, by whom presumably she meant Catherine Marsh, who had been involved in missions to

---

[152] Farningham, W*ill you take it?* p. 16.
[153] Farningham, Life, p. 243.
[154] Farningham, Life, p. 242.
[155] For an overview, see Wilson, *Zeal,* pp. 204–20. J.H. Lenton, 'Labouring for the Lord, Women Preaching in Wesleyan Methodism 1802–1932. A Revisionist View', in R. Sykes, ed, *Beyond the Boundaries: Preaching in the Wesleyan Tradition*, Wesley Westminster Series No 8 (Oxford, 1998), pp. 58–86, provides an interesting insight into Methodist women preachers.
[156] Hope, *Grace Darling,* p. 10.
[157] Hope, *Grace Darling,* p. 16.

railway navvies.[158] Preaching was clearly, for Marianne, not outside the remit of women. Yet when does refer to women as preachers, it is in the same breath as women in other professions, so she must have realised that it was a controversial issue. Although she mentioned preachers in a discourse encouraging women to move beyond the artificial boundaries society places around them, she did not concern herself with promoting their role any more than, for instance, that of female doctors. It was the Sunday school, rather than the church, which functioned as a third sphere for Marianne, as will be discussed in the following chapter. She does not seem to have been particularly concerned with the general role of women in the church, although she clearly approved of women preachers as part of her general affirmation of any active role which furthered genuine Christianity, peace, or care for the needy, pursued in any sphere by either men or women.

Conclusion

Marianne portrayed Grace Darling as epitomising all that was admirable about women: love of home and respect for parents, strength both of character and body, self-control, and the ability to act in the face of opposition when God prompted. One suspects that in practice Marianne would not have stayed at home as docilely as Grace Darling supposedly did. Yet Marianne saw the whole of life, private or public, in terms of mission, calling, and obedience to God. When God provided an occasion or opportunity to act, women should take it, she believed, regardless of the opinions of others: otherwise, they should continue doing the work they have always done, whether paid or unpaid. Thus whilst Marianne adhered unthinkingly to a basically patriarchal view of the family, or indeed society, like Sarah Ellis she wanted to see the influence of women spread beyond the home, although, unlike Ellis, she believed paid work was not just acceptable, but desirable. Hence, for Marianne, love of the home and the urge to be involved in the wider world beyond the home were all part of a woman's response to God.[159] In some situations this would involve being conventional, making the best of a mundane job in order to support oneself, but in others it might necessitate 'being singular', as for instance when Grace Darling rescued shipwreck survivors, Elizabeth Fry visited prisons or Mary Somerville grappled with advanced mathematics. For Marianne, therefore, support of the domestic priority was entirely compatible with her declaration that women should not be 'afraid to be singular' in rising to the challenges of life. Part of the connection lies in the concept of service. Cobbe also portrayed work in society in terms of service, but for Marianne service was linked to obedience to God, with the need to be bold to take hold of opportunities, and to be faithful in serving, but not to be limited by other people's paradigms of

---

[158] C. Marsh, *English Hearts and English Hands; or the railway and the trenches* (London: 1858).

[159] Chapter 7 explores Marianne's spirituality more fully.

suitable behaviour. The conflict for her was not between public and private but between the perceived need and other people's opinions. She bemoaned the lack of courage which prevented women responding to that need. Hers was an integrated world view, rooted in evangelical faith, which included subversive elements.

Marianne's fairly conventional views about domesticity were tempered from the beginning by a working-class pragmatism. She believed that single woman should be financially independent, and that all women should be willing and prepared to respond to the needs they saw around them, whether that meant rowing a lifeboat, looking after a family, preaching the gospel or becoming a doctor. She hinted that she had become a 'woman's rights woman', yet never questioned the basic status quo of society, or lost her belief in the importance, and indeed the primacy, of the domestic arena for women. The imperative to follow an individual call from God could, and did, lead women either to conventional living or to actions that subverted societal norms, or on occasions to a mixture of the two.[160] Marianne's advocacy of women's primary role as homemakers, the financial independence of single women and all women's obligation to react to needs, is an example of such a mix. Above all, she believed, women should be ready to respond to God's initiative. Marianne regarded this as a possibility to be expected and prepared for, believing as she did that the whole variety of work, paid or unpaid, was a call from God. Women needed courage, in her view, to be faithful in an unobserved role, day after day, or to take initiative boldly, regardless of public opinion.[161] The very faith that was the bulwark of respectability also had the potential to undermine convention. Thus the explanation for her mosaic of beliefs is to be found in the driving force of Marianne's life, her faith. For her, serving God was all, and the lost opportunities of many women who were trapped by convention, were not only lost in terms of earning power and self-fulfilment, but in terms of availability to serve God and humanity. No woman, she argued, 'ought to be content to pass her life in cutting holes to mend them up again; in playing a little, reading novels, and visiting. There ought to be some real tangible good done.... The first thing necessary, then, is to seek that religion which comes from above...'.[162] It was for godly service that women, she believed, should summon up their courage, and not be 'afraid to be singular'.

Marianne's combination of beliefs about the private and public roles of women demonstrates how hard it is to pigeonhole nineteenth-century women according to twenty-first century categories. Marianne is interesting precisely because, whilst she did not move in what could be termed the feminist world,

---

[160] For further discussion see L Wilson, 'Constrained by Zeal: Women in mid-nineteenth century Nonconformist churches', *Journal of Religious History* 23.2 (June 1999), pp. 185–202.

[161] Hope, *Grace Darling*, pp. 300–303.

[162] Hope, *Grace Darling*, pp. 300–303.

she reflected some of its attitudes.[163] Despite her advocacy of domestic priority, it can be argued that she was both an evangelical and a feminist. The belief system she shared with her readers gave her an opening to influence the opinions, and to engage the sympathy of, the Nonconformist public with regard to the role of women, in a way that someone with a more overtly feminist stance could never have done. As a journalist, Marianne was in a particularly advantageous position to contribute to such a process. Given her wide influence, her writings about women and women's role are of especial interest. Whilst rarely engaging directly with the contemporary debate about the 'woman question', her commonsense approach and mild version of hoping for new opportunities for women, almost certainly contributed to shaping and changing attitudes within the evangelical community regarding women's role.

---

[163] As Caine indicates, defining feminism is itself becoming increasingly difficult. (Barbara Caine, *English Feminism 1780–1980* (Oxford: Oxford University Press, 1997), pp. 2–4.

Chapter 4

'A Great Work': Marianne and Sunday Schools

> It is a great work that has to be done, so great that it cannot be overrated.[1]

It has been suggested that Sunday schools were 'perhaps the most important, but are now among the most neglected, of nineteenth-century religious and educational subjects',[2] and Marianne would surely have agreed with that estimate of their significance. The Sunday school movement, she believed, was a major means of facilitating the training up of young people to be good citizens and active believers in the Christian faith. Towards the end of her paper, 'Sunday Schools of the Future', published in 1871, she outlined her understanding of the consequences of the responsibility carried by a Sunday school teacher:

> It means less leisure, less rest, and in some cases even less self-culture. It means anxious solicitude, and weariness. It means working while others rest, and praying while others sleep. It means, in a word, thorough and entire consecration to God....
> It is a great work that has to be done, so great that it cannot be overrated.[3]

This 'great work' of training was one of Marianne's driving passions, and therefore she gave much of her energy to the cause. A considerable amount of her public activity, such as early public speaking engagements, was connected with her experience of Sunday school work, which arguably functioned as a 'third sphere' for Marianne, a borderland between the public and private worlds. In addition, much of her writing was inspired by her desire to see the lives of young people developing in what she considered healthy ways, whilst her personal involvement with her girl's class dominated her spare time. Her long editorship of the *Sunday School Times*, from the beginning of 1885 to her death over twenty years later, meant that she was not only a participant in, but a shaper of the movement over many years.

As the previous chapter has indicated, Marianne's definition of useful

---

[1] M. Farningham, *Sunday Schools of the Future* (London: Hodder & Stoughton, 1871), p. 133.
[2] K.D.M. Snell 'The Sunday-School Movement, in England and Wales', in *Past and Present,* No 164 August 1999 pp. 122-168, p.122.
[3] Farningham, *Sunday Schools of the Future*, p. 133.

occupations included both paid and unpaid work, and she had a firm belief that people should take up tasks when they needed doing, neither waiting for a role that suited them better, nor refraining from becoming involved because the job involved challenging cultural and gender norms.[4] She was eager to instil in others this same enthusiasm for work rooted in faith, taking every opportunity to stress that people should set the direction of their lives when young, so that they could reach their potential. Addressing young women in 1869, for instance, she insisted that 'Your whole future, the entire success or failure of your womanhood... all hinge very much upon what you are, and what you will do now.'[5] Similarly, the following year she wrote of her hope that young men, through good teaching, could be added to those who are the 'hope of England' because of the quality of their lives and behaviour.[6]

The Sunday School Movement

Whilst the extent of Marianne's dedication to Sunday schools was comparatively rare, her teaching role, and her belief in the importance of the school, reflected practice and attitudes common to much contemporary evangelicalism. It has been argued that these schools are one of the reasons for the 'cultural ascendancy' of evangelicalism in the second half of the century.[7] Certainly, nineteenth-century evangelicals were generally positive and enthusiastic about Sunday schools, with many church members becoming teachers, whilst MPs and other public figures boasted that they still taught classes despite their many other commitments.[8] In a study of nineteenth-century Nonconformists, a high proportion of men and women were recorded as having taught Sunday school classes at some stage in their lives. Out of a sample of 240 women in four denominations whose obituaries were recorded in their denominational magazines, just over 31% had been involved in such teaching, whilst in a comparative sample of men the total was slightly lower at 28%, although there was some denominational variation.[9] In the Baptist sample, 33% of both men and women were recorded as having some Sunday school responsibilities, slightly more than average. For many evangelicals, men and women, especially Baptists, involvement in Sunday schools was a significant

---

[4] See Chapter 3, p. 80, p. 81.
[5] M. Farningham, *Girlhood* (London: James Clarke, 1869), pp. 4-5.
[6] M. Farningham, *Boyhood* (London: James Clarke, 1870), p. 6.
[7] D.W. Bebbington, *The Dominance of Evangelicalism* (Leicester: IVP, 2005), p. 96.
[8] P. B. Cliff, *The Rise and Development of the Sunday School Movement in England 1720-1980* (Nutfield, Surrey: National Christian Education Council, 1986), p.165 quoting M.J. Street, *The Hundredth Year: the Story of the Centenary Celebrations of the Sunday School Union* (London: Sunday School Union, 1903), p. 166.
[9] L. Wilson, *Constrained by Zeal: Female Spirituality amongst Nonconformists 1825-75* (Carlisle: Paternoster, 2000), p. 190.

aspect of the outworking of their faith.

Such involvement was, however, a comparatively new development. Sunday schools had been initiated less than a century before Marianne began to instruct her Northampton class, by Robert Raikes and others as recently as the late eighteenth century. They quickly became widespread and influential until by 1850 there were two million working-class children enrolled in the schools.[10] The initial focus of the movement was literacy: the teaching of reading, and sometimes writing, to children who worked or were for other reasons unable to attend regular schools, and also to illiterate adults. For many people, this was all the schooling they ever received. All was mediated through the use of simple primers, the Bible and religious stories, and it was hoped that as well as gaining a rudimentary education, those who attended would develop a religious faith and become church members.[11] Whilst they were largely unsuccessful as recruitment agencies, Laqueur's argument that the schools 'sustained a Christian culture amongst working-class children' is as true for the later nineteenth century as for the earlier period which was the subject of his study.[12] Schools were usually aimed at the poorer segments of society, and Briggs believes that their success was often due to the involvement of men and women from the working classes,[13] although there is debate over the extent to which the schools were run by, rather than for those classes.[14] By the later nineteenth century, however, especially once schooling was much more widely available following the 1870 Education Act, the nature of the schools had changed considerably from their early days, and their primary goal became spiritual education. It was in this task that Marianne was an enthusiastic participant.

The College Street Class

Marianne expressed her personal commitment to Sunday schools in a variety of ways, ranging from composing verses intended to encourage children in their faith, through contributing to and eventually editing the *Sunday School Times*, to lecturing about the future of Sunday schools. Most importantly, however, her enthusiasm was worked out through practical, hands-on involvement with a class of older girls at College Street Baptist Chapel in Northampton, a role which always had a special place in her priorities and thinking. 'No theme', commented a friend many years later, 'could so inspire Miss Hearn as "my

---

[10] T.W. Laqueur, *Religion and Respectability: Sunday Schools and Working Class Culture 1780-1850* (New Haven and London: Yale University Press, 1976), p. 145.
[11] Cliff, *Rise and Development*, pp. 58-67.
[12] Laqueur, *Religion and Respectability*, p. 160.
[13] J.H.Y. Briggs, *The English Baptists of the Nineteenth Century* (A History of English Baptists, 3; Didcot: The Baptist Historical Society, 1994), p. 313.
[14] Snell, 'The Sunday-School Movement', pp. 132-33.

girls".[15] Although it was unpaid, this work was as important to her as writing. In the spring of 1867, shortly after giving up professional teaching in order to develop her journalistic career, Marianne started leading this small group of girls on what was intended to be a temporary basis, when the teacher, a Miss Shrewsbury, who had been taking it, was unable to continue due to ill health. The class was attended by young women aged between 16 and 24, an age at which, Marianne believed, there were 'many dangers' and significant choices to be made.[16] When she started leading the class it was held in a corner of one of the chapel galleries with just a handful of attenders. It quickly grew, however, until on one estimate it eventually included nearly two hundred young women.[17] A Northampton newspaper commented in 1907 that the 'success and the influence she extended' through the class 'does not need to be enlarged upon to Northampton people',[18] whilst on the day of Marianne's funeral, according to the *Northampton Daily Chronicle,* 'if one fact struck the observer more than any other about the personnel of the congregation it was the very large number of ladies who had come under Miss Hearn's teaching in her Class'.[19] Nationally, she might have been known as a writer, but locally, she was also thought of as the leader of her girl's Sunday school class.

Marianne led this class for some thirty-four years, and so there were many 'old girls' to mourn her passing, some of them women with married daughters who had also been class members. The labelling of these mourners as Marianne's 'old girls' indicates that in later life the identity of her ex-students remained linked with the formative period they spent in her class, and their presence at the funeral suggests a continuing affection for her. This was largely because the class was distinguished by a strong sense of community. On one occasion Marianne commented to her friend Jennie Street that her group of girls was not so much a class as a sisterhood.[20] This is an interesting reflection, containing as it does elements of mutual care and concern, as well as dedication and a sense of duty. Philippa Levine, discussing the lives of feminist women in Victorian England, has argued that all her subjects had strong networks of relationships, usually within their extended families.[21] In developing a class based on friendship, Marianne created a similar network for 'her' girls, a base for mutual support that would sustain them in their endeavour to live out their faith in everyday life.

---

[15] W. Glandwr-Morgan , *Marianne Farningham in her Welsh Home* (Birmingham: Ellesmere Press, 1923 [first edition James Clarke 1909]), Chapter 3.
[16] Farningham, *Sunday Schools of the Future*, p. 102.
[17] Farningham, *Life*, p. 116.
[18] *Northampton Independent* 20 April 1907
[19] *Northampton Daily Chronicle* 20 March 1909.
[20] M. J. Street in the *SST* 26 March 1909.
[21] P. Levine, *Feminist Lives in Victorian England* (Oxford: Blackwell, 1990), p. 28.

First Lessons

When Marianne was first asked to take the class, there was little indication that this would become one of the major enthusiasms of her life. Indeed, her lifelong commitment to her class started somewhat inauspiciously. In the introduction to a paper given at the Sunday School Union Conference in May, 1877, Marianne recounted the history of her involvement, stressing that she 'did not feel any special call to the work, and certainly possessed no particular fitness for it'.[22] She later recollected how she was persuaded rather against her will to take this class. She had previously taught at Sunday schools in Eynsford, Bristol and Gravesend, as well as being the head of a daily infant school. Assuming that because of this experience, she knew how to teach, she neglected to prepare for the lesson, which turned out to be a major mistake.[23] Recounting this first lesson, she once commented 'I am a very little woman, and they were such very big girls. I was so frightened that I scarcely knew how to speak at all...'[24] Many years later she gave a fuller account of this unfortunate first lesson:

> Scarcely ever have I experienced such deep humiliation as during that afternoon. One of the girls knew much more about the lesson than I did. She contradicted me several times, she put questions to me which I could not answer, and smiled scornfully... I reached home with a violent headache, thoroughly miserable, and spent the evening full of shame and remorse.[25]

Determined, however, not to be beaten, she resolved to try again, this time preparing more thoroughly. According to the account in her autobiography, when she faced this class again the following week, her first action was to admit her shame at her earlier fiasco 'and I think the girls liked me the better for that'.[26] As she told this story on several occasions, and the girls involved would have easily read her account, it may be assumed that her recollections were accurate.

This was the beginning of the long association which became a focus for much of Marianne's spare time. Once she overcame her initial fears and hesitation, she quickly discovered that, by temperament and inclination, she was suited to the task. Elizabeth Sharwood later commented of her aunt that 'of all her work, her class of young women at College Street easily held the first place in her heart'.[27] Marianne was free to give time to these girls in ways, and

---

[22] M. Farningham, *Will you take it?* (London: James Clarke, 1877), p. 5.
[23] Farningham, *Life*, p. 69 and p. 112.
[24] *Sunday School Chronicle* May 9, 1877, pasted in to Sunday School Union General Committee and Annual Meeting minutes, 15 May 1874 - 26 April 1878.
[25] Farningham, *Life,* p. 112.
[26] Farningham, *Life,* p. 113.
[27] *Souvenir of the Centenary of College Street Sunday School Northampton, 1810–1910*, p. 45.

with a consistency, which would have been difficult if not impossible for a married woman with her own family. Taking responsibility for this class over several decades also ensured that Marianne remained connected with the realities of teaching. Her lectures and writing thus gained the authority of hands-on experience, whilst her role first as a contributor to, then as editor of, the *Sunday School Times*, meant that she was in touch with a wide cross-section of teachers, and of necessity kept up to date with the latest educational developments, which would have contributed to her practical expertise. The fact that her class was the subject of several articles both in the Christian press and the local papers, indicates that it was not the ordinary, run-of-the-mill Sunday afternoon class like thousands of others, but that it had a distinctive character worthy of comment.

Building Community: The Nature of the Class

Her students were drawn from a variety of social backgrounds. Many of them were working girls, contributing earnings to the household income. A few were married. One woman, recalling the composition of the class at the time she joined it in 1874, stated that one of the participants 'came from a draper's establishment, and brought ten in her train, and another brought six or seven. Some were workers in shoe-factories.'[28] In 1877, Marianne described the women who were then class members, saying that 'the class numbers some 180. Out of that number there are eight domestic servants; fifty factory girls, and there is a large number of assistants and pupil teachers.'[29] The mix seems to have been similar a few years later in 1882, when an article in the *Sunday School Times* indicated that the majority of the girls in the class 'work in the shoe-factories of Northampton, but there are also pupil-teachers, assistant mistresses in board School, artists, music teachers, drapers' assistants, milliners etc, and perhaps half a dozen servants'.[30] The group thus consisted of quite a cross-section of local women, but all, like Marianne, individuals who needed to earn their own living, although none were extremely poor. This followed the pattern of other schools, which gradually became more respectable as the century continued.[31] Her working-class background and her own experience as a Sunday school student, as well as her continued role as a wage-earner, would have given her common ground with these young women. Some observers have suggested that not many teachers had themselves been pupils, and that few of these were clearly working-class. [32] If this is an accurate assessment, Marianne is unusual on both counts. In 1871, anticipating an increasing level of general

---

[28] Quoted in Farningham, *Life,* p. 127.
[29] *Sunday School Chronicle* 9 May 1877.
[30] *SST* 1882, quoted in *Life* p. 118.
[31] Cliff, *Rise and Development,* p. 144.
[32] Snell 'The Sunday-School Movement', p. 133.

education, Marianne suggested that schools containing a mixture of social classes, even including some from the upper classes if their parents would allow them, might be a good idea. In her usual over-optimistic fashion, she was hopeful that class divisions would fade in the wake of universal education.[33] She believed that people should attend Sunday school until the age of 20, easing the passage into Church membership. In fact, it appears that at least some of her girls remained involved beyond this age, well into their twenties, further evidence of their attachment to the group and to Marianne herself.

The main meeting for the girls was a Bible Class on Sunday afternoons. Marianne had a strong belief that the Bible should be the only text book, and that all of it should be used.[34] As the class grew larger, funds were raised for a permanent meeting place for the class, which was opened in 1887. She was in the forefront of a trend to improve the often inadequate accommodation which had housed Sunday schools.[35] Here, Marianne's fame as a writer aided the cause, for while the students managed to raise £100 themselves, there were other generous benefactors from far beyond Northampton, including the Crossley family of Halifax, who donated a carpet from their factory. Later a library was added, consisting largely of books donated by Marianne's editor James Clarke and including the complete works of Emma Jane Worboise.[36] In this new context, and with growing numbers, the Sunday afternoon sessions of necessity became fairly formal. Asked by an interviewer what method she adopted in teaching the class, Marianne explained 'We commence by singing a hymn. I then pray with the girls, and we sing again. Then I give the International Lesson. The class is too large to be carried on, on the conversational system.'[37] This more formal approach was, however, no doubt tempered with Marianne's warmth and sense of humour. She also made a point of saying good-bye to each girl, by shaking hands with each one as they left the room.[38] Even in this larger gathering, maintaining a personal touch remained important to her. In a speech to female Sunday school workers given in 1903 as part of the centenary celebrations of the Sunday School Union, Marianne commented that she knew something of the practical side of teaching. She added that she had 'had forty happy years of work among girls, and I have been calculating that during that time I have known, intimately and confidentially, over a thousand girls'.[39] She had a significant capacity for pastoral care and friendship.

Indeed, as her niece Elizabeth suggested, the Sunday meeting, 'was only the

---

[33] Farningham, *Sunday Schools of the Future*, pp. 116-118.
[34] Farningham, *Sunday Schools of the Future*, p. 37.
[35] Cliff, *Rise and Development*, pp. 178-81.
[36] Farningham, *Life*, p. 124.
[37] *Baptist Monthly*, September 1899.
[38] Farningham, *Life*, p. 260.
[39] Farningham, 'Girl's Bible-Classes', in Street, ed., *The Hundredth Year*, p. 122.

nucleus of all she did for her class'.[40] Marianne commented on one occasion that leading the class was not always easy. Because of its social composition it was 'a difficult class to manage, but we have succeeded in keeping up that kind of social friendship and interest which after all is the secret of success'.[41] Both by inclination and design, Marianne was a builder of community with the girls. After moving in with her sister Hephzibah and her family in 1871, where she had her own sitting room, she held a regular mid-week meeting. This gathering started off as a prayer-meeting but developed to include Bible study and discussion as well as prayer. It was a season which Marianne looked back on with fondness, when many young girls made a Christian commitment. Conversion, she believed, was the first aim of a class such as hers, but that was not sufficient: a life of discipleship had to follow.[42] This is evident in her recollections of their evening gatherings:

> My sister's room was a sanctuary consecrated by the prayers of the girls. I am today filled with joy, as I often was then, at the memory of those first prayers of young Christians, which were touchingly beautiful. My heart is full of unspeakable gratitude for the numbers of girls who gave themselves to Jesus at this time and who are today in many places and circumstances living the Christian life.[43]

It appears that many of these girls, guided by Marianne, were still pursuing the life of faith in 1907, when she wrote these words, and no doubt had been encouraged in this by their Tuesday evening gatherings. Discussion topics on these occasions included such vexed questions as whether to follow fashion, and whether a Christian woman could ever marry a man who was 'upright and moral' but not a Christian. Marianne had a liking for practical subjects.

A visit to her class could make a deep impression. One of her students described the first time she attended one of these Tuesday evenings, in 1874:

> That night there must have been at least sixty present – sometimes there were as many as eighty. The girls sat on chairs, couch, hassocks, floor... We had a prayer meeting in the twilight and ten girls prayed. Simple, earnest, wonderful prayers they were, which stirred me to the very depths and made me long to live a more consecrated life.[44]

These meetings, as on this occasion, often finished in twilight or by firelight. Marianne discovered that the girls were less timid, and more likely to talk about their own lives and problems, when their faces were more hidden from each

---

[40] *Souvenir of College Street Sunday School*, p. 47.
[41] *Sunday School Chronicle* 9 May 1877.
[42] Farningham, *Sunday Schools of the Future*, p. 55.
[43] Farningham, *Life*, p. 115.
[44] Farningham, *Life*, pp. 126-27.

other, commenting that 'some of our happiest and most sacred times have been when the room was full of faces of girls in shadow, and the Spirit of Peace seemed to brood over us'.[45] Those involved agreed that there was a special, intimate atmosphere on those evenings. Various features of the class are evident here: the informality of meeting in a home; the encouragement to the girls to be involved in the class; and the depth of spirituality which also characterised Marianne's own life. These factors created an atmosphere which was welcoming and stimulating, and which encouraged participants to keep coming. However, the main ingredient was evidently Marianne's own personality and enthusiasm. One observer commented that it did not take him very long to find out the secret of her class: 'Between herself and her scholars there was a relationship…the young people in her class directly they entered the room seem to gravitate towards her as to a centre'.[46] In many ways, the class had its real existence in these informal gatherings, later continued in her own home. The intimacy and informality of the domestic setting would more easily have encouraged a sense of belonging and the development of community and friendship than would the more formal setting of a purpose-built meeting room.

Even these weekday meetings, however, were not the sum total of her involvement with the girls. One observer, who described how Marianne was in touch with them throughout the week, mentioned these Tuesday meetings, when she was in the habit of 'throwing her home open' but noted other connections, too, such as attending with them the prayer meeting and weeknight service of the church, seeing them individually on Thursdays, and travelling with them on Saturdays'.[47] She herself recalled that she 'gave them much time. Except to the week-night services I seldom went out in the evening, that I might be at home with them.'[48] She was the girls' confidante, always available. Her ideal of a teacher was someone who was never 'too busy to give half and hour to one of the children who are in need of some help or advice' and she appears to have fulfilled her own ideal.[49] 'They told her about their love affairs, and when they married they still considered themselves "her girls"'.[50] One ex-scholar, Agnes Groves, recalled that 'the girls found any excuse to visit Miss Hearne at her home'.[51] Agnes, twenty-five years younger than Marianne, became a School mistress. She remained in close contact, and in Marianne's will was given 'the low chair presented by my girl's class' and a Bible. Some

---

[45] Farningham, *Life,* pp. 280-81.
[46] Sunday School Union Minutes, 1877.
[47] *SST* 26 March 1909.
[48] Farningham, *Life*, p. 113.
[49] Farningham *Sunday Schools of the Future*, p. 112.
[50] *SST* 26 March 1909.
[51] Farningham, *Life,* p. 283. This final chapter was written by an unnamed colleague at The Christian World, and so this quotation was not chosen by Marianne herself.

of the friendships with her girls lasted a lifetime. This was not without personal sacrifice: according to one of her nieces, only those closest to her knew the cost to her of her involvement with the class.[52]

Marianne believed that other activities were as important as spiritual training. In her novel *Nineteen Hundred,* young men and women in 'Darentdale' are found taking botany classes and supervising outdoor games, believing that 'in all this they were doing the Lord's work as certainly as when they were teaching in the Sunday School'.[53] She put this into practice: one class member wrote of attending parties in the winter in Marianne's own home, to which groups of girls were invited, when 'the house was ransacked to provide dresses and things for charades and other games', whilst in the summer their teacher took some of the girls on nature walks in the nearby countryside. On one such occasion one young woman saw primroses for the first time.[54] Some of the older members took holidays together, saving a shilling a week to pay for it.[55] Jennie Street recalled one such occasion when a holiday for 70 girls had been arranged, describing the young women gathered in the drawing room of the boarding house where most of them were staying. They were

> filling sofas and chairs, nestling in window-seats and sitting on hassocks and rugs. Outside was the sunlit bay, dancing under the blue; inside a more effective and enduring sunshine radiated from the face of the teacher, as she made them laugh, set them singing happy hymns, led them in prayer, and then in a tender little talk... (she) made it plain that the religion of Jesus was woven in one with the sunshine and the sea.[56]

Given the sense of fun that several of Marianne's friends have commented on, the activities and the opportunity for friendship on a holiday like this must have helped to create a strong sense of belonging.

Active Participation

When, in 1877, Marianne gave a talk to the Sunday School Union on leading a young women's class, she recommended giving more experienced Christians a larger role by means such as creating a committee to organise social events, or having a treasurer, as well as giving every Christian girl the name of a non-Christian to pray for.[57] This was undoubtedly her own practice. Their shared

---

[52] *Centenary of College Street Sunday School,* p. 45.
[53] M. Farningham, *Nineteen Hundred? A forecast and a story* (London; James Clarke & Co), 1892
[54] Farningham, *Life,* p. 128.
[55] Farningham, *Life,* p. 122.
[56] M.J. Street in *SST* 26 March 1909.
[57] Farningham, *Will you take it?,* p. 20. In the subsequent discussion, another Sunday school worker, a Mr Butcher, commented that her paper was not mere theory, as he had

holidays were organised by a committee of the girls, so that Marianne could say these times were a great pleasure for her, because she had very little responsibility for organising them, 'for I had such a splendid committee of helpers among my girls'.[58] Delegation, it seems, was a natural part of the way that Marianne ran her class. Others were involved in prayer. One participant recalled that 'There was a little inner circle of girls who used to stay behind and chat with their teacher after the others had gone... (they) used to hold special meetings for prayer whenever trouble or sickness visited any member of the class'.[59] Marianne knew how to develop the girls' abilities by giving them responsibility, creating a sense of shared ownership. This was an important aspect of her concept of a girls' organisation, as was demonstrated by a comment made in the *Christian World*. Writing in 1900 of the newly formed Girls' Friendly Society, which was Anglican, she stressed that she did not want the Free Church Girls' Guild to be similarly undemocratic, insisting that 'Free Church girls, though easily moved by kindness, will not be patronised'.[60] Harrison understands her comments as part of a trend towards 'secularization, egalitarianism and feminism'.[61] Whilst Marianne would have been supportive of the latter, and sympathetic with some egalitarian ideals, she was no secularist, indeed she would have preferred some kind of voluntary Christendom, as *Nineteen Hundred* indicates. It is more likely that consciously her comments reflected a Nonconformist tendency of independent thinking. That does not, however, prevent her preferences representing a trend which she herself would have repudiated.

Sometimes practical help was appropriate. Girls in the class were encouraged to help each other financially, giving regularly into a fund available to those who were ill or in difficult circumstances. Some, however, were reluctant to receive such help. At the time of a strike at the local shoe factories, fifty of her girls were struggling with hardship, but refused to accept help from the others: only one did so. Nonetheless, there is evidence of the creation of a network of relationships and of Christian community.

Mutual Benefit

Marianne had the ability to develop strong friendships with the girls in her class, and this was indeed part of the 'secret' of her successful teaching. She herself came to depend on this community of relationships. 'The confidences of

---

himself seen Marianne's work.
[58] Farningham, *Life*, p. 123.
[59] Farningham, *Life*, pp. 126-27.
[60] *CW*, 22 Mar 1900, quoted in B. Harrison 'For Church, Queen and Family: The Girl's Friendly Society 1874-1920', *Past and Present,* No 61 (November 1973), pp. 107–138, p. 134.
[61] Harrison, 'For Church, Queen and Family', p. 134.

the girls were very precious to me' she commented in her autobiography, written in 1907.[62] A friend recalled Marianne having tears in her eyes when receiving a letter from a student which began 'Dear little mother',[63] and in her autobiography she referred to a photograph of herself with the class in which she looked 'like a poor widow with a large family'.[64] For a single woman who had never had the opportunity of motherhood, her girls provided an extended family with the girls as her surrogate children. The class also led to one of her best known works, *Girlhood,* which initially appeared as a series in the *Sunday School Times* and was subsequently published in book form in 1869. It was written for the class in its early years, drawing on their shared experiences and discussion. These short pieces consisted of advice about how life as a young Christian woman should be lived, addressing a variety of topics including work, leisure, friendships, and health.[65] It proved to be one of her most popular works, indicating that there was a beneficial relationship between the class and the writing process. Another aspect of their mutuality was the way in which Marianne was supported by the girls in her other responsibilities. She often travelled in connection with her work, and in so doing she felt 'encircled with love, and borne as on wings by the prayers of my girls. In all my works, journeyings and undertakings, and especially in times of danger or difficulty, I have felt as if they were guarding me by their prayers'.[66] A kind of symbiosis was at work: the class shaped and supported Marianne as much as she developed the lives of the participants. Although it was costly, there were benefits for her as well as for the girls.

Initially, Marianne had insisted that she would only teach the group for three months, but she found both the times of study by way of preparation, and the developing friendship with the girls, enriched her life so much that she decided to continue. She had been planning a move away from Northampton, in order to further her writing career, but when the time came for a decision, she felt she could not leave because of the class. Many years later she commented that her choice had 'no doubt cost me something' in terms of the development of her writing career.[67] No doubt there were also benefits of staying: Northampton had been a good place to live, less expensive than some, and a useful centre to reach other parts of the country. Yet it was clearly the girls who kept her in the town.

---

[62] Farningham, *Life,* p. 113.
[63] M.J. Street in *SST* 26 March 1909.
[64] Farningham, *Life,* p. 115. (see also Evans, 'Marianne Farningham', p. 10)
[65] Farningham, *Girlhood,* pp. 5, 15, 19, 68. Amongst other advice, she recommended a cold bath every morning.
[66] Farningham, *Life,* p. 262.
[67] Farningham, *Life,* pp. 94-95.

Development of the Class

The success of Marianne's class was no doubt partly dependent on the general atmosphere at College Street and the support she received from the minister, John Turland Brown, whom she described as being 'ever kind and sympathetic' to the class, as were 'most of the deacons', although when she was raising funds for the new Schoolroom, not everyone in the church approved. Probably this had more to do with her fund-raising methods rather than the class, but it does indicate a difference of opinion.[68] A history of the College Street Sunday school mentions 'complaints that the church did not take sufficient interest in the school'.[69] It is interesting to note that in Marianne's utopian novel *Nineteen Hundred,* she comments on the relations between church and Sunday school in her fictional town of Grantchester, noting that the teachers had had 'a pet grievance... that their old minister was never seen in the school', yet when the new one declared that 'the Sunday school is, of course, a part of the church', and he wanted to become closely involved, they were not sure about this development either.[70] Given Marianne's familiarity with Sunday school issues, she was no doubt drawing on personal knowledge of such differences, though possibly not of College Street during the time of Turland Brown, given his sympathetic attitude towards the school.

Indeed, there must have been considerable co-operation, as Marianne's oldest niece, Elizabeth, recalled how during the 1870s and 80s 'scores of us were loved into the kingdom of Christ' by the teachers and the pastor, Rev. Turland Brown, indicating a partnership between pastor and school. One aspect of this was a regular Sunday tea hosted by the head of the girls' Sunday school, William Grey, for whom all the girls had 'a real personal affection'. He regularly invited several girls to his house for tea on a Sunday, when they were 'treated as honoured guests: the conversation was cheerful' but also serious.[71] Another woman commended by Elizabeth was Mary Williams, who led another Young Women's Bible Class. As well as being 'the true and trusted friend of the young women she taught week by week', Mary had an unofficial pastoral ministry, often visiting people in difficulties in the church as a whole, being known by some as 'Mr Brown's curate'.[72] It is significant that female pastoral ministry was encouraged within the chapel. Marianne was not the only active woman teacher and compassionate carer in the College Street congregation.

---

[68] Farningham, *Life*, p. 123.
[69] *Souvenir of College Street Sunday School*, p. 37.
[70] Farningham, *Nineteen Hundred?*, p. 177.
[71] *Souvenir of College Street Sunday School*, pp. 43-44. Also see Chapter 2, pp. 34-36 for more background to College Street Chapel. Cliff believes that this phrase 'loving them into the Kingdom' covered 'lack of preparation or knowledge' but that is unlikely to be the case in this instance. (Cliff, *Rise and Development*, p. 182.)
[72] *Souvenir of College Street Sunday School*, pp. 44-55.

Conversion and Church Membership

It has been pointed out that the continuation of a denomination is dependent on communicating faith to a new generation, and that Sunday schools were a prime means of doing this.[73] Yet, although conversion was a foundational experience for evangelicals, some were uncertain about expecting such a response from children. Marianne, however, argued that it was not inappropriate to expect conversion at an early stage. This is a debate that others have also engaged in, with some commentators questioning the validity of early commitment, whilst others have suggested that it should be expected and encouraged.[74] In fact Marianne recommended that it was something teachers should aim for, arguing that 'the conversion of the children to God is, and must every be, then, the one chief end and aim of all our work'.[75] Some children, she pointed out, have been told that praying and reading the Bible 'will make them good', yet this is not the 'way of salvation'. Her suggestion was to 'first bring them to the Saviour', and the teacher who already knows the child, would be the best person to lead them in this.[76] Yet she also made a point of encouraging those who have prayed, and wept, yet seen no tangible result, by insisting that results were not everything. Sometimes the work of a teacher involves sowing, not reaping, and it is best to find reward enough in just doing the work: 'if we are willing and loving servants all will be well... nothing in all the world can make us so happy as working for Jesus'.[77] Her world-view left little room for loose ends or uncertainties, but contained a simple trust that God was at work even when no results were evident. Thus it was not inconsistent to urge teachers to seek conversions, yet encourage them not to be discouraged if no-one had such an experience whilst under their care.

In the early phase of class teaching, Marianne herself felt rather reticent about speaking to the girls concerning a definite commitment to Christ. She wrote of herself at that time that 'she had a great dread of the forcing process in religion' which prevented her from 'putting close personal questions, and pressing for immediate decision'.[78] In her friendships, too, she was cautious about raising the subject of conversion. When writing to a former pupil teacher who had worked alongside her in the British School in Northampton, having

---

[73] Snell, 'The Sunday-School Movement', pp. 137-38; Laqueur, *Religion and Respectability,* pp. 166-69.

[74] For instance, Harry Sprange, *Kingdom Kids* (Fearn, Ross-shire; Christian Focus Publications, 1994), argues from historical examples that children can be expected to make early commitments and play an active role as young Christians.

[75] M. Farningham, 'The nation in the Sunday-school, a paper read on Good Friday at the Annual Conference of the Gloucestershire and Hereford Sunday-school Union' in *SST,* 10 April, 1885.

[76] Farningham, *Sunday School of the Future,* pp. 52-56

[77] *SST* 15 January, 1875.

[78] Farningham, *Will you take it?,* p. 7

encouraged her to consider the blessings of God, she added 'I trust that you have already made Him your Friend',[79] indicating that despite their obviously close working relationship, they had not actually discussed the question of religious commitment. In retrospect, however, she regarded this reticence as a mistake, after another woman took her girls' class one Sunday, and helped a girl, who had been wanting to find Christ for herself, to become a Christian.[80] Marianne's response was a strong sense of failure that she had not 'had the great joy of leading individual members of the class to the Saviour', and a resolution to approach the issue differently.[81] Within a few weeks, she held a evening at her house on a Tuesday evening for those seeking or unsure of their salvation to which five or six girls came. For some of them, that evening was the time when 'by faith they were saved', and this experience was followed by further Tuesdays when they received some basic teaching.[82] Marianne overcame her fear of forcing religion on others and found fulfilment in leading girls into the same relationship with God that she enjoyed.

Conversion by itself, therefore, was only a stage on the journey. On one occasion Marianne declared that 'if there was anything she was proud of, it was that five or six of her girls were now conducting young women's classes. These girls were not much bigger than their scholars, but they were doing good work.'[83] Her aim in teaching was not only the conversion of her girls, but their active involvement in the ongoing life of the church. Her ultimate measure of success was when a girl herself became involved in teaching and training the next generation, thus perpetuating the Christian faith. She commented that one of the most successful classes she knew of, that she herself had been a student in, was led by 'a poor young woman, in a paper-mill, who had no time, and few opportunities, who could not speak correctly, and who knew very little but her Bible, but I believe all her girls are members of churches'.[84] In using church membership as a measure of the success of a Sunday school class, Marianne was sharing an aim with others in the movement.[85] She was well aware that many of those who attended Sunday school never made this transition, and this worried her, as it did many of her fellow-workers. There was a common concern that many of those who started off in Sunday school left around the age of fourteen. Snell labels this desire for transition 'denominational control' in contrast to social control: the desire to see children socialised into the same denomination as the Sunday school, although Marianne's ecumenical inclinations would have almost certainly meant she would have been happy

---

[79] Letters to Pollie, (1) 17 April 1863.
[80] Farningham, *Will you take it?* p. 8.
[81] Farningham, *Will you take it?*, pp. 8-9.
[82] Farningham, *Will you take it?,* p. 9.
[83] *Sunday School Chronicle* 9 May, 1877.
[84] *Sunday School Chronicle* 9 May, 1877.
[85] Farningham, *Sunday School of the Future*, p. 53; Farningham, *Will you take it?* p. 23.

with their involvement in any church.[86] Cliff highlights it as an issue as early as 1853, in the response of teachers to the census findings,[87] and it continued to be a matter of concern for those involved in schools. Marianne lamented the fact that because of this, teachers were unable to reap what had been sown in the lives of the young scholars.[88] Cliff, however, believed that expecting church members to be recruited from the ranks of the schools had always been a flawed aspiration, and contrary to Raikes' original intentions. In Cliff's view, schools should have been providing education for the masses, not preparation for church membership.[89] He argued that the movement never directly led to students becoming church members, suggesting that at no time in its history did more that one percent of students move directly from Sunday schools to become church members or communicants.[90] The stress on spiritual development rather than basic skills had, he considered, been a wrong turning for the schools. Marianne would have taken exception to that claim, as she believed that the aim of a Sunday school was not only to teach children the Bible, but to lead them to the point of conversion and to 'know Jesus' and then to encourage them to join a church as soon as possible.[91] Her attitude, epitomising all that Cliff believes was mistaken about the Sunday school movement, would have been shared by the majority of evangelical practitioners within both churches and Sunday schools. The Congregationalist R. W. Dale, for instance, approved the later development of schools into a 'religious force', a 'great evangelistic agency' which gradually became the focus of much of the 'evangelistic zeal' of the churches.[92] Cliff's perspective would have made little sense to the main practitioners of Sunday school teaching during the second half of the nineteenth century.

In common with many teachers, Marianne understood her primary role as being not an educator but a spiritual mentor. She shared the common evangelical view that if young people left Sunday school without making a Christian commitment, as in fact frequently happened, the system had failed.[93] This was at the heart of her argument that young people must be encouraged to continue in classes beyond the age of fourteen when many of them left day school. Marianne acknowledged that to those older pupils, often earning their own living, Sunday school could seem childish, yet her belief was that this was not an insurmountable problem. The answer, for her, lay in dedicated teachers,

---

[86] Snell, 'The Sunday-School Movement', p. 138, and pp. 164-66. See Chapter 7 pp. 218-221 for discussion of Marianne's ecumenical sympathies.
[87] Cliff, *Rise and Development,* p. 139.
[88] Farningham, *Will you take it?* p. 13.
[89] Cliff, *Rise and Development,* p. 19.
[90] Cliff, *Rise and Development,* p. 19, and p. 322.
[91] Farningham, *Sunday Schools of the Future,* p. 35
[92] R.W. Dale, *History of English Congregationalism* (London: Hodder and Stoughton, 1907), p. 600.
[93] Farningham, *Sunday Schools of the Future,* p. 109.

older classes, and deliberate, if gentle, challenges to conversion. Whilst teachers should have 'well-informed minds', 'sanctified hearts' were equally important, if this task was to be fulfilled.[94] Yet it might be argued that more than this was needed, and that it was her emphasis on hospitality, and on her own availability to befriend and counsel students, which made the difference in her class, in addition to the elements which she identified. To be fair, she was giving the lecture which contained this argument before her own class had really developed and matured into the successful community it later became. The fact remains, however, that Marianne lived out the principles she believed in.

Cliff's assertion that family, and the larger family of church, were where children and young people should and do 'catch faith' would not have been disputed by Marianne. He believed that a simple Bible teaching class could not communicate the essence of a living faith. In many ways Marianne shared that viewpoint, as she did not only teach Scripture, but lived it, did not only see her students for an hour on a Sunday, but shared many hours of her life with them, allowing them to catch something of her own passions. Her role was not to stimulate intellect, or communicate information about God, but to make disciples by both teaching and example. The *Sunday School Chronicle* stated after her death, that 'None will ever compute the good she wrought in quiet and self-sacrificing ways among the girls of her great Bible-class'.[95] Had her form of Sunday school teaching been more common, Cliff might not have had such a strong antagonistic attitude towards it.

Marianne also appears to have been an eternal optimist, sharing the Enlightenment belief in progress that influenced nineteenth-century evangelicalism.[96] Thus, in the wake of the 1870 Education Act she expected Sunday schools still to have a bright future, actually anticipating that more rather than fewer children would attend, because they would no longer be embarrassed about their illiteracy. With more children literate when joining classes, she suggested, the teacher's task would be easier in some ways.[97] She was, however, aware of the challenge the 1870 Act presented to Sunday school teachers, and added calls for more training for teachers, better environments for classes, and more dedication on the part of teachers, imagining the result as having 'hosts of young spirits who are strong in the faith, who know the right and mean to do it' an admirable aspiration.[98] There was still a significant role in the future, she believed, for Sunday schools, and for some years, at least, that was the case. Although many children did not make the transition to church membership, their attendance meant that Christian values permeated much of

---

[94] Farningham, *Sunday Schools of the Future,* p. 16.
[95] *Sunday School Chronicle* 25 March 1909.
[96] Bebbington, *Evangelicalism,* p. 144.
[97] Farningham, *Sunday Schools of the Future,* pp. 1-3.
[98] Farningham, *Sunday Schools of the Future,* p. 40.

society.[99] She could not, however, have anticipated the decline that took place in attendance throughout the twentieth century.

Retirement

When she took over the editorship of the *Sunday School Times*, Marianne commented that many years of involvement in Sunday schools and of the 'responsibilities and possibilities' connected with the work has 'so endeared it' to her that she hoped teaching a class would 'be the last of all the life-tasks to be laid down when the evening shadows fall'.[100] This was not to be, however, and it was with great reluctance that Marianne eventually felt she had to retire from her class in 1901 at the age of sixty-seven. In her autobiography she described how for several years she had known she could not take the class much longer, as she was finding the mile-long uphill walk home from the classroom to her house increasingly tiring, and was frequently resorting to using a cab. She also found winters a difficult season, and yet she believed it was the best time of year for working with the girls. She was able to postpone the inevitable for some years because a friend, Miss Ashton, came to help in 1891 and took on most of the work, although it remained 'Miss Hearne's class' until her retirement. When Miss Ashton married and had less time to help, there was little choice for Marianne but to resign. So at the beginning of 1901 she finally made the decision 'to do almost the hardest thing possible for me, namely to give up the class which for thirty-four years had been mine'.[101] She took the last class, not telling the girls that it was the final one: 'I had not the strength and courage to tell them, being afraid that the trouble would be nearly as great to them as to me, and quite too much to bear.' Indeed in the days following she found that 'the wrench was terrible'.[102] As she read the letters the church and individual girls sent to her on her retirement, she recalled weeping over them. In many ways she had given the best of herself into the generations of girls who had passed through, encouraging them and easing the passage from girlhood into adulthood, often helping them find faith as they did so. That she gave up so reluctantly, despite her increasing frailty, is a mark of the passion of her involvement. But also, she seems to suggest that the role of surrogate mother to so many girls filled a space in her own life, as well as having a significant impact on others.

Sunday School as a Third Sphere

The number of teachers required to sustain the late nineteenth-century Sunday

---

[99] Bebbington, *Dominance of Evangelicalism*, p. 98.
[100] *SST* 2 January 1885.
[101] Farningham, *Life,* pp. 259-60.

school population was considerable, and over half of those teachers were women. Their teaching experience took place in a space that, it can be argued, comprised a borderland, or third sphere, neither fully public nor quite private.[103] Indeed, Laqueur noted of the pre-1850 schools that as part of a 'distinct religious subculture' they 'provided a new and unprecedentedly wide sphere of lay activity'[104] and this continued to be true of the schools throughout the century. Involving as they did children and young people, they were recognisably an extension of work women were used to doing at home, yet developed skills that could be useful in other contexts, such as committee work or pubic speaking. Many churches, and their related Sunday school, were experienced by their members as extended families, and into these comparatively secure and friendly settings women carried skills of the home, such as organisational abilities and explaining the Bible to children. This is not to deny that there could be strong disagreements within churches, or between churches and their related School, rather to suggest that both were usually experienced as a secure place within which serving God led to personal development, whether consciously or unconsciously pursued. Such church involvement clearly fell within the parameters of conventional behaviour for women, and thus into the category that has been labelled 'the Angel out of the House'.[105] Other skills, such as praying in public, or involvement in committee work, shaded into activities which were pushing at gender boundaries. Indeed, for some women, involvement in this third sphere was a stepping stone into a genuinely public role. This was the case for Marianne. I have argued elsewhere that the church can be best understood in this way, providing a forum especially for women, but also for some lay men, where gifts were developed that would otherwise have remained dormant.[106]

Although the degree varied to which Sunday schools were integrated into the church, or were independent of them, the same principle applies. Work within the Sunday school was also, perhaps even more than some church work, neither in the public nor the private sphere. Marianne spent many hours befriending and mentoring young women, which was very much a private role, but also taught them in the church building, and later in a hall on Sundays, a situation which verged on the public, especially as her class grew. At the very least, it occupied a grey area between the two spheres, and acted as a useful training ground, preparing her for other public opportunities. In her memoirs she explained that speaking regularly to a large number on Sunday afternoons meant that she lost most of her nervousness over speaking in public.[107]

---

[103] See Chapter 3, p. 68.
[104] Laqueur, *Religion and Respectability*, p. 244.
[105] E.K. Helsinger, R.L. Sheets, and W. Veeder, *The Woman Question*, Vol 1 (Chicago: University of Chicago Press, 1983), p. xv. See Chapter 3, p. 79. for further discussion.
[106] For further discussion of this see Wilson, *Zeal*, Chapter 7, pp. 174-211.
[107] Farningham, *Life*, p. 153.

Although she was already writing for the evangelical public, and was thus a well known name, it was through the Sunday school that she was able to develop and hone her various public skills. For Marianne, the experience gained with her class was invaluable when she later came to have a more clearly public role, particularly with her lecturing tours.

Sunday school teaching was, for many women teachers, one of their main activities outside the home. It is possible to discover one woman here, and another there, who like Marianne took extreme care over their preparation, making prayer for their pupils a priority, and meeting with their classes midweek either for prayer or for practical lessons, but these are rare enough to merit mention in an obituary.[108] It is easy to view these women, often the wives of pastors, as frustrated ministers themselves, who in another age could have found a wider area of ministry in church leadership. For Marianne, however, the role of teacher of a young people's class was not a second-rate calling, but a vitally important primary task: that of shaping the future generation. She suggested on one occasion that teachers genuinely dedicated to the task would reject the opportunity for more apparently prestigious roles, preferring the satisfaction of shaping the lives of young people.[109]

Her interest in Sunday schools also provided Marianne with the opportunity to move into a more clearly public arena. Although her fame within evangelical circles as a writer was probably the key that opened the door, it is significant that her first public appearance was connected to her experience of teaching a Sunday school class. In 1877 she read a paper to the Sunday School Conference which was subsequently published, and this appears to be one of the first of her many talks in public. Not long after, she chose to undertake a lecture tour.[110] She was no longer the same woman who had been afraid to pray before a dozen or so teenage girls. For Marianne, teaching a class was both an end in itself and the means of creating new opportunities, not that she would ever have thought of it in quite those terms.

'Unfilled hearts and unemployed hands'

Whilst Marianne was aware of the significance of being a woman in a public role, her main concern in moving beyond her own class was to increase the profile of Sunday schools and encourage others to become involved with them. Thus, she campaigned tirelessly on behalf of such participation, insisting that if people wanted to explore opportunities for Christian work, they could do little better than dedicate themselves to Sunday school teaching. Whilst teaching did have a high profile amongst evangelicals, there was always a need for more volunteers. Her concern for the young people who needed befriending and

---

[108] Wilson, *Zeal*, p. 192.
[109] *SST* 9 January 1885, editorial.
[110] See Chapter 5, pp. 155-161 for details of her lecture tours.

training was matched by a concern for older single women who had time on their hands and little to do with it.[111] Two of the major interests in her life coincided here. In her view 'taking a class' was both a way in which individuals in general, and women in particular, could find fulfilment by working for God, and the means by which young people could be encouraged and trained in understanding and living out the Christian faith.

Marianne's support of Sunday schools was a common evangelical attitude, but it was also a very personal enthusiasm. She took many opportunities, both through writing and speaking, to encourage other people, especially women, to become involved with Sunday school teaching, following her practical approach that one should do what came to hand, rather than waiting for some sign from heaven. She used her own experience to illustrate this. When it was suggested to her that men could also take girls' classes, especially when there was a shortage of suitable women teachers, she was clear that she considered this second best, and said that she would be stubborn and stick to her belief that women are better for girls' classes, though she wished the men success. She considered that the men have not tried hard enough to persuade women to be teachers.

> Of course a woman says 'No,' but if you are half as clever as I think you are, you can make a good many of them say 'Yes!' .... I was asked to take a class, and being a woman I said 'No'. The superintendent said 'You must' and I said 'I can't: there is really so much to do, and I should not like to enter upon anything I could not thoroughly carry out: I am sure I'm not the woman to take it.'[112]

The implication was that there were many women able to take such classes, if only they were asked forcefully enough to do so. People's responsibility, she suggested, was to take a step of faith and do the work that is needed, and they will be trained by God 'if only we try in simple faith to take the step that we see, he will make the next clear to us'.[113] Many women, she suggested, particularly single women like herself, would themselves benefit from such an opportunity. Commenting on the fact that it was often said there was no-one to do the job of taking a class she added that 'there are hosts of women with unfilled hearts and unemployed hands, women who love Christ and wish to serve him' and who would otherwise join sisterhoods or settle down as 'old maids'.[114] This is an interesting comment which illustrates the plight of unmarried women during this period, and is one of the few instances of Marianne commenting on the single state which she shared with many contemporaries. She implied that many wasted their lives, at a loss both to the individuals and to the churches and Sunday schools which might have made

---

[111] Farningham, *Will you take it?* p. 15.
[112] *Sunday School Chronicle* 9 May 1877 (Hearn History)
[113] Farningham, *Will you take it?* p. 5.
[114] Farningham, *Will you take it?* p. 16.

use of their capacity to love and to serve. She also recognised that such women could be uncertain of their own abilities, and needed drawing out. Implicit in this statement was her belief that every woman needed work or service of some kind to give themselves to, and a sense of purpose in their lives.[115] They might feel diffident about volunteering, but could look after a few girls. These women never reached their potential because they were not offered the opportunity to do so, and were too reticent to take the initiative themselves. The main qualifications teachers needed, she argued, were not education, but cheerfulness and love.[116]

On occasions, Marianne found herself in difficulties on the question of these essential characteristics of teachers. On the one hand, she was eager for teachers to develop themselves intellectually, and be able to engage with current theological debate. She recognised the need to become familiar with these developments, especially as the children themselves became more educated. It has been suggested that a problem with Sunday schools towards the end of the nineteenth century was that older teachers, who had taught for between thirty and fifty years, lost connection with the younger generation.[117] Writing in 1871, in the wake of the 1870 Education Act, Marianne indicated that she was aware that this might become a problem, as older teachers lacking 'intellect and scholarship' might be unable to learn new ways and to engage with modern scholarship in a way that more educated children would require.[118] Yet on the other hand, she firmly believed that the spiritual aspect of the work was the most important, so that character, and depth of faith, could outweigh any lack of intellectual sophistication. She resolved this tension by suggesting that, even in this new era, personal faith and the ability to befriend the children, were more important than scholarship.[119]

Marianne thus gave the impression that willingness was the main criterion for a teacher. Presumably she stressed this because of women's generally low opinions of themselves, and because of her own experience of having an uncertain beginning to her teaching. But in so doing she made the unwarranted assumption that others, if they took on the role, would share her experience of satisfying work after a shaky start. Possibly she under-emphasised her own gifts and abilities, believing that if she could make a success of a class, then anyone could. Yet the evidence suggests that she was particularly skilled as a teacher. One observer commented that

> He did not know of a class in the whole country which presented more pleasant features than the class over which she presided; and if they could find a Miss

---

[115] See Chapter 3, pp.80-88.
[116] Farningham, *Will you take it?* p. 16.
[117] Cliff, *Rise and Development*, p. 182.
[118] Farningham, *Sunday Schools of the Future*, p. 124.
[119] Farningham, *Sunday Schools of the Future*, pp. 126-28.

Farningham in every town, he believed they would find classes equally successful.[120]

Marianne seemed unable to understand the difficulties that might deter a potential recruit. It is true that she believed that that the educational background required was quite limited, because the general standard of education, even after 1870, was still quite low. However, Marianne was also unusual in the amount of time she was willing to give to the role, and the standard of commitment she set for taking a successful girls' class was extremely high, including a considerable sacrifice of time. Whilst she gave the impression that there were many women who, if asked, would happily and successfully take on a small class, it is hard to see how many could have filled her demanding criteria, which must surely have been a deterrent to some of her listeners and readers.

The Challenge of Sunday School Teaching

From the same paper, for instance, we gain some insight into the level of dedication that Marianne believed was necessary for the task. She suggested that teachers should 'be prepared constantly to give time and money, thought and love'. Giving advice to others starting as teachers of girls' classes, she argued that a teacher needs to be someone who is cheerful, and who loves her students. She should take plenty of time for the preparation of her Sunday lesson, both in prayer, and by thorough study and research, but she should also visit her students, and invite them for tea. Visiting, Marianne suggested, should take place when students were ill, or when they had stopped attending, it should be in private, and it required 'great and peculiar gifts'.[121] Here again there is a tension: on the one hand the main qualification is to be willing, but on the other a high standard is needed.

Marianne advised teachers of girls' classes to write letters to their students. Suitable occasions for this, she suggested, might be their birthday, or when a reprimand or congratulations are in order, or when girls are away on holiday. She also encouraged them to keep in touch with former students through letters.[122] In addition, they ought to hold meetings on week-day evening for prayer, sewing, or conversation, the main purpose being to bring the girls together and bring them under their teacher's influence.[123] They should be readily available at other times, too.[124] None of this advice was particularly

---

[120] *Sunday School Chronicle*, 9 May 1877, an account of the discussion following Marianne's paper *Will you take it?* given to the Sunday School Union in 1877.
[121] Farningham, *Sunday Schools of the Future*, p. 66.
[122] Farningham, *Sunday Schools of the Future*, pp. 57-61.
[123] Farningham, *Will you take it?* pp. 21-23.
[124] Farningham, *Will you take it?* p. 23; Farningham, *Sunday Schools of the Future*, p. 112.

innovative. Indeed, in the discussion that followed her paper, at least one other teacher claimed that she was already following most of this advice. Unfortunately we have no indication whether her paper inspired any more women to take up the challenge, although as she gave it at the Sunday School Union Conference, it is likely she was preaching to the converted. The difficulty, though, of following in her footsteps is highlighted by a comment in the *Sunday School Times* after her death, that 'there was no brighter Sunday afternoon gathering in the United Kingdom'.[125] Marianne's example was a challenging one to follow.

Marianne's opinions concerning the nature of teaching were formed early, and maintained throughout her life. In an early edition of the *Sunday School Times*, she wrote a little piece entitled 'Too Busy'. This concerned a fictional 'Mr A' who had been too busy to do his Sunday school preparation properly: he had missed the 'useful hints' at the preparation class, failed on Saturday night to pray at home, at a certain time for the next day's class, as all the other teachers had agreed to do. Faced on Sunday afternoon with two new difficult boys, he was unprepared.[126] This was a little story with a clear moral, typical of her early work with its sentimental naivety, which in later years develops into a more mature, and less trite (if still rather simplistic) attitude.

Whilst there were no doubt others who were as diligent, they were probably the exceptions. For instance, teachers were generally expected to visit persistent absentees, and Marianne encouraged this, but the records of these visits create the suspicion that teachers could be less than thorough in these duties, just recording 'not found' against several of the absent children.[127] Marianne also believed that teachers ought to make the class their priority. For the sake of their students, it would be better if they did nothing else within the church, refusing invitations to take Mothers' meetings and cottage meetings, to collect for missionary societies, or get involved in any of the myriads of church and philanthropic activities available. She argued was that 'those who attempt too many things do nothing altogether well', and pointed to the example of Jesus who spent his time with a small group of people 'not more interesting or important than our scholars, and yet He thought it worth while to give His life to them'.[128] This is another instance of Marianne's understanding of the importance of relational discipleship and nurturing. She believed in the value of making a priority of investing time in individuals at a critical stage of their lives. In practice, however, active women tended to be engaged with many projects, leaving them less time to concentrate fully on their classes.[129]

Marianne was far from being alone, of course, in her dedication to Sunday

---

[125] *SST* 26 March 1909.
[126] *SST* 16 March 1860.
[127] Stroud Congregationalist Sunday School Book, Gloucester Record Office.
[128] Farningham, *Will you take it?* p. 23.
[129] See Chapter 3, p. 92.

school teaching. Sunday schools may have declined to an embarrassing degree by the late twentieth century, catering for the children of church members instead of drawing in children from the streets, but they were highly regarded in the Victorian era and many people gave their time in the cause. The demands of taking a class were considerable, if one followed Marianne's lead, and might seem like the counsel of perfection, were it not a reflection of her own practice. It seems that her 'girls' always had a special place in her heart, and the evidence suggests that she did live out the level of commitment to her class that she commended to others.

Marianne as Pastor

It could be argued that this class, more than College Street Baptist Chapel, was to a large extent Marianne's church. Her role can be compared to that of a youth pastor, or a leader of a form of alternative church. Lacking was the multi-generational element, sacraments, professional ministry and denominational structure, yet many elements of a church were present. There were strong relationships and fellowship, prayer and mutual support, Bible teaching, worship and discipleship: shared faith and shared lives. She was much more than just the teacher of a Sunday afternoon class. Significantly, a minister made just this point following the paper Marianne gave in 1877. After she had described her class, and the way she built relationships with her girls, there was a discussion concerning the importance of forming friendships with scholars and a contributor, one Rev. Henderson, urged the leaders of young people's classes to see their group not as a class 'but rather their church and their pastorate. The class should be their flock…'.[130] With such encouragement, it is quite probable that Marianne did see herself in that light. Evans has suggested that Marianne's dedication to her class represented the 'self-sacrificial manner required of the perfect Victorian mother',[131] but whilst there is some truth in this observation, in that the mother-child relationship was one element in the mix, I believe it is more accurate to say that her work reflected the model of the minister with his flock. The quotation on the previous page reinforces this, as it indicates a degree of pastoral care and concern which would be appropriate in a minister.

There is a further indication that Marianne might herself have understood her role in this way, in the introduction to her biography of Grace Darling. Here she commended an unnamed London woman who regularly spoke to eight hundred members of a Young Woman's Bible Class 'of things pertaining to their present and eternal welfare', and compared her to the famous Quaker

---

[130] *Sunday School Chronicle* 9 May 1877.

[131] Evans, 'Marianne Farningham', p. 10.

Elizabeth Fry and other female preachers.[132] Given that Marianne, too, was regularly speaking to a large girls' class, there would seem to be an unspoken further identification of herself with the other preachers she mentions: in other words, that she understood her regular lessons given to the Bible Class as a form of preaching. It is probable, therefore, that she did consider herself, and not without cause, to be a pastor and preacher to her girls' class. This makes her mid-career 'breakdown' all the more interesting, following as it does the pattern of many ministerial careers.[133] Marianne in effect successfully developed and pastored a church of between one and two hundred young women for a period of over thirty years, another aspect of her life which has feminist overtones.

Sunday Schools in the Late Nineteenth Century

There is some disagreement concerning the actual situation of Sunday schools at the close of the nineteenth century. Cliff has suggested that not only were schools failing to keep up with the growth in population but by the end of Marianne's lifetime the attendance was actually starting to decline. He claimed that statistics in 1900 indicated that although the population had risen by 300,000, there had been a 30,000 decline in the numbers of scholars.[134] Part of the reason for this, he believed, was that as the middle classes moved out of the centre of cities, the inner-city Sunday schools lost their key workers.[135] More recently, however, Callum Brown has energetically challenged Cliff's assertions, arguing that the statistics of attendance have been inadequate and wrongly interpreted. Drawing on earlier work from Gilbert and McLeod, he has pointed out that working class church attendance was much higher in the later nineteenth century than some historians have asserted.[136] He has demonstrated that whilst actual church attendance was steadily in decline from the 1880s, church allegiance was still extremely high, and this involved a high level of Sunday school attendance, as parents despatched their offspring to Sunday school, as they had been sent themselves. Thus, in 1900, the vast majority of children in Britain, over 75%, still attended Sunday schools. Whilst there is

---

[132] E. Hope, *Grace Darling, Heroine of the Farne Islands* (London: Walter Scott, 1875), pp 10-11.
[133] See Chapter 2, p. 51.
[134] Cliff, *Rise and Development,* p. 197.
[135] Cliff, *Rise and Development,* p. 200.
[136] C. Brown, *The Death of Christian Britain* (London: Routledge, 2001), Chapter 7, especially pp. 166-69, H. McLeod, *Religion and Society in England, 1850-1914* (Basingstoke: MacMillan Press, 1996), A. D. Gilbert, *Religion and Society in Industrial England: Church, Chapel and Social Change, 1740-1914* (London, Longman, 1976), p. 63. Snell also indicated the large number of children attending in 1911, and was aware of Cliff's work, but as his focus was more on the 1851 census he did not take issue with Cliff's findings. Snell, 'The Sunday-School Movement', p. 126 .

room for disagreement with some of Brown's overall thesis, this part of his argument is a convincing reinterpretation of the statistical evidence backed up by research from oral history.[137] Thus Marianne's hopeful assessment of the situation was actually nearer the truth than might previously have been thought. She was still naïve, however, in expecting that a response of faith from many people was all that was needed to meet the new post-1870 challenges. At least she did not just shout encouragement from the sidelines: during the period of transition following the 1870 Act, Marianne was heavily involved in the development of the schools, helping them to adapt to the new situation.

Cliff's argument that the real role of Sunday schools had always been that of education, and that it was no surprise that Sunday school numbers declined once education was free and available to all, is thus undermined by Brown's presentation of the evidence. Far from being in decline, Sunday schools were at the height of their popularity and influence at the end of the century. The evangelical understanding of Sunday schools, shared by Marianne, as a place for the communication of the Christian faith and early training to be a follower of Christ, was in practice an acceptable one which drew many parents to send their children, even though they themselves were not churchgoers. There was still a shared culture and an identification with the Christian religion by churchgoers and many non-churchgoers alike. Marianne played a small, but significant part, in the maintenance of that Christian culture.

Other Sunday School Involvement

Over the years, Marianne demonstrated her support for the movement in various other ways. One major aspect, as contributor to and then editor of the *Sunday School Times,* will be explored in the following chapter, but this was not her only other contribution. She wrote many hymns which were used at various functions, ranging from a poem on a leaflet she gave to all her girls one new year, to hymns written for major Sunday school conferences. They were a part of her large output of hymns, which whilst of variable quality, bear witness to her enthusiasm for the cause.[138] She was also for some time a member of the National Council of the Sunday School Union as well as a frequent speaker at Union events. The Union had been founded in 1803 to be a resource for London Sunday schools, but had gradually become a national body as other local Unions became affiliated to it. The affairs of the Union were under the direction of a General Committee consisting of the President, Vice-President, Treasurer, Secretaries and 20 members, elected at the annual meeting, and

---

[137] Brown, *Christian Britain,* pp. 166-69, including statistics on p. 168.
[138] See Chapter 5, pp. 135-139.

representatives from the Committee of each Metropolitan Auxiliary.[139] Marianne was one of the elected members, initially as a representative of the Sunday School Unions of Northamptonshire.[140] Cliff comments that not many women 'ventured onto' the committee, suggesting that this might have been because they had no vote in the Union meetings.[141] This is an indication that Marianne's participation was unusual enough to be distinctive and therefore significant. It was one of several areas in which she was a pioneer, not in the sense of being the first woman to engage in a particular activity, but rather a participant when it was still culturally questionable. She was one of those whose actions helped to open the way for a greater role for women in public life, as the next chapter explores more fully.

It is difficult to assess the extent to which Marianne was an active member of the Council, as unfortunately no records from that period of the Council survive. She did comment in her autobiography that she continued on the Council for many years, joining committees, attending numerous festivities, and reading numerous papers at different meetings.[142] Her attendance is attested to by a comment made by Jennie Street, that another friend always tried to watch Marianne's face at the Council meeting.[143] Elizabeth Sharwood stated that her aunt spoke 'with authority' at the committee meetings, having become an expert through her 'life-long devotion to Sunday School work'.[144] Marianne would have had useful thoughts to contribute to the committee, and as she was well-known in Sunday school circles no doubt her opinions were respected.

Marianne was also one of three main speakers invited by Rev. Carey Bonner, the first full-time secretary of the Union, who was appointed in 1900, to address a women's conference on work with young people, which was part of the 1903 centenary celebrations of the Sunday School Union. He had asked her to speak on the subject of Girls' Bible Classes. He must therefore have known of Marianne and her girls' class, although it is unclear whether he knew her personally: she was clearly well known in Sunday school circles. Other contributors included Mrs Carey Bonner, and Mrs Hugh Price Hughes (Sister Katherine) wife of the well known Methodist minister, leader of the Methodist Forward Movement.[145] Marianne was in august company. As she came to speak, she was enthusiastically received by her audience:

---

[139] Constitution as given at front of minute book, 1874-78, Archives of *National Christian Education Council, formerly the National Sunday School Union*, Special Collections, Birmingham University.
[140] Farningham, *Life*, p. 195.
[141] Cliff, *Rise and Development*, p. 172.
[142] Farningham, *Life*, p. 195.
[143] *SST* 26 March 1909.
[144] *Souvenir of College Street Sunday School*, p. 45.
[145] C. Bryant, *Possible Dreams: A personal history of the British Christian Socialists* (London, Hodder & Stoughton, 1996), p. 230.

Again and again the storm of applause was renewed, and some moments elapsed before she was allowed to begin her address. It seemed as if her friends and fellow-workers could not sufficiently express their love and esteem for the singer of the Sunday School, who has cheered and counselled them with voice and pen for so many years.[146]

This account, and the speech itself, was later included with others in *The Hundredth Year*, a volume which described the centenary celebrations of the Sunday School Union. This was edited by her friend Jennie Street, and published the same year, 1903.[147]

The Union sought to extend its influence beyond supervision of the Sunday schools which were connected to it. It became involved in protesting to the press, and to parliament, over issues ranging from the treatment of Armenian prisoners, the content of the 1902 Education Bill, and the sale of cigarettes to children.[148] There is no particular evidence that Marianne was closely involved in any of these issues, but with regard to the main business of supporting and advising Sunday schools, her experience, wide knowledge and expertise would have been extremely valuable on this committee. In 1901 Marianne was presented with a diploma of honour given to those who had rendered signal service to the cause. She must have made a useful contribution to the Council, as she did for all the bodies with which she was involved.

Conclusion – the Sunday School Queen

Marianne was both a participant in and a shaper of the Sunday school movement in the later years of the nineteenth century. In 1999, Snell included her in a list of 'outstanding figures in the annals of working-class or religious history' who taught in a Sunday school, although his inclusion of a footnote indicating her autobiography suggested that he did not necessarily expect his readers to be familiar with her name.[149] She was closely involved in her girl's class for over thirty years, teaching, offering hospitality and friendship, and facilitating a network of relationships, some of which lasted for many years. Although it was costly for Marianne in both time and emotional investment, it had benefits for her too, as the girls provided a support network for her other work and she gained much personal satisfaction from helping them and seeing them develop. Her role with the class, which held 'first place in her heart' was similar to that of a pastor and congregation, and there are indications that she understood it in that way. Whilst her stress on the spiritual development of the young women, and their eventual inclusion in a church community, was

---

[146] Street, *The Hundredth Year*, p. 122.
[147] M. Farningham, 'Girl's Bible-Classes', in Street, *The Hundredth Year*, p. 122.
[148] Cliff, *Rise and Development*, p. 172.
[149] Snell, *The Sunday-School Movement*, p. 131.

according to Cliff part of the mistaken turn the Sunday school movement took in the later nineteenth century, contemporaries would have disagreed. More recently, Brown has demonstrated that in reality, the movement was still thriving at the turn of the twentieth century, justifying this adaptation of the movement to spiritual ends. In addition, this work gave credibility to her role as the editor of the *Sunday School Times,* which will be discussed in the following chapter.

She also helped to shape the movement by giving encouraging promotional and recruitment talks on the subject of girls' classes, although it was possible that she was usually preaching to the converted. She certainly believed that single women needed urging to be teachers, as they had much to give but might be reluctant to volunteer. There was a contradiction in her appeals, however: whilst she indicated that anyone could take a class, she set such high standards that most aspiring teachers must have been deterred from the task. She also sat on various councils and committees, where her experience and expertise, as well as her friendly manner, was valued and appreciated. She was, in short, involved in the promotion and development of Sunday school in a multiplicity of ways. Marianne's niece Elizabeth noted that after her aunt's death, a friend declared that she had been the 'Sunday School Queen',[150] a telling affirmation of her commitment and wide-ranging contribution, as well as of the extent of the appreciation of her fellow-workers.

This multifaceted role as 'Sunday School Queen' involved both the private and the public sphere. In many ways her class functioned as a 'third sphere' facilitating this transition. She moved from teaching a small class to preaching to two hundred girls, yet this was still within closed doors in an environment in which she felt confident and at home: a safe place. More than this, however, quite quickly her enthusiasm for the cause led her to give papers at conferences. Possibly her reception here encouraged her to believe that it was worth attempting a lecture tour, thus taking her thoroughly into the public arena. Her roles as editor, as speaker on the subject of Sunday schools, and as a member of various Councils, brought her increasingly into the public sphere, whilst her parallel career as a writer with the *Christian World,* and as Eva Hope, simultaneously eased the way for her to move into a more public role. Her lecturing tours, and her presence in later years on the Northampton School Board, were no doubt facilitated by a mixture of her Sunday school experience and her fame as a writer. The next chapter will explore her career as writer and editor along with other aspects of her involvement in public life, but it needs to be borne in mind that these roles were developing alongside her Sunday school activities. In one sense, her whole life was wrapped up with the schools: a private passion which helped to fuel her public career. She was, as Jennie Street wrote in 1903, 'the singer of the Sunday School…(who) cheered and

---

[150] *Souvenir of College Street Sunday School,* p. 45.

counselled them with voice and pen for so many years', [151] and in so doing she made a significant contribution both to the lives of many young people, and to the continued prosperity of the whole movement.

---

[151] Street, *The Hundredth Year*, p. 122.

Chapter 5

Marianne and Public Life

> ...those who love their work better than they love themselves are the most likely to win and wear the laurel-wreath of fame.[1]

Late in her life, Marianne published a volume of short pieces entitled *Women and their Work* in which she suggested that some of the women in the Old Testament were suitable for imitation, as being 'cultured and high-minded, gentle and patriotic, women who reigned in their homes and yet took part in public affairs'.[2] Marianne intended these women to be an inspiration to her readers encouraging them to become similarly involved in public life. As Chapter 3 has argued, whilst Marianne considered the domestic sphere should be women's priority, once all was in order and cared for at home, the way was open for them to take up whatever tasks, whether paid or unpaid, they were inclined to pursue. Women could, and should, move from the private to the public sphere, according to their talents and the perceived need, regardless of cultural conventions. It was necessary to seize opportunities when they arose and not to be constrained by public opinion.[3] Preparation for moving into a wider sphere often took place in the environment of church or Sunday school, which as the previous chapter has demonstrated, operated as a third sphere for many women, and also, on occasions, for men. It was to some extent through her involvement with Sunday schools that Marianne herself developed a public presence, as she accepted invitations to deliver papers and talks. Her membership of the Northampton School Board was partly a consequence of this local role, and partly because of her experience as an infant teacher. In her Board involvement in particular, as will be seen, she was aware of her identity as a woman and of the gender implications of her work. The other means by which the door to a wider sphere was opened was through her writing and editing career, which had already given her a public voice. Because she was already well-known it was comparatively easy for her to become a regular lecturer, whilst her experience in the Sunday school environment developed her confidence enough to attempt a series of talks. Throughout her life, therefore,

---

[1] E. Hope, *Great Modern Women* (London: Walter Scott Limited, 1886), p. 21.
[2] M. Farningham, *Women and their Work* (London: James Clarke, 1906), p. 116.
[3] See Chapter 3, p. 63..

she developed several strands to her public profile, beginning with the verses and short prose pieces she wrote for the *Christian World*.

Writing, Editing, and the Public Sphere

The writing of this prose and poetry, including hymns, is an ambiguous activity, not entirely public nor quite private. Whilst this is also true of working in the 'third sphere' of a church or Sunday school environment, there is a major, obvious difference between literary composition and church involvement, in that the latter is social whilst the work of a writer is usually solitary. The communication takes place between the writer composing work, perhaps in her own house, and the reader who also often reads in private, or in a limited family circle. Less clearly in the public sphere than being an employed editor, it was quite compatible with being a retiring and domestically-inclined woman, and some women had treated it this way. Yet, because the work is sold, in newspapers, magazines or contained in volumes in bookshops, writing is at the same time a public activity and it appears that this was how Marianne understood her work. In the preface to her first volume of poetry, *Lays and Lyrics of the Blessed Life,* she suggested a public location for her poems. She imagined the collection as a welcome guest in the homes of its readers. Acknowledging that some of these were more experienced than her in the life of faith, she continued that 'she ventures this *public* expression of her feelings in the hope that others may sympathize with them'.[4] It is significant that she regarded the volume, although it was to be read in private, as a public communication. There was, however, no need for an author to make an actual public appearance, and thus modesty and respectability could be maintained. In Marianne's case, she did choose to make the further steps into lecturing and editing, thus fully entering the public sphere. Prior to that move, however, she was more than merely a contributor, being consulted initially by Whittemore and later by Clarke on various issues connected with the production of the papers. She recalled, for instance, having long talks with Jonathan Whittemore concerning the possible launch of the *Sunday School Times*. Later, according to her own account, it was Marianne who first suggested a summer number of the *Christian World*, specifically to contain a story in two parts which she had written on the subject of capital punishment.[5] This 'sensational' story sold well, and she recalled being in a railway carriage while three other passengers were reading it, although one lady was very critical of the tragic ending, in which a man was mistakenly hung for murder.[6] Active behind the scenes, she communicated with her public primarily through the written medium, both as

---

[4] M. Farningham, *Lays and Lyrics* (London: James Clarke, 1861), p iv. My italics.
[5] M. Farningham, *A Working Woman's Life* (London: James Clarke, 1907), pp. 100 and 135.
[6] Farningham, *Life*, p. 136.

'Marianne Farningham' and under her second pseudonym, 'Eva Hope', and continued to do so until the end of her life, believing however that this was a public role. Indeed, it has been suggested that the periodical press, in enabling journalism to develop into a profession, 'created a space in which some women could earn their living "like men"'.[7] This was especially true of her later work as an editor, which took place unequivocally in the public sphere.

As early as the eighteenth century, and more frequently in the nineteenth, women had made their mark not only as contributors, but as editors of magazines aimed at their own sex. By the 1880s there were a number of magazines with women as editors which were targeting a female audience. Rarer, but not completely unknown, was the female editor of a Christian popular journal aimed at both men and women, even if the latter were likely to be the larger audience. One such was Emma Worboise, who edited the *Christian World's* companion, the *Christian World Magazine and Family Visitor*, from 1866-85, ceasing editorial work just as Marianne was starting.[8] Yet despite editing and journalism taking place within the public sphere of paid work, ambiguity over their role in society meant that women who were journalists and editors were still portrayed as 'essentially feminine' rather than professional.[9] Marianne's determination to be known as a 'working woman', although as much about class as gender, ran counter to this trend. As earlier chapters have demonstrated, she was determined to be financially independent and did not carry the inhibitions about earning that women of middle-class origins often appeared to struggle with. This motivation and stance, however was rarely apparent in her work especially when writing as Marianne Farningham (rather than Eva Hope) prior to the turn of the century. One exception was her encouragement to young girls that there was no need to regard earning their living as beneath them.[10] This was partly, as discussed in Chapter 3, because she held mid-Victorian views of the significance of domesticity alongside a growing conviction that talented women should develop a public role, and that all women should be willing to earn their living if necessity or providence dictated.[11] The subject matter also played a part here: many of Marianne's most popular hymns, poems and prose pieces, covered a range of subjects, sentimental, religious, natural, which rarely impinged on gender issues. Writing under the name of Eva Hope allowed more varied possibilities, as has been previously noted and will be explored further below.

---

[7] M. Beetham, *A Magazine of her own?* (London: Routledge, 1996), p. 43.
[8] B. Harrison, 'Worboise [*formerly* Worboys], Emma Jane [*known as* Mrs Etherington Guyton] (1825–1887)', *Oxford Dictionary of National Biography*, (Oxford: Oxford University Press, 2004) http://ww.oxforddnb.com/view/article/29966, accessed 7 Aug 2005.
[9] Beetham, *Magazine of her own?*, p. 129.
[10] See for instance M. Farningham, *Girlhood* (London: James Clarke, 1869), pp. 34-35.
[11] See Chapter 3 for discussion of these issues.

Marianne as Writer

The Baptist minister John Carlile commented after Marianne's death that 'the Baptists had in her one of their sweetest songsters'.[12] His personal friendship (he worked with her on the *Sunday School Times*) may have coloured his judgement, although as Mitchell indicates, she could 'write with rare beauty' on some subjects, adding that several of her poems 'are engagingly direct'.[13] Another Baptist, writing in 1899, commented on her 'well-written, chatty articles and charming verses'.[14] The Rev W. Glandwr-Morgan, Congregationalist pastor in Barmouth, who knew Marianne in her declining years, admitted that she was not in the same class as someone like Swinburne, who also died in 1909, yet declared that 'she appealed to all classes of the community, her strength lying in her confident sweetness and faith'.[15] He personally had been 'charmed by her writings' before ever meeting her.[16] His comments hint that her popularity lay as much in her spirituality as in her facility with words, but also indicates that she had a responsive Christian public who welcomed the style and content of her writing, which filled a need and reflected the concerns and desires of her readers.

One of the difficulties for modern readers when encountering Marianne's work is a feature which endeared her to her contemporaries, as recorded in an account of her literary work written in a local Northampton paper after her death by 'an admiring reader': 'All her works were written with a moral object, and have had considerable vogue. Her tales have a simple, homely pathos, and the lessons they teach are couched in wholesome language. Her verse is distinguished by its sincerity and its fervent religious tone.'[17] Her novels, too, were evidently written with a religious agenda. Although she regarded *Jane Eyre* as the ideal of fictional writing to be aspired to, her novels are very different from that masterpiece, having a laboured moral and a stilted style.[18] The former, however, was both common and acceptable at the time: indeed, it was the presence of such an element in a book which helped to make it acceptable in Nonconformist circles.[19] The popular Methodist author Silas

---

[12] J. C. Carlile, 'Marianne Farningham The Woman and her work', *Freeman and Baptist Times* 26 March 1909

[13] R. Mitchell, 'Hearn, Mary Ann (Marianne Farningham) (1834-1909)', *Oxford Dictionary of National Biography* (Oxford: Oxford University Press, 2004), www.oxforddnb.com/view/article/33789, accessed 4 July 2005.

[14] P. Morton, 'Marianne Farningham and her Work' in the *Baptist Monthly*, 1899, pp. 6-7.

[15] Rev. W. Glandwr-Morgan, *Marianne Farningham in her Welsh Home* (Birmingham: Ellesmere Press 1923 [first edition James Clarke 1909]), Chapter 1 (there are no page numbers).

[16] Glandwr-Morgan, *Welsh Home*, Chapter 2.

[17] *Northampton Daily Chronicle* 16 March 1909.

[18] Farningham, *Life*, p. 71.

[19] D.W. Bebbington, *The Dominance of Evangelicalism* (Leicester: IVP, 2005), p. 223.

Hocking, also unknown now but at one stage reportedly the most popular novelist in England, was equally didactic.[20] Emma Worboise similarly had moral points to make, as did Charlotte Yonge for a high church readership.[21] Having a clear moral purpose was likely to make Marianne's writing more popular with an evangelical readership, and in her own lifetime her writing was much appreciated. Nineteenth-century style was frequently more sentimental than we are comfortable with today, and Marianne's writing also illustrates this trend. Her work, initially composed for the weekly deadlines of the *Christian World* and the *Sunday School Times*, was then later issued as collections. *Girlhood*, for instance, was produced in this way.[22] Written with her Northampton class in mind, it became Marianne's most successful book, running to several editions and many thousands of copies. According to her own figures, when the new edition of *Girlhood* was produced in 1895, a total of 25,000 copies was printed.[23] *Boyhood* and *Home Life* were also first composed as a series of articles in the same paper. Through both the magazine and these collections of articles, Marianne's opinions reached a wide audience. One can see why she considered her work to be in the public domain.

More accurate than contemporary evaluations is the recent assessment of Greenall who has suggested that Marianne's writing was 'of no great literary or lasting merit... and rather dated'.[24] One might make exceptions for some of her later poetry and for her autobiography, but it has to be conceded that he has a point. Marianne was not an outstanding writer. She was aware of her own limitations, however, commenting in 1907 that 'it has never been in my power... to become a good writer of hymns, or a novelist'.[25] Accused by a publisher of having no style, she readily admitted it, whilst wishing she was more accomplished.[26] One could reply to Greenall that it was in her autobiography, finally, that Marianne found her own voice and the greatest freedom, with a highly readable, informative and amusing style. Perhaps this was because in writing it she was freed of all obligation to provide a moral, indicate a desirable course of action, or encourage a commitment to Christ (although there were a few pointers in that direction). Instead she was

---

[20] R.G. Burnett, 'Hocking, Silas Kitto (1850–1935)', *Oxford Dictionary of National Biography*, (Oxford: Oxford University Press, 2004), http://www.oxforddnb.com/view/article/33912, accessed 4 Aug 2006. See for instance S. K. Hocking, *Where Duty Lies* (London: Warne & Co, 1892) p. 345, when the protagonist discovered that fame was 'empty and unsatisfying'.

[21] See for instance C.M. Yonge, *The Heir of Redclyffe* (London: Macmillan, 1864), E. Worboise, *Evelyn's Story or Labour and Wait* (London: Hutchinson, 1864).

[22] See also Chapter 4, p. 108.

[23] Farningham, *Life*, p. 114.

[24] R.L. Greenall, Review of S.B. Black, *A Farningham Childhood* in *Northamptonshire Past and Present*, Vol 8 1989-90 No 1 p. 90.

[25] Farningham, *Life*, p. 202.

[26] Farningham, *Life*, p. 202.

concerned primarily with telling her story, re-imagining her past and justifying her own life, and the task proved a rewarding one.

Tastes in literature, including popular religious literature, change quickly and Marianne's writing has proved to be largely ephemeral. There are only occasional survivals of her verses in modern collections. One such is in an anthology of Northamptonshire poets, which alongside such noteworthy lyricists as John Clare and John Dryden, and lesser known but popular writers such as Felicia Hemans, has a galaxy of unknowns. To represent Marianne's poetry, Trevor Hold chose 'Geve Thanks to God Alwaeys' from the 1903 collection, *Harvest Gleanings*, suggesting that this was 'one of her more successful "serious" poems', a judgement which could be questioned.[27] Within a few decades of her death, her writing had lost its popularity.

During her lifetime, however, and for several years after her death, there seems to have been no shortage of people to praise her writing. An advertisement dated shortly after Marianne's death in 1909, for a new volume of her poetry, *Lyrics of the Soul,* which was for sale for the sum of 2s 6d, declared that it was 'her best volume of poetry yet' demonstrating 'a great gift of spontaneity'.[28] There is something in this judgement, as the collection does demonstrate a maturity, simplicity, and comparative lack of sentimentality compared to some of her earlier work. The advertisement also stated that her 'name is a household word in countless homes, where she is known and loved as a "sweet singer" on religious themes', and, quoting the *Westminster Gazette,* claimed that 'her messages of hope and spiritual consolation have brought much comfort to readers all over the world'.[29] There is some truth behind these claims, but even if slightly exaggerated, they are in themselves an indication that Marianne was both reflecting and shaping popular Nonconformist spirituality through her verses. This serves to emphasise the point that, for the purpose of this work, the main interest of her poetry is not literary, but as a historical source.

The Shortcomings of Journalism

It needs to be remembered too when reading her poetry, prose and fiction, that Marianne was primarily a journalist, writing not for posterity, but for weekly deadlines. The transient nature of journalism has contributed to her writings being largely forgotten, as much was written in a hurry. An account of her lecture on 'The Rush and Hush of Life' in 1881 noted her observation that because life was so busy, and 'the age was a tyrannical taskmaster' people

---

[27] T. Hold, ed., *A Northamptonshire Garland: An Anthology of Northamptonshire poets with Biographical Notes* (Northampton: Northamptonshire Libraries, 1989), p.79. M. Farningham, *Harvest Gleanings,* (London: James Clarke, 1903), p. 143.
[28] *SST* 1 January 1909.
[29] Advertisement in *SST* 1 January, 1909.

'worked far too rapidly to work perfectly'.[30] This also applied to Marianne herself in that her output was copious but the quality of her work extremely variable. In her favour, it has to be said that she was aware of this danger, commenting on 'mistakes that appear in print and have gone north, south, east and west, whence they can never be recalled'.[31] Her longer works were also subject to such flaws, especially the 'biography' of the heroine Grace Darling, as will be further explored below. She commented herself that she was very busy during this period, and that 'no doubt I was, then and always, doing too much to do it well'.[32] Marianne was an enterprising writer with a large capacity, but she was not always thorough in her research. In essence, she remained journalistic in her approach even when composing full-length books.

Her non-fiction prose ranged from pieces celebrating nature, or recounting travels, to series on a particular theme, which were later published as collections. Some of these pieces were light and superficial, whilst others dealt with more serious subjects. In her first short collection, *Life Sketches*, published in 1861, one of the lighter pieces is one written in praise of having a cup of tea at the end of the day. As the tea is drunk 'the day's accumulated bitterness melts away... It deserves to be ranked not among our smallest blessings'.[33] All, however, are didactic to some extent, as Marianne felt the need to finish with a worthy comment. The evangelical readership of the *Christian World,* like other readers, welcomed variety in their reading material, but it seems that everything needed a moral or at least a spiritual focus. In the case of the cup of tea, she was struggling to find something. All she could come up with was a wish that 'kind sentences and loving actions spring from its influences! And may "all malice, and all guile, and hypocrisies, and envies, and all evil speaking" be drowned in the tea-cup!'[34] Usually, however, her topics leant themselves more easily to a moral point or a spiritual analogy, particularly if she was describing an aspect of nature or paraphrasing a Bible story. From the account of Jesus stilling the storm in John 6:17 she drew the lesson that 'He is strong to save to-day',[35] and some years later she used the story of the woman at the well in John 4 to encourage personal evangelism, concluding 'Today I will tell someone. Lord, help me.'[36] On a different tack, she employed the story of David and Abigail[37] to stress the importance of women being peacemakers: 'In every home she is needed; in many churches and societies the opportunity is given.'[38]

---

[30] *Salisbury and Winchester Journal* 19 February 1881, p. 8.
[31] *SST* 9 January 1885.
[32] Farningham, *Life*, pp. 133-34.
[33] M. Farningham *Life Sketches* (1st series, London: James Clarke, 1861), p. 53.
[34] Farningham, *Sketches,* p. 54.
[35] M. Farningham, *In Evening Lights* (London: James Clarke & Co, 1897), p. 41.
[36] M. Farningham, *Women and their Saviour: Thoughts of a minute for a month of mornings* (London: James Clarke, 1904), p. 35.
[37] 1 Samuel 25.
[38] Farningham, *Women and Work,* pp. 87-90.

She also used Scriptural passages to emphasise many of her beliefs, ranging from standard evangelical doctrine to the role of women.[39] Yet she could draw the reader into scenes in which she portrays Christ as a genuine friend: hers was not a religion of morality but of a living relationship. Some of her compositions however, her later poetry in particular and her masterful autobiography, arguably her best piece of writing, can still call forth a positive response from the modern reader, and all of it illuminates her contemporary world, especially the Nonconformist milieu, as this book is seeking to demonstrate. A study of her most popular hymns also sheds light on the age she lived in, and her work as 'Eva Hope' complements in an interesting manner the rest of her writing.

Hymns

Following Marianne's death, a local Northampton newspaper claimed that her hymns were 'deservedly popular' and that they were sung in many countries 'with heart-inspiring fervour and devotion'. Whilst recognising that Marianne did not aspire to be a great poet, the piece declared that 'her verses embodied the feelings and needs of millions'.[40] Whilst this writer was probably guilty of exaggeration, even the fact he could contemplate such a claim indicates something of her popularity within Nonconformist circles, and thus her significance for this study. From quite early on in her career, Marianne was in demand as a writer of hymns and poems for special occasions. Several of these were connected in some way with the Sunday school movement. For instance, the annual conference of Sunday school teachers, which was held in Northampton on Good Friday, April 15 1870, opened with an appropriate hymn penned by Marianne. It asked for help from God for the 'band of workers' meeting together, who 'fain would feed Thy lambs', finishing with the cry

> Take fear, and sloth, and sin away;
> Let faith, and zeal, and love increase
> And give us, Lord, Thy light today![41]

In the days when Northants Sunday School Union held an annual Eastertide service in the Corn Exchange, Northampton, Marianne inevitably wrote a hymn for the occasion.[42] She was also regarded, as Evans has pointed out, as 'something of an authority on hymns' as in 1870 she headed the list of a Committee appointed by College Street Sunday School to 'arrange the hymns and select appropriate tunes'.[43] Her expertise in this area was recognised by

---

[39] See, for example, Chapter 3, p.76 and Chapter 6, p. 189.
[40] *Northampton Daily Chronicle* 16 March 1909.
[41] Programme of Meetings at the Annual Conference of Sunday School Teachers, 1870.
[42] *Northampton Daily Chronicle* 16 March 1909.
[43] College Street Baptist Chapel Sunday School Minute Book, 18 July 1870, p. 36, quoted in B. Evans, 'Marianne Farningham (1834-1909): Aspects of the Life of a Victorian Woman', (MA dissertation, University of Leicester, 1994).

those around her.

Her hymns and poems were not used only for Sunday school events, but for weddings, anniversaries and other special occasions. Her verse was certainly plentiful: she produced thousands of poems and prose pieces for the *Christian World* and *Sunday School Times*. The quality of her work no doubt suffered from being produced at such a rate, as Rosemary Mitchell has commented, making the realistic assessment that Marianne's 'verse was too plentiful to be uniformly good'.[44] Yet it remained in demand throughout her life. At least twice during the 1860s the yearly bill of mortality for a Northampton parish included, underneath the figures of people buried and baptised, a short poem by Marianne, a different one each time.[45] In 1871 a wedding service included one of her hymns,[46] whilst in 1897 she wrote a hymn for the Bicentenary of College Street Baptist Chapel, which began 'For centuries of blessing given'. A few years later she composed a hymn specially for the 1905 Baptist Union Assembly, which was inserted with her photograph in the Official Handbook, along with another of her hymns used in that year's Assembly.[47] Her verses spanned over half a century of Baptist life.

There is no sure way of knowing how often her hymns were actually used, or which ones were most sung, although the length of their endurance in hymn books is a good indication A volume written by Henry S. Burrage in 1883 on the topic of *Baptist Hymn Writers and their Hymns* includes a reference to Marianne.[48] At that stage, the most popular of her hymns was 'Waiting and watching for me', originally published in the *Christian World* in 1864, then included in *Poems* the following year. Introducing it, the author explained that the hymn was built on an 'old tradition (which) says that those whom we have served on earth shall be the first to welcome us to heaven'.[49] Its heart was the refrain 'Will any one stand at the Beautiful Gate/ Watching and waiting for me?' The first verse originally started with the rather weak 'When mysterious whispers are floating about' but for the hymn's inclusion in Sankey's *Sacred Songs and Solos* this was changed to the more satisfactory 'When my final farewell to the world I have said', and the final verse was removed. The basic sentiment remained the same. Marianne later commented that these verses were dashed off quickly when she was in a rush to meet her weekly deadline. If she had known how popular they were going to be, she would have spent 'half a

---

[44] Mitchell, 'Marianne Farningham', *Oxford Dictionary of National Biography*, www.oxforddnb.com/view/article/33789, accessed 4 July 2005.
[45] Northampton Yearly Bill of Mortality, (Northampton: Taylor & Son), 1866-67 and 1869-70.
[46] 'To Mr & Mrs James Gillitt, July 25th, 1871'.
[47] Baptist Union Official Handbook of the Autumnal Assembly, 1905.
[48] H.S. Burrage, *Baptist Hymn Writers and their Hymns*, (Portland, Maine: Brown, Thurston & Company, 1888), p. 206.
[49] M. Farningham, *Poems*, (London: James Clarke & Co, 1866) p. 33.

day instead of half an hour' on them and then 'they might perhaps have been more worthy of the career of usefulness and blessing accorded to them'.[50] Marianne was well aware that her verses were often lacking in polish. In 1892, when the revised Dictionary of Hymnology was published, these were still her most well-known verses,[51] as they were in 1898 when William Hearne of Missouri compiled a history of the Hearne family. His introduction to Marianne assumed that his American readers were familiar with this hymn, as he merely stated 'She is the Author of the hymn "Waiting and Watching for me" '.[52] Writing her contribution for this history, Marianne pointed out that many of her poems beside this one had been published in America.[53] This provides evidence for the claim of the advertisement mentioned earlier, that her writing was known overseas as well as in England. Indeed, inclusion in Sankey's collection, used as far away as Australia, would have immediately given her a large world-wide audience.[54]

Yet compared to those of contemporaries such as Mrs Alexander and Frances Ridley Havergal, Marianne's hymns have not, on the whole, stood the test of time, being for the most part too sentimental for modern tastes. Phrases such as 'in this vale of tears' (Anywhere with Jesus) or couplets like 'Let me play about Thy feet, Let me hear Thy whispers sweet' (Let the Children Come) have quickly dated. Even in her own day, with hymns being just one of her many creative outlets, she could not compare for quality, quantity or popularity with other female hymn writers. Julian mentions a total of just four of her hymns in common use in the late nineteenth century, two of them being hymns for children, and all written comparatively early in Marianne's career. In addition to 'Watching and waiting for me', he lists 'Hail the children's festal day', first published in the *Sunday School Times* in 1875, which was intended for Sunday school anniversaries, another hymn for children, 'Let the children come, Christ said'(1877), which was a rather over-sentimentalised hymn based on the saying of Jesus according to Matthew 'Suffer the little children to come unto me', and 'Father, who givest us now the new year', written in 1878. During the first world war, in a Congregationalist church in Birmingham, the young people were still singing 'Anywhere with Jesus' and another which proved to be the most resilient of her compositions.[55] This was 'Just as I am', not the more famous hymn of that name, although it is possible, as Trevor Hold

---

[50] Farningham, *Life*, p. 140.
[51] J. Julian, *A Dictionary of Hymnology*, (London: John Murray, 1892 [2nd edition 1908]), p. 502.
[52] W.T. Hearne, *Brief History and Genealogy of the Hearne Family*, 1907, Examiner Printing Company, Independence, Missouri, 'Mary Ann Hearn'
 http://www.cragun.com/brian/hearne/history/hh800m.html, accessed 12/02/2006.
[53] Hearne, 'Mary Ann Hearn', *Brief History*.
[54] Bebbington, *Dominance*, p. 89.
[55] Glandwr-Morgan, *Welsh Home*, Chapter 10.

suggests, that it was a conscious imitation of Charlotte Eliot's more famous verses.[56] Eliot's hymn was significant for Marianne,[57] and this one deals with a similar topic of consecration and surrender to God, and was suitable for both adults and children. It is the only hymn by Marianne which can still be found in some collections today, yet it was not mentioned by Julian, even in the revised edition of 1925. It has an attractive simplicity, and is free from the more obvious sentimentality which made many of her hymns outdated a couple of decades into the twentieth century.

> Just as I am, Thine own to be
> Friend of the young who lovest me
> To consecrate myself to Thee
> O Jesus Christ, I come.

This hymn can be found in collections as varied as the Children's Special Service Mission's (CSSM) *Golden Bells*, a selection for School Worship produced by the Congregational Union in 1926, the 1933 Methodist Hymn Book, 1964 Hymns of Faith, Redemption Hymnal and on various web sites. It was even given a new arrangement as late as 1961 by the composer William Lloyd Webber.[58] It was rare that one of her hymns was used in the Church of England, but in 1898 this was adapted as an Anglican confirmation hymn. The bishop of Truro had apparently written to Marianne saying he hoped to use it in his diocese. A local paper, the *Northampton Reporter*, was amused by this, and commented on the irony of a local Nonconformist writer producing a confirmation hymn.[59] Evans recalled that it was still in use for this purpose in the 1950s.[60] Whilst one or two other verses can still be found with difficulty, this hymn is the only one of Marianne's compositions to have been regularly sung in the century following her death.

It is reported that R.W. Dale, the Birmingham Congregationalist minister, once said 'Let me write the hymns of a Church and I care not who writes the theology'.[61] Marianne produced a lot of hymns in her time, and would, therefore, have influenced many people's theology. At the time of the Centenary of College Street Sunday School, it was noted that 'Her hymns sung at the Easter gatherings in the Corn Exchange, and at other anniversaries, have

---

[56] T. Hold, *A Northamptonshire Garland: An Anthology of Northamptonshire Poets with Biographical Notes* (Northampton: Northamptonshire Libraries, 1989) p. 78-79.
[57] Farningham, *Life,* p. 142.
[58] W. Lloyd Webber, *Just as I am Thine own to be, Hymn Anthem for Unison voices and SATB* (London: Novello & Co, 1961).
[59] *Northampton Reporter* 12 April 1898.
[60] Evans, 'Marianne Farningham', p. 36.
[61] Quoted in L.E. Elliott-Binns, *Religion in the Victorian Era* (London: Lutterworth Press, 1934 [1964]), p. 374.

never been forgotten, but linger in the memory and stir the heart'.[62] Marianne's hymns may not have generally stood the test of time, but they were influential during her lifetime. For the most part, apart from the occasional quirk, they expressed traditional evangelical beliefs, with any divergences indicated by what was omitted rather than by what was said: for instance, concerning her beliefs in the afterlife, as explored in the next chapter. She primarily wrote, in any case, to encourage and inspire, not to be controversial. She took pleasure in believing, from the responses she received and the comments people made to her when she travelled, that her writing most appealed to the working-classes, but it is not possible to gauge the reality of that assumption.[63] It is true to say, however, that her writing under the name of Eva Hope, gave much more scope for the expression of more unusual ideas, alongside many commonplace attitudes and platitudes.

Eva Hope

Marianne Farningham was so much a part of Mary Ann Hearn that the two were indistinguishable at times. From an early stage, she signed herself in private Marianne F Hearn on at least one occasion, and she became known locally by that longer name of Marianne Farningham Hearn.[64] Possibly, as Evans suggests, in adopting that name as herself she was indicating that she had moved on from the ignorant country girl that she had been, and was now a professional woman[65] In using the second pseudonym of Eva Hope, however, whilst the origin of the name was clearly a question of convenience, there was opportunity for a little more distance between the persona of the writer and Marianne herself. Or, perhaps it might be truer to say, this pseudonym allowed her to express personal opinions which she would have felt reluctant to air so clearly in print under her better known pen name which was much more publicly connected with her own self. Hence, as Chapter 3 has demonstrated, she was able to discuss the role of women in her biography of Grace Darling, with a frankness found rarely in her other printed work. One has to allow that it might have been merely the subject and the opportunity, and if she had written that book as Marianne Farningham she might have written the same words: unfortunately this can never be known. The books written as Eva Hope, however, are interesting in themselves as a distinctive and influential section of Marianne's output.

A didactic flavour was still evident in this work but unlike in her hymns, and

---

[62] Souvenir of the Centenary of College Street Sunday School Northampton 1810-1910, p. 35.
[63] Farningham, *Life*, p. 269.
[64] Writing to 'Pollie' in 1863 she signed herself Marianne F. Hearn, although the two later letters were signed merely Marianne Hearn.
[65] Evans, 'Marianne Farningham', p. 68.

more than in much of her writing as Marianne Farningham, it is possible to discover in these books elements that appear subversive of contemporary attitudes. These were mainly biographies, although she also edited some books of poetry. Her biographical subjects ranged from Grace Darling to General Gordon, from Charles Spurgeon to Queen Victoria, and are rather obviously evangelical journalism writ large. She recalled the work as being enjoyable and easy. She appreciated the atmosphere in the British Library reading room where she did her research and noted that the work 'was not a great mental strain...I had only to select facts and describe them in my own language'.[66] This simplistic comment reveals that she never thought to question or analyse her sources. The quality of these biographies, as a result, was extremely variable. They were not works of thorough research or careful composition, but were intended to be popular, having a didactic purpose and aiming to inspire a response. In her first biography, of Grace Darling, first published in 1875, Marianne commented that 'it would be of little use either to write or read any biography or record of deeds and lives, unless some good lessons could be learnt from the same'.[67] In this instance, she expected that the 'lessons' would primarily be of use to 'members of her own sex'. When composing the life of the popular Baptist preacher C. H. Spurgeon, she had a similar aim, this time directed at young men. Her stated intention was to 'show what a fine example to young men Spurgeon presents'.[68] These biographies were evidently aimed at young people rather than adults and the role models presented were often, but not exclusively, gender-specific. For Marianne, the purpose of writing biography was to provide inspiration for her readers through presenting men and women whose lives were worthy of imitation.

In writing with this aim, her accounts fall in a tradition of inspirational Christian biography. Such lives have been constructed as examples since the days when Athanasius wrote his Life of Anthony and inspired generations of monks. Whether written as hagiography, or in a more gritty and truthful style, the aim of such accounts has often been to portray a life that is worth imitating. Even today, in a time when biography is often more about uncovering scandal than recording good character, popular Christian biography serves the purpose of inspiring and encouraging its readers, and this was certainly the case in the nineteenth century. Biography contributed to popular spirituality during this period.

Grace Darling, Marianne's first attempt at writing biography 'had a very large sale, both at the time and afterwards'.[69] The success of this book led to a series of others on a wide range of subjects including Queen Victoria and General Gordon as well as two books containing shorter lives, *New World*

---

[66] Farningham, *Life*, p. 134.
[67] E. Hope, *Life of Grace Darling* (London, Walter Scott & Co, 1875), p. 293.
[68] E. Hope, *Spurgeon The People's Preacher* (Kilmarnock: John Richie, nd) p. 10.
[69] Farningham, *Life*, p. 132

Heroes and *Queens of Literature*. Marianne had added a second career to that of journalist. Fitting this task into her already full life, however, proved problematic, and as indicated above, the quality of her work could suffer. This was certainly the case with her life of Grace Darling, which was far from accurate. Armstrong, who did not know the author's real identity, referring to her as 'Mrs Hope', labelled the work as 'bad beyond belief'.[70] He noted that it was largely based on an 1839 biography by Jerrold Vernon which the latter had privately acknowledged contained a large amount of fiction.[71] Undoubtedly Marianne's composition barely qualifies as a biography, although the author considered it to be one, apparently remaining ignorant of the many factual errors it contained which ranged from the actual geography of the Farne Islands to the details of Grace's life and family.[72] The book was filled out with chapters on other subjects, such as the history of Northumberland, descriptions of various lighthouses, and accounts of assorted shipwrecks. The close similarity between her style, and that of her various prose stories, especially when describing conversations, also supports the probability that much of the book was largely the product of her imagination. Yet Marianne's 'biography' ran through several editions, becoming, according to Armstrong, accepted by the world 'as the last word, authoritative and indisputable, on the "girl with the wind-blown hair" '.[73] It is still the most easily available of her works and can be found in various forms and combinations: a search of second-hand bookshops on the internet easily found forty copies of the *Life of Grace Darling*. This work was popular despite its limitations as history. There are also signs of carelessness and cutting corners in Farningham's other biographies: for instance in that of Spurgeon some passages were repeated (although that could be a printing error), whilst in the account of Stanley whole pages at a time were copied from other sources. The pressure that her books appear to have been written under was detrimental to their quality and accuracy. Marianne was not a perfectionist, not someone who worked thoroughly, and she never learnt the basics of thorough primary research.

Marianne's stated aim was to record lives from which 'good lessons' could be learnt, but what kind of good lessons did she have in mind? Armstrong complained in a rather jaundiced way that her moralistic tone was almost unbearable:

---

[70] R. Armstrong, *Grace Darling: Maid and Myth* (London: J. M. Dent & Sons, 1965), p 10.

[71] Armstrong, *Maid and Myth,* p. 180.

[72] For instance, Grace's date of birth and the name of her father were both incorrect.

[73] Armstrong, *Maid and Myth,* p. 10.

She moralises with dreary, sickly sweetness and prodigious pomp on every page, and reading her has a great deal in common with wearing a hair-shirt and eating boiled fish in Lent.[74]

This is a little unfair, in that the aspects considered worthy of imitation are not all as conventional as one might suppose, especially where the women were concerned. Her portrayal of Grace Darling, for instance, emphasises an interesting mixture of attributes, as Chapter 3 has indicated. It included ones which might be expected from a Victorian evangelical: an emphasis on duty to parents, feminine accomplishments, and the role of faith. Darling was portrayed as loving her home, preferring it to the excitement of society, yet at the same time she was able to take initiative and was physically strong and healthy.[75] This desire to provoke imitation of lives which are to some degree unconventional is even more evident in Marianne's selection for *Queens of Literature*, reprinted as *Great Modern Women*, first published in 1886. Her choices demonstrate that she aimed to encourage women to imitate a wide range of activities. In this book she described and commented on the lives of Mary Somerville, Harriet Martineau, Elizabeth Barrett Browning, Charlotte Bronte, George Eliot and Felicia Hemans, all women at the forefront of their field. Once again, she insisted on their love of domesticity, but also stressed the ways in which they broke new ground for women.

The lessons she hoped readers would learn from her brief life of Mary Somerville are particularly interesting. As with Darling, she highlighted conventional female accomplishments as well as different, almost subversive aspects of the subject's life. She stressed Somerville's especially feminine attributes, quoting one contemporary who emphasised her modesty, commenting that it 'takes off all the dread of her superior scientific learning'.[76] Marianne portrayed her as fulfilling her role as a mother by being sympathetic to her children, and as a hostess by allowing people to interrupt her while she was working. Yet most of the space in this brief life, as one might expect, is taken up with an explanation of Somerville's intellectual accomplishments. Marianne outlined her life and publications and from this catalogue of achievements drew an important lesson which she wanted her readers to remember, namely that women are just as capable intellectually as men. Today's women who have BScs, she asserted, 'owe much to this pioneer heroine, who went before them where hitherto no foot of woman had ventured to tread, and who demolished, once for all, the idea that a woman's brain is less strong than that of a man's'.[77] She finished her mini-biography by insisting that 'Honest endeavour is certain to be rewarded by some success; and those who

---

[74] Armstrong, *Maid and Myth*, p. 7.
[75] Hope, *Grace Darling*, p. 152, p. 275, p. 56.
[76] E. Hope, *Queens of Literature* (London: Walter Scott & Co, 1886), p. 18.
[77] Hope, *Queens*, p. 3.

love their work better than they love themselves are the most likely to win and wear the laurel-wreath of fame'.[78] This last sentence could equally well be a comment on her own life: perhaps, indeed, it was just that. These biographies are an interesting mix of the conventional and unconventional, and were also the source of a useful extra income.

Writing Male Lives

Valerie Sanders makes the interesting observation that feminist literary criticism has been more concerned with how women have been represented by men, rather than vice versa.[79] It is interesting, therefore, to consider the way in which Marianne represented the men she chose as biographical subjects. These lives, intended for young men to emulate, were with the exception of Spurgeon, characterised as 'heroes'. At one point in the narrative of General Gordon's life (published in 1901) she listed the qualities 'out of which all heroes are made': singleness of purpose; diligence and self-help; a strong common sense; kindness and love to others, and godliness.[80] 'Diligence' included for Marianne both a sense of duty and the desire to be active. Thus a desire for usefulness was commended in the young Spurgeon,[81] and Gordon's preference for action over inaction was regarded approvingly, when he wrote 'I prefer life amidst sorrows, if those sorrows are inevitable, to a life spent in inaction'.[82] This was not just a male characteristic, however: both her biographies and her journalistic writing reveal that, although she believed in the importance of leisure, Marianne had a strong view about the necessity of work, whether paid or unpaid, as the primary way of serving God. The activism which Bebbington sees as one of the four main characteristics of evangelicalism was clearly part of Farningham's consciousness.[83]

It is interesting that Marianne wrote male biographies at all. As Sanders has remarked, writing about Mrs Oliphant, it was rare in the nineteenth century for women to compose accounts of men's lives: 'Biography was still essentially a male preserve when Oliphant was writing'.[84] The first Dictionary of National Biography had only four or five female contributors to each volume, and most female biographers wrote about women, or about men who were long dead, or

---

[78] Hope, *Queens*, p. 21.

[79] V. Sanders, 'Women writing men's lives: Margaret Oliphant's dethroned kings' in M. Hewitt, ed, *Representing Victorian Lives* (Leeds: Leeds Centre for Victorian Studies, 1999), p. 64.

[80] E. Hope, *Life of General Gordon* (London: Walter Scott & Co, 1901), p. 362.

[81] Hope, *Spurgeon*, p. 24.

[82] Hope, *Gordon*, p. 172.

[83] D.W. Bebbington, *Evangelicalism in Modern Britain* (London: Unwin Hymen, 1989), pp. 3-17. See also Chapter 6, p. 230.

[84] Sanders, 'Women writing', p. 63- 88, p. 64-65.

else biographies of their fathers or husbands, and Oliphant, writing between 1862 and 1891, had no role models to follow in writing about men.[85] As Marianne's male biographies were written in a similar period, this also applied to her. The similarity, however, stopped there. All Oliphant's subjects were, in Sanders' words, 'gullible, erratic, but brilliant',[86] whilst for Marianne it was important that men were strong, caring, and able to take initiative. The impression is that Oliphant was presenting flawed men, reflecting something of her own unfortunate experience, whilst Marianne was attempting to create heroes. Thus she remarked of Stanley that he was 'good as well as great, kind as well as strong',[87] whilst Spurgeon's talks to the Annual Conference at his college were described as containing 'fire and energy... tempered by the tenderest, most father-like love' for those listening.[88] Tenderness was unashamedly a male attribute in this biographer's eyes. She also admired men who were unaffected by fame or fortune, but maintained a sense of humility in either situation. Thus she repeated a remark made of President Lincoln that although he was weighed down with responsibilities, he was unaware of distinction or power: 'under all circumstances he was precisely the same – plain, unostentatious, truth-loving, pure and good'. Likewise, when Gordon found himself in Gravesend from 1865-71 after his escapades in China, he adapted himself easily, according to Marianne, to a different type of life.[89] It is interesting that the characteristics she looked for in men were often a more forceful version of those for women. Women's lives should be centred on domesticity in a way that men's were not, and she emphasised duty to parents more in her women's lives, but apart from that the characteristics were similar: duty, an obligation to find useful work, strength and determination, and gentler aspects such as tenderness, compassion, and care for the poor. Above all, they should share the same faith, and it was this faith that the author hoped her readers would be stirred to emulate.

In her male, as in her female biographies, Marianne emphasised the faith of her subjects. So because there was some doubt about Lincoln's exact beliefs, she cited a quotation in which he referred to God, and then told a tale of him addressing some Sunday school children, 'which gives additional evidence that his heart was right'.[90] Marianne was in many ways a Romantic, more concerned with a person's heart than the exact orthodoxy of their doctrine.[91] She explained that Gordon had various problems, such as being alone in his responsibility in China, as at times neither the English nor Chinese governments were

---

[85] Sanders, 'Women writing', p. 65.
[86] Sanders, 'Women writing', p. 66.
[87] E. Hope *Stanley and Africa* (London: Walter Scott, 1890), p. 4.
[88] Hope, *Spurgeon*, p. 116.
[89] Hope, *Gordon*, p. 116.
[90] Eva Hope, *New World Heroes* (London: Walter Scott, 1893), p. 69.
[91] See Chapter 6, p. 174.

sympathetic towards him, but throughout it all he 'never forgot whose servant he was. He was in himself an illustration of the truth that the Christian is the highest type of man. Because he served God he served his fellows also.'[92] Faith was a vital part of the lives to be imitated, just as it was the bedrock of Marianne's own life.

Marianne clearly constructed these lives for a purpose, choosing her material accordingly. Whilst some of the attributes she wished people to emulate were gender-specific, not all are. Women should be obedient and submissive as well as independent and innovative: not an easy combination. Men should, like women, be hard-working and dutiful, and also tender and compassionate. But all should be fuelled and inspired by faith, and have a sense of their own relationship with God. Her admiration for women who pioneered in areas such as education and medicine led her to stretch a point more than a little concerning their religious commitment. Her accounts were at times inaccurate, hurried, and sentimental. It appears that at the time they had a wide readership. Presumably some of her readers learnt 'good lessons' from reading these biographies, and we gain from them further understanding of an evangelical approach to biography and, indeed, to life.

The *Sunday School Times*

Another way that Marianne contributed to contemporary evangelical culture, and in particular the perpetuation of Sunday schools, was through her involvement with the *Sunday School Times and Home Educator*. Her writing in the *Times* helped to nurture, encourage and shape teachers long before 1885, when she took over the editorship. The first edition of this weekly was produced on Friday, January 6, 1860, as a small magazine with eight pages, selling for a halfpenny. It was described later as 'a cheap little paper... an acceptable visitor in the homes of the people and a sympathetic helper of Sunday-school Teachers and scholars'.[93] As in the case of the *Christian World*, the idea originated with Jonathan Whittemore. According to Marianne, Whittemore had a genuine desire to encourage the work of Sunday schools. Whilst there were other Sunday school magazines, Whittemore had spotted a niche in the market which the Sunday School Union had not yet filled. Apparently many of his friends thought that selling it at such an unusually low cover price would ruin him, but the gamble paid off and the paper was a great success.[94] Marianne helped to shape it from the beginning, and was involved in long discussions with Whittemore about the magazine's production. She contributed ideas for the title format and the design for the block which headed the front page, as well as suggestions for the content. She was encouraged by

---

[92] Hope, *Gordon*, p. 100.
[93] *SST* 2 January 1885 (Marianne's editorial address).
[94] Farningham, *Life*, p.101.

Whittemore to become a regular contributor,[95] which she did, also involving a friend, Miss Gordge, later Mrs Euren, who wrote a column with suggestions for lessons. (This was the woman whose invitation led to Marianne's move to Northampton.) Other contributions included articles by Emma Jane Worboise, various serials in instalments, and both prose and poetic contributions from Marianne herself. It was a varied and moderately successful formula.

Careful advance publicity was aimed at ministers and Sunday school Superintendents, so that when the paper arrived, Marianne suggested, 'it was at once felt by thousands to be a boon' and was welcomed 'as a true friend' in both large towns and little villages.[96] Evidence that this popularity was real, and not just the opinion of one very much involved in the project, is that the circulation reached 25,000 in the first year of publication. Unfortunately, Jonathan Whittemore died during that initial year, and never lived to see the continuing success of the paper he had launched. James Clarke followed him as publisher of both the *Sunday School Times* and the *Christian World*, and built on the promising beginnings. Marianne later commented that not only did the paper 'at once made room for itself in the crowded world of literature' but over the years it managed 'to grow in favour and gain in power and influence'.[97] It undoubtedly filled a gap in the market. As has been noted earlier, much of Marianne's writing which was later published in book form first appeared as weekly offerings in the *Sunday School Times*. Her writing helped to nurture, encourage and shape teachers and the way they taught long before 1885, when she took over the editorship of the *Times*.

Where James Clarke pioneered, other publishers followed, and a few years later, in 1874, the *Sunday School Chronicle* joined the fray. The *Chronicle* became the better known of the two papers, eventually absorbing its rival in 1925, by which time the market no longer existed for two such publications. Cliff only sees fit to mention the launch of the *Chronicle* in his history of the Schools, despite the earlier starting date of the *Times* and its significant circulation.[98] One of the Chronicle's regular contributors, Jennie Street, was a good friend of Marianne's. On Marianne's appointment as editor, the editor of the rival *Sunday School Chronicle*, Benjamin Clarke, was apparently the first to write and welcome her |'into the ranks of those whom I had afar off regarded as kings – the worshipful Company of editors'.[99] Both papers were concerned for the promotion of the Sunday school cause, and both editors frequently attended Sunday School Union events. After Marianne's death, the editor of the *Chronicle* claimed:

---

[95] Farningham, *Life*, p.100.
[96] Farningham, *Life*, p.103.
[97] *SST* 2 January, 1885.
[98] P.B. Cliff, *The Rise and Development of the Sunday School Movement in England 1720-1980* (Nutfield, Surrey: National Christian Education Council, 1986), p. 170.
[99] Farningham, *Life*, p. 195.

it is to the honour of proprietors and editor alike that from that time to the day of her death their mutual relations were of the happiest character..... . The two papers have had no rivalry except in the desire to serve most fully the teachers of the land, and we cordially recognise the services rendered to the schools for nearly fifty years by our contemporary, particularly in the villages.[100]

Indeed, throughout her time as editor, Marianne regarded her relationship with the editor of the *Chronicle* as being 'in some senses rivals', yet 'in every sense friends'.[101] If this seems contradictory, it does demonstrate Marianne's determination to look on fellow-believers with charity, and is an indication that the cause of promoting Sunday schools was greater in her eyes than any rivalry between the two publications.

Marianne as Editor

According to her own account, the invitation to become editor of the *Sunday School Times* took Marianne completely by surprise. Her main concern was whether it would mean moving to London, but after careful thought she nevertheless decided to accept the post. To her relief, James Clarke considered Northampton was in close enough touch with the capital for her to continue living there. She took on the role with enthusiasm as well as some trepidation, continuing in the post until the end of her life and steering the paper through years of transition in Sunday school teaching. Her aim, as stated in her first editorial, was that it would be 'a friend cordially received, warmly recommended, and well-beloved'.[102] A letter sent to Marianne twenty-three years later suggests that for some readers, at least, it had been such a friend. Her correspondent said that she had been reading the *Times* since she was a girl, forty years ago, and that for her it was 'next to the Bible'. Moreover, on a visit to America she looked in vain for an equivalent, and was grateful on her return to discover that the copies she had missed had been saved for her.[103] Marianne implied that this was only one of many such letters, and that the *Times* did indeed have a place in many people's hearts and lives. She also claimed for it that it featured the best Sunday school lessons 'written in this or any other land'.[104] As editor, however, her view was somewhat biased.

Although she had been a professional journalist for some years, taking on the mantle of editor was a significant development in Marianne's career. Most of the key evangelical publications had male editors, although Emma Worboise had successfully edited the *Christian World Magazine and Family Visitor* for nearly twenty years. Marianne described her colleague as 'a good deal less

---

[100] *Sunday School Chronicle* 25 March 1909.
[101] Farningham, *Life*, p. 195.
[102] *SST* 2 January 1885.
[103] *SST* 1 January, 1909.
[104] *SST* 1 January, 1909.

impatient than many editors are prone to be'.[105] In her discussion of the job, there is no mention of any gender awareness, so she must have felt comfortable as a woman in her new position, as on at least one occasion she did comment on being female in a male dominated environment.[106] Nor is there any indication that she was uncertain about her abilities. Given that when explaining how she became a teacher, she was always open about her misgivings and early mistakes, this would seem to suggest that she was confident in her new role as editor. Marianne's task was made easier because she already had many friends and acquaintances within the Sunday school movement. Travelling extensively within the United Kingdom as part of her journalism, and later her lecturing work, she had made a point of connecting with others involved in Sunday schools. She asserted that she had 'a wide personal knowledge of Sunday schools, north, south, east, and west, in cities, towns, and villages, and I knew and loved hosts of their teachers'. Indeed, she insisted that 'comradeship with teachers' was 'almost a passion for me'.[107] No doubt this network was extremely valuable to her in her role as editor, for it gave her a personal connection with the grass roots of the movement beyond her own area of Northampton.

There was no immediate dramatic alteration under her editorship, as Marianne was mainly concerned with keeping continuity and maintaining the success of the paper. According to a local commentator looking back at her work after her death, as editor 'she showed the same striking ability, the same appealing voice, as she had done before, and the paper benefited greatly from her help'.[108] She chose to make her mark on the paper with the introduction of a few small changes, one of which was a page designed for children to read, with short sermons and other features including a monthly competition.[109] For five years her youngest niece contributed a monthly competition to this under the name of 'Aunt Patty' Marianne also initiated a correspondence column so that those who were 'engaged in actual Sunday School work' could make a contribution which 'would be helpful to us all'.[110] This was not, however, a very successful venture, presumably because not many letters were received, and the column quietly faded away. A more long-lasting new section was devoted to Bands of Hope, one of her particular concerns. These were started in 1847 and aimed to encourage teetotalism in children. Bands met weekly and were taught, sang songs, and later in the century enjoyed magic lantern presentations, all with the intention of stressing the evils of drink. Regular attenders were expected to sign the pledge not to drink alcohol. By its Silver

---

[105] Harrison, 'Worboise', http://ww.oxforddnb.com/view/article/29966.
[106] See p. 163 below.
[107] Farningham, *Life*, p. 194.
[108] *Northampton Daily Chronicle* 16 March 1909.
[109] Farningham, *Life*, p. 201.
[110] *SST* 2 January 1885.

Jubilee in 1897, there were over ten thousand Bands, and was prestigious enough to have Queen Victoria as its patron for that year.[111] Marianne recognised that teetotalism could be a controversial issue, advising readers 'who do not approve of these societies' to avoid reading that section. This highlights another of her characteristics: an open-mindedness to the views of others. Despite her credentials and her experience, and her clear opinions on certain issues, Marianne herself continued to be open to new ideas, engaged in the process of learning.

At times she commented on some of the frustrations and pleasures of being an editor, noting the quantity of materials that arrived to be read. Sometimes these were illegible, whilst others were in need of correction.[112] On becoming editor, when asking for contributions, she reminded 'future correspondents to remember that our columns are very small, and words must be few... it really is wonderful how much can be told on one side of a sheet of paper when we have plenty to say and very little space in which to say it'.[113] Marianne's own economical style was one she wanted to encourage in others. Always concerned for others, she took the time when rejecting a contribution to send 'a note ringing with sympathy and encouragement' rather than a stereotyped letter.[114] She found that the work increased over the years, as more and more aspiring contributors sent in their offerings. By 1907, she was receiving over 500 contributions a year in the form of serials, short stories, sketches, articles and poems, all of which she considered and responded to. For Marianne, this could make her job 'difficult and strenuous' at times.[115] Producing the paper every week must have been a considerable pressure, but she obviously considered it worthwhile, as she continued in the job for many years.

Issues Addressed by Marianne

For some years Marianne wrote lengthy editorials in addition to her other contributions and the actual work of editing. The topics she chose indicate her priorities. She followed an introductory leader with an enthusiastic panegyric on the role of a Sunday school teacher, and this in turn was followed by a series on the importance of prayer. Other subjects tackled in editorials over the months and years that followed included topics as varied as prayer, the importance of taking Sunday school children to see the country, a tragedy at a Gateshead theatre which resulted in many deaths, the benefits of working for

---

[111] www.hopeuk.org/history.htm, accessed on 25 May 2006. The organisation has now become Hope UK, a drugs education charity.
[112] Farningham, *Life*, p. 200.
[113] *SST* 2 January, 1885.
[114] Morton, 'Marianne Farningham and her work', *Baptist Monthly*, 1899, pp. 7-8.
[115] Farningham, *Life*, pp. 199-201.

Fry and Cadbury and speculation as to what the new century might bring.[116] In later years she eschewed long editorials in favour of several short paragraphs communicating news and items of interest. On 13 January 1905, these included comments on the recent surrender of Port Arthur to Japan by Russia, and a suggestion for feeding poor children in Whitechapel, whilst the following week her topics were the benefits to unemployed men of being engaged in road-mending, and discussion of the Welsh revival.[117] Whether this change of style was because she believed shorter items were now preferred by her readers, or because her concentration and energy were waning, is not clear.

One issue which Marianne addressed at an early stage was the thorny one of the use of International lessons in Sunday schools. This idea had originated in America, where a Committee chose the readings, aiming to cover the whole Bible in six years.[118] A report on the Birmingham schools in 1888 indicated that well over half used the International Lessons. Marianne acknowledged that there had been much opposition to this system of learning, especially in England. She quoted from a critic who questioned whether the passages used, mainly New Testament letters and Old Testament history, were the best selection, and especially whether they were suitable for infants, and from a supporter who enthused about the lessons. She made it clear that she supported their use (indeed there is evidence as we have seen that she used them herself),[119] and was eager for the Anglicans and the Wesleyans to join the Baptists and Congregationalists in following the lessons. Whilst acknowledging that there were some faults with the system, she suspected that if left to their own devices, teachers would choose the same favourite passages and never look at others, and she loved the thought that thousands of people all over the country were studying the same Bible passage each week. Marianne concluded that teaching standards were higher than before the International Lessons were introduced, an argument intended to disarm their critics.[120] In her autobiography she mentioned Dr Peake, the Primitive Methodist theologian, who had, not long before, written and spoken convincingly in favour of a different system, and although a decision was made not long after to continue with the lessons, at this stage Marianne herself appeared less certain of their value, suggesting that at the very least the system would need modifying.[121]

Marianne was a safe pair of editorial hands for the little weekly for nearly twenty-five years. She used the freedom the editorials gave her to comment on many national and international events, as well as on the progress of Sunday schools and the responsibilities of their teachers, but she was careful not to

---

[116] *SST* 4 July 1890, 8 January 1892, 8 February 1895, 12 January 1900.

[117] *SST* 13 and 20 January 1905.

[118] Cliff, *Rise and Development*, p. 166 and p. 183.

[119] Morton, 'Marianne Farningham and her work', *Baptist Monthly*, September 1899.

[120] *SST* 27 March 1885.

[121] Farningham, *Life*, pp. 253-54.

abuse her privilege and move too far out of her readers' comfort zones. She could usefully talk about peace as many of her readers would have shared similar sentiments, but she did not, for instance, use the *Times* as a platform for her progressive views on the vote for women. She was not an innovator, able to reshape the magazine for the challenge of the new century. Ultimately this failure led to its demise and absorption by the *Chronicle*, but she maintained it successfully for a good number of years. Marianne's appointment had been a judicious move on the part of the proprietors.

Her editing work was a major area in which Marianne was a shaper of the movement. She had a key role as consultant and contributor from the launch of the paper, culminating in her years as editor. She did not make dramatic changes, but stamped on it her love of the schools, her awareness of the wider world and her concern for social justice. In her editorials she engaged with contemporary society and culture in many different ways, from significant political topics to small details. Whilst the publication might not have been 'next to the Bible' for all its readers, it no doubt played a significant role in resourcing and encouraging many Sunday school teachers. She also championed the International Lessons, encouraging their spread and influence. Female writers were becoming increasingly common, but women editors of magazines aimed at both men and women were less so, and in this respect Marianne helped to pioneer a role for women in the public area of journalism. These roles, as author, journalist and editor, opened the way for her to take a yet more obviously public role as she embarked on another career, that of lecturer.

Women and Public Speaking

It has been noted that lectures were a 'significant feature of nineteenth-century urban culture' and an important means for the communication of ideas. Speakers ranged from Samuel Taylor Coleridge to John Ruskin and William Morris.[122] Frank Prochaska has highlighted the development of women's involvement in public speaking, tracing it from the early years of the century when it was rare for women even to attend a public meeting, far less speak at one, to more general acceptance of their inclusion by the early twentieth century. He argued that these changes came about gradually as women, passionate about their chosen topics, addressed 'charity meetings, social science congresses, and trade union gatherings', thus making such activity more acceptable.[123] Marianne contributed in her own way to this gradual

---

[122] R. Williams, 'The press and popular culture, a historical perspective' in G. Boyce, J. Curran and P. Wingate, eds, *Newspaper History from the Seventeenth Century to the Present Day* (London: Constable, 1978), pp. 41-50, p. 46.

[123] F. Prochaska, *Women and Philanthropy in Nineteenth-Century England* (Oxford: Clarendon Press, 1980), p. 2.

erosion of prejudice by becoming a frequent speaker at Sunday school events, and embarking on a series of lectures. Interestingly, she refers to these public engagements as a speaking career, an indication that she was self-aware regarding her role as a woman in the public sphere.[124] In the 1881 census her occupation was listed as 'author and lecturer', a possible indication that she was claiming a higher status than that of journalist, although ten years later, when she was no longer lecturing, she was content with being recorded as a journalist and author.[125] Marianne later gave the impression that she had harboured no ambitions to speak in public, asserting in her autobiography that she had 'never meant to be a public speaker until I found myself started on the career'.[126] It is hard, however, to entirely believe this reconstruction of her past, as there is a hint in one of her early prose pieces that the idea of addressing an audience had long had an attraction for her. Her first published collection of articles, published in 1861, contained a short piece entitled 'Pleasure Life' in which, amongst other pleasures, she contemplated the joys of giving a talk:

> A remarkably pleasant thing it must be for a lecturer to look down upon a sea of upturned faces, all hanging upon his word. And as he skilfully plays upon the mass of hearts beneath him, he may see reflected in their eyes sorrow or joy, solemnity or mirth, as he pleases. And very pleasant it is too, to be so worked upon by the lecturer; to spend an hour in perfect self-forgetfulness, our thoughts concentrated upon an interesting subject.[127]

Such an occasion, she suggested, was something for which to be grateful to God. These sentiments reflect the popularity of lectures at the time, but also appear to contain an assumption that lecturers are male, although this might equally indicate a blindness to gendered language. This piece could represent a temporary flight of fancy, rather than a consistent aspiration, and might have been forgotten. Alternatively, it could be an indication of ambition that was nurtured for some years before it found fulfilment. Perhaps even as late as the early twentieth century, when she was composing her autobiography, Marianne was reluctant to admit to such ambitions in case they seemed inappropriate. Given that she demonstrated a confused mixture of being an advocate for women's rights, and a supporter of women as demure and restrained, this is a genuine possibility. Although she describes herself as 'shy and retiring',[128] she was certainly attracted by the possibility of lecturing.

---

[124] Farningham, *Life*, p. 154.
[125] 1881 census, www.nationalarchives.gov.uk/census, 1891 census http://content.ancestry.co.uk.
[126] Farningham, *Life*, p. 154.
[127] M. Farningham, *Life Sketches* (London; James Clarke & Co), 1861, pp, 22-23.
[128] Farningham, *Life,* p. 155.

Preparation for Public Speaking

As with many women who found themselves in such a role, Marianne was not initially confident speaking in front of others: her competent and relaxed style developed over a period of time. Her early work as an infant teacher would have meant she was used to the sound of her own voice amongst a group of small children. It was a large step, however, to then take a Sunday school class of young women, far more critical than a group of children.[129] In particular, she found praying out loud in front of these women a nerve-wracking experience. In her autobiography, Marianne implied that for women this presented a particular difficulty, remarking that 'most women know what a difficult thing it is to pray aloud and before others, and it is certainly not made more easy by the fear of criticism'.[130] There is an assumption here that any women who pray in front of others will feel awkward and self-conscious, an opinion that was probably based on reality for most women at that time. Evidence from denominational obituaries suggests that at the time Marianne started taking her class, to hear women praying in public was unusual, as it merited comment on the part of the obituary writer.[131] A generation earlier, a woman could question whether praying out loud with a neighbour was going beyond the boundaries of propriety.[132] It is not surprising, therefore, that Marianne initially found any kind of speaking, including praying, hard to do in front of others, and was fearful of possible negative remarks from her hearers. Her initial difficulties were thus not unusual, but the development of a public speaking role was rarer.

The Transition to Public Speaking

As her Bible Class became larger, Marianne's ability and confidence in speaking and praying out loud in front of larger numbers grew with it. She commented that 'for many years the number was so large that I lost most of my nervousness'.[133] No doubt this was made easier by the relationships she developed with the girls. It almost became a public occasion, as friends and visitors also slipped in to her classes, although she made sure that no men were admitted. At times she would have been speaking to almost two hundred

---

[129] See Chapter 4, pp. 101.

[130] M. Farningham, *Will you take it?* (London; James Clarke & Co), 1877, p. 4.

[131] L. Wilson, *Constrained by Zeal: Female Spirituality amongst Nonconformists 1825-75* (Carlisle: Paternoster, 2000) pp. 199-202.

[132] J. Lightfoot, *The Power of Faith: Life and Labours of Mrs Porteus* (Leeds: R Davis, Conference offices) p. 29. Mrs Porteus recalled, on being asked to pray with a sick neighbour, that she had no ability to pray and 'besides, I am a woman, and I cannot think it right for a woman to engage in any public capacity', thus indicating a mindset that believed any ministry outside the home, even in a neighbour's house, could be construed as 'public': however, this incident took place late in the eighteenth century.

[133] Farningham, *Life,* p. 153.

women. The class was thus, in many ways, a training ground for her later, truly public, lectures, in which she spoke to men as well as women. She herself made this distinction between the girls' class and true public appearances, writing of her 'first appearance in public' being in 1877 at the Sunday School Union's annual meeting.[134] The class had prepared her for that development.

This awareness of the training her class provided was, as one might expect, largely retrospective: looking back, she interpreted the process as being 'led' by a 'guiding hand'.[135] The journey from being so shy that she was reluctant to pray with a small Sunday school class, to comfortably speaking to several hundred people, was not one which she had pre-planned, either from ambition or perceived necessity. Her perspective was that it was a journey in which God encouraged her along a step at a time: 'God trains his servants as they work; and if only we try in simple faith to take the step that we see, he will make the next clear to us'.[136] Such a theology, of course, saved her from the responsibility of promoting herself in what might have still been for some readers a controversial area for women, but there is no reason to doubt that it was her genuine perspective, as it is in tune with her beliefs in the nature of God and his involvement in the lives of individuals.

Marianne had a second advantage in this transition in that she was by no means unknown when she started speaking in public. Rather, she was given opportunities to lecture because she was already known in certain circles as a writer, composer of hymns, and as the leader of the aforementioned girls' class. She thus came to this more public role by two routes simultaneously. Her experience of speaking to a growing group of young people combined with her increasing fame in evangelical circles through her writing, and both factors encouraged her to take further steps. The reality developed when Marianne's class experience and role as a journalist brought her invitations to talk publicly about the work of Sunday schools, and as she was passionate about it, she took advantage of these opportunities. According to her autobiography, the first time she spoke in public was in response to an invitation to give a paper at the annual meeting of the Sunday School Union, on the title of 'How to Retain our Elder Scholars', in May 1877. It was later published under the title of *'Who will take it?'* This talk, which drew on her own experience, provoked a lot of discussion and a warm response, as recorded in the Chronicle:

> Mr Hartley said on behalf of the Committee, he begged to say they were exceedingly obliged to Miss Farningham for her admirable paper. He thought there never had been submitted to them a more practical paper or one that was

---

[134] Farningham, *Life*, p. 153.
[135] Farningham, *Life*, p. 154.
[136] Farningham, *Will you take it?* p 4.

likely to be of more use, and he felt sure the Committee would do everything they could to circulate it extensively.[137]

This occasion led to regular opportunities to speak, and Marianne became a regular conference speaker on the topic of Sunday school teaching, encouraging people to become involved, or addressing the changes which the 1870 education act brought to Sunday schools. A memorial of her life in the *Sunday School Times* claimed that:

> For many years there was no more attractive and stimulating speaker at Sunday school Union Conferences than Marianne Farningham. She never spoke without offering practical suggestions, and she spoke in ways so lucid and attractive that she charmed the teachers, and sent them home often with a new ideal of what Sunday school teaching might be.[138]

Giving Lectures

In addition to giving a number of papers on the topic of Sunday schools, Marianne also embarked on a series of lectures, presumably with the twin aims of entertaining and instructing people, and of supplementing her income. Her own estimate is that she gave around a hundred lectures a year over six or seven winters. The first series was delivered just a few months after her initial paper, during the winter of 1877-8, under the title of 'The Women of Today'. It is significant that she portrays this as being her own initiative, in so doing stressing her independence as a 'working woman'. It came about, she explained in her autobiography, because she been provoked by her interest in the subject of women's rights to consider what she might want to say on the subject. Initially she considered writing a series of articles, but decided to see if a lecture would be well received. She started with a trial one at Daventry, not far from Northampton, and although she recalled being nervous, her talk seemed to be appreciated, and she found that her voice was strong enough to fill the hall. as lecturer. A reporter recalled many years later that this lecture 'was rich in epigram, humour and anecdote, and was honeycombed with wise advise and exhortation'.[139] She next contacted a friend at Derby, and gave the same talk there. In fact, she was forced to repeat it twice in the same venue, as so many people were eager to hear her that there was not room for all of them in the YMCA lecture room. Almost immediately, she recalled, invitations from other

---

[137] *Sunday School Chronicle* 9 May, 1877, recorded in W. T. Hearne, *Brief History and Genealogy of the Hearne Family,* 1907, Examiner Printing Company, Independence, Missouri, http://www.cragun.com/brian/hearne/history/hh800m.html accessed 12/02/2006.

[138] *SST* 26 March, 1909.

[139] *Northampton Daily Chronicle* 16 March 1909.

parts of the country arrived, and she realised this could turn into something larger. 'From nearly all large towns some committee sent me an invitation.'[140] At this point she portrayed herself as uncertain as to whether she should accept this and continue to lecture. This was, apparently, less because she felt the need for male legitimacy for her venture – in the first place she appears not to have done so – than because she was afraid that, having met her, a 'plain little woman', the readers of the *Christian World* might not want to read her pieces any more. Consulting her editor James Clarke was therefore the next logical step before making a decision. The outcome of that discussion is evident, as she continued to give many more lectures, by her own estimation over a hundred each winter for several years following the first series.[141]

Marianne appears to have been a popular speaker. On November 13, 1877, the Bristol paper the *Western Daily Press* included a report of a lecture on her initial subject, 'The Women of Today' given by 'the well-known author' Marianne Farningham.[142] The account is peppered by words in brackets such as 'laughter' and 'applause', as was the contemporary style. Marianne's rather disingenuous assessment of her lectures was that they were 'poor things'[143] but she knew how to handle her audience. The reporter noted that she began her talk by explaining to the men present that her remarks were not addressed to them:

> those who were married would be almost sure to know what women's lectures were – (laughter) – and those who had no knowledge of that kind would the more readily forgive her, if instead of presuming to lecture them – she daresay they often deserved it (laughter) – she endeavoured to lecture their lecturers (Renewed laughter and applause).[144]

This lecture dealt with the serious topic of women's rights, and other favourite themes, giving examples of women who had pioneered in different areas, and stressing that idleness and frivolity were inappropriate ways for a woman to pass her time. There were also comments on the varied topics of servants, men's and women's clothes, 'heroines' such as Grace Darling, Elizabeth Fry, and Florence Nightingale, and even about cats, Marianne insisting that

> no woman need be lonely: she was never meant to be alone. They must have something to love, if only a cat. (Great laughter) She thought that sometimes there

---

[140] Farningham, *Life*, p. 158.
[141] Farningham, *Life*, p. 170.
[142] It is interesting that an identical report, from the *Christian World*, is cited in Marianne's autobiography. It rather looks as though the *Christian World* has lifted this directly from the *Western Daily Press*.
[143] Farningham, *Life*, p. 170.
[144] *Western Daily Press* Tuesday 13 November, 1877.

was a good deal of affection wasted on cats; let her suggest that the place for the cat was on the rug and not in a woman's arms. (Laughter and applause) She never saw one of her own sex kiss a cat without thinking what a waste of good material it was – ('hear hear' and much laughter) – because they should remember how many miserable people there were who would only be too thankful for the caresses lavished on these animals.[145]

No doubt the *Western Daily Press* reporter included more of the humorous parts of the lecture than of the serious sections, but this excerpt helps to explain why these lectures were extremely popular. The same talk was reported a few months later in the *Cheltenham Examiner,* which as well as noting her comments on conventional emphases such as modesty, visiting the poor and 'sweetness of temper' mentioned the need of many women to be breadwinners and to 'acquire strength', a combination typical of Marianne.[146]

As this extract demonstrates, in all her public speaking, Marianne's approach was to begin by trying to get people to laugh. This was partly because it gave her some feedback on whether her audience could hear her clearly, but also because it helped them to 'be free and friendly together'. She deliberately spoke to the people furthest away, using their response as a guide to the volume of her voice.[147] On the occasions where the venue was a chapel she felt it appropriate to ask the minister beforehand to forgive her if they laughed, an indication that some might have thought laughter inappropriate in a place of worship. Marianne clearly enjoyed the rapport she experienced with her various audiences, and the appreciation she received, commenting that 'there is no sight quite so beautiful as that of hundreds of bright young faces looking with welcome and eagerness into the face of a speaker for whom they have an affectionate regard'.[148] In many ways she had come full circle, from contemplating the joys a (male) lecturer might feel, to being herself an experienced handler of audiences. There is little indication that she was a reluctant speaker, so the comment of the *Northampton Daily Chronicle* that 'The modest, retiring little woman had almost to be forced onto the public platform',[149] is a little puzzling. Either it is making assumptions about female behaviour and transferring them on to Marianne, or she portrays herself in her autobiography as having more, not less, confidence and assurance than she really possessed. In that case it would be yet another indication that she is attempting to be a different kind of female role model.

Henry Burrage, who in 1883 wrote an entry on Marianne for his book on Baptist hymn writers, observed that as a lecturer 'Her addresses are characterized by the modesty and quiet earnestness of her manner, as well as by

---

[145] *Western Daily Press* Tuesday 13 November, 1877.
[146] *Cheltenham Examiner* 13 February, 1878.
[147] Farningham, *Life*, p. 165.
[148] Farningham, *Life*, p. 263.
[149] *Northampton Daily Chronicle* 16 March 1909.

the clearness of her utterance, and the appropriateness and justice of her sentiments'.[150] In these words, similar to those frequently used of women in public roles such as preaching, we see the expectations of the public face of pious women. There was nothing here about her mischievous sense of humour. Hidden in this conventional language, however, was another positive assessment of Marianne's lecturing skills, both in the delivery and content of her material.

Certainly, she quickly developed an easy rapport with her listeners. According to her friend Jennie Street, Marianne's style of public speaking was warm and intimate. Writing after Marianne's death, Jennie recalled that whilst Queen Victoria complained that Gladstone talked to her as if the Queen was a public meeting, Marianne in contrast 'would talk to the biggest public meeting as if it were just one of her friends, to be chatted with, and entertained, and counselled and cheered'.[151] Elsewhere Jennie described a particular occasion when 'She took her hearers into her confidence, and chatted with them, out of the fullness of her large heart and wide experience, in a way that was wonderfully fascinating'.[152] Jennie was suggesting that Marianne was entirely relaxed on the public platform, but had a distinctive style which not only put her audience at ease, but both amused and challenged them. The above example bears this out, and this style is also reflected in her autobiography, making the readers feel as if they too are being confided in by a friend. Another commentator, writing in a somewhat laboured style, described Marianne as speaking 'with the calm self-possession, the intense earnestness, the tactful grace that riveted her hearers' attention and caused them to see her ideals as she saw them and endeavoured to realise them'.[153] Whether because of this speaking style, or due to the eagerness to see in reality someone whose written words had been read over many years, the lectures turned out to be very popular, and she continued to lecture every winter for six or seven years.

The topics for subsequent years were 'The Rush and the Hush of Life', 'Help-meets and Hinderers', 'The Women of Yesterday', 'The Women of the Bible' and 'Two Queens: Elizabeth and Victoria'. Of these 'The Rush and Hush of Life' was apparently the most popular: Marianne recalled giving that particular one over two hundred times, more than twice as often as some of the others. It was obviously a pertinent topic in the busy world of late Victorian England, and in addressing the subject Marianne regretted the fast pace of life, particularly in the cities, yearning for a more peaceful and slow way of life. She 'strongly commended patient, persistent plodding'. Probably she was

---

[150] H. S. Burrage, *Baptist Hymn Writers and their Hymns* (Portland, Maine: Brown, Thurston & Company, 1888), p. 206.
[151] *SST*, 26 March 1909.
[152] M.J. Street, *The Hundredth Year: the Story of the Centenary Celebrations of the Sunday School Union* (London: Sunday School Union, 1903), p. 122.
[153] *Northampton Daily Chronicle* March 16 1909.

addressing herself as much as others, for elsewhere she commented about the busyness of her own life.[154]

Evans has suggested that Marianne was at great pains to justify her lecturing tours by stressing in her autobiography the invitations she had received, the fact that she never travelled alone, the people she stayed with and the response she received. She argues that Marianne was pre-empting disapproval from her readers by stressing how many 'worthy bodies' had encouraged her lectures, by insisting that this was an extension of her Sunday school work and by noting that this travelling provided her with useful material for her journalism.[155] It is hard to say with certainty whether this was the case, and if so, whether the intention was operating at a conscious or unconscious level. It is clear from other comments that she relished speaking in public, and she virtually admitted to manipulating an audience, which does not sound as if she was wary of the reaction of readers to this role. The listing of friends and eminent people visited could equally be an demonstration of Marianne's love of networking, and perhaps indicative of a little insecurity in her friendships, so that she felt a need to state them clearly. Many writers of autobiographies, of course, tend to name-drop to make their text more interesting. It is possible, however, that she was protesting too much, and if this was the case even when she was writing in the 1900s, it indicates how much ground still needed to be taken if someone like Marianne, well known and at ease in public situations, still felt the need to defend her actions, albeit unconsciously.

Marianne recalled only a few bad experiences during her lecturing tours, usually connected with the travelling conditions rather than the actual talks. For instance, en route in the winter of 1880 to deliver a lecture in Merthyr Tydfil, she and her unnamed companion became stranded in a train which was trapped by snow, and had to walk up the line late at night to the station where, along with many others, they stayed the night, only being rescued the next afternoon.[156] There was one occasion, however, where the difficulty was directly associated with the lecture itself. At Whitehaven, following a week's lectures, she was staying with some good friends, and being asked to stay on to the Sunday, she found herself unexpectedly talking to 2000 people from all over the town and a platform-full of choirs. She was worn out, and had no notes prepared, as she was expecting only to say a few words. 'Never before or since have I been so frightened,' she commented later.[157] As an experienced public speaker, Marianne could still find herself in a situation in which she felt out of her depth.

After she stopped her winter lecture tours, Marianne still gave talks in support of causes she admired, for which she probably received no

---

[154] Farningham, *Life*, pp. 213-15. See also Chapter 2, p. 52.
[155] Evans, 'Marianne Farningham', p. 35. Farningham, *Life*, pp. 154-59.
[156] Farningham, *Life*, pp. 160-63.
[157] Farningham, *Life*, p. 168.

remuneration. In February 1889, she was asked by some friends in Sheffield to give a lecture, and it was whilst doing this that she became ill with exhaustion and had to take a long recuperative holiday.[158] Another example is given by Philip Morton, who interviewed her for the *Baptist Monthly* in 1899. This interviewer noted that when the newspaper editor W.T. Stead came to Northampton on his Peace Crusade there was a large meeting with 'several first-rate speakers' yet the 'palm for' the speech of the evening was given to Miss Hearne, more evidence that Marianne was a capable and skilful speaker.[159] Ten years before she died, Marianne decided she was too old to give even these occasional talks in public, but she still had many invitations, which she found very hard to refuse. In 1903, for instance, she made a presentation speech on the retirement of Rev. Gwynoro Davies, Calvinistic Methodist minister, as Chairman of the Borough District Council, a speech which Lloyd George, who was also present, said 'it was a delight to hear'[160] and two years later she spoke at a prize day of the County School in Barmouth.[161] The lure of public speaking remained a real one.

On the whole, Marianne appears to have relished the opportunities she had for public speaking, writing that she 'found much pleasure' in speaking. Yet she had no great opinion of her own ability, claiming not to believe the flattering things that were said when votes of thanks were proposed after her talks, because 'my best was very poor, as no one knew better than I myself'.[162] Commenting on the number of times she had delivered 'The Rush and the Hush of Life' she wished 'it had been more worthy of so great an opportunity!'[163] Such modesty, whether genuine or false, was frequently a feature of Marianne's appraisal of her own abilities, a characteristic perhaps typical of women at the time. Yet in other ways she appears to have been closer to a male, rather than a female, pattern of behaviour. Lecturing, for Marianne, was an extension of her role as an editor and author, and was a mixture of religious calling and an aspect of her career, and as such a means of earning her living. In this she was distinct from some of the more dedicated campaigners, such as Josephine Butler, or Elice Hopkins, who only gave public talks in support of a cause they passionately believed in. It was her name, not her topic, which drew the audience, and thus she was closer to the male type of a famous figure who used his fame to increase his income. Dickens, for instance, took to giving popular

---

[158] Farningham, *Life*, pp. 212-13. See Chapter 2, 51-53 for more details about her breakdown.

[159] P. Morton, 'Marianne Farningham and her Work' in the *Baptist Monthly* 1899, pp. 6-7 Stead was involved in peace campaigns over several years. www.oxforddnb.com/view/article/36258, accessed 12 July 2006.

[160] Glandwr-Morgan, *Welsh Home*, Chapter 4. (Chapter 6 indicates Lloyd George's chapel allegiance.)

[161] Glandwr-Morgan, *Welsh Home*, Chapter 5.

[162] Farningham, *Life*, p. 154.

[163] Farningham, *Life*, p. 165.

dramatised readings of extracts from his novels when he needed to raise his income. Marianne was able to buy her own house in Northampton with the profits of her lecture tours. Indeed, it was as she termed it, a career, part of her life as a 'working woman'.[164]

Northampton School Board

In contrast to her lecturing, Marianne's participation on Northampton School Board was not a paid but a voluntary position: yet she was offered it because of her stature as a woman who was competent in the public sphere: an ex-teacher, and one known for her experience with young adults. The provision of School Boards was one of the measures introduced by the 1870 Education Act, which was designed to make primary education a possibility for every child. The function of these elected Boards, 'the most democratic organs of local administration of the century', in theory if not in practice,[165] was to manage schools for children aged between five and twelve in areas where existing voluntary schools did not provide enough places. They were to be funded from a mixture of local rates and government grants. Attendance was initially neither compulsory nor free, although Boards could pay fees for poor children. Marianne was invited to stand for membership of the Northampton Board when it was first introduced, which demonstrates how, at a comparatively early stage in her career, she was already considered a woman of some significance in the town. However, she had a difference of opinion with the Liberals, who had approached her regarding the job, over the issue of religious education in schools. They wanted no religious teaching at all in schools. One of these men, was, to her surprise, a 'devoted member' of her church, and a local preacher. She declined the opportunity to stand on this occasion as she did not share their extreme views on the separation of church and state: as ever, being the practical woman rather than the theoretician or theologian, she wanted to maintain the emphasis on Scripture in the British school system, because she 'could not bear the thought of an infant school in which the little ones were taught nothing of Him who said "Suffer the children to come unto Me, and forbid them not" '.[166] In her biography of Spurgeon, she makes a point of highlighting him as championing this same cause, speaking to a meeting in Exeter Hall at which a resolution was passed that the Bible should be read in National Schools.[167] She felt so strongly about this issue that she was unable to stand for election to the Board. When, many years later, however, she was approached again, the question of religious education was no longer a current topic, so she consented

---

[164] Farningham, *Life*, p. 154.
[165] J. Lawson and H. Silver, *A Social History of Education in England*, (London: Methuen & Co, 1973), p. 314, pp. 319-20.
[166] Farningham, *Life,* p. 96.
[167] Eva Hope, *Spurgeon*, p. 135.

to stand, albeit as an Independent. In January 1886 under her real name of Miss Hearn, Marianne was elected to the School Board of Northampton, where she remained for two terms of office, a total of six years, thus becoming one of an elite band of female Board members. By this stage another Act, in 1880, had made attendance up to the age of ten compulsory, and during her involvement, in 1891, elementary schooling also became free. Marianne was a part of her local Board during an important time of transition for national education.

John Carlile, a friend and prominent Baptist minister, wrote many years later that Marianne 'went on the School Board at the request of many of Northampton's best citizens'.[168] Her own version is that it was teachers who approached her and in particular, female teachers. Perhaps they were the 'best citizens' Carlile referred to. A woman had previously been a member of the Board, but that was some years earlier and 'Northampton missed the advantage of having a woman member'.[169] Patricia Hollis has noted that 'progressive' boards tended to have women members, and this would fit the profile of Northampton politics.[170] It is interesting to have evidence that the female teachers in particular wanted to be represented on the Board by one of their own gender. This made Marianne's appointment of particular significance, in that she genuinely had the support of women. Whether this was because there were particular issues concerning women that needed to be raised, or whether the impetus was the lack of representation of women on the Board is unknown, but the local teachers obviously believed that Marianne could fill the role.

It has been suggested by Patricia Levine that 'the public nature and competitive manner of election was... antipathetic to prevailing notions of femininity'.[171] It is perhaps significant, therefore, that Marianne stressed her non-involvement in the actual campaigning: 'I determined to have no canvassing, nor to address any public meetings, but to print a letter, and send it round to the voters'.[172] This could not have been because she was uncomfortable speaking in public, as her lecturing skills have already been noted. More likely it indicated a reluctance to promote herself, and an allegiance at least in this respect to traditional understandings of what was appropriate for women. Despite this low-key approach, when the votes were counted, her name headed the poll. The minutes of the first meeting list the members and the number of votes they received, and Marianne received 6,667, over a thousand more votes than any of the other members. The next was Mr Adkins, who became the Chairman, with 5,611, then Mr Clayson with 5,246,

---

[168] *SST* 26 March, 1909.

[169] Farningham, *Life*, p. 90.

[170] P. Hollis, *Ladies Elect – Women in English Local Government, 1865-1914* (Oxford: Clarendon Press, 1987), p. 192.

[171] P. Levine, *Feminist Lives in Victorian England: private roles and public commitment* (Oxford: Blackwell, 1990), p. 40.

[172] Farningham, *Life*, p. 97.

whilst all the rest had less than 5,000 votes each. These statistics indicate that she was well-known and popular in Northampton, and that people trusted her judgement on the matter of education, presumably because of her long-standing involvement in a local Sunday school.

Although the numbers of women on School Boards rose steadily during the period of the Boards' existence, they were only ever a tiny minority, and Marianne remained the only woman on the Northampton Board during the six years of her involvement. During the 1880s nearly 90 women were serving at any one time on local Boards, whilst a contemporary estimated that in 1898 there were 188 women members of the various area Boards. This grew to 220 in 1903. In London the situation was rather better, with women making up around ten percent of the whole, but this achievement was never equalled in the provinces.[173] However, according to Hollis, by the time Marianne was elected, the role of Board member was becoming an easier one for women to fulfil. By the 1890s, only a few years later, she believes that they were regarded as 'more valuable and less threatening' than had initially been the case.[174] Yet we must not underestimate Marianne's achievement in becoming a female member of one of these influential bodies.

Marianne was certainly very conscious of her role as the only woman in the Board meetings, recalling in her autobiography that:

> I was not at all sure that all the members of the Board were glad to have me there – I fancy that most women who occupy public positions with men have the same doubt – but they were all courteous, and we worked together harmoniously.[175]

This comment demonstrates a gendered awareness on Marianne's part, a sense of being on male territory where perhaps she might be considered to be trespassing. According to Hollis, women members generally had a clear view that 'by standing for elected office they were staking out the claims of women to a wider public and political life',[176] and, given her sympathy to this aspect of feminism, it is likely that Marianne, too, had such a consciousness. This quotation also indicates, however, that her actual working experience was a cordial one, unlike that of Florence Fenwick Miller who also wrote of the difficulties of being a woman in a public situation:

> To be looked on as an oddity, and an unpleasant one, too... to be presumed to have not taste in feminine matters, no capacity for dressing well, no ability for

---

[173] J. Martin, *Women and the Politics of Schooling in Victorian and Edwardian England* (London: Leicester University Press, 1999), p. 2.
[174] Hollis, *Ladies Elect*, p. 185.
[175] Farningham, *Life*, p. 98.
[176] Hollis, *Ladies Elect*, p. 185.

housekeeping, no childward tenderness, no inclination for the ordinary pleasures of life...[177]

Perhaps because Marianne was already well known in the town, and presumably to the other members of the Board, by reputation if not in person, and because it was now a few years later, she was not subjected to such ridicule. Indeed, she describes her time on the Board as 'very pleasant years'.[178] Her fears of not being accepted were more due to self-doubt, and to the uncertainties of venturing as a woman into public space, than to her actual experience.

The possibility of becoming an elected Board member was, indeed, a new kind of opportunity for women. As Jane Martin has stressed in her work on women involved with the London School Board, this opportunity created by the 1870 Education Act was the most responsible elective position so far available to women. It was a significant opportunity in the public sphere for English women which had no contemporary equivalent in Europe or America,[179] and the role could be seen as a training ground for political involvement. Indeed, Martin has argued that most women were involved because they wanted a political voice and were eager to breach 'male bastions' of power, although later she concedes that not all these women shared a feminist ideology.[180] There is no indication that Marianne was interested in this political dimension. From her perspective, the role was one of 'being of service to teachers', and having been a teacher briefly herself, and continuing to be heavily involved in Sunday schools, she understood the issues from a teacher's perspective. Hollis has noted that women Board members usually had extensive school experience, having run Sunday schools or taught in day schools, and that in addition they knew the town and could speak for its needs.[181] Marianne would have fitted this profile well.

Martin has also pointed out that women involved in this work tended to be an elite, not because of the qualifications (they only had to be ratepayers, with no property qualification), but because in practice they had to have enough leisure to have time available, and the financial independence to make use of it: 'financial security, as well as stamina and dedication' were needed. The majority, therefore were spinsters or widows, and almost none of the women had young children.[182] Several women on the London Board were journalists,

---

[177] Martin, *Politics of Schooling*, p. 111.
[178] Farningham, *Life*, p. 98.
[179] Martin, *Politics of Schooling*, p. 137.
[180] Martin, *Politics of Schooling*, p. 31, p. 68.
[181] Hollis, *Ladies Elect*, p. 137. 'On the board, they could speak of the town's social geography, the streets, ... the buildings, the traffic, the families and the homes in a way few men could rival and all of them came to respect.'
[182] Martin, *Politics of Schooling*, p. 60.

including Annie Besant and Emily Davis.[183] In all these respects, Marianne fits the profile of a typical London female Board member: an unmarried journalist, with Liberal sympathies, and a ratepayer with financial security.

Hollis, however, who investigated women in public life across the country, has suggested that the majority of women in such roles were 'relatives of prominent Liberal men, invariably suffragist, mostly Nonconformist, and at least nominally teetotal'.[184] Marianne partly fitted this profile: she was Nonconformist, strongly teetotal, and becoming increasingly sympathetic with the suffragist movement, although in a very restrained, non-confrontational way. Her sympathies were also Liberal, although she steadfastly refused to ally herself with a particular political party. Hollis misquotes Marianne on this question of political allegiance, citing her as saying 'Of course I am a Liberal' by which she meant much more than allegiance to a party.[185] Marianne did make that comment in her autobiography, but she continued to explain 'I cannot feel great enthusiasm for a Political Party. I can always see something good on the other side, and I think the two parties should more often agree to work together for the common good',[186] a very modern attitude to confrontational politics! Her assertion that 'of course' she was a Liberal was a reflection of what has been called the Nonconformist Conscience: the late nineteenth-century identification of Nonconformity with Liberalism which culminated in the Liberal landslide in 1906 which saw 181 Nonconformists gaining seats.[187]

Hollis also noted that women who were earning their own living and had published their own books were unusual amongst Board women, and she observed that Marianne fell into this category.[188] Most women who became Board members owed their position to family connections: Hollis mentions 'the wives, sisters and daughters of solicitors, doctors, ministers and newspaper editors', middle-class women who were usually highly educated.[189] Instead, Marianne had had a humble education, and she was a participant on her own account, because of her own reputation and achievements rather than because of any family connections or inherited wealth, and thus, more than some of the others, in her membership of a School Board, she was a pioneer for women in public roles.

---

[183] Martin, *Politics of Schooling*, p. 37.
[184] Hollis, *Ladies Elect* p. 134..
[185] Hollis, *Ladies Elect*, p. 135.
[186] Farningham, *Life*, p. 278.
[187] D.W. Bebbington, *The Nonconformist Conscience* (London: George Allen & Unwin, 1982).
[188] Hollis, *Ladies Elect*, p. 135.
[189] Hollis *Ladies Elect*, pp. 134-35.

Marianne's Work on the Board

School Boards had an extremely responsible role. They dealt with everything pertaining to the schools, including overseeing the building of premises, the appointment of teachers and arrangement of salaries, and making general policy decisions. Matters discussed at their meetings ranged from arranging for coal deliveries to deciding on the subjects to be taught. The demands on Marianne and her fellow Board members in Northampton were rather less than the demands on those on the London Board, who tended to be involved with several committees each week in addition to regular weekly meetings of the full Board. Not surprisingly, Martin records that after the first three year term, half of the London female members did not stand again.[190] Although less demanding than the London Boards, the workload of the Northampton Board would still have been considerable.

Outside of London, Hollis has suggested that whilst for men, Board membership was part-time work, for women, such involvement 'was their duty, their faith and their delight'.[191] If this assessment is accurate, Marianne was closer to the male model of involvement. Typically, a School Board in a provincial town would meet fortnightly, but the Northampton Board assembled less frequently, usually monthly, although there were other committees in between. This made it more realistic for Marianne to be a member: the time commitment needed for a London Board would have been out of the question for her. As it was, she was unable to attend every meeting, only being present at about fifty per cent of the monthly meetings. There was a period in the spring of 1889 when she attended no meetings for an extended period, but this can be explained by her personal circumstances. In November 1888 she learnt of the death of her brother in South Africa, and she suffered a form of breakdown in February 1889, followed by a period of recuperation on the continent.[192] When present, she made suggestions and sat on various sub-committees, such as the Bye-Law committee. According to the minutes, she occasionally took the initiative in the main Board meetings by making a proposal, but what is impossible to ascertain is how frequently she joined in the discussion. She also chaired the Board on one occasion, indicating that her fellow members respected her and considered her capable of such a role. Whilst she does not appear to have played a leading role in the Board meetings, Marianne was an active and conscientious member as far as her other commitments allowed.

Marianne's Proposals

Marianne made the first proposal in the first meeting she attended, that Mr

---

[190] Martin, *Politics of Schooling*, p. 47.

[191] Hollis, *Ladies Elect*, p. 192.

[192] See Chapter 2, pp. 51-53 Evans brought the timing of this to my attention: Evans, 'Marianne Farningham', p. 56.

Adkins be made the chairman. Quite possibly this was to prevent herself being chosen for this role, as she had received the most votes, whilst he had the second largest number, but in any case it indicates that she was not shy in a new situation where she was the only woman present. Apart from that occasion, the proposals connected with Marianne's name were generally either of a courteous nature, such as a vote of thanks, or connected with specific issues, primarily cookery lessons, evening classes, or temperance. In these concerns, according to Hollis, she was typical of many women Board members.[193] Out of a total of five proposals made by Marianne, four were seconded by the Rev J Gasquoine, a Congregational minister in the town, who eventually stood down at the same time as Marianne. One can speculate that these two influential Nonconformists may have discussed Board matters in advance, and that there was even some mutual discussion over their leaving. One reason for the paucity of Marianne's proposals can be deduced from the minutes: on occasions when she did make proposals, she was included in the plans which resulted. After proposing evening classes in September 1887, she became part of the committee which organised them, and having suggested cookery lessons two years later, she was also minuted as being involved in making plans for the implementation of those lessons.[194] Perhaps, being very busy, she was wisely cautious about how often she made proposals, given that when she did make them her commitments were increased. She made sure that she only became involved in carefully selected issues.

Martin has commented that the growing focus on cooking and sewing owed as much to female influence as to narrow male thinking, and an examination of Marianne's Board involvement supports this claim. In 1889 she proposed that older girls should be taught some plain cookery, and her resolution was carried by seven to two. She was then seconded to the management of the schools in question 'with power to act'. There is no indication in the minutes that this was a particularly controversial measure, but Marianne's recollection was that her 'greatest opposition' was over this question of cookery lessons. She was remembered locally as a pioneer of cookery classes in the schools so her forceful attitude was successful.[195] One of the Labour members apparently objected to the resolution at the time, although she observed in 1907 that, 'he is now as pleased and proud as anybody with the girls' achievements in cookery'.[196] This small controversy even merited a comment in her obituary in the *Northampton Daily Chronicle,* which increased the scale of the debate in suggesting that she was 'surprised to find herself opposed by Labour members on this'.[197] Marianne, a firm believer in women being capable of running a

---

[193] Hollis, *Ladies Elect,* p. 188.
[194] Northampton School Board Minutes, 19 September, 1887.
[195] *Northampton Daily Chronicle* 16 March 1909.
[196] Farningham, *Life,* p. 98.
[197] *Northampton Daily Chronicle* 16 March 1909.

home well, was determined to give girls the domestic skills they would need later in life: she would not have considered such training, given only to women, as being demeaning or prejudiced, but as wise and practical.

In her second year on the Board, Marianne proposed that there should be 'one or two evening classes of a recreative and an instructive character'. All the Board members voted for this, and a sub-committee was created to facilitate this which included her, as well as the Chairman and several other people. Martin has noted that some women challenged the educational establishment in their support for recreational and educational evening classes.[198] In this instance, however, as everyone appears to have been in agreement, it is hard to see this as a challenge to the establishment, which was represented by the Board: however, this suggestion was clearly a contribution by Marianne. It is not always necessary to interpret every interaction in terms of challenges, as if women were in essence opposed to the status quo, rather than working for the most part in harmony with men of similar outlook for the benefit of the community. In so doing, they were changing the nature of women's role, but this was not always conscious, and to imply that Marianne was following some sort of subversive feminist strategy in her proposals is to read too much into her attitude towards the processes of the Board. In many ways, she was very much part of the Establishment. Yet in another area, she challenged established ideas. At the meeting of 19 December 1887, Marianne voted in favour of a proposal to remove a previous resolution to the effect that women teachers had to resign on marriage. Although this failed, it is indicative of Marianne's attitude to working women: she clearly believed that marriage should not prevent women continuing in professional paid work. The marriage bar in teaching remained in state schools until 1945. In this respect, Marianne was clearly pursuing a feminist agenda.

The other major proposal Marianne was involved with derived from her lifelong support for teetotalism. In 1890 she seconded a proposal that half hour lessons be given on 'Drink and strong Drink'. This was obviously a measure which caused some controversy, as another member tried to weaken it by suggesting it would be unwise to adopt a 'class of teaching in particular to the advantage of a party' when not everyone in the community would approve. This amendment was defeated, and the original suggestion of the temperance lesson was carried.[199] There is no indication how the children responded to this teaching.

Marianne's major responsibility was as part of the management team of the schools. When this became divided between the Board members, she was a manager for two schools, Vernon Terrace and Military Road. This involved meeting on the second and fourth Friday afternoon of each month respectively and keeping a close watch on a wide range of issues, including the fabric of the

---

[198] Martin, *Politics of Schooling*, p. 147.
[199] Northampton School Board Minutes, 21 April 1890.

buildings. Martin, whilst admiring women's increasing public role, did not always approve of the way their influence was exercised. She regarded the schools' attempts to civilise the poor, by imposing standards of cleanliness and behaviour on them which were sometimes resented by the parents, as a form of social control.[200] This was a perspective which would not have occurred to Marianne.

Marianne served on the Northampton Board for a total of six years, two separate terms, although there was no election at the end of the first three year period. As she commented 'nobody appeared to turn us out', so they all continued. After another three years, however, in 1892, she was feeling pressed for time, and finding the walk from her home to the Town Hall rather long on winter evenings. She was 58, and obviously felt that she had done her share of work for the Board. Possibly the fact that by 1891 she was involved in two extra committees contributed to her decision not to stand again the following year. In her autobiography, she explained that she would have liked to continue, but it cannot have been that high a priority, as she continued going into Northampton for several more years to take her girls' class, using a cab when she found it impossible to walk.[201]

Assessing Marianne's Contribution

Is it possible to evaluate Marianne's contribution to the Northampton Board? Carlile's assessment was that 'on the School Board, for many years, she was one of the most progressive spirits, interested equally in promoting educational efficiency and the welfare of the teachers'. He also noted that she 'was a zealous advocate of higher grade schools, and one of the first to urge the establishment of day training colleges for girls'.[202] As there is no evidence in the minutes to substantiate this claim, nor to disprove it, all we can do is note Carlile's opinion that Marianne played a significant role during her involvement with the Board. The evidence of the minutes suggests a less significant role than Carlile claimed for her. She does not appear there as one of the leaders of the Board, although as anyone knows who has read the minutes of a meeting at which they were present, much could have taken place in personal interaction which was never recorded. What is clear is that she did make a substantial contribution to the development of education in Northampton. One newspaper commented concerning her contribution on the School Board that 'every one of her colleagues recognised in her that she was a hard worker, with the cause of education at heart'.[203] Marianne's integrity and willingness to work were recognised as admirable characteristics. These were

---

[200] Martin, *Politics of Schooling*, p. 117.
[201] Farningham, *Life*, p. 259.
[202] *SST* 26 March 1909.
[203] *Northampton Daily Chronicle* 16 March 1909.

not particularly feminine characteristics: Martin has rightly challenged the contemporary assumption 'that School Board work was particularly suited to women's domestic skills and interests,' when, in fact, women were similar to their male colleagues in practicing an ethic of service.[204] They were, however, extremely valuable assets in a Board member, and must have aided the development of schools in the town.

More generally, her presence as a woman was in itself significant. Martin has argued that through involvement in the School Boards, women were able to play an active public role in late Victorian and Edwardian England, and make a positive contribution to the formation of a state education system, helping to shape policy.[205] She suggested that

> The fact that education was a field in which women began to engage in public activity in the later years of the nineteenth century, suggests a transfer of the authority and influence exercised by women in the private world of the home to the public arena of the Board.[206]

Marianne played a significant role in this transfer of authority, both by the work she did as an active member of the Board, and by her involvement in such a public role. She was not one of the first pioneers, but her participation was still unusual and noteworthy, a comment that could be made of much of her work.

Education Committee

When the 1902 Education Act reorganised the administration of schools, phasing out the Boards and replacing them with Education Committees, the Town Council made Marianne a co-opted member of the new body. Hollis has noted that it was in recognition of the work of women on the Boards that the town councils were requested to co-opt women onto the new LEAs.[207] This new role for Marianne was a recognition of the valuable work she had done in her years on the Board. The way John Carlile described this development in his memorial article gave the impression that she moved straight from Board to Committee where, he explained, she 'gave two years of devoted service to the cause of education'.[208] However, her own account, supported by the Board minutes, indicates that she only served on the Board for six years, thus having a break of ten years before being briefly involved with the new Committee. She left the latter after only two years because she 'was able to do so little, in

---

[204] Martin, *Politics of Schooling*, p. 29.
[205] Martin, *Politics of Schooling*, p. 147.
[206] Martin, *Politics of Schooling*, p. 92.
[207] Hollis, *Ladies Elect*, p. 167.
[208] *SST* 26 March 1909.

comparison with what I felt a woman member ought to do'.[209] There is no mention in her account, however, of the controversy the proposed 1902 Act caused amongst Nonconformists, who objected to the suggested abolition of School Boards, holding large meetings to object to the 'tyranny of the State Church' which they saw acted out in the planned Bill. This was partly the loss of the democratic Boards, but also the obligation the new Act put on local councils to bear the cost of voluntary schools, leading to Nonconformist and labour councils funding Anglican institutions.[210] It is likely that the feeling stirred up against the Tories by this Act was partly responsible for the Liberal election victory in 1906.[211] Marianne was quite elderly by the time she resigned, and would soon withdraw from other responsibilities, so it is no surprise that she only stayed a short time, and there is no indication that it was linked with the negative reaction of her fellow-Nonconformists to the Act. Probably, ever responsive to the wishes and needs of others, she was persuaded against her better judgement to become involved in the first place.

Marianne's involvement with the Board, and later the Education Committee, was a further example of how she became involved in the public sphere, in a way that was both consistent with her faith, and yet pioneered new areas for women. In so doing, as well as contributing to the development of education in the town, she was helping to increase the acceptance of women in public life. Yet it could be argued that there was a contradiction at the heart of Marianne's public work: at the same time both reflecting, and subversive towards the dominant ideology. Martin highlights this contradiction when she comments that notions of women's nature and mission were used to justify their presence on the political platform. This was storing up potential problems for the future, because, whilst women sought to enter public life on the same terms as men, their presence was also based on a 'culturally determined theory of sexual difference'.[212] Marianne, however, would not have recognised this as a contradiction. Whilst her support of women in unusual public roles or vocations was in tune with feminist thinking, for her, whether a woman was working in the public or private sphere, paid or unpaid, was less significant than whether she was using her God-given abilities to serve others, and doing it because her life was rooted in an intimate relationship with God.[213]

Conclusion

Marianne had a strong consciousness of being a woman in an increasingly

---

[209] Farningham, *Life*, p. 99.
[210] Lawson & Silver, *Social History*, pp. 369-71.
[211] Lawson & Silver, *Social History*, p. 371.
[212] Martin, *Politics of Schooling*, p. 112.
[213] See Chapter 3 for discussion of her attitudes to women and their roles, and Chapter 6 for a discussion of the spirituality which underpinned all her life and work.

public role. In her autobiography, she gives the impression that she had a gendered awareness since childhood. Yet she commented that 'I never meant to be a public speaker'.[214] There seems to be an ambiguity here: on the one hand, she supported women's encroachment into the public arena, whilst on the other, she still displayed some of the uncertainty and reserve that might be expected of a woman in a public role: an indication that she was very much of her time. Initially, therefore, Marianne found any kind of speaking, including praying, hard to do in front of others, and was fearful of possible negative remarks from her hearers. As the last chapter outlined, her Sunday school class was a clear example of the church environment providing a third sphere which eased the transition from private to public role.

Through her writing, and even more with her lecturing and membership of the Board, Marianne was clearly venturing into the public arena. Whilst there is no discussion of this distinction in her writing, she was clearly aware of moving beyond what many women were comfortable with. When first taking her class, she found praying out loud a trial, but within a few years she was addressing audiences in many halls all over the country, including Exeter Hall in London where the annual May gatherings were held, and apparently relishing the experience. Marianne drew on Scripture for support in this public role. She had a rather idealised view of the life of women in the society portrayed in the Old Testament, using for instance the life of Deborah to infer that women were not inferior, but able to take part in public life, prophesying and speaking in a public context.[215] It is significant that the book containing these thoughts, which are an attempt at a Biblical justification for a public role for women, was published in 1906, towards the end of Marianne's life. Although she was not a pioneer for women in public speaking, her role in this, especially when she first started, was still unusual. It is significant too that this venture appears to have been her own initiative, demonstrating that she was not afraid of breaking new ground for herself. In the last chapter, reference was made to one of Marianne's friends, Jennie Street, who commented of Marianne's Sunday school work that she had 'cheered and counselled... with voice and pen for so many years'.[216] In her roles as lecturer and Board member, as well as a writer and editor, she used that voice, and in so doing played a not insignificant part in taking ground for women in public life.

---

[214] Farningham, *Life*, p. 154.
[215] Farningham, *Women and Work*, p. 43.
[216] Street, *The Hundredth Year*, p. 122.

Chapter 6

Marianne's Spirituality

> We cannot talk with God without receiving inspiration, nor think of Jesus without being stirred to some emotion. And real feeling leads to action. Work of necessity follows prayer.[1]

Marianne noted in *Women and their Saviour* that God was to her 'an accessible, everyday friend'.[2] This was not simply a question of domesticating God, for elsewhere she made reference to his power.[3] Rather, it was an understanding of the nature of relationship with God, which she perceived as one of intimacy as well as of strength and support. Her faith was based not merely on a dutiful response, but on an intimate friendship with a living and loving God, in which the experience of the heart was more central than intellectual belief. Gordon, exploring the topic of evangelical spirituality, has similarly suggested in that for Christians the 'will to obedience' partly derives from an inner experience of Christ,[4] and this was clearly the case for Marianne, who understood the life of faith as an active response to God's love. 'To sit at Jesus' feet and hear His word,' she declared in 1904, 'is the true preparation for active service', so that 'we may live our lives, and do our work, strengthened by the assurance of His presence and blessing'.[5] This emphasis on relationship has also been convincingly demonstrated by Ian Randall. Randall regards the centrality of a relationship with Jesus as 'an overriding theme' of evangelicalism, and Marianne's writings indicate that this is the correct focus.[6] The synergy of faith and action encapsulated both in her recollection of her childish responses and in this comment was one of the distinguishing features of Marianne's writing and an indication that her spirituality was formed in an evangelical milieu.

Previous chapters have explored how Marianne worked out her beliefs

---

[1] *SST* 23 January 1885.
[2] M. Farningham, *Women and their Saviour* (London: James Clarke, 1904), p. 25.
[3] For example, in the poem 'The Storm' in M. Farningham, *Songs of Sunshine* (London: James Clarke, 1878), p. 186, Marianne refers to God speaking from his 'throne above'.
[4] J. M. Gordon, *Evangelical Spirituality* (London: SPCK, 1991), p. 2.
[5] Farningham, *Saviour*, pp. 76-77 and p. 95.
[6] I.M. Randall, *What a Friend we have in Jesus: the Evangelical Tradition* in Traditions of Christian Spirituality Series (London: Darton, Longman and Todd Ltd, 2005), p. 15.

through various means including journalism, a passionate allegiance to Sunday schools and her public work as a lecturer and on the Northampton School Board. In Marianne's faith, too, the various aspects of her belief and practice which might otherwise appear contradictory are reconciled. Thus, she believed both in the primacy of women's role in the domestic sphere and in the imperative for them to use their talents in a public, even a paid role, because she assumed that God, who had given men and women certain abilities, expected these gifts to be exercised, regardless of social mores.[7] Faith fulfilled an integrating role in Marianne's life. This chapter explores Marianne's spirituality in greater depth, considering how it reflected and mediated the changing nature of Nonconformist evangelicalism during the later years of the nineteenth century.

The Heart of Spirituality

In old age, Marianne recalled an interview with the church elders of Eynsford Baptist Chapel who were considering her application to become a church member. Although she remembered giving the 'right' answers to questions about faith and works, her focus was on the heart response of her fourteen-year-old self. She wrote of a girl, who, despite the lack of a distinct conversion experience, 'loved and trusted the Saviour... I wanted, above all else, to serve and please Him. My impulse and desire were towards religion.'[8] This account illustrates two central aspects of Marianne's spirituality: focus on relationship with God and a practical emphasis. This stress on experience rather than doctrine can be traced back to the Evangelical Revival, whilst also being an indication of her debt to the influence of the Romantic movement. Right belief was not unimportant to her, but she regarded a personal knowledge of God, and a life spent in practical service as one of his followers, as the heart of a life of faith. Activism, a notable feature of Marianne's spirituality, is also one of the four elements of Bebbington's now ubiquitous definition of evangelicalism, and in combination with the three other characteristics: conversionism, biblicism and crucicentrism, it is indicative that her spiritual home was evangelicalism.[9] It is important to note, however, that these characteristics should be understood in the context of Christianity being essentially a developing relationship.

Encouragement to her readers to connect with God in the ordinary working environment and to be obedient to him in the simple practices of daily life, fills Marianne's prose and poetry pieces, demonstrating that her spirituality was not primarily abstract or doctrinal, but practical and concrete, although based on

---

[7] See Chapter 3.
[8] M. Farningham, *A Working Woman's Life* (London: James Clarke, 1907), p. 54.
[9] D.W. Bebbington, *Evangelicalism in Modern Britain* (London: Unwin Hyman, 1989), pp. 3-17.

invisible reality. Her expertise was in this application of faith to life in the everyday world. The stress on faith as a personal relationship outworked in practice was at the heart of her spirituality and was a recurring motif throughout the years Marianne was writing. It will be useful, therefore, to explore in more detail the beliefs and devotional practices that underpinned her active spirituality.

Marianne's belief in God was based on a Trinitarian orthodoxy, and she referred to all three persons of the Trinity. There were many occasions where there was no differentiation in her writing, but only 'God' is mentioned. Thus 'God takes' a Christian who dies, in an early poem, whilst the reader is encouraged to 'choose and make God your choice' in another poem, dating from 1878, and to 'speak the word that God gives' in a third published in 1903.[10] It can be argued that this usage generally implied a reference to the Father, but this is not conclusive. Frequently, however, the Father was specifically noted as being the focus of the relationship, according to Bebbington an indication of the influence of Romanticism.[11] In *Boyhood*, 1870, for instance, Marianne urges her readers to tell the Father about the details of their lives: 'Oh it would be a great thing indeed if you were to learn now to consider God as your Father, and tell Him of all your failures and fears, your losses and sorrows, your pain and loneliness.'[12] Many of her poems also refer to God as Father: in *Songs of Sunshine*, for instance, there are titles such as 'Our Father' and 'The Father's promise' and lines which address God as Father: 'Shall we not praise Thee, O Father most tender?', and 'We thank Thee, Father!',[13] whilst in *Harvest Gleanings* the first section of fourteen poems are gathered under the heading 'Songs of the Father's Love',[14] and *Lyrics of the Soul* (1908) has several references to the Father, including a poem about God's love entitled 'Our Father'.[15] This spread, covering the whole range of Marianne's career, suggests that the love of the Father permeated her life. She felt safe in his care and was eager to understand what he had to teach her each day.[16] She was not amongst those who only highlighted Jesus.[17]

References to the Holy Spirit, however, were comparatively unusual. One rare example was in an early poem, 'O Lord, Revive Thy Work!' which contained the appeal 'Holy Spirit, hear, O, hear us!' in the context of longing

---

[10] M. Farningham, *Lays and Lyrics* (London: James Clarke & Co, 1860), p. 139, Farningham, *Sunshine*, p. 95 and M. Farningham, *Harvest Gleanings and Gathered Fragments* (London: James Clarke, 1903), p. 172.

[11] D.W. Bebbington, *The Dominance of Evangelicalism* (Leicester: IVP, 2005), p. 171.

[12] M. Farningham, *Boyhood* (London: James Clarke, 1870), p. 47.

[13] Farningham, *Sunshine*, p. 196 and p. 323, p. 1 and p. 198.

[14] Farningham, *Harvest*, pp. 15-28.

[15] M. Farningham, *Lyrics of the Soul* (London: James Clarke, 1908), p. 23.

[16] Farningham, *Harvest*, pp. 15-16.

[17] Bebbington, *Dominance*, p. 80.

for a purer church.[18] This was published in 1860, at a time when revival was a current topic, indeed a present reality, in some sections of the wider church in Britain and thus Marianne was reflecting a contemporary awareness of the Spirit. On other occasions she mentioned the leading of the Spirit. One poem from the early twentieth century alluded to 'the Spirit's wise leading' whilst in her autobiography Marianne commented on learning about the Spirit's guidance.[19] A late collection, *Lyrics of the Soul,* contained two poems on the subject of Whitsuntide, one of which celebrated the 'indwelling Spirit'.[20] There was recognition of the Holy Spirit in Marianne's writings, yet without any major emphasis on his activity, a reflection of the situation within many Baptist congregations at the time.

Focus on Jesus

More frequently her relationship to God was focused on Jesus, and frequent illustrations of this can be found in her writings. This balance was similar to that found in my study of female and male obituaries from the mid-nineteenth century, in which over half the references were to Jesus, many were to the Father, but only a minority mentioned the Spirit.[21] The situation was actually more complex than might appear, in that Marianne held the conventional Christian doctrine that Jesus revealed the Father to humanity, and therefore to a reference to Christ could also be an allusion to the Father. This was explicitly stated in one poem:

> How may we know the Father and his grace?
> By looking into Jesus' life and face.[22]

The persons of the Trinity were intimately connected in Marianne's thinking.

Elsewhere, for instance in *Women and their Saviour*, the focus is solely on the Son. Here Marianne enthused about knowing Jesus: 'No joy is like that which I find in Thee'.[23] Whilst one would expect a focus on Jesus in a book of meditations with such a title, the same emphasis is also found in other works. In one short piece she called him 'the Saviour – ever our Comrade and Companion as well as our Master', [24] whilst in her autobiography Marianne asserted that Jesus is 'always our Saviour, Protector, and Guide, is nearer than our nearest friend, and even more accessible'.[25] This was a consistent opinion

---

[18] Farningham, *Lays and Lyrics,* p. 212.
[19] Farningham, *Harvest*, p. 172, and *Life*, p. 149.
[20] Farningham, *Lyrics of the Soul*, p. 141.
[21] L. Wilson, *Constrained by Zeal: Female Spirituality amongst Nonconformists 1825-75* (Carlisle: Paternoster Press, 2000), pp. 101-106.
[22] Farningham, *Harvest,* p. 22.
[23] Farningham, *Saviour*, p. 9.
[24] M. Farningham, *In Evening Lights* (London: James Clarke, 1897), p. 116.
[25] Farningham, *Life,* p. 280.

expressed over many years. In her earliest published prose collection, *Girlhood*, Marianne encourages young women to make a commitment to Jesus, because 'feeling this love, you shall be no longer either friendless or lonely'.[26] The presence of Christ, in her observation and experience, made a significant difference to a person's life.

This was true whether one was busily engaged in work, or restricted because of illness and age. Whilst she wrote in *In Evening Lights*, published in 1897, which contained an unusual strand of melancholy, that 'old age shuts the doors on friends and joys that a little while ago we thought we could not do without',[27] elsewhere she suggested that even the difficulties of old age and the grief of dying could be alleviated by finding help from Jesus:

> The sight of his face, and the assurance of His presence occupy us, heart and soul, and there is nothing left to wish for. Indeed, we feel that he has shut us in with Himself that He may chase away our fears and fill us with his peace. No friend can do what he does for the lonely soul.[28]

Friendship with Jesus was thus a source of personal strength and support for Marianne, one she constantly recommended to her readers. Taking time to develop the intimacy of a personal relationship with the Triune God was a key evangelical trait which she fully embraced. This relationship was not primarily one of the intellect, but of the heart. For Marianne, spirituality was primarily about a connection with the divine which provided purpose, encouragement and a sense of identity as it was worked out in daily life. This was the form of Christianity which she mediated to her readers through her prose, poetry and editorials, a focus which supports Randall's assertion that relationship was at the heart of evangelical spirituality.

The Importance of Joy

According to Marianne one direct result of this relationship, and a characteristic feature of the Christian life, was joy. She was irritated by Christians who deterred others from belief because of their own lack of joy, writing to a friend who was unhappy that 'God sends us so many blessings, we should try to let our lives be as happy as possible'.[29] In writing of George Eliot, for instance, Marianne argued that Eliot's difficulties with faith had been emotional rather than intellectual. Describing Eliot's letters to her aunt, and her religious doubts, Marianne wrote 'Dreamy, romantic, repressive, and austere, she needed greatly

---

[26] Farningham, *Girlhood* (London: James Clarke, 1869), p. 7. Whilst the second person of the Trinity is not named on this page, it is clear from the rest of this little piece that it is Christ who is referred to.
[27] Farningham, *Evening Lights*, p. 109.
[28] Farningham, *Evening Lights*, pp. 108-109.
[29] Letters to Pollie, (1) 1863.

a little more brightness in her religious life; and if she could have had it, it is probable that more steadfastness would also have characterised her during this epoch.'[30] Her suggestion that Eliot turned away from her teenage evangelical enthusiasm primarily because of the narrow and dreary nature of the style of evangelicalism she encountered is a credible one.

> Her religion had too little or real Christian joy in it to content her long. Probably if during this time of transition she had been thrown among those whose Christianity was of a healthy, gladsome sort, instead of among rigid Calvinists or Unitarians, her thoughts might have taken a different turn.[31]

This picture of a 'narrow and dreary' religion is all too often the image we now have of Victorian evangelicalism, mediated as it frequently is through fictional representations in the novels of the time.[32] Indeed, Price and Randall argue that, prior to Keswick, evangelicalism was not characterised by 'confidence and joy, but rather by a negative introspection which created a dreary atmosphere of gloom and guilt'.[33] This, no doubt, was just the sort of religion Marianne was objecting to, but to suggest that it was the uniform face of Nonconformity in the mid-nineteenth century is to make too negative an assessment of the situation. Certainly it had not been her own experience. Marianne's first church was a Strict Baptist Chapel where the lives of the members were attractive to the young girl despite the narrowness of their theology. She remembered that 'their Christian joyousness was wonderful, and I longed to be as they were'.[34] Joy was part of what drew Marianne into Christianity, and it remained an essential ingredient of her spirituality, both before and after her significant Brighton experience, discussed below. Her experience might not have been typical, but Price and Randall's assessment needs qualification.

Conversion: The Gateway to a Relationship with God

Throughout her life, Marianne held the belief that conversion was the usual starting point of the life of faith, and that it was therefore important to encourage people to make a clear response to the gospel and to God. In this she was reflecting common evangelical belief and practice. It has already been noted that David Bebbington has identified conversion as one of the key characteristics of evangelicalism.[35] Other writers such as David Gillett and

---

[30] E. Hope, *Great Modern Women* (London: Walter Scott, 1886), p. 198.
[31] Hope, *Modern Women*, p. 204.
[32] Examples include Mr Chadband in *Bleak House*, and Nicholas Bulstrode in *Middlemarch*.
[33] C. Price, and I. Randall, *Transforming Keswick* (Carlisle: Paternoster, 2002), p. 22.
[34] Farningham, *Life*, p. 55.
[35] Bebbington, *Evangelicalism*, p. 5, and *Dominance*, p. 77.

more recently, Ian Randall, have explored the topic further.[36] Randall suggests that 'the classic evangelical understanding of conversion (is) as a personal encounter with Christ',[37] and this was certainly Marianne's expectation of the experience. In the final pages of *Girlhood,* written in 1869, Marianne challenged her young readers with the thought that life is short, and must end one day, and therefore they should consider the world to come.[38] Girls should respond to the one 'who has waited ever, with loving kindness in His eyes...(those) who yield themselves to the Lord, need not fear death'.[39] In 1885 she declared in a *Sunday School Times* editorial that 'the conversion of the children to God is, and must ever be, then, the one chief end and aim of all our work'.[40] It has been demonstrated already that she believed even quite young children could be encouraged to make a response to God and be converted.[41] In the Sunday school context, the best person to do this was the class teacher whom they already knew, rather than the more distant and possibly intimidating minister.[42] Towards the end of her life, Marianne was still stressing this necessity for a clear commitment. She took the opportunity in the closing pages of her autobiography to emphasise the reality of knowing Christ, and the importance of making a response to Him when one is young. She did not adopt the notion rooted in Coleridge, which began to affect some evangelicals, that children were born innocent and did not need to be challenged to respond to Christ.[43] The expected nature of conversion had changed over many years, however, from the protracted Puritan process with little hope of eventual assurance, through the crisis experience, albeit often preceded by an extended period of repentance, advocated by Wesley, to the abrupt event recommended by the American evangelist Charles Finney in the mid-nineteenth century.[44] Marianne was uncomfortable with extremes and was wary of a long period of consideration of one's sin which had accompanied some forms of conversion, regarding this as 'unhealthy habits of morbid introspection' which was 'a caricature of Christianity' and, indeed, more than that, was 'a disease'.[45] Yet she was equally suspicious of sudden, pressurised conversions, arguing that it

---

[36] D.K. Gillett, *Trust and Obey: Explorations in Evangelical Spirituality* (London: Darton, Longman and Todd, 1993), pp. 23-39, Randall, *What a Friend,* pp. 25-39.
[37] Randall, *What a Friend,* p. 33.
[38] Farningham, 'The End of Life' in *Girlhood,* pp. 131-36.
[39] Farningham, *Girlhood,* p. 235.
[40] *SST* 10 April 1885.
[41] See Chapter 4, p. 110-113.
[42] M. Farningham, *Sunday Schools of the Future* (London: James Clarke, 1871) p. 56.
[43] Bebbington, *Dominance,* p. 253-54.
[44] See B. Hindmarsh, *The Evangelical Conversion Narrative: Spiritual Autobiography in Early Modern England* (Oxford: Oxford University Press, 2005) for a useful discussion of conversion narratives in the eighteenth century, including some from College Street Baptist, Northampton.
[45] Farningham, *Sunday Schools,* p. 52.

was sensible to take time to consider the issues before making a commitment. In an editorial on the subject in the *Sunday School Times* she claimed that 'the great danger in regard to some of the young people when under the excitement of mission services or revival meetings is that they should make the confession before they have the faith, and that when the excitement dies down, their religion should die down also'.[46] This appears to be a criticism of the appeal for instant responses practiced by Finney which had influenced some behaviour in England.[47] Marianne's preferred method of conversion was a decision arrived at gradually through careful consideration. In the same editorial she cited with approval Edwin of Northumberland who declared that because 'his reason must go with his heart', he would take time to examine the faith before making a commitment.[48] She commented that

> a too hasty decision is frequently altered. It is just here, we think, that the Salvation Army makes a mistake. Feeling is wrought upon, and perhaps is sometimes mistaken for faith; and people are invited to step at once into the kingdom of joy whether they have or have not passed through the valley of repentance.[49]

There was not the same danger, to her mind, with seeking a commitment from Sunday school scholars, as here there was a progressive work from infants on, and therefore they should have been aware of what they were committing themselves to. 'They are never asked to accept the Christian religion otherwise than intelligently, and after much prayerful searching and consideration.'[50] This article reveals Marianne's understanding of conversion as part of the process of developing a relationship with God. Whilst it was a necessary doorway into a lifetime as a believer, it was only one element, and although emotion was involved, so was rational thought. An interesting light is shed on her belief by a suggestion she made in 1870 that if there were prayer meetings, that might lead to 'a great outpouring of the Holy Spirit' and conversions.[51] Individual conversion was understood as resulting from both the work of the Holy Spirit and human response.

As always, however, her stress was on the ongoing relationship that followed conversion, rather than on the decision itself: 'You will not be long in discovering that Christ who is able to save you is also able to keep you'.[52] That such a commitment did not always need to begin with a crisis is highlighted by her own experience, in that she herself did not know if she was converted 'or

---

[46] *SST* 13 March 1885.
[47] Randall, *What a Friend*, p. 34.
[48] *SST* 13 March, 1885.
[49] *SST* 13 March, 1885
[50] *SST* 13 March, 1885
[51] Farningham, *Sunday Schools*, p. 70.
[52] Farningham, *Life* p. 279.

had ever been', having grown up within the faith. The significant issue was, rather, whether a person was developing a life of discipleship in the context of an ongoing relationship with God.[53] For Marianne, this result was more important than any specific conversion event, an attitude that still placed her clearly within an evangelical framework.

In Marianne's thinking conversion affected more than merely the individual who had made a commitment. In 1885, following the Parliamentary Reform Act of 1884, which had given another two million male householders the vote, she suggested in the *Sunday School Times* that it was evident that the future would see the rule of the majority. In her opinion, not surprising given her working class origins, it was not class that mattered, but character: 'it does not matter so much which class rules, as that the ruling-class should be Christian'.[54] Given that many of those who would be influential in the future were from the working classes, it was evident to Marianne that 'we have, to all intents and purposes, the future House of Commons in the Sunday-school', and also 'the future mayors and magistrates, merchants and mechanics, authors and artists, speakers and workers'.[55] Marianne's longing to see these future citizens trained as Christians was not just for their own salvation, but for the good of the country: 'it is righteousness that exalts the nation'.[56] She anticipated a modern form of Christendom, which is an interesting assumption coming from a Baptist, a group traditionally on the margins of society.[57] A similar sentiment was expressed at more length in her novel, *Nineteen Hundred*, in which she explored her vision of a Christian country.[58] Similarly, in a late poem 'Thy Kingdom Come', Marianne expressed a longing for God's kingdom, which would begin when 'men let love reign over them, not hate... And God shall find on earth His home'.[59] Marianne shared the postmillennial vision of a transformed society, and constantly imagined she saw the signs of this becoming reality, writing enthusiastically of 'the growth of great causes', or anticipating in 1900 that 'the new Century will certainly be in many ways the best the world has ever known'.[60] In one late poem she still wrote of believing that 'the world is getting better', urging her readers to help to 'free men's hands from every fetter'[61] whilst in an editorial on the RSPCA in 1890 she suggested

---

[53] Farningham, *Life*, p. 55. Also see Chapter 2, p. 25.
[54] *SST* 10 April 1885.
[55] *SST* 10 April 1885.
[56] *SST* 10 April 1885.
[57] See S. Murray, *Post-Christendom, Church and Mission in a Strange New World* (Carlisle: Paternoster Press, 2004), for a historical overview of the development and demise of Christendom.
[58] M. Farningham, *Nineteen Hundred, A Forecast and a Story* (London: James Clarke, 1892).
[59] Farningham, *Harvest*, p. 21.
[60] Farningham, *Life*, p. 241, *SST* 12 January, 1900.
[61] Farningham, *Harvest*, p. 120.

that 'if we would hasten the coming of his kingdom we must develop kindness and mercy'.[62] This revealed a belief that the future kingdom could be brought closer by the actions of Christians, a classic postmillennial belief. Despite the waning of such beliefs towards the end of the nineteenth century, partly due to the rise of premillenialism,[63] at this stage they were still held by a significant proportion of evangelicals, only becoming untenable following the first world war. Another poem published in 1908 indicates that she continued to hold this viewpoint at the end of her life: 'thus shall His kingdom be ushered in, As the light in the Eastern sky...'.[64] Marianne continued to anticipate a future heavenly kingdom on earth. Nevertheless, individual salvation remained of great consequence: the same editorial which discussed the possible transformation of the nation finished with a conventional comment concerning heaven. Writing of those children who become Christ's, she stressed that '[Christ] will give them joy and gladness here and take them to His home for ever at the last'.[65] Whatever her dreams for the nation, personal conversion, leading to a lifelong relationship with God, took precedence, and in this she was reflecting the priorities of her evangelical audience.

Developing the Relationship: Personal Devotions and Prayer

The Practice of Devotions

James Gordon has suggested that Christian spirituality 'presupposes the practice of spiritual disciplines',[66] and indeed regular devotions provided an anchor for the rest of Marianne's life, and were in one sense, the most authentic aspect of existence. She believed that 'the royal moments of life are those we spend at His feet'.[67] Devotional times enabled the relationship with God which was at the heart of evangelical Christianity, to be expressed and developed. In an article written in 1884 she stressed the importance of times of devotion, insisting that above all things 'it is essential that we have our own quiet times in quiet places' because 'communion with Him will alone bring the strength and light we need'.[68] She continued this theme in the first series of articles she wrote in 1885 on becoming editor of the *Sunday School Times* was on the subject of prayer. In one of these she suggested that 'He who has had the hour

---

[62] *SST* 1 August 1890.
[63] Bebbington, *Dominance,* p. 151.
[64] Farningham, *Lyrics of the Soul,* p. 45.
[65] *SST* 10 April 1885.
[66] Gordon, *Evangelical Spirituality,* p. 4.
[67] Farningham, *Saviour,* p. 77.
[68] *SST* 29 February 1884.

of communion with God goes forth from the study like a new creature'.[69] In making such remarks Marianne was reflecting and reinforcing common evangelical teaching about the need for regular times of prayer, expressed not as a doctrine, but as a deeply felt personal need.

Prayer is not, of course, an evangelical distinctive, being central to all forms of Christian spirituality, but as Randall argues, it has not always been recognised that within the evangelical tradition there is a history of prayer being regarded 'with great seriousness'.[70] Certainly Marianne considered it to be vital. In one of her editorials in the *Sunday School Times,* she noted that a national week of prayer for young people had just taken place, observing that 'if we did not believe in the efficacy of prayer we should scarcely have added our names to the list of Christian workers'.[71] Prayer was for Marianne an essential support for any work undertaken by Christians. She believed, however, that it was also much more than that, being the means by which a relationship with God was maintained and developed, as well as an opportunity to learn and to share the deepest secrets of the heart. In an earlier article she had urged her readers to pray by suggesting

> Shall we not try for ourselves to bring everything to Him, and find in Him our Counsellor, our guide, our Friend? He will teach us how to work, and how to rest. He will let us understand when to speak and when to keep silent. Happy are those who put their trust in Him![72]

This highlights one of the key aspects of prayer for Marianne, which was to tell Jesus everything, including 'doubts and fears, our ignorance and weakness, our sins and sorrows and all the problems of life that distress us'.[73] Whilst she had many friends, she regarded her deepest relationship as being with God, and it was through prayer that this was expressed. She was aware that prayer was difficult at times, when an effort was needed to 'arouse us from our lethargy and warm our cold hearts into love' but for Marianne these were usually only temporary difficulties.[74] Prayer was not only about gaining personal strength and inspiration, but about requesting help for the people that one was concerned about. She herself continued to pray for her girls long after they had left her class.[75] Thus mothers were urged to 'besiege His throne' on behalf of their children whilst Sunday school teachers were encouraged to pray for their scholars.[76] Prayer featured in her fiction too, prayer both for self and for others.

---

[69] *SST* 23 January 1885.
[70] Randall, *What a Friend*, p. 91 and p. 76.
[71] *SST* 16 January 1885.
[72] *SST* 29 February 1884.
[73] Farningham, *Saviour*, p. 61.
[74] *SST* 23 January 1885.
[75] Glandwr-Morgan, *Welsh Home* , Chapter 3.
[76] Farningham, *Saviour*, p. 73, *SST* 16 Jan 1885.

In *Brothers and Sisters* the family is concerned about one son, Frank. Their communal prayer for him leads to his return home, although disaster later follows.[77] Whilst there is an indication that as time went on Marianne increasingly stressed the importance of the relationship rather than the discipline, there was otherwise little change or progression in her belief of the importance of prayer during her working years.

Varieties of Prayers

Marianne embodied something of the diversity in forms of prayer found within evangelicalism.[78] She encouraged the girls in her class to pray aloud in their own words, and clearly valued extempore prayer when it was done well, that is, when it was 'short and specific'.[79] Too often, she warned, such prayers could instead be 'long and effusive', which if offered by the Sunday school Superintendent when all the children were present could have the effect of undermining the good teaching that had just been given. Many public prayers, Marianne suggested, were 'remarks... opinions and meditations upon God or ourselves' rather than prayers pleading and imploring God for something 'that we really long for', a comment on the length of many evangelical prayers.[80] It is easier to be sincere in a short prayer, she argued.[81] She was not averse to the cautious use of set prayers: in the same article, Marianne suggested that Nonconformists 'have been too much afraid' of written prayers. Many people did this anyway, she believed, by quoting Scripture or hymns when they prayed, and there were prayers available which at times could more exactly express what was in an individual's hearts than his or her own words, both in a Sunday school context and in private prayer. In this, she was in tune with developments within some Nonconformist denominations, especially Congregationalism.[82] Nevertheless, she was also wary of the dangers of 'mechanical repetition taking the place of the earnest supplication',[83] but the implication in this article is that she used set prayers herself on occasions. In similar vein, a few years later she commended a family prayer book as being a good resource for those who 'do not feel able to make a prayer' but who would 'very gladly offer one'.[84] Prayers could take many forms, and Marianne was happy to explore these: the focus for her was on God, the reason for prayer,

---

[77] M. Farningham, *Brothers and Sisters* (London: James Clarke, 1873), p. 96.
[78] Randall, *What a Friend*, pp. 79-82.
[79] *SST* 16 January 1885.
[80] Bebbington, *Dominance*, p. 79, notes that prayers of 15 or 20 minutes duration were common in prayer meetings.
[81] *SST* 16 January 1885.
[82] Bebbington, *Dominance*, p. 151. He links this development with the influence of the Romantic movement and the desire for 'beauty and dignity'.
[83] *SST* 16 January 1885.
[84] *SST* 19 September 1890.

rather than on any particular method, and she used any means to encourage her readers to develop in their faith through prayer.

Realistic Patterns of Prayer

Marianne's opinions on the importance of prayer did not necessarily mean, however, that she personally spent a long time in prayer every day. Her life was busy, and she was well aware that the same was true for many others. For women in particular setting aside a lengthy time for devotions could be problematic. She was a pragmatist who recognised the reality of her readers' situations, and addressed these, rather than highlighting some impossible ideal. This was probably part of the reason why her readers found her writings so helpful. In her earliest published work she suggested that in the 'busy, bustling week, we have only had snatches of the promises – hasty glances into the loving face of the Redeemer'.[85] Over forty years later, addressing women in particular, she demonstrated a similar practicality, suggesting that 'if they can snatch a few minutes to spend with Him in the morning the entire day is more serene'.[86] Such a focus, if brief, put the whole day into perspective, and was the foundation for an ongoing relationship during the day a 'sense of His gracious companionship'.[87] Thus this time of prayer, the means of sustaining a Godward orientation throughout the day, need not be a lengthy affair: it was more an attitude of heart.

Neither should prayer be confined to a certain part of the day, but could be interwoven throughout everyday life, even in the middle of other tasks. In one poem, 'A Suggestion', Marianne mentioned suddenly thinking of someone who was 'miles and years away', and suggested that the reason a person came to mind might be because they were in need of prayer. 'And so, in case he needs my prayer, I pray.' She asked the reader to do the same for her if she should come to mind in a crowded day, and

'Give me a moment's prayer, as interlude;
Be very sure I need it, therefore pray'. [88]

This indicates that it was her practice to pray spontaneously when working, and that she expected others to similarly consider prayer a normal response to a sudden thought. On one occasion, when out with friends for the day to visit the new dam in the Elan Valley, near Barmouth, the group was discussing some navvies they passed on the road and those who tried to reach them with the gospel. Marianne spontaneously thanked God for the missioners, a

---

[85] Farningham, *Sketches*, (1861) p. 10.
[86] Farningham, *Saviour*, p. 5.
[87] Farningham, *Saviour*, p. 5.
[88] Farningham, *Harvest*, p. 62.

demonstration that she practiced what she preached.[89] For Marianne, the bedrock of the Christian life was thus a continuous relationship with God, mediated through prayer in a mixture of specific times of devotion and an ongoing awareness of his help and presence during the rest of the day. Her readers would have appreciated and aspired to this approach which represented a homely and practical evangelical spirituality.

Developing the Relationship: The Role of the Bible

Marianne remained a regular reader of Scripture all her life, always insisting on its importance. Writing for children, she described it as being 'that wonderful book which God has sent for us, which tells us about himself, and Jesus Christ, and heaven',[90] thus demonstrating the centrality of Scripture and of Jesus, as well as the importance of heaven, in her belief system. She was concerned about young people who made flippant remarks about the Bible, hoping that before it is too late, they 'learn to look at things as they really are', a sign that for her, Scripture provided the basis of reality, not an escape from life.[91] In *Home Life* she expressed the desire that the Bible was read more in the family circle, for poetry, history, romance, biography, suggesting even at that early stage she had an awareness of the different types of literature found within the Scriptures.[92] Many years later, in *Homely Talks* she was still encouraging her readers not to neglect their Bible reading, which probably indicates that there was a tendency for many to do just that. She commended the example of General Gordon, who was 'a loyal and loving student of the Bible, and had its words in his memory and in his heart'.[93] Her writing, especially her poetry, was steeped in Biblical terminology and allusions, which both highlights the importance of Scripture in her understanding and her expectation that her readers were biblically literate and would recognise the references. Many examples could be given, but a few can illustrate the point. One poem is entitled 'He giveth His Beloved Sleep', without citing the reference,[94] whilst in a later poem, 'Through Tribulation' Marianne refers to people in heaven 'who out of tribulation came', expecting her readers to know the passage in Revelation which this refers to.[95] Similarly, in her autobiography, she included the phrase 'serve my generation, and fall asleep' in perfect confidence that her

---

[89] Glandwr-Morgan, *Welsh Home*, Chapter 2.
[90] M. Farningham, *Little Tales for Little Readers* (London: James Clarke, 1869), p. 43.
[91] Farningham, *Girlhood*, pp. 120-21.
[92] M. Farningham, *Home Life* (London: James Clarke, 1869), p. 54.
[93] M. Farningham, *Homely Talks about Homely Things* (London: James Clarke, 1886), pp. 19-20.
[94] M. Farningham, *Poems*, (London; James Clarke, 1866), pp. 36. The reference is to Psalm 127:2.
[95] Farningham, 'Through Tribulation', *Harvest,* p. 50. See Revelation 7:14.

readers would already be familiar with the quotation.[96] If Biblicism was a measure of being evangelical, then it was one which Marianne fulfilled.

Marianne believed in reading long sections of the Bible in preference to short excerpts or isolated verses which led to a fragmented understanding. In *Boyhood,* for instance, she encouraged her youthful readers to read whole books[97] and in a short piece for children, published the previous year, Marianne made a similar point in telling a story about an eight-year-old girl named Susie, who was initially disappointed to receive a Bible for her birthday, but came to enjoy it. Her mother suggested that rather than read a few verses, she could treat it like any other book, by continuing to read to find out what happens. Indeed, Susie kept reading it 'not a few verses here and there, but a complete story, when she had time'.[98] In another piece in the same collection, a different young girl, Lily, was described as finding 'the Bible the most interesting book she had. She was never tired of reading about little Moses'.[99] This was no doubt written to inspire young readers, but incidentally revealed Marianne's personal reading style and her own enjoyment of Scripture. She expected even young readers to be able to make sense of the text with divine aid. When the fictional Susie read the Bible, she 'could not always understand it, but she asked God to teach her. And he did'.[100] According to Marianne, the Bible should be the only text book in Sunday schools, and all parts of it should be taught to the children so they have more than just a superficial knowledge.[101] This does not mean, however, that she regarded the use of commentaries as misguided: she was very complementary about Spurgeon's commentaries on the psalms, and appreciative of any aids which made the Sunday school teacher's job easier.[102] There are suggestions that Marianne may not have regarded all Scripture as carrying equal weight. In 1874 she published a book of Bible studies, containing 86 sessions based on the teaching she had given to her girl's class on a Sunday afternoon, covering the gospels. This demonstrates that she considered Scripture important, but also suggests that she prioritised the gospels in her thinking, as this is the only such study she published. It could also mean, however, that she was following lesson schemes after this and thus there were no notes available to produce separately. Much later in her life she did produce two other studies intended for women, based on various Bible passages, *Women and their Saviour* (1904) and *Women and their Work* (1906). An appreciation of the Bible was central to Marianne's Christian experience, a primacy which would have reflected and reinforced its place within

---

[96] Farningham, *Life*, p. 275. The reference is to David, see Acts 13:36.

[97] Farningham, *Boyhood*, 1870, p. 11.

[98] Farningham, *Little Tales*, p. 15.

[99] Farningham, *Little Tales*, p. 43.

[100] Farningham, *Little Tales*, p. 15.

[101] Farningham, *Sunday Schools*, pp. 37-40.

[102] E. Hope, *Life of C. H. Spurgeon* (Kilmarnock: John Ritchie, nd), p. 272.

evangelicalism.

Marianne was also open to reading new translations, making use of the new Revised version when working on her meditations for *Women and their Work*. She suggested that the Song of Deborah, which 'has surely never been equalled by any subsequent poet, man or woman', should be read in both Authorised and Revised versions, taking note of the margins, and when considering the story of Martha and Mary in Luke, the margin of the Revised version was to be preferred.[103] This Revised version, which had resulted in much controversy, was not entirely new, having been published in the 1880s.[104] F.F. Bruce considered the Revised New Testament to be a great improvement in its representation of the Greek text, but not entirely useful as a translation, whilst the Revised Old Testament was in his estimation 'from all points of view an excellent achievement'.[105] Whether Marianne was aware of the controversy surrounding its publication,[106] and of the comments of her friend Frances Power Cobbe on the new translation, as having an abusive attitude to women,[107] is uncertain, but her use of the Revised version is an indication that hers was a thoughtful Biblicism.

Marianne's relationship with God was thus sustained by the practice of personal devotions, with regular times of prayer and Bible reading, as well as through regular church attendance. She did not regard the practice of these disciplines in themselves, however, to be all that a Christian life entailed: teaching needed to be worked out in everyday life. In an early item on gossip, Marianne commented that the Bible was full of directions we disregard, such as being slow to speak.[108] In a piece from *Women and their Saviour*, concerning the gospel story of Martha and Mary, she argued that Martha was faithful in service whilst Mary was contemplative, and suggested, in a slight alteration to Jesus' emphasis, that 'the blending of the two makes the perfect woman.... to sit at Jesus' feet and hear His word is the true preparation for active service'.[109] This was no life of contemplation: prayer was not an end in itself. A response was required, and that led directly to action.

---

[103] M. Farningham, W*omen and their Work* (London: James Clarke, 1906), p. 48 and p. 75.

[104] The Revised New Testament was published in 1881, the Old Testament in 1885. See F. F. Bruce, *The English Bible* (London: Lutterworth Press, revised edition 1970), pp. 139-140, and 148-153, for discussion of the controversies following publication.

[105] Bruce, *English Bible,* pp. 138-44.

[106] There was controversy regarding both the Greek text used and the translation itself: see Bruce, *English Bible,* pp. 138-44.

[107] P. Levine, *Feminist Lives in Victorian England: private roles and public commitment* (Oxford: Basil Blackwell, 1990), p. 11.

[108] Farningham, *Sketches*, (1861), pp. 50-51.

[109] Farningham, *Saviour*, pp. 76-77.

The Cross

There is general agreement that Jesus' death on the cross is at the heart of evangelical spirituality. Bebbington places crucicentrism as the fourth side of his quadrilateral, and writers on evangelical spirituality, including Randall and Gillett, also stress the importance of the cross within the evangelical belief system,[110] with Gillett citing the well-known Baptist minister C.H. Spurgeon who declared that the atonement was 'the essence and marrow' of evangelical belief.[111] Marianne's early work represents this conventional evangelical emphasis on the cross, and it featured comparatively frequently in Marianne's writing in her early years. Out of just over 200 poems in her first book of poetry, *Lays and Lyrics*, twenty-three mention the cross. A few of those refer to Calvary whilst several have a passing reference to the blood of Jesus. Of the twenty-three, a handful focus on the cross as their main topic, including the long poem, 'Light from the Cross', which begins the collection, and mentions how, when 'God's just wrath shall round about us sweep', we will be rescued by 'the spotless Lamb who once was slain'.[112] The resurrection is not mentioned in this poem. Thus there is an indication that at this early stage, Marianne understood the atonement to at least partly involve the appeasing of the Father's anger by the son. In one of these early poems, 'The Story of the Cross', Marianne recounts a Sunday school teacher telling the story to his class, concluding with the rather sentimental couplet:

> There's nothing so sweet and beautiful
> As the story of the cross.[113]

The indication is that, at this stage of her life, Calvary was the focus of her Christian faith.

In later collections, however, the cross was mentioned less frequently, losing the prominence it had in *Lays and Lyrics*. In *Harvest Gleanings and Gathered Fragments*, for instance, published in 1903, there were merely eleven mentions of the cross out of a total of 170 poems, approximately half the number compared to forty years earlier, and *Lyrics of the Soul* has a similar paucity of references. In *Harvest Gleanings,* any references to the cross were merely a minor part of the composition, and there was only one which referred to the blood of Christ. This was in the context of a poem about heaven as portrayed in the book of Revelation, where it is a quite appropriate reference.[114] Other mentions include one poem which referred to Jesus as the 'Crucified one', whilst in another a mother encouraged her son to see 'the Christ who died for

---

[110] Bebbington, *Evangelicalism,* p. 14; Randall, *What a friend,* pp. 93-110, Gillett, *Trust and Obey* pp. 66-93.

[111] Gillett, *Trust and Obey,* p. 69.

[112] Farningham, *Lays and Lyrics*, p. 3.

[113] Farningham, *Lays and Lyrics*, p. 122.

[114] Farningham, *Harvest*, p. 212.

thee'.[115] A rare example is the poem 'Be Reconciled' from the collection which contains the verse

> Come home to God, nor be afraid;
> Your sins were on your Saviour laid.
> He lived, and died, and rose to win
> All men from trespasses and sin.
> On God's behalf, with you He pleads;
> He heeds your sorrows, knows your needs.[116]

This stanza indicates that in the early years of the twentieth century Marianne still held to a recognisably evangelical doctrine of Jesus' death, stressing that he took the wrongdoings of the people on him, and that the purpose of his death and resurrection was deliverance from personal enslavement to sin. Yet there had been a subtle shift: the Father was now seen as, if not quite a participant, a willing partner in the enterprise of redemption. In this, Marianne was reflecting the developments that took place within evangelicalism concerning the doctrine of the atonement during the later years of the nineteenth century.[117] This does not of itself, however, necessarily explain why there was a decrease in her emphasis on the cross.

One obvious explanation is that Marianne's later books of poetry contained poems written on a far wider selection of topics than found in *Lays and Lyrics*. More were written on nature. *Harvest,* for instance, included titles such as 'March Violets', 'September', whilst other poems celebrated places she had visited: 'Jungfrau', 'Kynance Cove, Cornwall', or people she wished to commemorate: 'Ruskin' and 'John Bunyan' being two of these.[118] Whilst most, although not all, of these examples contain a reference to God, as Marianne continually sought to earth her experience in her understanding of God, this broader range of subject matter in her later work is one contributing factor to the lack of references to the cross. Another possibility is that belief in an evangelical doctrine of the cross was such an integral part of her thinking that she felt no need to spell it out. This might well be the most logical explanation, but one difficulty with it is that on many other subjects she communicated basic ideas and beliefs with regularity: for instance her appreciation of nature, or her longing for heaven, suggesting that the cross was possibly less at the heart of her spirituality than in the first years of her journalistic career. It is most likely, therefore, that her focus had shifted slightly from an appreciation of the cross towards a celebration of the resurrection, and this is borne out by investigating her poetry. In *Songs of Sunshine,* for instance (1878), in which the poems follow the pattern of a year, those which refer to Easter place more stress on the resurrection than the crucifixion. 'The Easter Message' re-tells the Easter story,

---

[115] Farningham, *Harvest,* pp. 56, 57.

[116] Farningham, 'Be reconciled' in *Harvest,* p. 27.

[117] Bebbington, *Dominance,* pp. 157-58.

[118] Farningham, *Harvest,* pp. 89, 108, 155, 149, 138, 139.

with the same last line on each stanza 'Jesus is risen, he goeth before', and the climax of the poem looking forward to 'a second Easter, our resurrection'.[119] The preceding poem 'A Thought for Passion Week', does cover Jesus' last days, and his death, but also ends with a declaration that the resurrection, rather than the crucifixion, should be the focus of attention:

> And why should we think of our Master, dying,
> And going down to the darksome tomb?
> Death could not hold Him, He lives to-day,
> And because He rose we shall live for aye.[120]

At the stage when this collection was published, it seems that the resurrection held a greater significance for Marianne, a position closer to that of Eastern than of evangelical spirituality. Another poem entitled 'Good Friday' in the late publication *Lyrics of the Soul,* begins 'Why keep Good Friday mournfully?' encouraged rejoicing on that day.[121] Another indication in this direction is that, in her later poems, when Marianne mentions Jesus she does not usually state or imply that that involves a focus on the cross. For instance, in 'The accessible friend' in her final collection, she writes about a longing for intimacy with Christ, and how he invites people to come to him, but the cross is not mentioned.[122] Conventional belief in the atonement continued to be important for Marianne throughout her life, but it appears that in later years it was less prominent in her thinking, compared with approaching the risen Jesus as a friend.

All the ingredients of the now-famous 'evangelical quadrilateral' were thus present in some measure in Marianne's writing. The focus of her spirituality, however, was more on the constant experience of a relationship with God, than on these four elements in themselves. All were either the means of developing a relationship with God, or the way that relationship was outworked in practice. Usually, when discussing the Christian life, Marianne chose to stress the importance of developing a relationship with God, and the discipline of a consistent life, rather than particular experiences. She did, however, highlight one major landmark in her spiritual journey, one which added an additional dimension to her spirituality which greatly affected the understanding and practice of her faith.

Developments in Spirituality: Marianne's Brighton Experience

This exception was a conference Marianne attended in Brighton during 1875 in

---

[119] Farningham, *Sunshine* pp. 12-13.

[120] Farningham, *Sunshine*, pp. 11-12.

[121] Farningham, *Lyrics of the Soul*, p. 136: 'Dear hearts, accept the joy of spring/Think of the harvests of the cross,/Christ's death meant every gain, not loss;/ For it was Calvary made Him King!'

[122] M. Farningham, *Songs of Joy and Faith* (London: James Clarke, 1909), pp. 68-70.

her capacity as a journalist with the *Christian World*. Following a small gathering at Oxford in the late summer of 1874, which had a significant impact on those who attended, a series of meetings was held the following May 'for the Deepening of the Spiritual Life'.[123] This was the forerunner to the successful Keswick Convention, which became such an influential strand within evangelicalism in subsequent years.[124] Marianne found the whole conference extremely helpful, commenting that the prayers and talks at the meetings 'were like nothing which I had ever heard', but it was the teaching of Hannah Pearsall Smith which, she recalled many years later, made the most dramatic impact on her.[125] The Pearsall Smiths, an American couple with a Quaker background, stressed the need for an experience of 'full surrender' and thereafter 'resting in Christ', beliefs which drew on the 'holiness' experience of sanctification and became characteristic of the Keswick movement.[126] For Marianne, this teaching was apparently life-changing:

> These meetings made a great impression on me, and I was never quite the same after them. Religion was much more real to me, and I perceived a little of the meaning of the Higher Christian Life. Christ as my Saviour I had long known, but Christ as my King I saw for the first time. During that wonderful week certain truths grasped me which have not to this day loosened their hold – the fullness of salvation, the guidance of the Spirit, the constant presence of Christ, the unreasonableness of care and anxiety, and deeper than all, the wonderful love of God so little comprehended before.... I am profoundly thankful for the joyousness which then entered into my personal experience.[127]

This approach to faith with its Romantic overtones, stress on personal surrender and on joy within the Christian life, and more generous theology of salvation, drew a ready response from Marianne, and laid the foundation for her ongoing spirituality. After Brighton she claimed to have felt a new freedom from concerns and anxiety.[128] Incidentally, she never mentioned the incident in which Robert Pearsall Smith was suspected of impropriety and had to return to America: a typical example of Marianne ignoring that which was unpleasant or unsavoury.[129] As Bebbington and others have highlighted, Keswick was an extremely influential movement.[130] Whilst remaining evangelical, it had a distinctive flavour reflecting Romantic sensibilities and a love of poetry, which

---

[123] Price and Randall, *Keswick*, p. 28.
[124] D.W. Bebbington, *Holiness in Nineteenth-Century England* (Carlisle: Paternoster Press, 2000) p. 90.
[125] Farningham, *Life* pp. 149-50.
[126] Price and Randall, *Keswick*, p. 27, Bebbington, *Dominance*, p. 195.
[127] Farningham, *Life*, pp. 149-50.
[128] Farningham, *Life*, p 149.
[129] Price & Randall, *Keswick*, pp. 29-30.
[130] Bebbington, *Dominance*, p. 194; Price and Randall, *Keswick*.

Bebbington comments had been rare within Evangelicalism. He also noted that various protagonists in the movement had a dislike for doctrine.[131] It is not surprising, considering that Marianne wrote poetry, had a deep appreciation of nature, and a suspicion of rigid beliefs, that she felt at home with this distinctive expression of spirituality. There is no indication, however, that she ever attended a Keswick conference, and some aspects of Keswick belief were never adopted by her: for instance, she remained a postmillennialist all her life, rather than adopting the premillennialism typical of Keswick followers,[132] neither did she embrace its tendency towards conservative theology. Indeed, as has been seen, she was travelling in the opposite direction.[133] In many ways, however, she was a firm adherent of what became Keswick spirituality. Certainly, Bebbington's description of it as 'heroic but restful spirituality' is a good summary of Marianne's own teaching on Christian living. A whole section in *Harvest Gleanings* is devoted to 'Songs of Endeavour' with titles such as 'Christ's Knight' and 'Endure and Hope'. The latter begins

> Stand firmly. Do not yield or quail!
> Force back the cry, let Hope prevail;
> Or brace thyself the worst to meet
> Even defeat. [134]

Such verses epitomise the heroic aspect of Marianne's teaching, in which she encouraged readers, especially young people, to give their lives wholeheartedly in following Jesus. Alongside this, the concept of resting in Christ was also thoroughly threaded through her work. In the same collection, a poem entitled 'God Loves the World' indicated that God's love is affecting many people. In the middle of rush and hurry, she suggested, men have found a place of rest, so that 'while the crowded street they trod/ Have rested in the love of God'.[135] Another poem, 'Time to Rest', in the collection *Songs of Joy and Faith*, has as its subject people who believe there is too much work to do for God to be able to rest, then asks forgiveness for not taking time for rest, finally asking for God's presence in a season of rest, and expressing hope that there might be more work to do in the future.[136] This reads like an autobiographical account of her own experience, one which her readers would have identified with. Rest became an important aspect of her spirituality.

It is interesting that Marianne had already been using the language of consecration and surrender prior to Brighton. The final piece in her first

---

[131] Bebbington, *Holiness*, p. 78, p. 84.

[132] Bebbington, *Holiness*, p. 83-84 discusses the premillenialist teaching of Keswick. Farningham, *Nineteen Hundred*, is an illustration in novel form of Marianne's own beliefs.

[133] Bebbington, *Dominance*, p. 200.

[134] Farningham, *Harvest*, p. 166.

[135] Farningham, *Harvest*, p. 23.

[136] Farningham, *Joy and Faith*, pp. 44-45.

published collection of prose pieces encouraged readers that if they had wandered from God and been restored, 'let us never forget it. Let our whole lives be thank-offerings. May we be entirely consecrated to him', whilst in *Girlhood* young women were urged to live 'consecrated lives'.[137] Ten years later, in 1871, she similarly declared that being a Sunday school teacher involved 'thorough and entire consecration to God',[138] whilst at the end of *Boyhood,* published in 1870, Marianne urged any reader who did not already 'know Jesus as King' not to 'put it off another minute. You may lay down the book you are reading, and say at once, "O Lamb of God, I come".' [139] It thus appears a little strange that she later claimed that the idea of Jesus as King was new to her in 1875. However, the teaching of the Pearsall Smiths and others which became a distinctive feature of the Keswick movement may have built on earlier teaching and experiences, but it had a distinctive and new flavour, partly shaped by the Romantic movement.[140] These concepts were not new as such, but at Brighton, and later at Keswick, they were presented in a way that led their adherents to talk of a fresh and deeper experience of God. For Marianne this created a significant spiritual landmark.

Although activism continued to be at the heart of Marianne's spirituality, there was a transition in her attitude following this experience. The mixture of ideas she imbibed then remained important to her many years later, including 'the fullness of salvation, the guidance of the Spirit, the constant presence of Christ, the unreasonableness of care and anxiety, and ... the wonderful love of God, so little comprehended before' including a new understanding of heaven.[141] In her own estimation, the 'verses' she wrote then from then on contained 'an underflow of new life'. There was a noticeable shift in her thinking away from legalism, anxiety and a need to prove oneself to God towards a relationship based on love, a more trusting and restful approach. Thus many years earlier in 1861, we find her almost recommending salvation by works: 'No one has a right to believe himself a Christian, unless he is doing something for the common cause of Christianity... Then we might, indeed, look for a revival'.[142] By contrast, in a much later piece, with the pressure of a sense of earning God's love removed, she expressed things rather differently. Commenting on Mark 1:31 she explained that 'I am to let him heal me, and then I am to show my gratitude to Him by my works'.[143] Brighton was an important stage in her developing belief that action flowed out of intimacy, and that surrendering to Christ brought joy.

---

[137] Farningham, *Sketches,* (1861), p. 184, *Girlhood*, p. 136.

[138] Farningham, *Sunday Schools,* p. 133.

[139] Farningham, *Boyhood*, p. 134.

[140] Price and Randall, *Keswick*, pp. 45-47.

[141] Farningham, *Life,* p. 149.

[142] Farningham, *Sketches* (1861), p. 46.

[143] Farningham, *Saviour,* pp. 28-30.

This attitude is encapsulated in a poem included in the selection *Songs of Sunshine*, published in 1878, only three years after Brighton. The name of the collection in itself is an indication of a change in the writer's perception of life, and several of the poems contain sentiments about finding rest and peace through trusting in Christ.[144] In 'The Lord is Thy Keeper' she wrote about a spirituality based on serving Christ, but full of anxiety and fear, being changed into one of joyfulness and trust in God:

> ...I toiled and laboured from morn till night,
> For how could I take my rest?...
> And my heart was sad with a heavy care,
> For I knew I should often fail...
>
> But a message of gladness came at last,
> One day by the shining sea,
> That I need not cling with my trembling hands,
> For the Master was holding me.
> 'Tis the King who fights for the victory,
> 'Tis the Shepherd who tends the sheep...
>
> The sorrow is over, the weary strife,
> I rest me in God's great love.[145]

It is extremely likely that in this poem she was recounting in poetic language her experience at Brighton. This is one more indication that the event enabled Marianne to build her security on the fresh foundation of the acceptance and love of God. This form of spirituality remained with her for the whole of her life. When she composed her autobiography in the early years of the next century, she still regarded the occasion as a watershed. Whilst it is possible that, as happens to others following a significant experience, she had a tendency to stress the discontinuity with her own past, rather than the continuity, there had clearly been a major change in her thinking. Always troubled by versions of evangelicalism which focused on introspection and tended towards both sadness and legalism, yet struggling with similar issues in her own life, she embraced this teaching with relief and enthusiasm.

Marianne and Developments in Evangelical Theology

Other changes Marianne encountered she found more problematic. The nineteenth century was a time of change and disruption for evangelical theology and Marianne's position on the staff of the *Christian World* meant that she was aware, and at times involved with, contemporary theological controversies. It has been shown that by the end of the century both higher

---

[144] Farningham, *Sunshine*, including 'A Whisper' p. 30, and 'A thought of peace', p. 97.
[145] Farningham, *Sunshine*, pp. 69-71.

criticism and evolution had been generally accepted within Nonconformity, but the process was a painful one.[146] Inevitably the focus of much of the change during Marianne's lifetime was the issue of Biblical interpretation. One view which emerged in the 1840s and 50s was the concept of Biblical inerrancy, the belief that every word was inspired, and that there were no factual errors in the text. Bebbington suggests that this developed in response to the Romantic idea that poetry could be divinely inspired, leading to the need for a clear distinction between the Scriptures and other literature.[147] In opposition to this conservatism James Clarke, editor of the *Christian World,* championed 'a more generous theology' in a leader in May, 1873. Clarke challenged several common evangelical assumptions, suggesting, for instance, that 'neither the Bible nor common sense sanctions the whole figment of universal, verbal, infallible inspiration', as well as questioning various doctrines such as the nature of hell.[148] Marianne's comment on this leader was that 'nothing that has ever come into my life has made me more sorry, or more fully of anxiety'. She professed to act 'a coward's part' and not to 'try to solve the great problems for myself', using busyness as an excuse to avoid grappling with the issues.[149] Yet her disclaimers were a little disingenuous, since, despite her protests, she did engage with these ideas. Some years later she insisted in an editorial of her own that 'Thoughtful persons must not ignore all that is going on in these days' especially concerning attitudes towards the Bible. Even so, she was cautious about such conversations, arguing that 'homes and firesides' should not be the place for theological conversations.[150] These important issues, she believed, should be handled with care.

Although she responded reluctantly to theological developments rather than grappling with them enthusiastically, Marianne's gentle prose and pious poetry often mediated such ideas to a wider public. She did not seem threatened by developments in doctrine. On the contrary, it is probable that Marianne's own lack of education led her to accept too uncritically the pronouncements and opinions of those who were well-educated, without stopping to understand the implications for her faith, or to discover whether all educated people shared the same viewpoint. Marianne was also eager that Sunday school teachers, as far as possible, were aware of fresh developments in theology. This, she believed, was especially important following the 1870 Education Act, which meant that Sunday school children would be coming into classes considerably better-educated. Thus there was also a need for teachers educated to a higher standard, although their spirituality was still of primary significance.[151] Late in life she

---

[146] Bebbington, *Dominance*, p. 165, p. 168.

[147] Bebbington, *Dominance*, p. 165.

[148] *CW* 2 May 1873 (not 3 May as Marianne suggested).

[149] Farningham, *Life*, pp. 136-38.

[150] *SST* 19 December 1890, editorial.

[151] Farningham, *Sunday Schools*, pp. 123-27.

commented with approval that teachers had become 'less resentful of Biblical criticism' than formerly, learning not to panic if they 'should be obliged to readjust some ideas in regard to theology'.[152] One such issue was the historicity of the book of Genesis. In 1906, Marianne commented on Genesis that 'Our children may call it legend or poetry, though our grandmothers called it history', but it was still splendid. She insisted that the first verse was the most important (In the beginning, God created), and that whilst she could not be sure how many thousands or millions of years it took for the earth to be ready, in the end it was and man was created.[153] Marianne had adapted herself to new developments, as many evangelicals did.[154]

In this new climate, everyday explanations had to be found for Biblical miracles. It has been suggested that this was in part due to the influence of Romanticism: if God was always involved in creation, then specific interventions could appear less necessary.[155] In *Women and their Work*, Marianne recounted the story of the Israelites crossing the Red Sea, quoting from the Jewish writer C. G. Montefiore who described the miracle as due to the winds causing a temporary passage, in such a way as to suggest she accepted that explanation. She also pointed out that the song of Moses could not have been written in the New Testament era 'being very different from Christ's command to love our enemies'.[156] This indicates a comparatively sophisticated, Christocentric hermeneutic rather than a naïve assumption that all Scripture should be regarded as equally useful for contemporary application. Marianne, a simple believer in the ideal of progress as well as in the salvation story, seemed to have few difficulties with the new developments. Possibly this indicates that she welcomed a more nuanced Christianity, although it could also be as she herself had suggested, that she did not have the intellectual capacity to grapple with some of the issues. The former explanation is suggested by her reaction to the Downgrade Controversy, a disagreement that erupted in 1887 when Charles Spurgeon resigned from the Baptist Union because no action had been taken over his concerns about changes in teaching within Baptist churches.[157] Her description of the events implied that Spurgeon regarded the *Christian World* as 'on the down grade', indeed as one of the leaders of that trend, yet Marianne's sympathies were apparently with her editor, James Clarke. She admired Clarke's 'advanced views', declaring that 'He believed in the free expression of opinion, and in fearlessly facing the problems of the age. He was not afraid of that which was new, and though there was great reverence

---

[152] Farningham, *Life*, pp. 252-53.

[153] Farningham, *Work*, p .1.

[154] H. McLeod, *Religion and Society in England, 1850-1914* (Basingstoke and London: Macmillan Press, 1996), p. 191.

[155] Bebbington, *Dominance*, p. 170.

[156] Farningham, *Work*, p. 36.

[157] Bebbington, *Dominance*, p. 245.

in his nature, he did not hesitate to attack any dogma merely because it was old.'[158] The implication is that Marianne, too, was not bound by tradition but open to new possibilities. She respected James Clarke's honesty and sincerity, and could not speak too highly of him as a man of faith. 'His own faith seemed always beautifully sincere and simple, and its outcome was a brave and blameless life... Often have I wished that those who said bitter things of his theology could have known the real man.'[159] With great relish she described an accidental meeting she witnessed between Clarke and Spurgeon, which she interpreted as showing that relationships were more important than doctrine. Encountering each other on a train, the two men shook hands 'in true brotherhood' despite the fact that 'at that very time a fierce theological war was going on between them'.[160] This was typical of Marianne's attitude, more concerned with maintaining friendships than with particular doctrines. Bebbington's comment that the solvent of Romanticism led in at least one instance to relationships between Christians being based on 'spiritual sympathy rather than theological agreement' is an accurate description of her position.[161] This primacy of friendship contributed to her avoidance of theological disputes.

Simply by continuing to write for the *Christian World*, however, Marianne showed a sympathy with developments in theology. Her tendency to embrace new ideas was demonstrated when she employed Samuel Cox, a controversial Baptist minister and author, to write some of the commentaries on the International Lessons for the *Sunday School Times*. And despite her earlier misgivings, she came to believe that questioning was important. In a *Sunday School Times* editorial of 1890 she suggested that those who reacted to modern Biblical criticism 'with a cry of fear' had not followed the debate, explaining that 'if these sacred books are indeed the title-deeds of our faith, it will be the most fatal policy to decline to have them investigated'.[162] Towards the end of her life, the Congregational minister in Barmouth, Rev Glandwr-Morgan, recorded her as joking about a young supply preacher who attacked higher criticism, declaring that he was sorry for its proponents. Marianne's reaction was, 'with a merry twinkle in her eye' to comment that 'it had long struck me that the Higher Critics would have been very sorry for him'.[163] She was not uncritical, however, and referred approvingly in the same editorial to the Bishop of Ripon who had recently written an article on modern criticism, in which he suggested people should be open to the truth without swallowing 'any rash theory'.[164] How much was new to her readers, and indeed how much they

---

[158] Farningham, *Life*, pp. 209-10.
[159] Farningham, *Life*, pp. 209-10.
[160] Farningham, *Life*, p. 210.
[161] Bebbington, *Evangelicalism*, pp. 144-45.
[162] *SST* 19 December 1890, editorial.
[163] Glandwr-Morgan *Welsh Home*, Chapter 3.
[164] *SST* 19 December 1890, editorial.

were aware of some of these nuances in her work, it is difficult to evaluate. What is evident is that whilst Marianne was a woman with typically evangelical priorities and concerns, she was also open to new ideas, even if these took her over the boundaries of traditional evangelical doctrine.[165]

Another example of this was given by Glandwr-Morgan, who recalled several conversations in which Marianne 'revelled in pointing out the goodness of human nature'. It is easy to believe that Marianne thought of human nature as essentially good, but the minister may have been interpreting her comments in that way because of his own theological perspective.[166] Indeed, as early as 1863 she was encouraging a friend to 'look constantly on the sunny side of people as well as things',[167] so her remarks may have been the result of a disposition to think positively of people rather than a change of theology. If the latter was true, however, and she had abandoned belief in original sin, it is one more demonstration of the theological distance she had travelled from her origins. In making such a journey she was not alone: other evangelicals were reassessing various aspects of their theology and in the process evangelicalism gradually became an even larger umbrella term than earlier in the century.[168]

The Development of Marianne's Theology: Heaven, Hell and 'the larger hope'

One way in which this was reflected was in the development of a wider range of opinions concerning the nature of heaven and hell. For Marianne, this was rooted in the Brighton experience which had led her to re-evaluate some aspects of her belief system. In particular, after her time at the conference, she changed her ideas on the scope of salvation and the nature of hell, on which she developed strong and controversial beliefs. For some years she was reticent to express herself clearly in writing on the matter, presumably because of a desire to preserve unity, but her autobiography indicates that it was at Brighton that her fear of hell was removed, although it was likely that some of these ideas were already familiar to her given James Clarke's developing theology. As a child Marianne absorbed the conventional evangelical picture of hell. In Sunday school in the late 1830s and early 40s she learnt a hymn containing a verse which began 'There is a dreadful hell, and everlasting pain', and

---

[165] There are some similarities here with the Christian feminist campaigner Josephine Butler, who was better educated, and therefore, it might be expected, less naïve, yet whilst Butler reflected non-evangelical attitudes to the Bible that would have been beyond what Marianne was comfortable with, she nevertheless believed that revelation could take precedence over criticism. See L. S. Nolland, *A Victorian Feminist Christian: Josephine Butler, the Prostitutes and God* (Carlisle: Paternoster, 2004), p. 47.
[166] Glandwr-Morgan *Welsh Home*, Chapter 3.
[167] Letters to Pollie (1) 1863.
[168] Bebbington, *Dominance*, p. 165.

imagined that the entrance to the inferno was through a crack in the road just outside her village, which she was afraid she would fall into, running 'over it in breathless haste and with panting prayers'.[169] It is not surprising, given this background, that during her early years as a Christian and as a writer, Marianne appears to have held to traditional doctrine on this matter, although she usually referred to it rather discreetly. One of the clearer examples was in her first published prose collection, *Life Sketches,* where she said that those who are only 'trifling, sinning the hours away' will have to pay the penalty, 'death and destruction'.[170] A few years later, in the series of pieces which became *Girlhood*, Marianne wrote more circumspectly about the dangers of not knowing Christ: 'there is no hope for those who have not fled to Him for refuge: there is no light for them who persist in sitting in darkness'.[171] Here hell was portrayed as an absence of hope and light, rather than as a place of torment. This lack of clarity probably reflected the fact that Marianne, in common with many of her contemporaries, was becoming increasingly uncomfortable with the usual evangelical doctrine of hell. Her autobiography suggested that she had never been totally comfortable with the concept, although whether there is a touch of hindsight there it is difficult to say. She explained that the 'larger hope' had already attracted her some time before she attended the Brighton conference,[172] another indication that she was strongly influenced by Romantic sensibilities.[173] Her approach to changes in theology tended to be to chew them over slowly, expecting that a solution would eventually emerge. Certainly by the time she wrote about her childhood fears, she had long since ceased to believe in such a hell, although it was not an easy passage.

In this process Marianne was on a similar journey to many of her fellow-believers, as during the second half of the century there was a gradual shift regarding hell, in Nonconformist circles as much as in the wider church, as people became less comfortable with such a violent doctrine.[174] It has been suggested by Hugh McLeod that in the later years of the century questioning conventional teaching on hell was 'one of the chief touchstones in the battle between conservatives and liberals in the various churches'.[175] This impacted on Marianne because a debate on the subject of eternal punishment was taking place in the columns of the *Christian World*, led by Samuel Cox and Edward White, both of whom held unorthodox views on the subject. The editorial in May 1873 which caused Marianne such anxiety suggested that amongst the theological beliefs which should be jettisoned were the 'un-Christlike tenets of

---

[169] Farningham, *Life,* p. 29.

[170] Farningham, *Sketches* (1861), pp. 113-14.

[171] Farningham, *Girlhood,* p. 135.

[172] Farningham, *Life*, p. 138.

[173] Bebbington, *Dominance*, p. 161.

[174] Bebbington, *Dominance*, p. 159-61.

[175] McLeod, *Religion and Society,* p. 184.

the theology of blood, and brimstone, and fire'.[176] Despite her confusion over the issues, she was interested in the topic, recalling that ' "The larger hope" had already attracted me, and I decided to wait, hoping and praying that the light which it was necessary for me to have would come to me gradually'.[177] Marianne was open to new ideas, but cautious about embracing them too hastily.

The uncertainty was resolved for her two years later, at the Brighton Conference in 1875, when as has been argued earlier, the speakers, and in particular the American Hannah Pearsall Smith, had a strong influence on the development of her spirituality. Afterwards, she recalled, never 'did I find it possible to be afraid of everlasting punishment, so assured was I that love would find some other way. A great hope arose within me that there might be unread meanings in some of the words of the Lord Jesus, which as yet we had not fully understood.'[178] In this she was following the lead of her editor, and also reflecting a significant minority within evangelicalism. There was, however, much disquiet in evangelical circles around this topic, as Pearsall Smith's son recalled: 'by expressing her disbelief in eternal torment,' he asserted, '(Hannah) had risked her acceptability as a preacher in England'.[179] Many people for whom hell was a problematic issue, however, found the idea of an alternative to traditional belief very attractive. Marianne commented that after the Brighton Convention, she found an opportunity to talk all this over with her father, and that she found to her 'great joy' that 'his outlook was wider than that of many, and that he had great hope of the world, through the Life, Death and Resurrection of our Saviour'.[180] This opinion on the part of a deacon from a rural, working-class, Calvinist Baptist church indicates that disquiet concerning the traditional evangelical teaching on hell had permeated to the grass roots more than has generally been realised.

The Larger Hope became the title of a book by Cox in 1883, his second on the topic of the nature of salvation. Cox argued in both his books that because atonement is intended for all, it must extend to all. Discipline and judgement, remedial in this life, will continue to be so after death.[181] Hell is the fire which purges people for an eventual heaven.[182] Although he insisted that he was teaching a biblical version of the atonement, his arguments sound very like justification for a doctrine of salvation by works with a form of purgatory for those less than perfect. It seems, however, that he found a sympathetic audience

---

[176] Farningham, *Life*, p. 137.
[177] Farningham, *Life*, p. 138.
[178] Farningham, *Life*, pp. 149-50.
[179] L. P. Smith, Ed., *A Religious Rebel, The letters of HWS (Mrs Pearsall Smith)* (London, Nisbett & Co Ltd, 1949), p. xviii.
[180] Farningham, *Life*, p. 150.
[181] S. Cox, *Salvator Mundi* (London: Henry S. King, 1877), p. 195.
[182] S. Cox, *The Larger Hope* (London: Kegan Paul, Trench, 1883), p. 16 and p. 34.

within a section of the evangelical community, including Marianne. Yet it is still surprising to find in her writing the assumption that certain individuals are in heaven – apparently without a period of intermediary discipline – despite being avowed agnostics, or in the case of Harriet Martineau, even atheist, during their lives. One can imagine some of them being rather surprised or even dismayed to find themselves eternally in the company of Christians! This is most noticeable in a book published under the name of Eva Hope, *Queens of Literature of the Victorian Era*, in later editions *Great Modern Women*. As with her opinions about women, it seems that she felt free to be more frank about her beliefs when using this pseudonym than when she wrote under her own name. When discussing women she admired, the mixture of her more liberal beliefs and her natural sentimentalism meant that she could not conceive of those women not enjoying heaven, even if they had been antagonistic to Christianity during their life. She was fully aware that some of them had not shared her faith. For instance, in her account of Harriet Martineau, Marianne commented that it must have been easier to arrive at agnosticism from Unitarianism than if she had believed in the divinity of Jesus Christ 'and trusted in Him for salvation'. Yet she was impressed by the firm nature of Martineau's beliefs, stressing that 'she had real convictions, and the courage to act upon them,' and that Martineau 'lived for others, and she died in quietness; and we cannot better conclude our sketch than in the words of Florence Nightingale "O, how she must be unfolding now in the presence of that supreme Goodness and Wisdom, who must welcome her as one of His truest servants" '.[183] It appears that sincerity and selflessness were, in Marianne's eyes, almost the same as an evangelical faith, a perspective that would have appeared decidedly suspect to many of her fellow believers. Although, early in the twentieth century, she also confessed to believing in a 'second chance' after death, she was still influenced enough by her early doctrine to add that 'my early theological training almost seals my lips on the question',[184] an indication that she was entirely aware how far she had travelled since her teenage membership of Eynsford chapel.

Evidence for a sympathetic attitude to Christianity is similarly slim in the case of George Eliot, whom Marianne also greatly admired, regarding her as the greatest novelist of her era. She declared that readers of Mr Cross's biography must feel

> that the old woman's heart must have found some rest at last in the old faith. Perhaps she had never wandered so far from it as she herself imagined. Mr Cross tells us that they read the Bible together, and she read it aloud as if she enjoyed it. We confess to a profound wish that the great writer had been different in some

---

[183] Hope, *Great Modern Women*, p. 87 and p. 101.
[184] Glandwr-Morgan, *Welsh Home*, Chapter 3.

things; but for all that was good, and generous, and honourable – and there was very much of these in her character and life – we may well be thankful.[185]

George Eliot's appreciation of the Scriptures needs to be seen in the context of another comment by Cross that it was 'difficult to ascertain, either from her books or from the closest personal intimacy, what her exact relation was to any religion'.[186] Whilst Marianne clearly had a sympathetic attitude towards George Eliot, and was always inclined to interpret people's responses in a way that was favourable to religion, it seems that she was still stretching credulity here. This extract seems to indicate that despite her belief in the 'larger hope' she still shared the Victorian yearning for a deathbed affirmation of faith.

As she appears to have included in the after-life anyone whom she admired, whatever their personal beliefs, why did she believe that anyone should live the disciplined life of a believer? Her approach perhaps reveals her kind, slightly sentimental way of looking at life more than raising a major intellectual difficulty. The idea that anyone who had done some good in this world should be prevented from enjoying a blissful after-life, whatever their attitude to Christianity, did not sit easily with her desire that everything should be well with everyone. However, if some of her comments were taken in isolation, one would be justified in questioning whether she was still evangelical in later life. In other matters, however, Marianne still maintained comparatively conventional beliefs, for instance in her Christology. Evangelicalism in the late nineteenth century could be unexpectedly fluid at times, which was no doubt partly why the conservative Spurgeon protested so strongly in what became known as the Downgrade controversy. Marianne reflected the alternative trend towards a broader theology, especially when she wrote as Eva Hope.

Heaven

The concept of heaven was central to evangelical piety and beliefs, closely linked with the idea of redemption, which concerned not just forgiveness now, but a future hope for a life after death.[187] This was usually conceived not in terms of bodily resurrection on a renewed earth, but eternity in a somewhat idealised heaven. It was the strength of this belief which led Elie Halevy, followed by E. P. Thompson, to unfairly blame Methodism for preventing a proletarian revolution.[188] Although life expectancy was increasing during the nineteenth century, surviving to old age was still uncertain, and people carried

---

[185] Hope, *Great Modern Women*, p. 258. The reference is to J.W. Cross, ed., *Life of George Eliot, Vol 3* (London: William Blackwood and Sons, 1885?), p. 369.

[186] Cross, *George Eliot, Vol 3*, p. 375.

[187] Wilson, *Zeal*, pp. 59-63.

[188] E. Halévy, *A History of the English People in 1815* (London: T. Fisher Unwin, 1924); E. P. Thompson, *The Making of the English Working Class* (Middlesex: Penguin Books, 1980 edition).

more of an awareness of death from a young age than they do today. Most would have known family members or friends who had died, and Marianne would not have been unusual in losing her mother, an infant brother and a younger, teenage sister before she reached her twenties. Such experience gave the anticipation of heaven an immediacy lacking in our contemporary western culture.

This interest was reflected strongly in Marianne's writing. For instance, in a late poetry collection, *Harvest Gleanings*, published in 1903, out of a total of 170 poems 14 are substantially or entirely about heaven, whilst a further 50 contain a reference to a future life. As this collection was published in her old age, it might be thought that her belief in, and anticipation of, a future life, was connected with her own approaching death. However, her very first book of poetry also contained a large number of references to heaven. In this volume, *Lays and Lyrics*, (1861) out of nearly 200 poems at least 22 are primarily about heaven, and a further 13 concern dying, all of which mention the afterlife, as do at least ten other poems. In comparison, only five poems feature the cross. A similar emphasis is found in Marianne's prose. In her first collection of prose pieces written for the *Christian World*, *Life Sketches* (1861), she asserted that life is preparation for death, 'the door by which heaven is entered'.[189] Many of those little pieces have references to heaven. At the end of a short novel, *Brothers and Sisters* (1878) one of the characters explains the Christian life: having found Christ, 'we have only to walk where he leads, and wait until he tells us to rest with him in heaven'.[190] Nearly 20 years later, she described the experience of friends dying, expressing frustration at being left alive which can seem as if 'the door has been slammed to in our faces, and we have been alone on the outside, baffled and distressed'.[191] Anticipating heaven in her old age, she expected that there will be new treasures and old loves waiting for us 'in the other home'.[192] The emphasis on heaven was thus not just connected with advancing age, but was a consistently integrated feature of her faith. Her friend Jennie Street, another Sunday school advocate, writing in the *Christian World* after Marianne's death, echoed this emphasis. She commented of Marianne that 'she did not love death; she was too healthy-natured, too vigorously alive for that. But I have never known anyone who took a more vivid interest in the life beyond, or who talked of it with a more trustful assurance.'[193] As her experience of bereavement would not have been unusual, this was more than a commonplace expression of generalised hope. The anticipation of heaven appears to have a reality to her: she lived in the expectation and awareness of a future beyond death.

---

[189] Farningham, *Sketches* (1861), p. 75.
[190] Farningham, *Brothers & Sisters*, p. 186.
[191] Farningham, *Evening Lights*, p. 112.
[192] Farningham, *Evening Lights*, p. 103.
[193] *CW*, 18 March 1909.

How did Marianne conceive of heaven? What kind of imagery did she use? From what we know of her already, we would expect her conception of heaven to be similar to that of other evangelicals of her time, possibly evolving a little over the years. It is no surprise, therefore, to find that in common with many of her contemporaries, Marianne regarded arriving in heaven as a kind of final home-coming. Henry Rack has suggested that this domestication of heaven increased throughout the nineteenth century, and Patricia Jalland similarly discovered that homely imagery of heaven was used increasingly from the 1860s, and expressed even more strongly by 1880.[194] Interestingly, however, in Marianne's writing the concept of heaven as home is as strong in 1860 as at the end of the century. In 1861 she wrote of the joy of 'a brighter, fairer home' where there is 'eternal rest', and a few years later she entitled a piece about heaven 'Going Home'. In it she comments that it is nice after a holiday amongst strangers to go home and see your loved ones again, but it is even better to think of 'a brighter, fairer home' and the greeting there.[195] In her writings the domestication of heaven thus seems to occur at a slightly earlier stage than in popular thought generally, an indication that, at least in this instance, Marianne is not only reflecting popular thinking, but helping to shape it. It is probable that this emphasis is more than domestication, but is an indication of the strength of Nonconformist belief in the fellowship of believers.[196] The imagery used, however, is frequently homely, inviting domestic comparisons.

A logical consequence of this imagery about heaven was the assumption that loved ones might be at the door to welcome newcomers. Thus in 1897 Marianne wrote poetically if somewhat ungrammatically of death as a journey in which 'we can sail gently away, with our eyes on the fading lights of the west, and our ears listening for the welcomes home with which they will greet us who have gone before'.[197] This idea of greeting on arrival in heaven produced one of her most popular poems 'Watching and waiting for me', although she commented that this was drawn from a legend, giving the impression that she did not necessarily believe it herself.[198] Heaven was understood as a place of reunion, where there would be no more partings.[199]

Of more significance even than meeting those who have 'gone before', however, was the thought of an encounter with Jesus. Describing the arrival of

---

[194] H. D. Rack, 'Evangelical Endings: Death-beds in Evangelical biography', in *Bulletin of the John Rylands University Library of Manchester* Vol 74, No 1, (1992), p 52, and Jalland, P, *Death in the Victorian Family* (Oxford: Oxford University Press, 1996) p. 273, p. 275.
[195] Farningham, *Sketches* (1861), p. 79.
[196] Bebbington, *Dominance*, p. 83.
[197] Farningham, *Evening Lights*, p. 74.
[198] Farningham, *Life*, p. 140.
[199] Farningham, *Sketches* (1861), p. 69.

a woman in heaven, Marianne imagines her kneeling before Jesus:

> He raised and folded her in His kind arms,
> And bade her welcome to her home in heaven![200]

Jalland has suggested that there were two dominant conceptions of heaven during this time, that of home and family, and of worship,[201] and Marianne's emphases tend to bear this out. Marianne was either unaware of, or unsympathetic to, the suggestion that the afterlife might provide an opportunity for further service. An extract from one of her own poems, which was printed on the back of the pamphlet for her memorial service, expresses these ideas of home and peace:

> When I go home it will be evening,
> And I shall hear my own dear people sing
> And see the lighted rooms and take my place
> As one with them, in that sweet time of grace.
>
> When I go home I shall be very tired
> Of struggling for the things that I desired
> But I shall be content to end my quest,
> Gaining the best things, peace and love and rest.[202]

Whether she herself chose these verses, or they were chosen by those close to her, it indicates their shared belief in heaven as home and a place of rest after a lifetime of work. Heaven thus played a significant role in Marianne's religious awareness. She frequently referred to it, and others recognised that the expectation of a future life impinged on her experience now. In this, she reflected the religious sensibilities of her contemporaries, and encouraged her readers in their own beliefs.

Unorthodox Beliefs

Marianne held some beliefs that were closer to popular religion than to official evangelicalism, although they are mentioned rarely, and mostly early on in her career. For instance, in an excessively sentimental early poem, 'The Wife's Farewell' a dying woman is made to say

> And I will ask to come
> And float around thee in thy sombre hours…
> And fan thy aching brow

---

[200] Farningham, *Lays and Lyrics*, p. 130.
[201] Jalland, *Death*, pp. 267-73. She argued that although the idea of a 'dynamic' future life was present in preaching, it was not part of popular belief. Also see Bebbington, *Dominance*, p. 83,
[202] 'When I go home it will be evening' in *Joy and Faith*, p. 206.

With the cool, soothing airs of Paradise[203]

This concept of an aspect of the afterlife is both naïve and theologically dubious. There is a similar instance in *Life Sketches*, in which Marianne encouraged a child to visit a cemetery, because lessons can be learned there, and it is well to 'have communed with departed spirits' once in a while.[204] It is not exactly clear if this was meant figuratively, as in the child imagining a discussion with someone who is dead, or literally, in other words that it was possible to actually have some communication with dead spirits by visiting a graveyard. Two pages later, she returns to the subject of spirits, asking 'How do we know what spirits of good or evil are floating around us? Perhaps we feel their influence, perhaps from many dangers they shield us; but we know them not – that wonderful ethereal world, that may be about us, is hidden from our view.'[205] Here it is unclear whether Marianne is referring back to the spirits of dead people as mentioned previously, or if this is now a discussion of the presence of angels and demons close to humanity, but it sounds more like popular superstition than orthodox Christianity, and it is hard to integrate this with her beliefs about heaven. It is interesting that there seem to be no later examples of such ideas, suggesting either that these were unthinking superstitions on which her views changed, or that she no longer expressed them in public.

In her autobiography there are other references to practices which seem unlikely for an evangelical Christian. One is concerned with the popular custom of 'telling the bees' when someone had died. Marianne's father kept bees, and when a cousin died, they went together for 'a curious little ceremony' in which her father tapped the hive, and told them his cousin was dead. Marianne recalled 'I felt a cold shiver pass over me, as I distinctly heard a wailing response like a buzzing moan from the bees'. This, apparently, was their way of expressing their sorrow.[206] She regarded this manifestation of popular religion as just an interesting custom, and her father obviously saw no conflict between this and his role as Baptist deacon. Another popular trend was reflected when she mentions a visit to a phrenologist as a girl, with no positive or negative comments, just as one of those things which people do. The fact that she seemed unselfconscious in mentioning these popular habits indicates that they were ideas shared by at least some of her evangelical contemporaries. It could also be an indication of a degree of syncretism in rural areas where local folk religion seemed to sit happily with Christian belief. Interestingly, there is no evidence of any interest on her part in Spiritualism, which became very popular during the nineteenth century.

---

[203] Farningham, *Lays & Lyrics*, p. 114.
[204] Farningham, *Sketches* (1861), p. 102.
[205] Farningham, *Sketches* (1861), p. 104.
[206] Farningham, *Life*, p. 16.

Doubts and Difficulties

It has been noted recently that evangelicals were 'often remarkably willing to admit' to doubts.[207] Certainly, Marianne freely acknowledged that not only were there difficulties in the Christian life, but that many people were troubled by doubts. In the novel *Nineteen Hundred*, Marianne has one character, the 'basket woman' lead another, Fanny, to the point of conversion, whilst commenting that 'she had often doubted, and sometimes been inclined to believe nothing; yet now that a soul looked to her for light all the doubts seemed strangely to vanish, and all the old lessons came back to her, as she told the story of the Christ'.[208] This tale of an individual's doubts dispelled by the simple act of sharing faith is one that some readers might well have identified with. Some, however, might consider the remedy a little trite. Perhaps it is an indication that, as she herself acknowledges, doubt was not a major problem for her. Late in life she wrote 'It has not been easy for me to doubt, and I have had no hesitation as to prayer'.[209] Although she was intelligent, and, as has been seen, interested in issues of the day such as hell, or approaches to Genesis, it seems as if little ever shook Marianne's faith. Her writings, however, indicate that this was not because she felt doubts ought to be excluded as inappropriate, but was more a question of her personality and own experience.[210] Nor was she amongst those who questioned the involvement of God in 'all the trivial decisions of everyday life'; rather, she continued to understand that such involvement was an essential part of the life of faith.[211]

Whilst she might not have experienced strong doubts, she certainly went through her share of difficulties, and she appeared to write about these times with honesty. Thus she commented in the *Sunday School Times* in 1885 that in difficult seasons it can feel as if we are 'lost in the tangled underbrush, and have no light to show us the way back to joy and peace'.[212] In one poem 'A Fulfilled Promise' she lamented that once the 'easy years' had passed 'Then the conflict fiercer grew, and I more of sorrow knew', whilst in a different poem in the same collection she implied that some days were difficult 'Even some Mays in mist are clad, And sorrow wakes as soon as I'.[213] Similarly, in a short piece commenting on a Biblical passage from Luke, in which Jesus healed a crippled woman, Marianne noted that he took the initiative because of the state of the woman, and that we can be like her at times: 'Bent and depressed, with no eyes for the heavens, we have lost our joy, and are of no use to ourselves or others,

---

[207] Bebbington, *Dominance*, p. 81.
[208] Farningham, *Nineteen Hundred*, p. 94.
[209] Farningham, *Life*, p. 279.
[210] *SST* 2 January 1885.
[211] McLeod, *Religion and Society*, p. 186.
[212] *SST* 2 January 1885.
[213] Farningham, *Harvest*, p. 25 and p. 16.

and least of all to God'.[214] She was under no illusions that the Christian life was an easy one, and she communicated her own experience, whether good or bad. It was this, no doubt, which helped to endear her to her many readers. She also gave the impression that she regarded questioning as an integral part of the journey of faith, rather than a sin to be repented of, recognising that many people, including herself, questioned God in times of trouble, asking

> Why is he not near us when we want Him? Why does he not heal our sick? Why does he not prevent sorrow and sin? Why is He so silent? Why does he not give the world some signs of His coming? Why does he not stop war and bring peace? Why is he so long absent? What is Jesus doing?[215]

Similar sentiments were expressed in a late poem 'The presence of Christ' (1908) with the initial lines

> He does not seem to answer
> All my prayers,
> Nor always lift the burden
> Of my cares'.[216]

Such issues, however, did not for Marianne ultimately lead to a loss of faith, but rather to a deeper trust in God. In the same poem she declared that 'If I know him near me all is well'.[217] Once again, relationship with God was the central focus of her spirituality and the answer to all problems. In the moment of most need, Jesus 'brings us light, leads us out of our distress, and guides us back to joy and comfort'.[218] The choice of this subject of the spiritual life for her first editorial in the *Sunday School Times* is an indication of the importance to her of this topic of finding help from God in both the difficulties and the joyful times of life. Whatever the questions, ultimately the answer was in an intimate relationship with the divine, with experience rather than rational discussion, a solution that could be identified as more influenced by Romanticism than Enlightenment.

Given that experience of God was so central to her spirituality, difficulties could arise when the subjective sense of that presence was lost. She recounted missing God's presence and 'searching and crying for Thee' but always with the assumption that 'in time, I shall find Thee'.[219] Marianne's down to earth, popular theology suggested that there was always a way forward: in her world view Jesus would always come and lead an individual back into the light and the place of faith. She provided hope and a sense of direction for those who

---

[214] Farningham, *Saviour*, pp. 66-68.
[215] Farningham, *Saviour*, pp. 13-15.
[216] Farningham, *Lyrics of the Soul*, p. 41.
[217] Farningham, *Lyrics of the Soul*, p. 41.
[218] *SST* 2 January 1885.
[219] Farningham, *Saviour*, pp. 14-15.

were struggling with life and faith. Ultimately, God was in control, and even when 'everything appears to be happening for the very worst,' disappointments and even bereavements could be 'blessings in disguise'.[220] For her, too, responding to difficulties appears to be connected with the approach to the Christian Life she learned at Brighton in 1875, of surrender to and rest in Christ. Thus she suggested that the appropriate response to difficulties is to let Jesus carry all one's worries, letting him choose the way ahead.[221] This can sound extremely passive, but it was a philosophy that seemed to work in practice for Marianne. Although her comments might sound a little trite, Marianne was writing out of her own hard-earned experience, so it is likely that it is the means of expression, rather than the ideas expressed, that can appear simplistic at times.

Her understanding of sickness developed during her writing career. In her earliest selection of prose pieces, she commented that we all have to contend with illness at some stage: 'Certainly it is one of our very greatest trials to be called away from the business and delights of life, and lie prostrate and helpless as an infant.' Our reaction, she suggests, is to rebel and have 'hard thoughts of the hand that has laid us there', but it would be better to 'set ourselves humbly to learn what he will teach' so that if we recover, we 'will sing his praises'.[222] By the end of her life, however, Marianne had come to believe that illnesses are not sent from God: 'Let us not suppose that when trouble and sickness overtake us God has sent them for punishment. I think that he is sorry for us. He will take us into His arms and comfort us, and will presently show us that the discipline of sorrow is the growth of the soul.'[223] She wrote, presumably out of her own experience, that the later years bring both joy and sadness: 'Broken friendships, broken plans, broken health, sometimes even broken hearts...We are very poor when we leave this world.'[224] But it was also easier to surrender to God: older people, she suggests, more easily 'give their worries all up, and are more than glad to lie in the arms of God, and grow quiet with the sense of an infinite repose. All is well with them at last, and they learn, as they never did before, that in returning and rest they shall be saved; in quietness and confidence shall be their strength.'[225] This concept of rest and trust, learnt in Brighton, seems to have served her well during her later years.

Although Marianne engaged with issues of doubt, therefore, it is as if she did so from the security of a safe harbour, rather than from sharing the danger of the storm. She certainly had some serious difficulties in her life, primarily bereavements, but there seems to have been no real danger of her faith being

---

[220] Farningham, *Sketches*, (1861), p. 73.
[221] Farningham, *Evening Lights*, pp. 9-10.
[222] Farningham, *Sketches* (1861), pp. 23-24.
[223] Farningham, *Life*, p. 280.
[224] Farningham, *Evening Lights*, p. 100.
[225] Farningham, *Evening Lights*, p. 73.

undermined by those events. Likewise with intellectual difficulties, although she questioned doctrines which led others to lose their faith – primarily over the question of everlasting punishment – the strong assurance she gained from her belief in a close personal relationship with God meant that she was able to revise her views without any danger of losing her faith. Yet her honesty is commendable: even today, some evangelicals struggle to be honest about their pursuit of faith amid the difficulties of life. Because of this she would have been a help to others in a similar situation, although it was quite late in her life when she finally wrote explicitly on the subject.

Changing Attitudes to Leisure and the Use of Time

Another area of spirituality in which Marianne's attitudes changed over the years, reflecting those of the evangelical milieu in which she lived, was the wise use of time. This was an area of some anxiety when Marianne was first writing. She was concerned about the ways that her readers, especially the younger ones, filled their leisure hours. Recreation was necessary, but pleasures had to be suitable and not sinful, however that was defined. She suggested to the young readers of *Girlhood* that a useful rule for leisure activities was to 'never engage in anything upon which you cannot ask God's blessing'.[226] Commenting about this aspect of early nineteenth-century evangelicalism, Doreen Rosman has argued that even those who believed in the value of leisure had 'unease about their use of time'. This, she observed, was particularly evident amongst dissenters.[227] In the 1850s and 60s, when Marianne Farningham was in the early years of her journalistic career, it could be argued that this unease had grown, and was verging on obsession. This was the period during which, as Bebbington has noted, 'the cult of duty, self-discipline and high seriousness was at its peak'.[228] In this climate, an anxiety existed amongst evangelicals which led them to insist on the importance of using every moment wisely, to work hard, and to be cautious about the way their increasing leisure was spent. Some of Marianne's early pieces demonstrate this sense of worry. In *Life Sketches*, for instance, she suggested that it was commendable to be constantly busy, because time must not be wasted. 'When tempted to be inert and slothful', she argued, 'let us remember that there is much to do; time is very short, and we have "not a minute to spare".'[229] Evangelicals were conscious that one day, each individual would have to give an account to God for their lives, and in an age of railway timetables and increased clock consciousness, they believed that part of this would be for the use of their

---

[226] Farningham, *Girlhood*, p. 43.
[227] D. Rosman, *Evangelicals and Culture* (London: Croom Helm, 1984), p. 121.
[228] Bebbington, *Evangelicalism*, p. 105.
[229] Farningham, *Sketches* (1861), pp. 39-40 and p. 66.

time.[230] She was fearful that her readers might be wasting some of their precious minutes. A rather trite poem dating from 1860 also encapsulates this fear–

> Only a day – a little day!–
> Full half its hours were wasted
> We trifled in its morning prime,
> Forgetting how it hasted...
>
> Only a day – we might have helped
> To stem the raging waters;
> We might have blessed and comforted
> Earth's wretched sons and daughters.[231]

Half a day spent relaxing with friends was thus portrayed as an unsuitable use of time, and the implication was that to enjoy leisure was sinful if there was work, especially philanthropy or mission, waiting to be done. However, Marianne also believed in the need for play: 'we do well to take all the happiness we can find in the world,' she wrote of the need for relaxation, 'seeing that our Father in heaven has sent it on purpose for us'.[232] Marianne's early views on the subject of work and leisure were strong and straightforward and would have struck a chord with her readers.

Such a sentiment did not appear in quite the same form in her later writings. The near-obsession with the use of time disappeared. What remained was a belief in a disciplined and careful use of time. Whereas in 1860 she had written urgently about the need not to waste time, and in 1861 with enthusiasm about the fast pace of life, only a few years later her writings reveal a more balanced approach. In *Home Life*, published in 1869, she suggested that 'we live too fast, we work too hard, there is too great a strain both on body and mind'.[233] Relaxation was not only permitted, but vital, to alleviate this strain, whether through reading aloud in the family circle, or taking a walk in the country. It did not even need a clear purpose. She did not 'believe that time absolutely given up to fun and nothing else is wasted. On the contrary, so it be free from sin, it is well spent.'[234] Approval of the need for leisure was thus given. As Marianne's early attitudes to the use of time mellowed, so that she was more comfortable with leisure, she was reflecting the experience of the evangelical community, and indeed, middle-class culture as a whole, as it came to terms with the extra time available for relaxation and worked out how best to fill it. Between 1870 and 1914, according to McLeod, there was a 'leisure revolution'

---

[230] Farningham, *Sketches* (1861), p. 17.
[231] Farningham, *Lays and Lyrics*, pp. 63-64.
[232] Farningham, *Girlhood*, p. 39.
[233] Farningham, *Home Life*, p. 38.
[234] Farningham, *Home Life*, p. 41.

which affected the whole of society, including the churches.[235] The subtle changes in Marianne's writing reflected the developments in evangelical attitudes over these years.

It is possible, however, to over-emphasise the change in Marianne's attitude. All through her life she taught that leisure time was a gift from God, which should be enjoyed for its own sake, as well as for the beneficial effect it could have on work. 'To those who live to purpose, who devote the far greater part of their time to *duty*, there come many pleasures', she wrote in a very early piece,[236] and in her autobiography she wrote at length about some of those pleasures, especially travel and the enjoyment of nature. Leisure always remained, in her view, something that came after the necessary work had been done. In one piece, entitled 'Drudgery', an early contribution, she discussed ordinary everyday tasks, asserting that leisure is only genuinely enjoyable if people have worked first.[237] Similarly in her biography of Grace Darling, Grace was portrayed as a good and cheerful worker, but Marianne suggested that 'it was a happy time for her when the work of the day was done, and she was able to sit down by the fireside, and read from her favourite books'.[238] Work was thus the purpose of life, and leisure the earned relaxation bodies and minds needed in order to work more effectively.

Marianne was also concerned about the ways that her readers, especially the younger ones, filled their leisure time. Recreation was necessary, but pleasures had to be suitable and not sinful, however that was defined. One of the most appropriate ways of spending leisure time was, for Marianne, in appreciation of nature. Romantic by inclination, and brought up in a Kent village, Marianne greatly appreciated the countryside, and she often referred to nature in her newspaper column.[239] 'Do you ever sit under the shade of a tree on a hill,' she wrote, 'and look over a beautiful landscape until your heart has grown full, and the tears have come unbidden to your eyes?'[240] She tended to believe that people brought up in the country had an advantage over those in cities. Thus in her biography of Spurgeon, his experience of tramping as a teenager through the countryside to his preaching appointments is portrayed as a strong advantage: 'God and His world of nature! What better could there be to fill the

---

[235] McLeod, *Church and Society*, pp. 196-201. Also see Peter Bailey, *Leisure and Class in Victorian England* (London: Routledge and Kegan Paul, 1978), Chapter 3, on the middle classes and the new leisure in the mid-Victorian period.

[236] Farningham, *Sketches* (1861), p. 22.

[237] Farningham, *Sketches* (1861), p. 67. A similar sentiment is expressed in *Home Life*, p. 88.

[238] E. Hope, *Grace Darling* (London: Walter Scott & Co, 1875), p. 56. See Chapter 5 pp. 61-63 for discussion of this biography.

[239] Two of many such examples can be found in Farningham, *Girlhood*, pp. 40-42, and 'The Woods' in Farningham, *Joy and Faith*, p. 122, which, like many of her publications, are collections of her weekly articles.

[240] Farningham, *Girlhood*, pp. 40-41.

young student's thoughts and inspire his imagination?'[241] Similarly, Grace Darling's time spent outdoors at the lighthouse is interpreted as the source of her strength.[242] Nature was, for Marianne, a true shaper of character and an important part of the lives she wrote about. The influence of Romanticism, which saw the immanence of God in creation, was evident in much of Marianne's poetry and prose.[243] In this she was reflecting a development within evangelicalism but, once again, because of her influence, she would have been contributing, if to a small extent, to the legitimisation of that trend amongst her readers.[244] Such an appreciation of nature could also be usefully coupled with another important element, exercise. During her years of full-time writing, her preferred pattern of work included a morning walk, and she also recommended this to others.[245] In 1869 she advised her young female readers to have regular cold baths, and frequent exercise in fresh air, suggesting at least one walk a day, preferably in the morning, although not before breakfast.[246] The following year she gave similar advice to boys, with the disconcerting suggestion that to sit in front of a fire with a book in winter could lead to mental illness.[247] Taking a walk thus combined two virtues: the need for exercise and fresh air and the enjoyment of nature.

Reading was another great pleasure for Marianne and she encouraged the habit in her own readers. Her advice indicates, however, that she remained extremely cautious about what constituted 'really good books', suggesting that some novels and periodicals were 'full of hidden stings and secret mischief', whilst others were 'silly and quite useless', or even 'vile'.[248] Her advice to girls was that if there were passages in a book which could not be read aloud to the men in the family without blushes the book should be discarded,[249] a comment which has been cited as an example of the 'proliferation of advice directed towards protecting girls from unsuitable books' found at that time.[250] The intriguing aspect of this, of course, is that as a child Marianne had herself been subject to such advice from other members of her chapel and had rejected it.[251] Her definition of a good book, the only sort worth reading, was restricted to one which had a moral purpose, a perspective shared in theory, if not practice, by many of her contemporaries. Marianne also believed in restricting time spent

---

[241] Hope, *Spurgeon*, p. 27.
[242] Hope, *Darling*, p. 14.
[243] Bebbington, *Dominance*, p. 170.
[244] McLeod, *Religion and Society*, p. 199.
[245] Farningham, *Life*, p. 139.
[246] Farningham, *Girlhood*, pp. 67-69.
[247] Farningham, *Boyhood*, p. 40.
[248] Farningham, *Home Life*, p. 54, Farningham, *Girlhood*, p. 46, Farningham, *Boyhood*, p. 54.
[249] Farningham, *Girlhood*, p. 46.
[250] K. Flint, *The Woman Reader 1837-1914* (Oxford; Clarendon Press, 1993), p. 89.
[251] Chapter 2

reading. To both young men and women she insisted that it was important not to read when there was still work to be done. 'Books can be so bewitching that everything else is neglected for them', she wrote in *Girlhood*, surely an indication of her own fondness for them. The remedy, she suggested, was to set aside part of the day for reading, and to be careful about keeping to it.[252] To boys she similarly suggested that young people should 'read only good books in a proper way, and at a suitable time'.[253] Thus an anxiety about the use of time, and leisure in particular, had been reduced by 1869 to advising self-discipline to control the potential dangers of free time. This was a perspective which Marianne continued to maintain, although by the time she wrote her autobiography it was less of a pressing issue.

Holidays, of course, gave scope for all these pleasures and more, and they became more common for the lower middle class during this period. Marianne believed that holidays were a good thing, suggesting frequent breaks, either by the sea or in the country.[254] She took plenty herself, though she usually worked when travelling, using what she saw as material for short prose pieces. On several occasions she also took some of her girls' class away together. Several of them had never seen the sea, 'holidays were not so easy and common then as now' and they apparently were thrilled at the sight.[255] Her own holidays ranged from short trips within England to a Cook's tour of the Holy Land, paid for by a friend.[256] But if these holidays were often more busy than relaxing, her cottage in Barmouth, which she rented from the mid-1880s, did provide a place for retreat, rest, and the enjoyment of nature. She was so thrilled with having 'a cot of my very own' where she could retreat when strength and health were at a low ebb, that she declared that she could not 'imagine why the plan is not more often tried'.[257] Whether through holidays or just regular walks, Marianne believed in the recuperative power of nature and exercise.

Marianne's Attitude to the Sabbath

Another facet of rest amongst evangelicals in this period was of course the Sabbath, and here too Marianne's slowly changing attitudes mirrored those of the wider Nonconformist community.[258] In her early writings, she is very particular about the use of Sunday, regarding it as a day given over to recuperation, and to thinking and reading about God. As with much of her early

---

[252] Farningham, *Girlhood*, pp. 44-45.
[253] Farningham, *Boyhood*, pp. 54-56.
[254] Farningham, *Girlhood*, p. 42.
[255] Farningham, *Life*, p. 122.
[256] Farningham, *Life*, pp. 179-187.
[257] Farningham, *Life*, pp. 230-34.
[258] J. Wigley, *The Rise and Fall of the Victorian Sunday* (Manchester: Manchester University Press, 1980).

writing (she was probably about 27 when she wrote this) it comes over as a little naïve, simplistic and sentimental, although one must not assume that she is being in any way dishonest. 'What a tranquil, sacred part of our life is that which is passed in the courts of the Lord!' she declared, when those who are worn out with work can find refreshment: 'what deep peace floats into the spirit! How easy it then seems to leave all events to our loving Friend!' Whilst in the 'busy, bustling week, we have only had snatches of the promises – hasty glances into the loving face of the Redeemer', but in comparison on Sunday there is time to 'sit and enjoy the good things spread before us to our hearts' grateful content'.[259] She believed that Sunday was a much-needed opportunity for refreshment, but at this stage she was quite rigid in her interpretation of the day of rest, criticising people who allow the postman to call on Sunday and who eat hot dinners cooked by someone else, calling this by implication a 'desecration of the Sabbath'.[260] Her early understanding of the Sabbath was conventionally evangelical and legalistic. In the same collection of pieces, Marianne commented that philanthropists, wanting people to have holidays, were suggesting that art galleries and gardens should be open on Sundays. She thought, however, that it would be better for people to take some time each day to meet friends and enjoy nature. Yet in the previous sentence she acknowledges that some employers keep young people working too long: fourteen or fifteen hours a day, until an hour is needed to do the work of half an hour. Where they were also supposed to find the time to visit a forest or a river is not clear. Her reason for suggesting spending time with nature on other days is so that on Sunday they were free to have a days 'of real rest; go and lie by the still waters and in the green pastures of the Redeemer's love'. Then the next day will find you refreshed and able to save time.[261] For Marianne, time spent in church clearly was a refreshing and invigorating experience, and she assumed that this was true for everyone.

As Chapter 2 has explored, church was for Marianne a significant part of her spirituality, which was not just an individualised experience, but included a network of relationships, and a sense of belonging to a community. This is seen most clearly in comments about her youth and the rural chapel she attended. As an adult she expressed it mainly through her girls' class. She wrote surprisingly little about her church involvement as an adult. Whilst she frequently mentioned the sermons of John Turland Brown at College Street, which provided her with ideas and inspiration for her writing, as well as personal spiritual encouragement, there is little about the current church community there. In the pages of the *Sunday School Times,* she discussed topics related to church life as it impinged on the schools, but either she regarded the subject of the local church as inappropriate for publication, or in her maturity it lost some

---

[259] Farningham, *Sketches,* pp. 9-11.

[260] Farningham, *Sketches,* p. 128.

[261] Farningham, *Sketches,* p. 40.

of its significance for her.

As the nineteenth century progressed, the attitude of some evangelicals towards Sundays softened.[262] Reflecting this, by the end of the century, Marianne's attitude had also changed. Personally, she spent her Sundays at College Street Chapel, and taking her girls' class on a Sunday afternoon, but wrote very little in later years, or in her autobiography, about the Sabbath, which in itself is interesting, indicating that its observance was no longer a major concern for her, and possibly indicating it was also becoming less of an issue for her readership. Significantly, in a later collection of her prose pieces *Homely Talks about Homely Things*, published in 1886, there was an item entitled 'Joyous Sunday' in which the writer envisaged the working-class spending time enjoying nature not as a distraction from true rest, but as a possible means of connecting with the God who created nature. Rather than lamenting their lack of church attendance, she suggested here that others should not judge them or assume that they have no spiritual experience. Who knows, she argued, how many of these people 'come crowding to Him in thought, and longing, and need, through the silence of the Sabbath. They do not say a word to us about it – why should they? – perhaps they do not even say a word to Him; but He understands.'[263] This is an intriguing passage, as it is hinting at more than just a question of how people should occupy themselves on Sundays, but at the whole nature of spiritual experience, and the possibility of knowing God without verbalising that belief to oneself or others. It is clear evidence of the permeating influence of Romanticism within Nonconformity. Similarly the 1903 collection *Harvest Gleanings* contains a poem entitled 'At Church in the Open', which appears to have been written on a Sunday spent amongst nature rather than at church, as she writes of her family worshipping as they always do, whilst she 'in Thy green aisles', asks for the 'tree and fern' to speak to her of God, finishing by asking

> May my Sabbath service rise
> From this church of birds and flowers
> Higher than the deep-blue skies
> And these consecrated hours
> be to me a fount of strength
> When my work-day dawns at length.[264]

She wrote here of her usual understanding of Sabbath: that it was a time for rest and recuperation in the presence of God, such that energy was given for the following week, but on this occasion it was derived not from a church service but from nature. Possibly it was written during a time of illness, as the impression is given that the work day, rather than being the following day, might be some time away. Another example of this is 'Whitsuntide' (1908) in

---

[262] Bebbington, *Dominance*, p. 225.
[263] Farningham, *Homely Talks*, p. 70.
[264] Farningham, *Harvest Gleanings*, p. 103.

which Marianne wrote of people visiting the countryside, and experiencing a 'whisper' of the Holy Spirit, even though

> They may not know
> Whence comes the better thought
> But in them, in the midst of play
> Some subtle change is wrought.[265]

Marianne's attitude towards the Sabbath thus developed, rather than remaining fixed in the rigid practice of her youth, influenced by and reflecting changes within both contemporary society and Nonconformity.

Evangelicalism and Ecumenism

Evangelicalism has always been an umbrella term incorporating much common ground, some variations of doctrine and a range of expressions of spirituality.[266] The nineteenth century saw the founding of the Evangelical Alliance and other initiatives of co-operation, but many people remained suspicious and at times overtly critical of fellow evangelicals who differed from them in belief and practice. In this area Marianne's attitude changed significantly during her lifetime. From her Strict and Particular background she gradually became open to a wide range of Christian belief and experience both within and beyond the evangelical camp. At the end of her life, she implied that she had never really been a Calvinist, distancing herself from the beliefs of her church origins.[267] She was certainly not alone in her journey from a narrow to a broader belief system. The Congregational leader R W Dale, for instance, was one of many who trod a similar path.[268] This development was one more facet of her life in which her experience mirrored that of a section of her evangelical contemporaries.

Although Marianne remained a Baptist all her life, she also toyed with Congregationalism. When she first arrived in Northampton, finding College Street Baptist not initially to her taste, she spent some weeks at a Congregational church, even joining the choir, and becoming friends with the pastor and his wife before returning in the end to her Baptist roots at College Street.[269] In later years when she rented a cottage in Barmouth, she became involved with the Congregational church there, attending on a Sunday during the winter when the English-speaking Baptist Chapel was not functioning. She also laid the foundation stone of the new Congregationalist building in 1896 and became friendly with the ministers, the Rev. Z. Mather and later the Rev.

---

[265] Farningham, *Lyrics of the Soul*, p. 142
[266] Randall, *What a Friend*, p.23.
[267] Farningham, *Life*, p. 55, in which she recalls giving an elder 'the answer he wanted' concerning good works and salvation.
[268] Bebbington, *Dominance*, pp. 126-27.
[269] Farningham, *Life*, p. 91.

W. Glandwr-Morgan.[270] Whilst she always remained a Baptist at heart, she was sympathetic to other churches, and in many way Congregationalist ecclesiology was closest to that of Baptists.

Marianne's sympathy, however, extended also to churches unlike her own. According to her autobiographical account, for example, she was well-disposed towards the Salvation Army at a time when they faced considerable opposition, no doubt impressed by their ability to evangelise. She considered Catherine Booth to be 'one of the most saintly and gifted heroines of the century'.[271] In her autobiography she portrayed herself as reassuring Catherine when the latter was heckled in a public meeting, thus indicating her support.[272] Shortly after Catherine's death, Marianne wrote an appreciation in the *Sunday School Times*, noting that 'her motherly influence has done more than can be imagined towards its success' and suggesting that 'no one who once saw and heard Mrs Booth, and talked with her about her work and its object, could speak slightingly of the motives which actuated her and her husband'.[273] Despite some uncertainties about their methods, Marianne obviously had no animosity or sense of rivalry towards the Army, but was generous in her appreciation of its strengths. This attitude was typical of her determination to see the best in others. She entertained the rather forlorn hope that disputes between Christians might gradually cease. Recalling towards the end of the century an occasion when Spurgeon provoked vocal opposition, she opined approvingly, if rather optimistically, that 'happily good people have found something better to do than to denounce the religious opinions of each other'.[274] As Glandwr-Morgan commented, she was 'first a Christian, then a denominationalist'.[275] Christian unity was more important to her than doctrinal precision.

This tendency to stress common values and friendships, rather than areas of disagreement, is also evident in her treatment of Spurgeon, who she clearly respected yet disagreed with, noting approvingly of her father that whilst he read Spurgeon's sermons, his theology 'was on a broader basis'.[276] When composing her biography of Spurgeon, Marianne did her best to ignore the Downgrade controversy, one of the most controversial aspects of his career, only mentioning it briefly in the main text and mostly consigning discussion to a short appendix, in which she deftly managed to take both sides of the dispute at once, by suggesting both that Spurgeon's 'protest was needed' and undertaken 'from the highest motives' but that he was also behind the times and

---

[270] Glandwr-Morgan, *Welsh Home*, especially Chapter 3.
[271] Farningham, *Life*, p. 242.
[272] Farningham, *Life*, p. 242. See Chapter 2, p. 93.
[273] *SST* 17 October 1890.
[274] Hope, *Spurgeon*, p. 120. This biography has no date but was probably written soon after the death of Spurgeon early in 1892.
[275] Glandwr-Morgan, *Welsh Home*, Chapter 4.
[276] Farningham, *Life*, p. 149.

unduly suspicious of his fellow Baptist ministers.[277] This desire to see the best in others, and to sympathise with them, at times led to her apparently supporting points of view which she actually disagreed with. In this biography she also took issue with some of Spurgeon's critics, giving the false impression that she was in sympathy with his theological views.[278] She was always more concerned about enjoying a good relationship with people than with finding total agreement.

Marianne's generous appreciation of her fellow-Christians ranged beyond evangelicalism and Nonconformity, and she openly drew on a wide range of influences in her work. There are indications that this tendency developed early, as in *Lays and Lyrics* she was already writing with hope of the future when 'party spirit' would not divide Christians and 'our grand cathedrals will not be/Closed to God's servants of another name'.[279] The same year one of her pieces for the Christian World, reprinted in *Life Sketches,* began with some verses by the high Anglican John Keble.[280] One poem in *Harvest Gleanings* has a very similar rhythm to a Celtic prayer: 'The love of Christ befriend you, The care of Christ attend you', whilst another indicates a knowledge of the mystics, declaring that in God's presence 'I have no good to crave, Desire shall cease'.[281] Her influences were eclectic. The clearest statement of her ecumenical beliefs can be found in her idealistic novel *Nineteen Hundred* in which the ministers from various churches sink their differences of opinion in the cause of furthering the gospel and social justice in the imaginary town of Darentdale. 'There was here, happily, no bitterness between the Clergyman and the Dissenting ministers... the men were brothers, who respected the good which they saw in each other, and carried together the burden of the souls of the people.'[282] In the novel, the way these men worked together led the way to an eventual establishment of a Christian social and political movement which transformed the country. Whilst this might appear a little extreme, not to say unlikely, the desire to work together with other Christians, at least evangelical Protestant ones, represented a section of evangelical public opinion at the end of the century.

Initially she did not extend this sympathy to Catholics. In her novel *The Cathedral's Shadow* (1871), the main theme is a dislike for Catholicism and the way people can be lured into its net, with deceit being employed to make converts. The Cathedral is an evil presence in the novel, a character in its own right. The desire to be a nun is described by one character as 'senseless', and the assumption is made that Catholics cannot pray directly to God. Discussing

---

[277] Hope, *Spurgeon*, pp. 327-30.

[278] Hope, *Spurgeon,* p. 56.

[279] Farningham, *Lays and Lyrics* (1861), p. 14.

[280] Farningham, *Sketches* (1861), p. 33.

[281] Farningham, *Harvest*, p. 65, p. 39.

[282] Farningham, *Nineteen Hundred*, p. 73.

the longing to know God, she wrote that 'with Romanists that want cannot be satisfied, and the heart often grows only sick with longing'.[283] Catholicism was at this stage considered by Marianne to be a 'poison' which prevented people from finding true faith.[284] In this she was in tune with fellow-Protestants, sharing an antagonism which, whilst reaching its peak in the mid-century, continued for several decades.[285] Yet even this attitude mellowed a little over the ensuing years. Visiting Rome in 1889, she noted 'Of course we spent Easter Sunday at St Peter's' but she was disappointed by the lack of reverence shown by the tourists during the service, clearly believing that she would have been able worship God in that context if the other visitors had been better behaved.[286] Following the death of Cardinal Manning early in 1892 she called him 'that great good man' and suggested that 'the nation sorrowed' for him.[287] Yet in *Nineteen Hundred*, published around the same time, in 1892, there is no suggestion that Catholics were involved in the great project to bring the Kingdom of heaven to earth in England, although there is no denunciation either. They are conspicuous by their absence in this novel, which indicates that Catholicism never became for Marianne genuinely a part of the Christian communion. There is some indication of a further change of attitude, however, in her final novel, *A Window in Paris* (1898). After the start of the Franco-Prussian war, there is a sympathetic scene where French women light candles to their favourite saints. The comment is made that 'there were vows that day by those whose hope was in God, though the prayer was made before the Virgin or St Laurent', a remarkable accommodation to the cult of saints.[288] Even Catholics were no longer entirely beyond the pale for her. This reveals an interesting sympathy towards Catholicism for a nineteenth-century Baptist and also reflects the changing attitude toward Catholics amongst many English evangelicals during the later nineteenth century. Her ecumenist tendencies were both a measure of Marianne's generous heart, and of how far she had travelled from her roots in a rural Strict Baptist chapel, a journey which indicates something of the changes which took place within Nonconformity in the second half of the century.

Was Marianne's Spirituality Gendered?

Whilst it has been proved that in the second half of the nineteenth century, as

---

[283] M. Farningham, *The Cathedral's Shadow* (London: James Clarke, 1871), p. 67 and p. 73.
[284] Farningham, *Shadow*, p. 131.
[285] J. Wolffe, *The Protestant Crusade in Great Britain, 1829-1860* (Oxford: Clarendon Press, 1991) p. 289; Bebbington, *Dominance*, p. 226.
[286] Farningham, *Life*, pp. 218-19.
[287] Hope, *Spurgeon*, p. 316.
[288] M. Farningham, *A Window in Paris* (London: James Clarke, 1898), p. 33.

indeed at other times, women attended churches in larger numbers than men,[289] the question as to whether female and male spiritual experience differed during these years is more problematic. I have demonstrated elsewhere that in general, within mid-nineteenth century evangelicalism, female and male spirituality was similar. In a sample of denominational obituaries, and a variety of biographies and autobiographies, the differences that emerged were usually based on denominational differences rather than on gender.[290] Marianne's opinions on the topic of spirituality provide an interesting comparison, especially because her writing was so influential. Marianne had a keen awareness of her gender, and of the implications of being a woman in various situations, whether as a child longing for a positive story about a girl, or as the only woman on the Northampton School Board.[291] She was sympathetic to many aspects of feminism, yet believed that although new opportunities and possibilities should be open to women, their basic identity should remain rooted in their domestic role. It is therefore interesting to consider whether there are any indications of a gendered spirituality in her writings: did she believe that women experienced God in the same way as men?

Much of Marianne's writing was addressed equally to men and women, and carried no obvious gendered distinctions. A few collections were gender-specific, but even in these there are few indications that she regarded women's relationship to God as different from that of men. Two early collections of prose pieces, *Girlhood* and *Boyhood* present an interesting comparison. Addressing boys, Marianne makes use of phrases one might associate with muscular Christianity. Thus, boys should be 'bold, courageous, generous, open, chivalrous, frank, firm and noble', and they needed to learn not to fight other boys, but to 'conquer sin and evil' which is a difficult task.[292] In contrast, girls were urged to develop 'love, and self-denial, and thought for others', and to 'be everywhere and to all around you a sunbeam and a blessing'.[293] Yet they, too, were urged to develop courage.[294] These are however, character traits rather than aspects of spirituality, and on that subject little is said in these volumes. In what is said, nothing indicates that she believed young men and women to relate to God differently, although she clearly believed one had to appeal to them in different ways in order to draw out the wholehearted response of an eager disciple. At the end of *Girlhood* she encouraged her readers to be amongst 'those who have given their hearts to the Saviour', whilst the boys were urged to 'trust in the Lord with all your heart...' [295] The language might

---

[289] McLeod, *Religion and Society,* p. 157.
[290] Wilson, *Zeal*, pp. 64-65.
[291] See Chapter 1, p. 8 and Chapter 5, pp. 161-170.
[292] Farningham, *Boyhood*, p. 13 and p. 28.
[293] Farningham, *Girlhood*, p. 14 and p. 18.
[294] Farningham, *Girlhood*, pp. 85-87.
[295] Farningham, *Girlhood* p. 136, *Boyhood*, p. 134.

have been slightly adapted, but the sentiment was the same.

In *Women and their Saviour*, however, published in 1904, there were a few comments which indicate a tendency towards a gendered spirituality. This collection was a series of short meditations on extracts from the Bible, intended to be used as daily readings. As one might expect from the title of this little book, the relationship in this instance is with Jesus, although as has been demonstrated above, the Father was also referred to frequently in Marianne's writings. Here Jesus was portrayed as understanding women, being not just Saviour but also a Friend who is always present. This relationship had a mutual element: 'He valued their love and devotion'. At the same time, their role in life originated in this relationship: 'he gave them their appointed ministries'.[296] Thus once again work was understood as originating with God and activism as being under girded by a relationship, not just a set of beliefs or values.

Commenting, in this collection, on the passage in Mark 10 when the disciples are portrayed trying to prevent mothers from bringing their children to Jesus, Marianne suggested that 'The disciples did not understand Him as well as the mothers did', thus suggesting that woman had a particularly intimate relationship with Jesus.[297] She also pointed out in several of the little meditations that some of the most significant words of Jesus were spoken to women, declaring 'It is remarkable that it was a woman to whom Jesus spoke surely the most profound truth He ever uttered', referring to the assurance to Martha after the death of Lazarus, that those who believed in him would never die.[298] Marianne also highlighted other examples of women's significance in the gospels, stressing for instance in the final meditation that it was a woman who was chosen to bring the news of the resurrection to the other disciples. She used this example to encourage women to preach the gospel to others, even if just timidly to a few: 'it will not matter... at all that we are but women'.[299] Whilst portraying women as weak in some senses, she encouraged them to disregard this and pursue the opportunities they are given.[300] There was clearly a gendered awareness here, and a feminist use of Biblical material to develop women's sense of self and encourage their action, but there is no real evidence that she considered female experience of God to be substantively different from that of men.

Thus, when she wrote in the same series of meditations that 'The real and precious things of life are service and humility, self-surrender, self-forgetfulness' she did not only intend that for women.[301] Other instances addressed either to men or to both sexes illustrate that she believed such

---

[296] Farningham, *Saviour*, p. 77.
[297] Farningham, *Saviour*, p. 39.
[298] Farningham, *Saviour*, p. 81.
[299] Farningham, *Saviour*, p. 94.
[300] Farningham, *Saviour*, p. 7. This was developed more explicitly in Hope, *Darling*.
[301] Farningham, *Saviour*, p. 86.

characteristics to be godly, rather than merely feminine. The point of the book was not to illustrate a different kind of spirituality, but to encourage women that they had a special place in God's purposes, a relationship of intimacy that needed developing, and work from him to do. The final phrase of the little volume was 'Whatsoever He saith unto you do it'. The themes are therefore the same ones that can be found throughout her work, and although she expected a woman's response to Christ to be in tune with her femininity, the essentials of that relationship were not essentially gendered.

Conclusion

Marianne was not an innovator or a great thinker, although her views did change along with those of the wider evangelical community. Her readers were men and women who, like Marianne herself, worked conscientiously, were self-conscious about their use of time, were becoming more relaxed about the beliefs of those from other traditions, and were enjoying the expanding variety of leisure available to them. Above all, however, they, like her, understood the whole of their lives in the light of their faith. The few sentences which head up this chapter, written in the *Sunday School Times* of 1885 encapsulate much of Marianne's understanding of the Christian life: 'We cannot talk with God without receiving inspiration, nor think of Jesus without being stirred to some emotion. And real feeling leads to action. Work of necessity follows prayer'.[302] At the heart of her spirituality was an experiential relationship, developed through devotional practices, and leading inevitably to an active lifestyle. Faith was the frame within which the tapestry of life could be comprehended; it was the motivation and the inspiration, the starting point and the goal in view. This faith was intensely personal, sustaining and supporting Marianne in her daily life, but it was also communal, expressed and at times discovered within the context of groups of believers, whether in a formal church context or the more informal gatherings of her girls' class or of friends, as well as at home. She commented realistically that perhaps 'we should speak of Him more than we do, but we know He is present'. A sense of this reality of spiritual things pervaded Marianne's everyday life, whether it was in her writing, or her home life. Marianne's brand of spirituality was straightforward and homely, expressed as a simple, trusting faith in God. It could at times appear almost naïve and simplistic but there are subtleties if one looks beyond the clichés. In the final pages of her autobiography, Marianne lapsed into what she admitted was a homily, in which she looked back on her life and singled out God's involvement in it as its most important characteristic. She reflected that she had known difficulties, but that more often 'peace and plenteous good (have) been sent to me' indicating that she regarded the good things in her life as having

---

[302] *SST* 23 January 1885.

their origins in God.[303] She also recalled that she had on several occasions been asked by young believers whether the Christian message is 'really real' to which her answer is 'Yes, absolutely. The power of Christ, and all that is claimed for it is the realest thing in life, the realest thing in the world...His help is real, whatever your need may be.'[304] Reality was, therefore, for Marianne, first and foremost spiritual reality, which was both intellectual and experiential, and was worked out in everyday life. Like many of her contemporaries, she interpreted the whole world through the lens of her evangelical understanding.

Marianne reflected the changing patterns of that belief, for instance with regard to hell and final judgement, attitudes to Catholicism, or the nature of the Bible, but she also reinforced a straightforward experiential spirituality which assumed that God was involved in every detail of life, and trusted that whatever the circumstances one found oneself in, ultimately all was in God's hands and would work out for the best. It was not naïve in its simplicity, however, for Marianne had experienced heartache and bereavement, and communicated an understanding and a sympathy for her readers, along with an enjoyment of life, which must have helped to keep them in the evangelical fold. Remaining a postmillennialist, despite her Brighton experience, she also expected that the kingdom of God would gradually appear and that society would improve, until that day when Christ would reign. This was a belief that she never modified, and in this she represented what was increasingly becoming a minority view within evangelicalism.

The writer ended her autobiography by quoting a hymn that she had often sung with her girls' class, 'when the room was full of faces of girls in shadow', at the end of a session. The final stanza declared—

O my Shepherd, Guardian true,
All my life is Thine to keep,
At Thy feet my work I do,
In Thine arms I fall asleep.[305]

The combination of consecration, intimacy and work indicated in this simple verse is an illustration and a useful summary of Marianne's own spirituality: surrender, trust, prayer, work and rest were at the heart of her uncomplicated response to the divine. This verse would have been, if not the testimony, at least the aspiration, of her wide evangelical readership.

---

[303] Farningham, *Life*, p. 278.
[304] Farningham, *Life*, p. 279.
[305] Farningham, *Life*, p. 281. The hymn was by Anna Waring, and was published in 1850, see J. Julian, *Dictionary of Hymnology* (London: John Murray, 1892), p. 1233.

Chapter 7

Conclusion

In the preceding chapters, I have argued that faith was the common thread in Marianne's life, drawing together apparently opposing strands in her writing and practice. On the one hand, she supported the Victorian ideology of domesticity, and frequently asserted that the home was the best place for women to focus their attention. Yet she also encouraged them not to be 'afraid to be singular' but to use their gifts and abilities, even if that meant flying in the face of contemporary opinion, both cultural and Christian. Thus she appears to have been declaring at one and the same time that women should be completely in line with contemporary attitudes, and that they should challenge conventional opinion.[1] She was able to hold both these aspects together because for her, the nature of duty and of work was rooted in faith and consisted of taking hold of opportunities. Thus, at least in theory, in her thought convention was not the issue: rather, it was making wise use of gifts and abilities which was important. Because both aspects were spiritual responses there was no dichotomy for Marianne: rather, for her, all should 'do what they can'. Such activism was the natural outworking of her spirituality, and was expressed through her writing career, her girls' class and her public activities, whether lecturing or sitting on a School Board. The evangelical piety reflected in her writings, through popular phrases and even platitudes and worked out in her life, meant that many readers found her to be in tune with their own Nonconformist spirituality. In the process, whilst Marianne reflected many traditional evangelical beliefs, she also exposed some of her readers to different ideas, both in theology and in relation to the place of women in society.

Marianne and Women

Marianne's perception of women and their role reflected the mixed heritage women derived from evangelicalism, and, no doubt, the varied experience of her readers. Her writing and lecturing on the controversial topic of women's role included both conventional and subversive elements. On the one hand, she championed the domestic ideology which reached its zenith in the years of her early womanhood, remaining influential throughout the century. The home,

---

[1] See Chapter 3, p, 68, p. 63.

Marianne insisted, was woman's first priority, and should command 'the first place in our affection'.[2] Many times, in prose, poetry and fiction, she stressed this primacy of domesticity and the importance of hospitality. She also believed in cultivating traditional feminine virtues, such as a 'meek or gentle spirit, and unselfish devoted affection'.[3] Her opinions on these matters remained constant throughout her life. Similarly, when Marianne wrote about motherhood, she consistently expressed a largely traditional perspective, and much of her prose, poetry and fiction on the home and women's role was entirely conventional. Her views on domestic and family matters were safely within the accepted, uncontroversial contemporary beliefs.

It is, however, inadequate to claim that Marianne was merely reinforcing patriarchy, as some critics have suggested. Her attitudes were more complex than such a statement would indicate, as the title of her autobiography demonstrates. There was a second strand to her opinions about women's role: Marianne believed that not only was it a necessity for some women to earn their own living, but that at times it could be a positive advantage. She applied this especially, but by no means exclusively, to single women, and included in it a wide range of jobs and vocations, from factory worker to preacher or doctor. Whilst such opinions concerning work were expressed in her writing at an early stage, her attitudes to women's rights in general, and the vote in particular, developed and changed over the years. Some of her more radical comments are to be found under the pseudonym of Eva Hope or in reports of lectures, rather than in pieces in the evangelical press with the familiar by-line of 'Marianne Farningham'. Marianne's complex mixture of attitudes was derived from a cocktail of middle-class evangelicalism, and her working-class roots, but they also reflected some of the more radical implications of the Christian gospel. To her, all these opinions were equally rooted in her Christian faith: she was not aware of any apparent contradiction between the ideal of female domesticity and the role of the independent wage-earner.

Ruth Watts has argued that radical feminist beliefs could never be birthed out of evangelicalism, but only out of the rational discourses of Unitarianism.[4] Perhaps that was true earlier in the nineteenth century, but as time went on, a broader and more liberal evangelicalism gave rise to women who embraced aspects of the feminist agenda, whilst denying some of the attitudes, especially moral stances, which some of the early feminists held. Marianne was one such woman, and her developing attitude to women's role was a small contribution to the 'woman question' and the changing place of women in society. She challenged the attitudes of her evangelical readers concerning women and work

---

[2] M. Farningham, *Home Life* (London: James Clarke, 1869), p. 1 and p. 8.
[3] E. Hope, *Grace Darling, Heroine of the Farne Islands* (London: Walter Scott, 1875), p. 279.
[4] Watts, R., *Gender, Power and the Unitarians in England 1760-1860* (Harlow: Addison Wesley Longman, 1998).

and the vote. Whilst it is possible to see in her life some of the characteristics identified by Vicinus in her study of single women, Marianne rarely mentioned singleness, and there is no evidence that she campaigned particularly on behalf of unmarried women, nor that she saw the existence of a large number of single women as in any way undermining the domestic ideology: single women could also be householders. Marianne was more aware of her identity as a woman than as a single person. She reassured her female readers, and the women in her lecture audiences, that their traditional domestic role was primary and significant, yet she also encouraged them to develop their God-given gifts and abilities however apparently unconventional, as long as all was rooted in faith and in the motive of service. There was no room for self-aggrandisement. In this she was weaving together the conventional and the radical strands of evangelicalism, always remaining within an evangelical framework.

Marianne and Sunday Schools

Sunday schools were a significant part of the later nineteenth-century religious landscape, yet little work has been done on them. In particular, they were part of the 'third sphere', between public and private worlds, in which women found opportunities to develop their skills outside the home, yet without intruding into the public, male world. This study has shown that Marianne contributed to Sunday schools at many levels. She was involved at the grass roots with nearly two hundred girls in her own class, opening her home to them and giving them much of her spare time and energy. As a teacher, she was an example of dedication which few others could have matched, although she continued to assert, rather implausibly, that anyone could do it. Admirable as this was, Marianne was much more than a local class leader. As the editor of the *Sunday School Times* she was well placed to aid both the maintenance and development of the movement, and to influence individual students and teachers as well as the wider movement. Marianne was an activist who also contributed to ongoing debates concerning the importance of Sunday schools, their future, and the nature of religious education. These schools were a major passion of Marianne's life and she was an enthusiastic propagandist on their behalf. As a Sunday school activist and School Board Member she contributed to ongoing debates concerning the importance of Sunday schools and the nature of education. She was also involved in consistent work at grass roots level, primarily with her girls' class. Marianne's contribution to the evangelical world and to the town of Northampton was considerable.

Public Life

The late nineteenth century was an era when new opportunities were becoming available to women, and Marianne was able to take advantage of this as an editor and later as a public speaker. Her choice of careers, teaching followed by writing, might have been extremely conventional, yet she expanded and developed the opportunities her writing and editing and her Sunday school connections gave her. Over a period of ten years she moved from being shy when having to pray before a few young women, to speaking in public at a Sunday school conference. She read her first paper at the 1877 conference, contributing to the general acceptance of women reading their own papers, and in the same year gave her first winter lecture series, and came to relish the rapport with an audience which she was able to establish. Whilst she was not a pioneer, in the sense of being the first woman to do a particular job, or to become involved in certain causes, taking the initiative in such a public role was not commonplace for women. She was one of the first women to make a public career for herself.

Another role which Marianne fulfilled, which was still comparatively unusual for women, was her position as a member of the Northampton School Board. This was the most responsible public role available to women at that time. She was not the first female member of the Board, but her presence was an unusual enough occurrence for her to assume that it might be an issue for the men, and indeed she indicates that her fellow-Board members were not entirely comfortable working with a woman. She was a very popular member, having received the largest vote, a thousand more than any other candidate, demonstrating her standing and popularity in her adopted town. During the six years she was on the Board, Marianne helped to shape and influence the development of education in Northampton, with a particular interest in the subjects taught to girls. Indeed, she has been hailed as 'one of the most progressive spirits' on the Board during that time.[5] Although she lamented that she gave the role too little time, others saw her contribution as of vital importance. Once again, Marianne was treading on comparatively fresh territory for women in making a useful contribution to public life. In this, she put into practice her belief that it was important to take hold of opportunities, whether or not they fitted closely to the conventional image of womanhood. She was at the forefront of a cultural trend, and was herself an example of a woman who took hold of the new opportunities.

Spirituality and Theology

As with her opinions concerning women's rights, Marianne's developing attitudes and experience mirrored the journey taken by a number of thinking evangelicals during this period. One aspect of this was her move from a close-knit village Strict Baptist community to a large town chapel. Always remembering the earlier community spirit with fondness, she left much of the traditional separatist attitudes behind, developing a strong belief in ecumenism and the need to cross denominational boundaries. Her theology also evolved, as

---

[5] *SST* 26 March, 1909.

she moved from the strictly Calvinist beliefs of Eynsford, which she claimed to have never been entirely comfortable with, to embrace an Arminian approach and teaching on 'the larger hope'. Her attitude to the Scriptures also changed, reflecting the impact of German scholarship, and she was quite relaxed about some of the new possibilities. Despite asserting that she wanted little to do with theological disputes, her sympathies were clear. A similar relaxation took place concerning Sunday observance, and leisure and culture in general. These developments in Marianne's beliefs reflected the issues which contemporaries grappled with, and to a large extent mirrored the attitudes of the *Christian World* during the second half of the nineteenth century. As an intelligent participant in many aspects of evangelical life and trends during this period, she encapsulated the transition experienced by many thinking evangelicals. Insisting that she would leave theology for those better qualified, she nevertheless indicated from time to time where her sympathies lay, and she encouraged the idea of fellowship built on a common loyalty to Jesus Christ, rather than a detailed agreement on doctrine.

At the heart of her spirituality, however, lay a continued belief in the importance of an intimate relationship with Christ, and an adherence to the evangelical emphasis on prayer, Bible reading, conversion, the centrality of the cross and activism. In addition, Marianne was influenced by the Romantic movement, and especially its embodiment in Keswick spirituality, which she found personally life-changing. Nature, as a means both of revelation and relaxation, was always important to her, and she drew from it many topics for her short journalistic pieces. Interestingly, Keswick theology did not, for Marianne, lead to a withdrawal from engagement with society, but co-existed with a strong activism, as her School Board membership indicates. Marianne also shared the common Enlightenment belief in progress, as did many evangelicals, and she confidently expected the twentieth century, when it dawned, to continue the march to a Christian utopia. Her unquestioned assumptions included a belief that everything was improving, that peace and harmony were possible in the world, and that the gospel would continue its spread throughout Britain and the world.

Changes within Evangelicalism

There were significant changes within evangelicalism during the years Marianne was working. Her journey reflected that of many in her denomination, from a strict Calvinist background to a more 'generous orthodoxy', especially in her understanding of heaven, hell and the nature of salvation.[6] She did, however, move too far for some evangelicals, as demonstrated when an admirer tried to persuade her to leave the *Christian*

---

[6] B. D. McLaren, *A Generous Orthodoxy,* (Grand Rapids: Zondervan, 2004). I can imagine Marianne and Brian McLaren having a fascinating conversation.

World because of its 'heretical' views.[7] Marianne would have been on the liberal side of the evangelical/liberal divide of the early twentieth century, whilst resenting such categories, camps and definitions.

Marianne also reflected the change in attitude towards women's role and in particular, the vote, giving public support to the campaign for the vote for women householders like herself. These changes were also mirrored in the *Christian World* itself, and presumably in its readers. Marianne was changing with the paper and its readership and whilst exactly who influenced whom is difficult to tell, with people choosing a paper which suits their perspective on life, it is probable that some readers had their attitudes challenged and even altered by the beliefs of Marianne and other writers in the paper. In other ways Marianne did not change. She continued to be influenced by Enlightenment optimism, not absorbing the increasing tendency to pre-millennialism. She hoped that the kingdom of God would come on earth and in particular in England. It is remarkable that despite close bereavements and an awareness of the reality of some social evils and contemporary wars, Marianne managed to maintain such a positive expectation, instead of developing the pessimistic attitude of some pre-millenialists. In this respect she remained true to her youthful beliefs.

A Plain Working Woman

A plaque on the wall in College Street Baptist Chapel declared that for 44 years Marianne was a member of the church and for 33 years 'the much loved leader of a class of young women'. It added that

> Her songs and writings are widely known and her consistent life and sterling qualities endeared her to all who came within the sphere of her influence. As Writer, Teacher and Friend she did more than can be told for the enrichment of many lives, and her sweet unselfish service was for the uplifting and blessing of others, and to the Glory of God.

Behind these rather anonymous comments lies the reality of not a 'plain', but an unusual woman who, it seems, had the gift of inspiring friendship. Marianne's brand of down-to-earth piety, of spiritual experience laced with a good dose of common sense, appealed to people who continued to regularly read her words. One can speculate that people who felt reassured and encouraged in their faith by her traditional approach to many aspects of Christian living, had their minds opened to new possibilities when she ventured an opinion on women's work, or the use of the bicycle, but it may just be that those who had chosen to read the *Christian World* were already of a more liberal evangelical persuasion. There is no doubt, however, that the

---

[7] M. Farningham, *A Working Woman's Life* (London: James Clarke, 1907), pp. 138-39.

combination of the rapid growth and development of popular publishing, and the pervasive influence of evangelicalism within society, resulted in her writing reaching many thousands of people at just the time when they would have had most appeal, thus making her a significant figure in nineteenth-century evangelicalism. To herself she was just 'a working woman', but to her many readers and even more, to the girls in her class, she was a mentor and a guide, an understanding friend in time of need, an encourager when faith faltered.

Marianne was not an original thinker, but she was interested in and open to new ideas, and contemporary issues were frequently reflected in her writings. She had a natural curiosity, and her sense of having had an inadequate schooling as a child, only encouraged her never to stop learning. Her work as a journalist also meant that she was continually looking for fresh and interesting things to write about. Yet she shied away from controversy and disagreement, being more interested in maintaining relationships than in developing unusual lines of thought. She kept some of her more controversial opinions for the pseudonym of Eva Hope, or until she composed her autobiography, by which time many opinions had mellowed and developed and hers no longer seemed unusual within evangelical circles. Whilst it is problematic to use twenty-first-century categories for nineteenth-century women, there is a sense in which she was both an evangelical and a feminist, despite her conventional understanding of social relationships and the priority of the home in women's lives. Her feminist sympathies developed because of, not in spite of, her deeply felt Christian belief, as well as her working-class background and her own position as a single woman making an independent living for herself. It was to some extent a natural extension of the self-help popular at the time, applied to women's lives but with a spiritual dimension.

In many ways Marianne was a woman of her time, who reflected trends within evangelicalism and to a small extent helped to shape them. Yet, despite being a household name within evangelical circles throughout the many years of her working life, she has previously been largely neglected by historians. This book has sought to remedy that, and to investigate the life and work of someone who by her own admission was only 'a simple woman worker'. Indeed, she was a hard worker, someone who loved her work and brought enthusiasm to all she did, yet she was much more than that. To many of her readers, she was a friend and an inspiration, who provided support for their own faith. To those involved in Sunday schools she was a contributor to discussions about progress and change within the movement. She was also at the forefront of the movement of evangelical women beyond the home, and beyond the third sphere of church activity, into public life. Marianne Farningham was a significant figure within evangelicalism in the later nineteenth century, and her contribution deserves to be recognised and included in the mainstream of religious history of the period.

The Last Word

It is fortunate that Marianne was already dead when war broke out in the summer of 1914. Her hope of a bright future would have been sadly shattered, although her faith in God, deep-rooted as it was, might well have survived. She would have struggled to match her concern for young people of all conditions, and her deep compassion, with the reality around her. Although always looking to the future, and open to new ideas, much of her value system was rooted in her nineteenth-century origins. She had no illusions, however, that her work would last beyond her own lifetime. Indeed, one suspects that she would have been surprised to discover that someone has written about her nearly a hundred years after her death. Researching Marianne's life and work has been a fascinating exercise. Some of her ideas, beliefs, and turns of phrase, seem an echo from a distant age, whilst others sound fresh and are couched in language still familiar in evangelical circles. Marianne has become a partner in the enterprise, and in many situations I have found myself wondering what she would have thought and how she would have reacted. In studying her, she has come alive for me.

Perhaps it would be appropriate to give Marianne herself the final word. She would appreciate the offer. Concluding the discussion which followed a paper given at the Sunday School Union in 1877, she commented 'It is exceedingly kind of you, Mr Chairman, to give me what every lady likes to have – the last word'.[8] Towards the end of her autobiography, she commented that she had always known she would not 'do any great thing which would impress the world, and cause me to be kept in remembrance'. Rather, she hoped 'to do a great many little things' which might have affected individuals.[9] This assessment, not withstanding some of the grand claims made by friends and contemporaries, is probably accurate. She did not make a great stir in the world, either as a writer, lecturer or a pioneer of women's issues, but she did make a considerable impact during her lifetime in Northampton and Barmouth, and in the lives of many who knew her personally or read her writings. She hoped to 'serve her generation and fall asleep', and it can be safely said that, in the eyes of many fellow-evangelicals, she fulfilled that aspiration. Marianne Farningham was rather more than 'a plain working woman'.

---

[8] *Sunday School Chronicle* 9 May 1877.
[9] Farningham, *Life*, p. 275.

Bibliography

Primary Sources

Manuscripts

Archives of the National Christian Education Council, formerly the National Sunday School Union, Special Collections, Birmingham University
Constitution, as given at front of minute book, 1874-78.

Northampton City Library
Marianne Farningham Hearn, Letters to 'Pollie' (uncatalogued).

Northampton County Record Office
Northampton School Board Minutes.
Northampton Yearly Bill of Mortality, (Northampton: Taylor & Son), 1866-67 and 1869-70
Wills, p. 138, no. 132.

Gloucester Record Office
Stroud Congregationalist Sunday School Book.

Marianne Farningham's Works in Chronological Order

Farningham, M., *Lays and Lyrics* (London: James Clarke,1860).
—, *Life Sketches and Echoes from the Valley* (London: James Clarke,1861).
—, *Life Sketches and Echoes from the Valley (2)* (London: James Clarke, 1868).
—, *Life Sketches and Echoes from the Valley (3)* (London: James Clarke, 1871).
—, *Morning and Evening Hymns* (London: John Cording, 1863).
—, *Poems*, (London: James Clarke, 1866).
—, *Chats by the Sea* (London: James Clarke, 1868).
—, *Girlhood* James (London: James Clarke, 1869).
—, *Little Tales for Little Readers* (London: James Clarke, 1869).
—, *Home Life* (London: James Clarke,1869).
—, *Boyhood* (London: James Clarke, 1870).
—, *The Cathedral's Shadow* (London: James Clarke, 1871).
—, *Sunday Schools of the Future* (London: James Clarke, 1871).
—, *Brothers and Sisters* (London: James Clarke, 1873).

—, *Leaves from Elim* (London: James Clarke, 1873).
—, *A Happy New Year for our Class*, pamphlet, (Northampton: Taylor & Son, 1874).
—, *Sunday Afternoons with Jesus* (London: James Clarke, 1874).
—, *What of the Night?* (London: James Clarke, 1876).
—, *Summer and Autumn of Life* (London: James Clarke, 1876).
—, *Will you take it?* (London: James Clarke,1877).
—, *Homely Talks about Homely Things* (London: James Clarke, 1878).
—, *Songs of Sunshine* (London: James Clarke, 1878).
—, *The Children's Holidays* (London: James Clarke, 1878).
—, *Nineteen Hundred? A forecast and a story* (London: James Clarke, 1892).
—, *A Story of 50 Years* (London: James Clarke, 1893).
—, *In Evening Lights* (London: James Clarke, 1897).
—, *A Window in Paris* (London: James Clarke, 1898).
—, *Harvest Gleanings and Gathered Fragments* (London: James Clarke, 1903).
—, *Women and their Saviour* (London: James Clarke, 1904).
—, *Women and their Work* (London: James Clarke, 1906).
—, *A Working Woman's Life* (London: James Clarke, 1907).
—, *Lyrics of the Soul* (London: James Clarke, 1908).
—, *Songs of Joy and Faith* (London: James Clarke, 1909).

Marianne Farningham's Work under the Pseudonym of Eva Hope

Hope, E., *Grace Darling, Heroine of the Farne Islands* (London: Walter Scott, 1875).
—, *Our Queen: A Sketch of the Life and Times of Victoria, Queen of Great Britain and Ireland* (London, Walter Scott, 1883).
—, (ed.) *Longfellow* (London: Walter Scott, 1884).
—, (ed.) *The Poetical Works of William Cowper* (London: Walter Scott, 1885).
—, *New World Heroes* (London: Walter Scott, 1893).
—, *Life of C.H. Spurgeon* (Kilmarnock: John Ritchie, nd).
—, *Great Modern Women* (London: Walter Scott, 1886), also published as *Queens of Literature of the Victorian Era*.
—, *Stanley and Africa* (London: Walter Scott, 1890).
—, *Life of General Gordon* (London: Walter Scott, 1901 [1884]).

Other Books and Pamphlets

Baptist Union Official Handbook of the Autumnal Assembly, 1905.
Cobbe, F., *Life of Frances Power Cobbe* (London: Richard Bentley & Sons, 1894).
Cox, S., *Salvator Mundi* (London: Henry S. King, 1877).
—, *The Larger Hope* (London: Kegan Paul, Trench, 1883).
Dale, R.W., *History of English Congregationalism* (London: Hodder and Stoughton, 1907).
—, (ed.) *The Life and Letters of John Angell James* (London: James Nisbett, 1861).
Dickens, C., *Bleak House* (London: Bradbury and Evans, 1853).
Ellis, S.S., *Women of England* (London: Fisher & Son, 1839).
Glandwr-Morgan, Rev W. *Marianne Farningham in her Welsh Home* (Birmingham: Ellesmere Press, 1923) [1909].

Gosse, E., *Father and Son* (London: William Heinemann, 1907).
James, J., *Female Piety* (London: Hamilton, Adams, 1852).
Landels, W., *Women's Sphere and Work considered in the light of Scripture: a book for young women* (London, 1859).
Latimer, J., *Annals of Bristol in the Nineteenth Century,* 1887 (Bath: Kingsmead Reprints, 1970).
Marsh, C., *English Hearts and English Hands: or the railway and the trenches* (London: 1858).
Official Handbook to a Grand Bazaar in aid of College Street Bi-Centennial Commemorative Fund, 1899.
Patmore, C., *The Angel in the House*, Frederick Page (ed.), (London: Oxford University Press, 1949).
Ruskin, J., 'Of Queens' Gardens' in *Sesame and Lilies* (London: Collins, 1864-69).
Pearsall Smith, L., (ed.) *A Religious Rebel, The letters of HWS (Mrs Pearsall Smith)* (London: Nisbett, 1949).
Programme of Meetings at the Annual Conference of Sunday School Teachers, 1870.
Souvenir of the Centenary of College Street Sunday School Northampton, 1810 – 1910.
Street, M.J., *The Hundredth Year: the Story of the Centenary Celebrations of the Sunday School Union* (London: Sunday School Union, 1903).
Wesley, J. Sermon 50, in A.C. Outler, *The Works of John Wesley Vol 2: Sermons 2 34-70,* (Nashville: Abingdon Press, 1985).

Newspapers and Periodicals

Baptist Monthly 1899.
Cheltenham Examiner 13 Feb 1878.
Christian Cabinet 21 November 1856.
Christian World.
Freeman and Baptist Times December 1907 and March 1909.
North British Review (February - May 1862).
Northampton Independent 1907, 1909.
Northampton Reporter 12 April 1898.
Salisbury and Winchester Journal 19 February 1881.
Sunday School Chronicle.
Sunday School Times and Home Educator.
The Times 17 March 1909.
Western Daily Press 13 November 1877.

Online Resources

1881 census, www.nationalarchives.gov.uk/census
1891 census, www.content.ancestry.co.uk
1901 census, www.1901census.nationalarchives.gov.uk

Selective Bibliography - Secondary Sources – Books

Armstrong, R., *Grace Darling: Maid and Myth* (London: J. M. Dent & Sons, 1965).

Bailey, P., *Leisure and Class in Victorian England* (London: Routledge and Kegan Paul, 1978).
Bebbington, D.W., *The Nonconformist Conscience: Chapel and Politics 1870-1914* (London: George Allen and Unwin, 1982).
—, *Evangelicalism in Modern Britain* (London: Unwin Hymen, 1989).
—, *Holiness in Nineteenth-Century England* (Carlisle: Paternoster Press, 2000).
—, *The Dominance of Evangelicalism* (Leicester: IVP, 2005).
Beetham, M., *A Magazine of Her Own?* (London: Routledge, 1996).
Binfield, C., *So Down to Prayers, Studies in English Nonconformity 1780-1920*, (London: J.M. Dent & Sons Ltd, 1977).
Black, S.B., *A Farningham Childhood* (Sevenoaks: Darenth Valley Publications, 1988).
Bradley, I., *The Call to Seriousness* (London: Cape, 1976).
Briggs, J.H.Y., *The English Baptists of the Nineteenth Century* (A History of English Baptists, 3: Didcot: The Baptist Historical Society, 1994).
Brown, C.B., *The Death of Christian Britain* (London: Routledge, 2001).
Bruce, F.F., *The English Bible* (London: Lutterworth Press, revised edition 1970).
Burnett, J. (ed.), *Destiny Obscure: Autobiographies of Childhood, Education and Family from the 1820s to the 1920s* (London: Routledge, 1994 [1982]).
Burrage, H.S., *Baptist Hymn Writers and their Hymns* (Portland, Maine: Brown, Thurston & Company, 1888).
Caine, B., *English Feminism 1780-1980* (Oxford: Oxford University Press, 1997).
Cliff, P.B., *The Rise and Development of the Sunday School Movement in England 1720-1980* (Nutfield, Surrey: National Christian Education Council, 1986).
Davidoff, L. and C. Hall, *Family Fortunes: Men and Women of the English Middle Class, 1780-1850,* (London: Routledge, 1987).
—, *Family Fortunes* (London: Routledge, 2002).
Elliott-Binns, L.E., *Religion in the Victorian Era* (London: Lutterworth Press, 1934 [1964]).
Flint, K., *The Woman Reader 1837-1914* (Oxford: Clarendon Press, 1993).
Gilbert, A.D., *Religion and Society in Industrial England: Church, Chapel and Social Change, 1740-1914* (London: Longman, 1976).
Gillett, D.K., *Trust and Obey: Explorations in Evangelical Spirituality* (London: Darton, Longman and Todd, 1993).
Gordon, J.M., *Evangelical Spirituality* (London: SPCK, 1991).
Helsinger, E.K., R.L Sheets and W. Veeder, *The Woman Question*, Vol 1 (Chicago: University of Chicago Press, 1983).
Hilton, B., *The Age of Atonement* (Oxford: Clarendon Press, 1988).
Hindmarsh, B., *The Evangelical Conversion Narrative: Spiritual Autobiography in Early Modern England* (Oxford: Oxford University Press, 2005).
Hollis, P., *Ladies Elect – Women in English Local Government, 1865-1914* (Oxford: Clarendon Press, 1987).
Hopkins, E., *Childhood Transformed: Working-class Children in Nineteenth-century England* (Manchester: Manchester University Press, 1994).
Jalland, P., *Death in the Victorian Family* (Oxford: Oxford University Press, 1996).
Jelink, E.C. (ed.), *Women's Autobiography: Essays in Criticism* (Bloomington & London: Indiana University Press, 1980).
Jones, E.R., *History of Barmouth and its Vicinity* (Barmouth: John Evans and nephew, 1909).

Julian, J., *A Dictionary of Hymnology* (London: John Murray, 1892 (2nd edition 1908).
Landow, G.P., (ed.) *Approaches to Victorian Autobiography* (Athens, Ohio: Ohio University Press, 1979).
Laqueur, T.W., *Religion and Respectability: Sunday Schools and Working Class Culture 1780-1850* (New Haven: Yale University Press, 1976).
Larsen, T. (ed.), *Biographical Dictionary of Evangelicals* (Leicester: IVP, 2003).
Lawson, J. and H. Silver, *A Social History of Education in England* (London: Methuen & Co, 1973).
Levine, P., *Feminist Lives in Victorian England: private roles and public commitment* (Oxford: Blackwell, 1990).
—, *Victorian Feminism 1850-1900* (London: Hutchinson, 1987).
Lloyd, Dr L.W., *Maritime Merioneth – the town and port of Barmouth 1565-1973* (Porthmadog, Gwynedd, Wales: Snowdonia Press, 1975).
Malmgreen, G., *Religion in the Lives of English Women 1760-1930* (London: Croom Helm, 1986).
Martin, J., *Women and the Politics of Schooling in Victorian and Edwardian England* (London: Leicester University Press, 1999).
McLeod, H., *Religion and Society in England, 1850-1914,* (Basingstoke and London: MacMillan Press, 1996).
Morgan, S., *A Passion for Purity: Ellice Hopkins and the politics of gender in the late Victorian church* (Bristol: Centre for Comparative Studies in Religion and Gender, 1999).
Munson, J., *The Nonconformists* (London: SPCK, 1991).
Noll, M., *The Rise of Evangelicalism* (Leicester: Inter-Varsity Press, 2004).
Nolland, L.S., *A Victorian Christian Feminist: Josephine Butler, the Prostitutes and God* (Carlisle: Paternoster, 2004).
Orchard, S. and Brigs, J.H.Y., *The Sunday School Movement* (Carlisle: Paternoster, 2007).
Pollock, J., *Forgotten Children: Parent-Child Relationships from 1500 to 1900* (Cambridge: Cambridge University Press, 1983).
Price, C. and I. Randall, *Transforming Keswick* (Carlisle: Paternoster, 2002).
Prochaska, F., *Women and Philanthropy in Nineteenth Century England* (Oxford: Clarendon Press, 1980).
Randall, I., *What a Friend we have in Jesus: the Evangelical Tradition*, Traditions of Christian Spirituality Series (London: Darton, Longman and Todd Ltd, 2005).
Rose, J., *Elizabeth Fry* (London: Macmillan, 1980).
Rosman, D., *Evangelicals and Culture* (London: Croom Helm, 1984).
Shoemaker, R., *Gender in English Society,1650-1850: The Emergence of Separate Spheres?* (London/New York: Longman, 1998).
Stott, A., *Hannah More: The First Victorian* (Oxford: Oxford University Press, 2003).
Thompson, E.P., *The Making of the English Working Class,* (London: Penguin, 1980 [1963]).
Tosh, J., *A Man's Place: Masculinity and the Middle-Class Home in Victorian England* (New Haven & London: Yale University Press, 1999).
Trevelyan, G.M., *The Life of John Bright* (London: Constable,1913).
Vicinus, M. (ed.), *A Widening Sphere* (London: Methuen, 1980 [1977]).
—, *Independent Women: Work and Community for Single Women 1850-1920* (London: Virago, 1985).

Wakefield, G. (ed.), *A Dictionary of Christian Spirituality* (London: SCM Press, 1983).
Watts, M., *The Dissenters Vol 2* (Oxford: Clarendon Press, 1995).
Wigley, J., *The Rise and Fall of the Victorian Sunday* (Manchester: Manchester University Press, 1980).
Wilson, L., *Constrained by Zeal: Female Spirituality amongst Nonconformists 1825-75* (Carlisle: Paternoster, 2000).
Wolffe, J., *The Protestant Crusade in Great Britain, 1829-1860* (Oxford: Clarendon Press, 1991).
—, (ed.) *Evangelical Faith and Public Zeal* (London: SPCK, 1995).

Articles and Pamphlets

Atkinson, B., *Ruskin's Social Experiment at Barmouth* (London: James Clarke, 1900).
Bebbington, D.W., *Evangelical Conversion c. 1740-1850*, North Atlantic Missiology Project, Position Paper Number 21, (Cambridge, 1997).
Counterslip Baptist Church: A Brief History 1804-2004
Harrison, B., 'For Church, Queen and Family: The Girl's Friendly Society 1874-1920', *Past and Present,* No 61 (November 1973), pp. 107–38.
Hold, T. (ed.), *A Northamptonshire Garland: An Anthology of Northamptonshire poets with Biographical Notes* (Northampton: Northamptonshire Libraries, 1989).
Jenkins, C., 'The major silence: autobiographies of working women in the nineteenth century', in J. B. Bullen (ed.) *Writing and Victorianism* (Addison Wesley Longman, Harlow, 1997).
Lee, A., 'The structure, ownership and control of the press, 1855-1914', in G. Boyce, J. Curran and P. Wingate (ed.), *Newspaper History from the Seventeenth Century to the Present Day* (London: Constable, 1978), pp. 117-29.
Lenton, J.H., 'Labouring for the Lord, Women Preaching in Wesleyan Methodism 1802-1932. A Revisionist View', in R. Sykes (ed.), *Beyond the Boundaries: Preaching in the Wesleyan Tradition*, Wesley Westminster Series No 8 (Oxford, 1998), pp. 58-86.
McGrath, A.E., *Evangelical Spirituality: past glories, present hopes, future possibilities* (London: St Antholin's Lectureship Charity, 1993).
Morgan, S., 'Women, Religion and Feminism: Past, Present and Future Perspectives' in S. Morgan (ed.), *Women, Religion and Feminism in Britain, 1750-1900* (Basingstoke: Palgrave Macmillan, 2002).
Sanders, V., 'Women writing men's lives: Margaret Oliphant's dethroned kings', in M. Hewitt (ed.). *Representing Victorian Lives* (Leeds: Leeds Centre for Victorian Studies, 1999), p 63- 88.
Smith, K.E., 'Beyond Public and Private Spheres: Another Look at Women in Baptist History and Historiography', *The Baptist Quarterly* (April 1991), pp. 79-87.
Snell K.D.M., 'The Sunday-School Movement', in England and Wales' *Past and Present,* No 164 (August 1999), pp. 122-168.
Rack, H.D., 'Evangelical Endings: Death-beds in Evangelical biography' *Bulletin of the John Rylands University Library of Manchester,* Vol 74, No 1, (1992).
Vickery, A., 'Golden Age to Separate Spheres? A Review of the Categories and Chronology of Women's History', *Historical Journal* , Vol 36, No 2, (1993), pp. 383-414.
Winston, E., 'The Autobiographer and her Readers: From Apology to Affirmation' in

E.C. Jelink (ed.), *Women's Autobiography: Essays in Criticism'* (Bloomington & London: Indiana University Press, 1980), p. 93.

Williams, R., 'The press and popular culture, a historical perspective' in G. Boyce, J, Curran and P. Wingate (ed.), *Newspaper History from the Seventeenth Century to the Present Day* (London: Constable, 1978), pp. 41-50.

Wilson, L., 'Afraid to be singular': Marianne Farningham and the role of women, in S. Morgan (ed.), *Women, Religion and Feminism in Britain, 1750-1900* (Basingstoke: Palgrave MacMillan, 2002), pp. 107-21.

Unpublished Theses

Knight, B., 'Strategy, mission and people in a rural diocese in a critical examination of the diocese of Gloucester' (PhD thesis, University of Gloucestershire, 2002).

Evans, B.M.A., 'Marianne Farningham (1834-1909) Aspects of the Life of a Victorian Woman' (unpublished MA dissertation, University of Leicester, 1994) (Held at University of Northampton).

Miscellaneous

Lloyd Webber, W., *Just as I am Thine own to be, Hymn Anthem for Unison voices and SATB* London Novello & Co, 1961.

Web Resources

A Short History of Eynsford Baptist Church 1775-1906,
www.pages.ukonline.co.uk/Eynsfordbaptist/hist1.htm

Burnett, R.G., 'Hocking, Silas Kitto (1850–1935)', *Oxford Dictionary of National Biography*, (Oxford: Oxford University Press, 2004),
http://www.oxforddnb.com/view/article/33912, accessed 4 Aug 2006.

Harrison, B., 'Worboise [*formerly* Worboys], Emma Jane [*known as* Mrs Etherington Guyton] (1825–1887)', *Oxford Dictionary of National Biography*, (Oxford: Oxford University Press, 2004)
http://ww.oxforddnb.com/view/article/29966, accessed 7 Aug 2005.

Hearne, W.T., *Brief History and Genealogy of the Hearn Family,* (Independence, Missouri: Examiner Printing Company, 1907),
http://www.cragun.com/brian/hearne/history/hh800m.html

Mitchell, R., 'Hearn, Mary Ann (Marianne Farningham) (1834-1909), *Oxford Dictionary of National Biography*, Oxford University Press, 2004,
www.oxforddnb.com/view/article/33789, accessed 4 July 2005

Royle, E., 'Bradlaugh, Charles, (1833-1891) *Oxford Dictionary of National Biography*, (Oxford: Oxford University Press, 2004),
www.oxforddnb.com/view/article/3183, accessed 12 July 2005.

www.Northampton.org.uk accessed 5 July 2005.

Index

Armstrong, Richard, 76
Aunt Patty. *See* Sharwood, Patty
Bands of Hope, 153
Baptist Times, 1, 5, 11, 58, 67
Barmouth, 3, 45, 49, 52, 56–59, 60, 92, 135, 165, 192, 205, 222–23, 226, 241
Bebbington, David, 5, 27, 70, 148, 180, 181, 185, 195, 199, 203, 205, 218
Binfield, Clyde, 5
Black, Shirley Burgoyne, 2, 16, 21, 27
Booth, Catherine, 97, 226
Bradlaugh, Charles, MP, 35–36
Briggs, John, 2, 103
Brighton Convention 1875, 184, 198–202, 206, 208, 217, 233
Bristol, 22, 30–31, 33, 92, 105, 161
Brown, John Turland, 36, 113, 224
Carlile, John, 5, 15, 53, 58, 135, 167, 174, 175
Christian World, 1, 3, 4, 6, 10, 32, 33, 37, 41–43, 54, 59, 66, 67, 111, 131, 133, 136, 138, 141, 150, 161, 198, 202, 204, 207, 211, 227, 238, 239
Clarke, James, 6, 42, 43, 55, 56, 68, 107, 133, 151, 152, 161, 203, 204, 206
Cobbe, Frances Power, 10, 52, 59, 70, 77, 92, 94, 95
College Street Baptist Chapel, 1, 19, 35, 36–37, 61, 84, 113, 114, 140, 224, 226, 239
Constable, Mary Ann (Pollie), 38, 41, 50
Cook, Thomas, 51, 222
Cotching, Emily, 45, 46, 53

Cox, Samuel, 205, 208
 The Larger Hope, 208
Davidoff, L. and Hall, C., 7, 31, 71–72, 78, 92
Duffield, Minnie, 45, 46
Eliot, Charlotte, 142
Eliot, George, 88, 147, 184, 209–10
Ellis, Sarah, 69, 71, 73, 80, 82, 98
Euren, Mrs. *See* Gordge, Miss
Evans, Barbara, 2, 39, 126, 140, 143, 144, 164
Eynsford, 20, 25, 33
Eynsford Baptist Chapel, 20–23, 28, 36, 76, 105, 180, 209, 238
Farningham, Kent, 15, 21, 25, 38
Farningham, Marianne
 A Working Woman's Life (autobiography), 8, 10, 11–13, 16–19, 23, 24, 25, 29, 38, 43, 44, 47, 51, 53, 56, 58, 60, 63, 64, 67, 68, 85, 92, 95, 97, 105, 112, 118, 128, 162, 163, 168, 170, 177, 183, 185, 202, 214, 220, 226, 232, 233, 240, 241
 Boyhood, 4, 81, 136, 181, 193, 200, 230
 Girlhood, 4, 63, 69, 76, 85, 90, 112, 136, 183, 185, 200, 207, 218, 222, 230
 Harvest Gleanings, 74, 137, 181, 196, 200, 211, 225, 228
 Homely Talks about Homely Things, 2, 47, 51, 63, 71, 73, 94, 192, 224
 Lays and Lyrics, 91, 133, 195, 196, 211, 227
 Life Sketches (1), 39, 43, 138, 207, 211, 214, 219, 227

Index 243

Lyrics of the Soul, 137, 181, 182, 196, 197
Nineteen Hundred, 40–41, 68, 110, 111, 113, 187, 215, 228, 229
Songs of Joy and Faith, 200
Songs of Sunshine, 181, 197, 201–2
Sunday Schools of the Future, 101
What of the Night?, 71, 74
Women and their Saviour, 52, 79, 179, 182, 195, 231
Women and their Work, 80, 132, 194–95, 204
female suffrage, 6, 66–68, 88, 95
Freeman and Baptist Times. See Baptist Times
Fry, Elizabeth, 66, 79, 84, 97, 99
Glandwr-Morgan, Rev W., 19, 53, 58, 60, 61, 135, 205, 206, 226, 227
Gordge, Miss, 33, 34, 36, 38, 50, 150
Gravesend, 33, 34, 38, 48, 51, 105, 149
Greenwell, Dora, 40, 54
Groves, Agnes, 37, 53–54, 110
Hearn,
  Ann, 16, 21, 28
  Geoffrey, 45
  Hephzibah (Heppie), 17, 32, 44, 47, 48, 108
  Joseph, 16, 17, 20, 24, 25–26, 28, 29, 31, 33, 42, 46, 47, 75, 208, 214, 227
  Margaret, 45
  Rebecca, 16, 17, 26, 28, 32, 48, 75, 83
  Rebecca (2), 17, 31
  Tom, 17, 54
Hearn, Geoffrey, 49
Hemans, Felicia, 18, 43, 137, 147
Hope, Eva, 2, 10, 44, 55, 88, 134, 135
  Great Modern Women, 43, 146, 209
  Life of C.H. Spurgeon, 145, 148, 149, 167, 194, 221, 227
  Life of C.H. Spurgeon, 146
  Life of General Gordon, 43, 145, 148, 149, 192
  Life of Grace Darling, 18, 43, 67, 73, 76, 84, 90, 95, 97, 98, 126, 144, 146, 220, 221
  Stanley in Africa, 43, 146, 148
James, John Angel, 85
Jenkins, Carole, 12, 24
Keswick movement, 184, 198, 199, 201, 238
Knight, Brian, 76
Levine, Philippa, 28, 40, 52, 70, 77, 78, 83, 90, 95, 104, 167
Lloyd George, David, 3, 165
Married Women's Property Act, 6, 92
Martin, Jane, 169, 171, 172, 174, 175, 176
Martineau, Harriet, 43, 88, 146, 209
Mitchell, Rosemary, 2, 4, 135, 140
Morgan, Sue, 78
motherhood, 25, 112, 235
Municipal Franchise Act 1869, 6
Noll, Mark, 11
Nord, Deborah, 17, 40
Northampton, 34–36, 45, 48, 51, 55, 59, 60, 75, 113, 140, 152, 166, 236, 241
  meeting with Catherine Booth, 97
  teaching, 38, 41
Northampton School Board, 1, 45, 94, 131, 132, 166–75, 237
Oliphant, Margaret, Mrs, 42, 148
Pearsall Smith, Hannah, 198, 201, 208
Petit, George, 49, 54

Prochaska, Frank, 37, 65
Randall, Ian, 4, 9, 179, 183, 184, 185, 189, 195
Rogers, Helen, 2, 20, 24, 25
Rogers, John, 20, 21, 28
Ruskin, John, 57, 64, 72, 156, 197
Sabbath, 6, 223–25
School Boards, 6, 87, 94, 166, 168
Sharwood,
   Frank, 45, 49, 60
   Herbert, 49
   Patty, 45, 49, 153
   Rebecca E, 46, 54, 106
   Rebecca E., 48
Sharwood, Elizabeth. *See* Sharwood, Rebecca E.
Sharwood, Minnie. *See* Duffield, Minnie
Somerville, Mary, 43, 88–89, 89, 99, 146–47
Spurgeon, Charles Haddon, 3, 10, 18, 52, 68, 195, *See also* Hope, Eva, *Life of C. H. Spurgeon*
downgrade controversy, 204–5
Street, Jennie, 19, 48, 52–53, 104, 110, 128, 129, 131, 151, 163, 177, 211
Sunday School Chronicle, 117, 151–52, 155, 159
Sunday School Times, 2, 4, 10, 19, 37, 42, 45, 48, 49, 54, 60, 61, 87–88, 94, 101, 106, 112, 118, 124, 133, 135, 136, 142, 150–56, 160, 185, 186, 187, 189, 205, 215, 216, 224, 226, 232, 236
Sunday School Union, 111, 124, 128–29, 150, 151, 158, 159, 241
Sunday schools, 10, 20, 22, 26, 43, 96–97, 98, 101, 132, 140, 143, 150, 152–56, 158, 159, 160, 190, 193, 200, 203, 206, 211, 236, 237, 240
Tosh, John, 82
Western Daily Press, 92
Whittemore, Jonathan, 3, 21, 32–33, 34, 36, 133, 150–51
Winston, Elizabeth, 11, 12, 13
Wolffe, John, 6
Worboise, Emma, 42, 107, 134, 136, 150, 152

Studies in Baptist History and Thought

(All titles uniform with this volume)
Dates in bold are of projected publication
Volumes in this series are not always published in sequence

David Bebbington and Anthony R. Cross (eds)
Global Baptist History
(SBHT vol. 14)

This book brings together studies from the Second International Conference on Baptist Studies which explore different facets of Baptist life and work especially during the twentieth century.

2006 / 1-84227-214-4 / approx. 350pp

David Bebbington (ed.)
The Gospel in the World
International Baptist Studies
(SBHT vol. 1)

This volume of essays from the First International Conference on Baptist Studies deals with a range of subjects spanning Britain, North America, Europe, Asia and the Antipodes. Topics include studies on religious tolerance, the communion controversy and the development of the international Baptist community, and concludes with two important essays on the future of Baptist life that pay special attention to the United States.

2002 / 1-84227-118-0 / xiv + 362pp

John H.Y. Briggs (ed.)
Pulpit and People
Studies in Eighteenth-Century English Baptist Life and Thought
(SBHT vol. 28)

The eighteenth century was a crucial time in Baptist history. The denomination had its roots in seventeenth-century English Puritanism and Separatism and the persecution of the Stuart kings with only a limited measure of freedom after 1689. Worse, however, was to follow for with toleration came doctrinal conflict, a move away from central Christian understandings and a loss of evangelistic urgency. Both spiritual and numerical decline ensued, to the extent that the denomination was virtually reborn as rather belatedly it came to benefit from the Evangelical Revival which brought new life to both Arminian and Calvinistic Baptists. The papers in this volume study a denomination in transition, and relate to theology, their views of the church and its mission, Baptist spirituality, and engagements with radical politics.

2007 / 1-84227-403-1 / approx. 350pp

July 2005

Damian Brot
Church of the Baptized or Church of Believers?
A Contribution to the Dialogue between the Catholic Church and the Free Churches with Special Reference to Baptists
(SBHT vol. 26)

The dialogue between the Catholic Church and the Free Churches in Europe has hardly taken place. This book pleads for a commencement of such a conversation. It offers, among other things, an introduction to the American and the international dialogues between Baptists and the Catholic Church and strives to allow these conversations to become fruitful in the European context as well.

2006 / 1-84227-334-5 / approx. 364pp

Dennis Bustin
Paradox and Perseverence
Hanserd Knollys, Particular Baptist Pioneer in Seventeenth-Century England
(SBHT vol. 23)

The seventeenth century was a significant period in English history during which the people of England experienced unprecedented change and tumult in all spheres of life. At the same time, the importance of order and the traditional institutions of society were being reinforced. Hanserd Knollys, born during this pivotal period, personified in his life the ambiguity, tension and paradox of it, openly seeking change while at the same time cautiously embracing order. As a founder and leader of the Particular Baptists in London and despite persecution and personal hardship, he played a pivotal role in helping shape their identity externally in society and, internally, as they moved toward becoming more formalised by the end of the century.

2006 / 1-84227-259-4 / approx. 324pp

Anthony R. Cross
Baptism and the Baptists
Theology and Practice in Twentieth-Century Britain
(SBHT vol. 3)

At a time of renewed interest in baptism, *Baptism and the Baptists* is a detailed study of twentieth-century baptismal theology and practice and the factors which have influenced its development.

2000 / 0-85364-959-6 / xx + 530pp

Anthony R. Cross and Philip E. Thompson (eds)
Baptist Sacramentalism
(SBHT vol. 5)

This collection of essays includes biblical, historical and theological studies in the theology of the sacraments from a Baptist perspective. Subjects explored include the physical side of being spiritual, baptism, the Lord's supper, the church, ordination, preaching, worship, religious liberty and the issue of disestablishment.

2003 / 1-84227-119-9 / xvi + 278pp

Anthony R. Cross and Philip E. Thompson (eds)
Baptist Sacramentalism 2
(SBHT vol. 25)

This second collection of essays exploring various dimensions of sacramental theology from a Baptist perspective includes biblical, historical and theological studies from scholars from around the world.

2006 / 1-84227-325-6 / approx. 350pp

Paul S. Fiddes
Tracks and Traces
Baptist Identity in Church and Theology
(SBHT vol. 13)

This is a comprehensive, yet unusual, book on the faith and life of Baptist Christians. It explores the understanding of the church, ministry, sacraments and mission from a thoroughly theological perspective. In a series of interlinked essays, the author relates Baptist identity consistently to a theology of covenant and to participation in the triune communion of God.

2003 / 1-84227-120-2 / xvi + 304pp

Stanley K. Fowler
More Than a Symbol
The British Baptist Recovery of Baptismal Sacramentalism
(SBHT vol. 2)

Fowler surveys the entire scope of British Baptist literature from the seventeenth-century pioneers onwards. He shows that in the twentieth century leading British Baptist pastors and theologians recovered an understanding of baptism that connected experience with soteriology and that in doing so they were recovering what many of their forebears had taught.

2002 / 1-84227-052-4 / xvi + 276pp

Steven R. Harmon
Towards Baptist Catholicity
Essays on Tradition and the Baptist Vision
(SBHT vol. 27)

This series of essays contends that the reconstruction of the Baptist vision in the wake of modernity's dissolution requires a retrieval of the ancient ecumenical tradition that forms Christian identity through rehearsal and practice. Themes explored include catholic identity as an emerging trend in Baptist theology, tradition as a theological category in Baptist perspective, Baptist confessions and the patristic tradition, worship as a principal bearer of tradition, and the role of Baptist higher education in shaping the Christian vision.

2006 / 1-84227-362-0 / approx. 210pp

Michael A.G. Haykin (ed.)
'At the Pure Fountain of Thy Word'
Andrew Fuller as an Apologist
(SBHT vol. 6)

One of the greatest Baptist theologians of the eighteenth and early nineteenth centuries, Andrew Fuller has not had justice done to him. There is little doubt that Fuller's theology lay behind the revitalization of the Baptists in the late eighteenth century and the first few decades of the nineteenth. This collection of essays fills a much needed gap by examining a major area of Fuller's thought, his work as an apologist.

2004 / 1-84227-171-7 / xxii + 276pp

Michael A.G. Haykin
Studies in Calvinistic Baptist Spirituality
(SBHT vol. 15)

In a day when spirituality is in vogue and Christian communities are looking for guidance in this whole area, there is wisdom in looking to the past to find untapped wells. The Calvinistic Baptists, heirs of the rich ecclesial experience in the Puritan era of the seventeenth century, but, by the end of the eighteenth century, also passionately engaged in the catholicity of the Evangelical Revivals, are such a well. This collection of essays, covering such things as the Lord's Supper, friendship and hymnody, seeks to draw out the spiritual riches of this community for reflection and imitation in the present day.

2006 / 1-84227-149-0 / approx. 350pp

Brian Haymes, Anthony R. Cross and Ruth Gouldbourne
On Being the Church
Revisioning Baptist Identity
(SBHT vol. 21)

The aim of the book is to re-examine Baptist theology and practice in the light of the contemporary biblical, theological, ecumenical and missiological context drawing on historical and contemporary writings and issues. It is not a study in denominationalism but rather seeks to revision historical insights from the believers' church tradition for the sake of Baptists and other Christians in the context of the modern–postmodern context.

2006 / 1-84227-121-0 / approx. 350pp

Ken R. Manley
From Woolloomooloo to 'Eternity': A History of Australian Baptists
Volume 1: Growing an Australian Church (1831–1914)
Volume 2: A National Church in a Global Community (1914–2005)
(SBHT vols 16.1 and 16.2)

From their beginnings in Australia in 1831 with the first baptisms in Woolloomooloo Bay in 1832, this pioneering study describes the quest of Baptists in the different colonies (states) to discover their identity as Australians and Baptists. Although institutional developments are analyzed and the roles of significant individuals traced, the major focus is on the social and theological dimensions of the Baptist movement.

2 vol. set 2006 / 1-84227-405-8 / approx. 900pp

Ken R. Manley
'Redeeming Love Proclaim'
John Rippon and the Baptists
(SBHT vol. 12)

A leading exponent of the new moderate Calvinism which brought new life to many Baptists, John Rippon (1751–1836) helped unite the Baptists at this significant time. His many writings expressed the denomination's growing maturity and mutual awareness of Baptists in Britain and America, and exerted a long-lasting influence on Baptist worship and devotion. In his various activities, Rippon helped conserve the heritage of Old Dissent and promoted the evangelicalism of the New Dissent

2004 / 1-84227-193-8 / xviii + 340pp

Peter J. Morden
Offering Christ to the World
Andrew Fuller and the Revival of English Particular Baptist Life
(SBHT vol. 8)

Andrew Fuller (1754–1815) was one of the foremost English Baptist ministers of his day. His career as an Evangelical Baptist pastor, theologian, apologist and missionary statesman coincided with the profound revitalization of the Particular Baptist denomination to which he belonged. This study examines the key aspects of the life and thought of this hugely significant figure, and gives insights into the revival in which he played such a central part.

2003 / 1-84227-141-5 / xx + 202pp

Peter Naylor
Calvinism, Communion and the Baptists
A Study of English Calvinistic Baptists from the Late 1600s to the Early 1800s
(SBHT vol. 7)

Dr Naylor argues that the traditional link between 'high-Calvinism' and 'restricted communion' is in need of revision. He examines Baptist communion controversies from the late 1600s to the early 1800s and also the theologies of John Gill and Andrew Fuller.

2003 / 1-84227-142-3 / xx + 266pp

Ian M. Randall, Toivo Pilli and Anthony R. Cross (eds)
Baptist Identities
International Studies from the Seventeenth to the Twentieth Centuries
(SBHT vol. 19)

These papers represent the contributions of scholars from various parts of the world as they consider the factors that have contributed to Baptist distinctiveness in different countries and at different times. The volume includes specific case studies as well as broader examinations of Baptist life in a particular country or region. Together they represent an outstanding resource for understanding Baptist identities.

2005 / 1-84227-215-2 / approx. 350pp

James M. Renihan
Edification and Beauty
The Practical Ecclesiology of the English Particular Baptists, 1675–1705
(SBHT vol. 17)
Edification and Beauty describes the practices of the Particular Baptist churches at the end of the seventeenth century in terms of three concentric circles: at the centre is the ecclesiological material in the Second London Confession, which is then fleshed out in the various published writings of the men associated with these churches, and, finally, expressed in the church books of the era.
2005 / 1-84227-251-9 / approx. 230pp

Frank Rinaldi
'The Tribe of Dan'
A Study of the New Connexion of General Baptists 1770–1891
(SBHT vol. 10)
'The Tribe of Dan' is a thematic study which explores the theology, organizational structure, evangelistic strategy, ministry and leadership of the New Connexion of General Baptists as it experienced the process of institutionalization in the transition from a revival movement to an established denomination.
2006 / 1-84227-143-1 / approx. 350pp

Peter Shepherd
The Making of a Modern Denomination
John Howard Shakespeare and the English Baptists 1898–1924
(SBHT vol. 4)
John Howard Shakespeare introduced revolutionary change to the Baptist denomination. The Baptist Union was transformed into a strong central institution and Baptist ministers were brought under its control. Further, Shakespeare's pursuit of church unity reveals him as one of the pioneering ecumenists of the twentieth century.
2001 / 1-84227-046-X / xviii + 220pp

Karen Smith
The Community and the Believers
A Study of Calvinistic Baptist Spirituality in Some Towns and Villages of Hampshire and the Borders of Wiltshire, c.1730–1830
(SBHT vol. 22)

The period from 1730 to 1830 was one of transition for Calvinistic Baptists. Confronted by the enthusiasm of the Evangelical Revival, congregations within the denomination as a whole were challenged to find a way to take account of the revival experience. This study examines the life and devotion of Calvinistic Baptists in Hampshire and Wiltshire during this period. Among this group of Baptists was the hymn writer, Anne Steele.

2005 / 1-84227-326-4 / approx. 280pp

Martin Sutherland
Dissenters in a 'Free Land'
Baptist Thought in New Zealand 1850–2000
(SBHT vol. 24)

Baptists in New Zealand were forced to recast their identity. Conventions of communication and association, state and ecumenical relations, even historical divisions and controversies had to be revised in the face of new topographies and constraints. As Baptists formed themselves in a fluid society they drew heavily on both international movements and local dynamics. This book traces the development of ideas which shaped institutions and styles in sometimes surprising ways.

2006 / 1-84227-327-2 / approx. 230pp

Brian Talbot
The Search for a Common Identity
The Origins of the Baptist Union of Scotland 1800–1870
(SBHT vol. 9)

In the period 1800 to 1827 there were three streams of Baptists in Scotland: Scotch, Haldaneite and 'English' Baptist. A strong commitment to home evangelization brought these three bodies closer together, leading to a merger of their home missionary societies in 1827. However, the first three attempts to form a union of churches failed, but by the 1860s a common understanding of their corporate identity was attained leading to the establishment of the Baptist Union of Scotland.

2003 / 1-84227-123-7 / xviii + 402pp

Philip E. Thompson
The Freedom of God
Towards Baptist Theology in Pneumatological Perspective
(SBHT vol. 20)

This study contends that the range of theological commitments of the early Baptists are best understood in relation to their distinctive emphasis on the freedom of God. Thompson traces how this was recast anthropocentrically, leading to an emphasis upon human freedom from the nineteenth century onwards. He seeks to recover the dynamism of the early vision via a pneumatologically-oriented ecclesiology defining the church in terms of the memory of God.

2006 / 1-84227-125-3 / approx. 350pp

Philip E. Thompson and Anthony R. Cross (eds)
Recycling the Past or Researching History?
Studies in Baptist Historiography and Myths
(SBHT vol. 11)

In this volume an international group of Baptist scholars examine and re-examine areas of Baptist life and thought about which little is known or the received wisdom is in need of revision. Historiographical studies include the date Oxford Baptists joined the Abingdon Association, the death of the Fifth Monarchist John Pendarves, eighteenth-century Calvinistic Baptists and the political realm, confessional identity and denominational institutions, Baptist community, ecclesiology, the priesthood of all believers, soteriology, Baptist spirituality, Strict and Reformed Baptists, the role of women among British Baptists, while various 'myths' challenged include the nature of high-Calvinism in eighteenth-century England, baptismal anti-sacramentalism, episcopacy, and Baptists and change.

2005 / 1-84227-122-9 / approx. 330pp

Linda Wilson
Marianne Farningham
A Plain Working Woman
(SBHT vol. 18)

Marianne Farningham, of College Street Baptist Chapel, Northampton, was a household name in evangelical circles in the later nineteenth century. For over fifty years she produced comment, poetry, biography and fiction for the popular Christian press. This investigation uses her writings to explore the beliefs and behaviour of evangelical Nonconformists, including Baptists, during these years.

2006 / 1-84227-124-5 / approx. 250pp

Other Paternoster titles relating to Baptist history and thought

George R. Beasley-Murray
Baptism in the New Testament
(Paternoster Digital Library)

This is a welcome reprint of a classic text on baptism originally published in 1962 by one of the leading Baptist New Testament scholars of the twentieth century. Dr Beasley-Murray's comprehensive study begins by investigating the antecedents of Christian baptism. It then surveys the foundation of Christian baptism in the Gospels, its emergence in the Acts of the Apostles and development in the apostolic writings. Following a section relating baptism to New Testament doctrine, a substantial discussion of the origin and significance of infant baptism leads to a briefer consideration of baptismal reform and ecumenism.

2005 / 1-84227-300-0 / x + 422pp

Paul Beasley-Murray
Fearless for Truth
A Personal Portrait of the Life of George Beasley-Murray

Without a doubt George Beasley-Murray was one of the greatest Baptists of the twentieth century. A long-standing Principal of Spurgeon's College, he wrote more than twenty books and made significant contributions in the study of areas as diverse as baptism and eschatology, as well as writing highly respected commentaries on the Book of Revelation and John's Gospel.

2002 / 1-84227-134-2 / xii + 244pp

David Bebbington
Holiness in Nineteenth-Century England
(Studies in Christian History and Thought)

David Bebbington stresses the relationship of movements of spirituality to changes in their cultural setting, especially the legacies of the Enlightenment and Romanticism. He shows that these broad shifts in ideological mood had a profound effect on the ways in which piety was conceptualized and practised. Holiness was intimately bound up with the spirit of the age.

2000 / 0-85364-981-2 / viii + 98pp

Clyde Binfield
Victorian Nonconformity in Eastern England 1840–1885
(Studies in Evangelical History and Thought)
Studies of Victorian religion and society often concentrate on cities, suburbs, and industrialisation. This study provides a contrast. Victorian Eastern England—Essex, Suffolk, Norfolk, Cambridgeshire, and Huntingdonshire—was rural, traditional, relatively unchanging. That is nonetheless a caricature which discounts the industry in Norwich and Ipswich (as well as in Haverhill, Stowmarket and Leiston) and ignores the impact of London on Essex, of railways throughout the region, and of an ancient but changing university (Cambridge) on the county town which housed it. It also entirely ignores the political implications of such changes in a region noted for the variety of its religious Dissent since the seventeenth century. This book explores Victorian Eastern England and its Nonconformity. It brings to a wider readership a pioneering thesis which has made a major contribution to a fresh evolution of English religion and society.

2006 / 1-84227-216-0 / approx. 274pp

Edward W. Burrows
'To Me To Live Is Christ'
A Biography of Peter H. Barber
This book is about a remarkably gifted and energetic man of God. Peter H. Barber was born into a Brethren family in Edinburgh in 1930. In his youth he joined Charlotte Baptist Chapel and followed the call into Baptist ministry. For eighteen years he was the pioneer minister of the new congregation in the New Town of East Kilbride, which planted two further congregations. At the age of thirty-nine he served as Centenary President of the Baptist Union of Scotland and then exercised an influential ministry for over seven years in the well-known Upton Vale Baptist Church, Torquay. From 1980 until his death in 1994 he was General Secretary of the Baptist Union of Scotland. Through his work for the European Baptist Federation and the Baptist World Alliance he became a world Baptist statesman. He was President of the EBF during the upheaval that followed the collapse of Communism.

2005 / 1-84227-324-8 / xxii + 236pp

Christopher J. Clement
Religious Radicalism in England 1535–1565
(Rutherford Studies in Historical Theology)
In this valuable study Christopher Clement draws our attention to a varied assemblage of people who sought Christian faithfulness in the underworld of mid-Tudor England. Sympathetically and yet critically he assess their place in the history of English Protestantism, and by attentive listening he gives them a voice.

1997 / 0-946068-44-5 / xxii + 426pp

Anthony R. Cross (ed.)
Ecumenism and History
Studies in Honour of John H.Y. Briggs
(Studies in Christian History and Thought)

This collection of essays examines the inter-relationships between the two fields in which Professor Briggs has contributed so much: history—particularly Baptist and Nonconformist—and the ecumenical movement. With contributions from colleagues and former research students from Britain, Europe and North America, *Ecumenism and History* provides wide-ranging studies in important aspects of Christian history, theology and ecumenical studies.

2002 / 1-84227-135-0 / xx + 362pp

Keith E. Eitel
Paradigm Wars
*The Southern Baptist International Mission Board
Faces the Third Millennium*
(Regnum Studies in Mission)

The International Mission Board of the Southern Baptist Convention is the largest denominational mission agency in North America. This volume chronicles the historic and contemporary forces that led to the IMB's recent extensive reorganization, providing the most comprehensive case study to date of a historic mission agency restructuring to continue its mission purpose into the twenty-first century more effectively.

2000 / 1-870345-12-6 / x + 140pp

Ruth Gouldbourne
The Flesh and the Feminine
Gender and Theology in the Writings of Caspar Schwenckfeld
(Studies in Christian History and Thought)

Caspar Schwenckfeld and his movement exemplify one of the radical communities of the sixteenth century. Challenging theological and liturgical norms, they also found themselves challenging social and particularly gender assumptions. In this book, the issues of the relationship between radical theology and the understanding of gender are considered.

2005 / 1-84227-048-6 / approx. 304pp

July 2005

David Hilborn
The Words of our Lips
Language-Use in Free Church Worship
(Paternoster Theological Monographs)

Studies of liturgical language have tended to focus on the written canons of Roman Catholic and Anglican communities. By contrast, David Hilborn analyses the more extemporary approach of English Nonconformity. Drawing on recent developments in linguistic pragmatics, he explores similarities and differences between 'fixed' and 'free' worship, and argues for the interdependence of each.

2006 / 0-85364-977-4

Stephen R. Holmes
Listening to the Past
The Place of Tradition in Theology

Beginning with the question 'Why can't we just read the Bible?' Stephen Holmes considers the place of tradition in theology, showing how the doctrine of creation leads to an account of historical location and creaturely limitations as essential aspects of our existence. For we cannot claim unmediated access to the Scriptures without acknowledging the place of tradition: theology is an irreducibly communal task. *Listening to the Past* is a sustained attempt to show what listening to tradition involves, and how it can be used to aid theological work today.

2002 / 1-84227-155-5 / xiv + 168pp

Mark Hopkins
Nonconformity's Romantic Generation
Evangelical and Liberal Theologies in Victorian England
(Studies in Evangelical History and Thought)

A study of the theological development of key leaders of the Baptist and Congregational denominations at their period of greatest influence, including C.H. Spurgeon and R.W. Dale, and of the controversies in which those among them who embraced and rejected the liberal transformation of their evangelical heritage opposed each other.

2004 / 1-84227-150-4 / xvi + 284pp

Galen K. Johnson
Prisoner of Conscience
John Bunyan on Self, Community and Christian Faith
(Studies in Christian History and Thought)

This is an interdisciplinary study of John Bunyan's understanding of conscience across his autobiographical, theological and fictional writings, investigating whether conscience always deserves fidelity, and how Bunyan's view of conscience affects his relationship both to modern Western individualism and historic Christianity.

2003 / 1-84227- 151-2 / xvi + 236pp

R.T. Kendall
Calvin and English Calvinism to 1649
(Studies in Christian History and Thought)

The author's thesis is that those who formed the Westminster Confession of Faith, which is regarded as Calvinism, in fact departed from John Calvin on two points: (1) the extent of the atonement and (2) the ground of assurance of salvation.

1997 / 0-85364-827-1 / xii + 264pp

Timothy Larsen
Friends of Religious Equality
Nonconformist Politics in Mid-Victorian England

During the middle decades of the nineteenth century the English Nonconformist community developed a coherent political philosophy of its own, of which a central tenet was the principle of religious equality (in contrast to the stereotype of Evangelical Dissenters). The Dissenting community fought for the civil rights of Roman Catholics, non-Christians and even atheists, on an issue of principle which had its flowering in the enthusiastic and undivided support which Nonconformity gave to the campaign for Jewish emancipation. This reissued study examines the political efforts and ideas of English Nonconformists during the period, covering the whole range of national issues raised, from state education to the Crimean War. It offers a case study of a theologically conservative group defending religious pluralism in the civic sphere, showing that the concept of religious equality was a grand vision at the centre of the political philosophy of the Dissenters.

2007 / 1-84227-402-3 / x + 300pp

Donald M. Lewis
Lighten Their Darkness
The Evangelical Mission to Working-Class London, 1828–1860
(Studies in Evangelical History and Thought)

This is a comprehensive and compelling study of the Church and the complexities of nineteenth-century London. Challenging our understanding of the culture in working London at this time, Lewis presents a well-structured and illustrated work that contributes substantially to the study of evangelicalism and mission in nineteenth-century Britain.

2001 / 1-84227-074-5 / xviii + 372pp

Stanley E. Porter and Anthony R. Cross (eds)
Semper Reformandum
Studies in Honour of Clark H. Pinnock

Clark Pinnock has clearly been one of the most important evangelical theologians of the last forty years in North America. Always provocative, especially in the wide range of opinions he has held and considered, Pinnock, himself a Baptist, has recently retired after twenty-five years of teaching at McMaster Divinity College. His colleagues and associates honour him in this volume by responding to his important theological work which has dealt with the essential topics of evangelical theology. These include Christian apologetics, biblical inspiration, the Holy Spirit and, perhaps most importantly in recent years, openness theology.

2003 / 1-84227-206-3 / xiv + 414pp

Meic Pearse
The Great Restoration
The Religious Radicals of the 16th and 17th Centuries

Pearse charts the rise and progress of continental Anabaptism – both evangelical and heretical – through the sixteenth century. He then follows the story of those English people who became impatient with Puritanism and separated – first from the Church of England and then from one another – to form the antecedents of later Congregationalists, Baptists and Quakers.

1998 / 0-85364-800-X / xii + 320pp

Charles Price and Ian M. Randall
Transforming Keswick

Transforming Keswick is a thorough, readable and detailed history of the convention. It will be of interest to those who know and love Keswick, those who are only just discovering it, and serious scholars eager to learn more about the history of God's dealings with his people.

2000 / 1-85078-350-0 / 288pp

Jim Purves
The Triune God and the Charismatic Movement
A Critical Appraisal from a Scottish Perspective
(Paternoster Theological Monographs)

All emotion and no theology? Or a fundamental challenge to reappraise and realign our trinitarian theology in the light of Christian experience? This study of charismatic renewal as it found expression within Scotland at the end of the twentieth century evaluates the use of Patristic, Reformed and contemporary models (including those of the Baptist Union of Scotland) of the Trinity in explaining the workings of the Holy Spirit.

2004 / 1-84227-321-3 / xxiv + 246pp

Ian M. Randall
Evangelical Experiences
A Study in the Spirituality of English Evangelicalism 1918–1939
(Studies in Evangelical History and Thought)

This book makes a detailed historical examination of evangelical spirituality between the First and Second World Wars. It shows how patterns of devotion led to tensions and divisions. In a wide-ranging study, Anglican, Wesleyan, Reformed and Pentecostal-charismatic spiritualities are analysed.

1999 / 0-85364-919-7 / xii + 310pp

Ian M. Randall
One Body in Christ
The History and Significance of the Evangelical Alliance

In 1846 the Evangelical Alliance was founded with the aim of bringing together evangelicals for common action. This book uses material not previously utilized to examine the history and significance of the Evangelical Alliance, a movement which has remained a powerful force for unity. At a time when evangelicals are growing world-wide, this book offers insights into the past which are relevant to contemporary issues.

2001 / 1-84227-089-3 / xii + 394pp

Ian M. Randall
Spirituality and Social Change
The Contribution of F.B. Meyer (1847–1929)
(Studies in Evangelical History and Thought)

This is a fresh appraisal of F.B. Meyer (1847–1929), a leading Free Church minister. Having been deeply affected by holiness spirituality, Meyer became the Keswick Convention's foremost international speaker. He combined spirituality with effective evangelism and socio-political activity. This study shows Meyer's significant contribution to spiritual renewal and social change.

2003 / 1-84227-195-4 / xx + 184pp

July 2005

Geoffrey Robson
Dark Satanic Mills?
Religion and Irreligion in Birmingham and the Black Country
(Studies in Evangelical History and Thought)
This book analyses and interprets the nature and extent of popular Christian belief and practice in Birmingham and the Black Country during the first half of the nineteenth century, with particular reference to the impact of cholera epidemics and evangelism on church extension programmes.
2002 / 1-84227-102-4 / xiv + 294pp

Alan P.F. Sell
Enlightenment, Ecumenism, Evangel
Theological Themes and Thinkers 1550–2000
(Studies in Christian History and Thought)
This book consists of papers in which such interlocking topics as the Enlightenment, the problem of authority, the development of doctrine, spirituality, ecumenism, theological method and the heart of the gospel are discussed. Issues of significance to the church at large are explored with special reference to writers from the Reformed and Dissenting traditions.
2005 / 1-84227330-2 / xviii + 422pp

Alan P.F. Sell
Hinterland Theology
Some Reformed and Dissenting Adjustments
(Studies in Christian History and Thought)
Many books have been written on theology's 'giants' and significant trends, but what of those lesser-known writers who adjusted to them? In this book some hinterland theologians of the British Reformed and Dissenting traditions, who followed in the wake of toleration, the Evangelical Revival, the rise of modern biblical criticism and Karl Barth, are allowed to have their say. They include Thomas Ridgley, Ralph Wardlaw, T.V. Tymms and N.H.G. Robinson.
2006 / 1-84227-331-0

Alan P.F. Sell and Anthony R. Cross (eds)
Protestant Nonconformity in the Twentieth Century
(Studies in Christian History and Thought)

In this collection of essays scholars representative of a number of Nonconformist traditions reflect thematically on Nonconformists' life and witness during the twentieth century. Among the subjects reviewed are biblical studies, theology, worship, evangelism and spirituality, and ecumenism. Over and above its immediate interest, this collection provides a marker to future scholars and others wishing to know how some of their forebears assessed Nonconformity's contribution to a variety of fields during the century leading up to Christianity's third millennium.

2003 / 1-84227-221-7 / x + 398pp

Mark Smith
Religion in Industrial Society
Oldham and Saddleworth 1740–1865
(Studies in Christian History and Thought)

This book analyses the way British churches sought to meet the challenge of industrialization and urbanization during the period 1740–1865. Working from a case-study of Oldham and Saddleworth, Mark Smith challenges the received view that the Anglican Church in the eighteenth century was characterized by complacency and inertia, and reveals Anglicanism's vigorous and creative response to the new conditions. He reassesses the significance of the centrally directed church reforms of the mid-nineteenth century, and emphasizes the importance of local energy and enthusiasm. Charting the growth of denominational pluralism in Oldham and Saddleworth, Dr Smith compares the strengths and weaknesses of the various Anglican and Nonconformist approaches to promoting church growth. He also demonstrates the extent to which all the churches participated in a common culture shaped by the influence of evangelicalism, and shows that active co-operation between the churches rather than denominational conflict dominated. This revised and updated edition of Dr Smith's challenging and original study makes an important contribution both to the social history of religion and to urban studies.

2006 / 1-84227-335-3 / approx. 300pp

David M. Thompson
Baptism, Church and Society in Britain from the Evangelical Revival to
Baptism, Eucharist and Ministry

The theology and practice of baptism have not received the attention they deserve. How important is faith? What does baptismal regeneration mean? Is baptism a bond of unity between Christians? This book discusses the theology of baptism and popular belief and practice in England and Wales from the Evangelical Revival to the publication of the World Council of Churches' consensus statement on *Baptism, Eucharist and Ministry* (1982).

2005 / 1-84227-393-0 / approx. 224pp

Martin Sutherland
Peace, Toleration and Decay
The Ecclesiology of Later Stuart Dissent
(Studies in Christian History and Thought)

This fresh analysis brings to light the complexity and fragility of the later Stuart Nonconformist consensus. Recent findings on wider seventeenth-century thought are incorporated into a new picture of the dynamics of Dissent and the roots of evangelicalism.

2003 / 1-84227-152-0 / xxii + 216pp

Haddon Willmer
Evangelicalism 1785–1835: An Essay (1962) and Reflections (2004)
(Studies in Evangelical History and Thought)

Awarded the Hulsean Prize in the University of Cambridge in 1962, this interpretation of a classic period of English Evangelicalism, by a young church historian, is now supplemented by reflections on Evangelicalism from the vantage point of a retired Professor of Theology.

2006 / 1-84227-219-5

Linda Wilson
Constrained by Zeal
Female Spirituality amongst Nonconformists 1825–1875
(Studies in Evangelical History and Thought)

Constrained by Zeal investigates the neglected area of Nonconformist female spirituality. Against the background of separate spheres, it analyses the experience of women from four denominations, and argues that the churches provided a 'third sphere' in which they could find opportunities for participation.

2000 / 0-85364-972-3 / xvi + 294pp

Nigel G. Wright
Disavowing Constantine
*Mission, Church and the Social Order in the Theologies of
John Howard Yoder and Jürgen Moltmann*
(Paternoster Theological Monographs)

This book is a timely restatement of a radical theology of church and state in the Anabaptist and Baptist tradition. Dr Wright constructs his argument in dialogue and debate with Yoder and Moltmann, major contributors to a free church perspective.

2000 / 0-85364-978-2 / xvi + 252pp

Nigel G. Wright
Free Church, Free State
The Positive Baptist Vision

Free Church, Free State is a textbook on baptist ways of being church and a proposal for the future of baptist churches in an ecumenical context. Nigel Wright argues that both baptist (small 'b') and catholic (small 'c') church traditions should seek to enrich and support each other as valid expressions of the body of Christ without sacrificing what they hold dear. Written for pastors, church planters, evangelists and preachers, Nigel Wright offers frameworks of thought for baptists and non-baptists in their journey together following Christ.

2005 / 1-84227-353-1 / xxviii + 292

Nigel G. Wright
New Baptists, New Agenda

New Baptists, New Agenda is a timely contribution to the growing debate about the health, shape and future of the Baptists. It considers the steady changes that have taken place among Baptists in the last decade – changes of mood, style, practice and structure – and encourages us to align these current movements and questions with God's upward and future call. He contends that the true church has yet to come: the church that currently exists is an anticipation of the joyful gathering of all who have been called by the Spirit through Christ to the Father.

2002 / 1-84227-157-1 / x + 162pp

Paternoster
9 Holdom Avenue,
Bletchley,
Milton Keynes MK1 1QR,
United Kingdom
Web: www.authenticmedia.co.uk/paternoster

July 2005

www.ingramcontent.com/pod-product-compliance
Lightning Source LLC
Chambersburg PA
CBHW070240230426
43664CB00014B/2363